STUDIES IN EARLY MODERN CULTURAL,
POLITICAL AND SOCIAL HISTORY

Volume 50

CIVIL RELIGION IN THE EARLY MODERN
ANGLOPHONE WORLD, 1550–1700

Studies in Early Modern Cultural, Political and Social History

ISSN: 1476-9107

Series editors

Tim Harris – Brown University
Stephen Taylor – Durham University
Andy Wood – Durham University

Previously published titles in the series are listed at the back of this volume

CIVIL RELIGION IN THE EARLY MODERN ANGLOPHONE WORLD, 1550–1700

Edited by
Adam Morton and Rachel Hammersley

THE BOYDELL PRESS

© Contributors 2024

All Rights Reserved. Except as permitted under current legislation no part of this work may be photocopied, stored in a retrieval system, published, performed in public, adapted, broadcast, transmitted, recorded or reproduced in any form or by any means, without the prior permission of the copyright owner

First published 2024
The Boydell Press, Woodbridge

ISBN 978-1-78327-784-1

The Boydell Press is an imprint of Boydell & Brewer Ltd
PO Box 9, Woodbridge, Suffolk IP12 3DF, UK
and of Boydell & Brewer Inc.
668 Mt Hope Avenue, Rochester, NY 14620-2731, USA
website: www.boydellandbrewer.com

A catalogue record for this book is available
from the British Library

The publisher has no responsibility for the continued existence or accuracy of URLs for external or third-party internet websites referred to in this book, and does not guarantee that any content on such websites is, or will remain, accurate or appropriate

Contents

	List of Contributors	vii
	Acknowledgements	x
	Introduction: Civil Religion in the Early Modern Anglophone World Adam Morton and Rachel Hammersley	1
1	Civil Religion: Two Traditions Mark Goldie	42
2	A Mutable Wall of Separation? Reconfiguring Ecclesiastical Civility, Mixed Polity, and Civil and Sacred Matter in Late Elizabethan England Polly Ha	71
3	Alexander Leighton and the Erastian fabric of early Stuart Puritanism Esther Counsell	92
4	Reading Machiavellian Civil Religion in Early Modern Britain Charlotte McCallum	119
5	Republicans and Independents: Debating 'National Religion' in Cromwellian England John Coffey	139
6	Henry Stubbe and Civil Religion Connor Robinson	159
7	Civil Religion on the Ground: Theory and Practice in Early Pennsylvania Andrew R. Murphy and Christie L. Maloyed	183
8	John Locke and Civil Religion John Marshall	203
9	Civil Religion and Early Modern Views of the Anglo-Saxon Church Jacqueline Rose	223
	Bibliography	243
	Index	279

Contributors

John Coffey is Professor of Early Modern History at the University of Leicester. His research addresses the relationship between religion, politics and ideas in the Protestant Atlantic world. He is the author of *Politics, Religion and the British Revolutions: The Mind of Samuel Rutherford* (1997); *Persecution and Toleration in Protestant England* (2000), *John Goodwin and the Puritan Revolution* (2006); and *Exodus and Liberation: Deliverance Politics from John Calvin to Martin Luther King* (2014). He has edited *The Cambridge Companion to Puritanism*, with Paul Lim (2008); *Seeing Things Their Way: Intellectual History and the Return of Religion*, with Alister Chapman and Brad Gregory (2009); *The Oxford History of Protestant Dissenting Traditions, vol. I: The Post-Reformation Era* (2020); and *Reliquiae Baxterianae*, 5 vols, with N. H. Keeble (gen. ed.), Tim Cooper and Thomas Charlton (2020).

Esther Counsell is a PhD candidate at Trinity College, Cambridge, and her thesis is titled 'Protestant jurisdictionalism and the nature of puritanism, c. 1560–1642' (forthcoming, 2024). She has co-edited a volume of essays entitled *Reformed identity and conformity in England, 1559–1714* (Manchester, 2024), and also has a forthcoming article on William Stoughton. Her research interests are the legal and political thought of the European reformations, and the history of English Parliament.

Mark Goldie is Emeritus Professor of Intellectual History, University of Cambridge, and Honorary Professor of Intellectual History, University of Sussex. He has published extensively on politics, religion, and ideas in early modern Britain. He has co-edited *The Historical Journal* and two volumes in the *Cambridge History of Political Thought*, has been Chair of the Cambridge History Faculty, and Vice-Master of Churchill College. His essays on Restoration England, *Contesting the English Polity, 1660–1688*, appeared in 2023. He is currently working on an intellectual biography of John Locke.

Polly Ha is Associate Professor of History in the Divinity School and History Department at Duke University and a MacDonald Senior Distinguished Fellow at the Center for the Study of Law and Religion at Emory University. Her current work explores the universalization of liberty among independent thinkers in the English Revolution, the longer-term impact of the Reformation, reconfigurations of the relationship between religion and politics, and broader intellectual change and social innovation in the sixteenth and seventeenth centuries. She has published widely on reformation reception and is chief editor of *The Puritans on Independence* and *Reformed Government*. Her earlier work challenged traditional assumptions about the range of alternative ecclesiastical polities in pre-civil war England and the social breadth of reformed communities by analyzing English exiles in the Netherlands and New England.

Rachel Hammersley is Professor in Intellectual History at Newcastle University. Her research has explored the history of political concepts such as republicanism, revolution and democracy and the ways in which ideas are transformed when they cross national boundaries. She has recently published an intellectual biography of James Harrington with Oxford University Press and a survey of the history of republican thought from the ancient world to the present.

Christie L. Maloyed is an independent scholar with research focuses on religion and politics, civic education, and American political thought. She works with public sector agencies to increase civic engagement. She earned her Ph.D. in Political Science from Texas A&M University.

John Marshall is Leonard and Helen R. Stulman Professor of History at The Johns Hopkins University. He is a British historian and an historian of political thought. He was awarded a bachelor's and master's degree from Cambridge University, where he has also been a Junior Research Fellow, a By-Fellow, and an Overseas Fellow. He has also been a Visiting Honorary Fellow at the Centre for the History of Political Thought at Queen Mary, University of London. He has a master's degree and a PhD from Johns Hopkins. He is a Fellow of the Royal Historical Society. He has written two books on the English philosopher and political theorist John Locke: *Locke: Religion, Resistance, and Responsibility* (Cambridge, 1994) and *John Locke, Toleration and Early Enlightenment Culture* (Cambridge, 2006). He has coedited two further books on religion and politics in seventeenth- and eighteenth-century Britain, and published many articles.

Charlotte McCallum recently completed a PhD at Queen Mary, University of London, entitled 'English Translations of Machiavelli's Political Works 1560–1675'. Her thesis considered the publication and translation of Machiavelli's works in sixteenth- and seventeenth-century England. Her work lies at the intersection between the history of the book, translation studies, and the history of political thought and her current research centres on the distribution of copies of Machiavelli's works in various languages in early modern England.

CONTRIBUTORS

Adam Morton is Senior Lecturer in the History of Britain at Newcastle University. He is an historian of the long-Reformation in England and has specific research interests in anti-popery, tolerance and intolerance, and visual culture. He is editor of *'Getting Along:' confessional politics, identity and non-conformity in early modern Europe* (Farnham, 2012); (with Feike Dietz, Els Stronk, and Marc van Vaeck), *Illustrated Religious Texts in Northern Europe 1500–1800* (Farnham, 2014); (with Helen Watanabe-O'Kelly), *Cultural Encounters as Political Encounters: Queens Consort and European Politics, c.1500–1800* (Abingdon, 2016); and (with Mark Knights), *The Power of Laughter and Satire in Early Modern Britain* (Woodbridge, 2017). He is currently writing a monograph, *Glaring at Antichrist: anti-Catholic images in early modern England, 1530–1690*.

Andrew R. Murphy is Professor of Political Science at the University of Michigan. His scholarship focuses on the relationship between religious and political thought and practice, in both historical and contemporary contexts. He is the author of, among other titles, *William Penn: A Life* (2019) and *Liberty, Conscience, and Toleration: The Political Thought of William Penn* (2016).

Connor Robinson recently completed a PhD in the Department of Politics at the University of York. His research interests are the history of political and religious thought of early modern Europe, particularly during the Puritan Revolution. He is currently working on a monograph adaptation of his doctoral thesis titled *The Quest for Settlement at the Twilight of the Puritan Revolution*.

Jacqueline Rose is a Senior Lecturer in History at the University of St Andrews. Her research explores early modern religious, political, and intellectual history. She has published *Godly Kingship in Restoration England: The Politics of the Royal Supremacy, 1660–1688* (Cambridge, 2011); edited a volume on *The Politics of Counsel in England and Scotland, 1286–1707* (*Proceedings of the British Academy*, 204, Oxford, 2016); and co-edited, with Colin Kidd, *Political Advice: Past, Present and Future* (London, 2021).

Acknowledgements

Professor Justin Champion had hoped to attend our conference and had agreed to write an Afterword for this volume. Unfortunately, in the end neither was possible. His death constituted a profound loss to early modern intellectual history, and he continues to be much missed. His presence, however, lies behind this volume through both the work he did on the complex interrelationship between political thought and religion in the late seventeenth and early eighteenth centuries and in his generous friendship and support to many of the contributors.

Our interest in civil religion began in 2016, when Katie East suggested we ran an informal reading group on the subject at Newcastle University. We owe Katie, and our other civil religionists Delphine Doucet and Federico Santangelo, a special thanks for inspiration and encouragement. The reading group led to a conference – 'Civil Religion: from Antiquity to Enlightenment' – held at Newcastle University 23–24 October 2019, and our volume has its origins in that event. Thanks must be given to Newcastle University for providing the funding that made the conference possible; and to Graham Barrett, Ronald Beiner, Andreas Bendlin, Stefana Cristea, Fabio Della Schiava, Oren Margolis, Julien Le Mauff, Manolis E. Pagkalos, Jorg Rupke, and Ashley Walsh for their stimulating papers at the event, some of which will appear in a special issue of *Intellectual History Review* edited by Katie East and Delphine Doucet. Ronald Beiner also spoke at a public event on toleration on the evening before the conference, and was generous with his time and his expertise on civil religion throughout the planning stages of the conference and during the conference itself.

Two things have happened since 2019 to delay the publication of this book: a global pandemic; and the birth of a child. We are grateful to our contributors, and Michael Middeke at Boydell & Brewer, for their patience. Everyone in question has been remarkably civil throughout.

Rachel and Adam, North Shields, July 2023

Introduction: Civil Religion in the Early Modern Anglophone World

Adam Morton and Rachel Hammersley

A history of civil religion would account for little more than the inconsistent application of an imprecise term. 'Civil Religion' refers to no particular faith or denomination, no codified theology or principles, and no specific model of the relationship between church and state. The term has as many definitions as it does advocates, and those definitions are often contradictory.[1] The 'civil religion' of modern America exists in a republic built on the absolute separation of church and state; conversely, the 'civil religion' of Thomas Hobbes depended on a Erastian union of church and state in one autocratic ruler.[2] Historians must consequently treat civil religion with care. We are not dealing with something as definite as an idea or as concrete as a form of government that applies that idea systematically. 'Civil Religion' refers to something looser, the religious dimension of public life through which a people saw their polity as guided by providence. It is descriptive, not prescriptive, and therefore depends on variations of interpretation in its historical applications.

Civil religion refers to the infusion of politics with religion to cultivate solidarity in a polity, galvanising the people in the myth that their society, politics, and history is an expression of the divine.[3] The expression might be

---

[1] For excellent overviews of civil religion across the centuries, see Steven M. Frankel and Martin D. Yaffe (eds), *Civil Religion in Modern Political Philosophy: Machiavelli to Tocqueville* (Penn State, PA, 2021) and Ronald L. Weed and John von Heyking (eds), *Civil Religion in political thought: its perennial questions and enduring relevance in North America* (Washington, DC, 2010).

[2] On America see Philip Goff, Raymond Haberski, and Rhys Williams (eds), *Civil Religion Today: Religion and the American Nation in the Twenty-First Century* (New York, 2021) and pp. 183-202 below. On Hobbes, see Richard Tuck, 'The Civil Religion of Thomas Hobbes', in *Political Discourse in early modern Britain*, eds Nicholas Phillipson and Quentin Skinner (Cambridge, 1993), pp. 120-38.

[3] See Rhys H. Williams and Todd Nicholas Fuist, 'Civil Religion and National Politics in a Neoliberal Era', *Sociology Compass*, 8 (2014), 929-38.

blatant (in the belief that their nation, city republic, or polity is guided by providence) or latent (in a tacit conviction that the laws and values of the polity refer to a morality that is transcendent to give a polity a loose form of sacred authority). Civil religion fosters patriotism by harnessing the zeal associated with religion into the service of politics – civil religion, notes the political scientist Ronald Beiner, is 'the empowerment of religion, not for the sake of religion, but for the sake of enhanced citizenship'.[4] This was as true of twentieth-century America as it was of ancient Rome.[5] In both cases a civil religion was the cement of a moral community, providing the symbols, language, and beliefs that express a society's idea of itself. People are bound to a community through an integration of morals and behaviour. When those morals have divine sanction, the integration is stronger – the people believe in the polity.

How does civil religion achieve this? It suffuses public life with symbols and languages that express the peoples' relationship to the divine. The divine is invoked in political speeches or on public monuments and buildings. 'Great' figures are venerated as martyrs to or pastors of the polity and exemplars of its values. Religious texts or ceremonies are used at political occasions, and reference to the divine is made in the founding myths of a people or a polity.[6] For this reason, civil religion has been seen as a precursor to totalitarianism. But many of its historical formulations show that it does not necessarily lead to state-worship.[7] In America, for example, civil religion has served to both legitimise and critique the state. It has done so because it is the foundation of the nation as a moral community.[8] As Bellah noted, civil religion holds a people to account to its own values. It is the 'subordination of the nation to ethical principles that transcend it and in terms of which it should be judged'.[9]

Because civil religion is concerned with political identity – rather than with a system of politics – its forms have been many and varied. We can trace

---

[4] Ronald Beiner, *Civil Religion: a dialogue in the history of political philosophy* (Cambridge, 2011), p. 2.
[5] On Rome, see Jörg Rüpke, *Pantheon: A New History of Roman Religion* (Princeton, 2018), chapter 13 especially; Jörg Rüpke (ed.), *Companion to Roman Religion* (Oxford, 2007); Andreas Bendlin, 'Religion in Rome', in *Themes in Roman Society and Culture*, eds M. Gibbs, M. Nicolic, and P. Ripat (Oxford, 2021), pp. 246–76; John North, *Roman Religion* (Oxford, 2000); and Mary Beard, John North, and Simon Price, *Religions of Rome*, 2 vols (Cambridge, 1998).
[6] For an excellent consideration of early modern material, see Gerald Parsons, *Perspectives on Civil Religion* (Aldershot, 2002).
[7] Mark Goldie, 'The Civil Religion of James Harrington' in *The Languages of Political Theory in early modern Europe*, ed. Anthony Pagden (Cambridge, 1987), pp. 197–222.
[8] Martin Marty, 'Two Kinds of Civil Religion', in *American Civil Religion*, ed. Russell E. Richey (New York, 1974), pp. 139–60.
[9] Robert N. Bellah, 'Civil Religion in America', in his *Beyond Belief* (New York, 1970), p. 168.

INTRODUCTION

civil religion back to Plato's *Laws*.[10] In characterising the Magnesian city he described, Plato outlined law and society in ways that were shaped by the civil religions of his time, showing how sacred space and political forums were critical to the practice of virtue and the cultivation of civic pride. Treatises by Cicero, Livy, Seneca, and Varro show that civil religion was equally vital in sustaining political unity and patriotism in the Roman Republic. Civil religion was so crucial to how Rome conceived of its politics that the early Church had to respond to charges that Christianity would undermine political unity; and the post-Constantinian church positioned itself as an alternative to civil religion equally capable of inculcating virtue and buttressing the civil power. As Augustine's *City of God* demonstrated, however, Christianity defined itself in part against civil religion – where civil religion had been valued because it was politically useful, Augustine defined Christianity as valuable because its claims about the supernatural were true.[11] If civil religion was vital in the ancient world, it was equally potent as an ideal in the modern one. English republicans flirted with civil religious alternatives to Christianity from the mid-seventeenth century; Francis Bacon saw civil religion as necessary to the cultivation of piety, patriotism, and reason in his utopian *New Atlantis* (1626); Hobbes deemed it a necessary fix for the religious warfare caused by rival churches; Rousseau presented it as the glue of the social contact he hoped would replace the *ancien regime* in Europe; and Alexis de Tocqueville saw civil religion as a symptom of the coming democracy to revolutionary America.

The range of civil religions in history, then, are diverse. As Ronald Weed and John von Heyking note, however, all versions of civil religion fall between two poles. One type of civil religion uses faith to legitimise politics through 'an acknowledged set of beliefs, drawing on familiar religious symbols and language, that sustain and reinforce a society's moral-political beliefs'.[12] Plato, Baruch Spinoza, Francis Bacon, John Locke, and Jean-Jacques Rousseau might be grouped in this category.[13] The second type of civil religion 'ascribes more significant theological motivations, though it garners by political means and maintains itself in political forms'.[14] The

---

[10] Plato, *The Laws*, ed. Trevor J. Saunders (Harmondsworth, 1970). See V. Bradley Lewis, 'Gods for the City and Beyond: Civil Religion in Plato's *Laws*', in Weed and von Heyking, *Civil Religion in Political Thought*, pp. 19–46.

[11] On Varro, see Augustine *City of God*, trans. Henry Bettenson (New York. 1984), books I–IV and see books VI–VII. Ernest Fortin, 'Augustine and Roman Civil Religion: Some Critical Reflections', in *Classical Christianity and the Political Order: Ernest Fortin's Collected Essays*, ed. J. Brian Benestad (Lanham, MD, 1996), II, pp. 238–56.

[12] Weed and von Hekyking, 'Introduction', in idem (eds), *Civil Religion in political thought*, p. 2

[13] Francis Bacon, *New Atlantic and Great Instauration*, ed. Jerry Weinberger (Arlington, IL, 1989); Baruch Spinoza, *Tractatus Theologico-Politicus*, chapters 3, 6.40, 8.46. On Rousseau, see below pp. 9–10.

[14] Weed and von Hekyking, 'Introduction', in idem (eds), *Civil Religion in political thought*, p. 2

civil religion of America's Puritans might be placed in that category. What all iterations of civil religion share is a potent capacity to bind together a people. For this reason, a growing body of scholarship in the social sciences is demonstrating that civil religions are flourishing in the contemporary world as a response to the growing atomisation of societies in the face of individualism and multiculturalism and the failure of secularisation to generate unity within polities through the creation of meaningful social identity based on shared values across its citizenry. To analyse civil religion, these studies argue, is to address a defining problem of Western society.[15]

The ambitions of our volume are more modest. We argue that developments in the political thought of sixteenth- and seventeenth-century Britain and America played an important and underappreciated role in the development of what would later be called 'civil religion'. Civil religion has been closely associated with the Enlightenment by both historians of political thought and by political scientists. It is logical to do so. The term 'civil religion' was coined by Rousseau and is the theme of the final chapters of his *Social Contract* (1762); and other leading Enlightenment political philosophers, including the Baron de Montesquieu, David Hume, and Alexis de Tocqueville, wrestled with the relationship between politics and religion in equivalent terms.[16] The Enlightenment takes centre stage in Ronald Beiner's important study, *Civil Religion: A Dialogue in the History of Political Philosophy* (2011), which presents an account of civil religion over the *longue durée* of the history of political thought. The distinct versions of civil religion offered by Niccolò Machiavelli, Thomas Hobbes, and Jean-Jacques Rousseau are at the centre of Beiner's account, but his study also takes in a much wider cast of characters ranging from the Enlightenment's leading philosophers to John Stuart Mill, Friedrich Nietzsche, and John Rawls. Beiner understands civil religion as a response to the fundamental challenge that religion poses to political authority – it is 'the appropriation of religion by politics for its own purposes' – and sets out to trace the 'centuries-long dialogue within the history of political philosophy' generated by that issue.[17] Though they lived in very different times and places, Beiner presents his cast of philosophers as tackling a common problem and as engaging in dialogue with one another.

We argue that the ideas that became 'civil religion' in the hands of Rousseau and others emerged in part from an earlier period, European history after the Reformation, and its themes of the godly magistrate, the confessional state, religious uniformity and persecution, and the development of liberty of conscience amidst the reality of religious pluralism. These were themes that the early modern political philosophers and religious reformers considered in

---

[15] *Ibid.*, pp. 13–14.
[16] David Hume, *Dialogues Concerning Natural Religion*; Montesquieu, *The Spirit of the Laws*, books 24–5.
[17] Beiner *Civil Religion*, pp. 1, 2. See also his 'Machiavelli, Hobbes, and Rousseau on Civil Religion', *Review of Politics*, 55 (1993), pp. 613–38.

INTRODUCTION

this volume – Richard Baxter, James Harrington, Richard Hooker, Alexander Leighton, John Locke, Marchamont Nedham, William Penn, John Stubbe, and the Independent Protestants of the 1650s – had to consider as they thought through the questions of the relationship between religion and politics, the structure of the church, and the role of the clergy in the state. We adopt a contextualist approach, focusing on civil religion specifically as it was understood in early modern England rather than in its more generic 'Enlightened' form. For early modern writers, civil religion was not merely a general reaction to the cosmic clash of religion and politics. Rather the specific and distinctive forms propounded by early modern thinkers reflected their particular attempts to engage with and resolve the religio-political issues that they witnessed around them such as the justification and organisation of royal supremacy, the proliferation of radical sects, and the construction of a new religious settlement to match the republican regime of the 1650s. Civil religion was, of course, not the only solution to these issues and, as will be demonstrated, its advocates engaged with other options that were propounded at the time including: theocracy; different versions of Erastianism; and calls for the complete separation of church and state.

Our volume makes three claims. First, it challenges the view that civil religion was fundamentally an Enlightenment concept, demonstrating that it owed as much to the Reformation as it did to the Enlightenment, and that the understanding of it that developed during the eighteenth century was grounded in an earlier history and phase of development. Second, it highlights the fact that the 1650s were a critical moment in the development and rise to prominence of the concept of civil religion in England. The British Revolutions of 1640–60 marked the culmination of a long period of growing tensions between religion and politics that had been initiated by the Reformation and the ways in which it had been enacted in England. The attempts to work out a settlement during the 1650s brought those tensions to a head. Third, the volume serves to put the religion back into civil religion, demonstrating that early modern thinkers saw religion as valuable in and of itself and not simply as a tool to bring about political ends.

The final point causes us to reconsider the *nature* of civil religion. Too often, it is approached cynically – the state appropriating religion to manipulate a population by recourse to their superstitions. When viewed in this way, there is a paradox in civil religion. As Beiner notes, 'precisely in celebrating the political instrumentalization of religion, one presents religion as a bag of tricks and impostures....A civil religion can never work as long as the ideas of civil religion have been articulated in a public medium to which the notional recipients of that civil religion have access'.[18] But this cynical approach to religion – the use of religion *solely* to enhance citizenship and political unity

---

[18] Ronald Beiner, 'Civil Religion and Anticlericalism in James Harrington', *European Journal of Philosophy*, 13 (2014), pp. 388–407, quotation at p. 388.

– was not widespread among advocates of civil religion in the period before 1700. The early Enlightenment in England was anti-clerical, not anti-religious. Its advocates made religion the subject of reason and scepticism not because they were *against* religion, but because they hoped to rescue religion from its corruptions at the hand of priests. Reason, they argued, would purify Christianity of the superstitions and creeds put upon it by the clergy to justify their power and influence, returning the church to its primitive state in the centuries after Christ and to the natural role of religion in human societies.[19]

That role was understood to be beneficial – indeed, necessary – to the health of a society. John Locke was deeply critical of the role of established churches in fomenting schism and persecution by insisting on strict adherence to what was Christian. But in calling for toleration of heterodox views as a way of limiting the capacity of religion to provoke unrest, he stopped short of permitting atheism – religion was too central to virtue and morality that the spread of unbelief threatened society.[20] Debates about the place of religion in society which took place in the fall out of the Reformation were sincere, not cynical. They were concerned with two things: the *civic* (the constitution and the relationship between politics and religion); and the *civil* (the role of religion in the moral health of society and, as the eighteenth century progressed, in the promotion of patriotism).[21] As Mark Goldie, Robert Ingram, and Ashley Walsh have argued, ecclesiology, the history of the church, and the legacy of the Reformation continued to be debated so vigorously in the early eighteenth century precisely because religion was so important to that society.[22] The debate was about religion's place in society, about *why* it mattered not *if* it mattered. Civil religion was one response to that problem.

---

[19] There is, of course, a counter-position which characterises that many of the claims made to 'improve' religion during the Enlightenment masked atheism. See David Berman, *A History of Atheism in England* (London, 1987); idem, 'Disclaimers as Offence Mechanism in Charles Blount and John Toland', in *Atheism from the Reformation to the Enlightenment*, eds Michael Hunter and David Wootton (Oxford, 1992), pp. 255–72; and Margaret Jacob, *The Radical Enlightenment* (London, 1981).

[20] On Locke, see John Marshall's chapter below, pp. 203–22.

[21] Ashley Walsh, *Civil Religion and the Enlightenment in England 1707–1800* (Woodbridge, 2020), pp. 20–5, 30–5, 43–8, 58–63, 117–27, 166–74, 193–4.

[22] Robert Ingram, *Reformation without end: religion, politics, and the past in post-Revolution England* (Manchester, 2018). See also Justin Champion, *The Pillars of Priestcraft Shaken: The Church of England and its Enemies 1660–1730* (Cambridge, 1992); Tim Harris, Paul Seaward, and Mark Goldie (eds), *The Politics of Religion in Restoration England* (Oxford, 1990); and Justin Champion, John Coffey, Tim Harris, and John Marshall (eds), *Politics, Religion, and Ideas in seventeenth- and eighteenth- century Britain: essays in honour of Mark Goldie* (Woodbridge, 2019).

INTRODUCTION

Approaches to Civil Religion

Our approach to civil religion is distinct from previous considerations of the topic. We might see these as twofold – top-down (regulated by the state) and bottom-up (developing organically from national experience). The two types have much in common. Civil religion fosters solidarity among a people, uniting them in allegiance to the nation despite social, cultural, class, and ethnic differences and distinctions. It imbues the people and their past with a religious quality – covenantal, providential, redeemed, or sacred – that gestures towards the transcendent or the divine to legitimise the nation-state in terms that are more than rational or constitutional and secures allegiance to that polity on the basis of emotion or identity rather than merely on formal or legal grounds. But there are significant differences between the two types of civil religion. Top-down civil religion sees elites impose a sacred morality on a population, manufacturing consent for the power of the state. Niccolò Machiavelli saw the political advantages of civil religion. He saw the sacralisation of the state as essential to coercing the populace to practice the virtuous citizenship necessary for a civic republic to thrive – religion was to be used to cultivate a civic consciousness. Bottom-up civil religion is integrative, not imposed. Shared religious sentiments develop organically within a society to suffuse the polity with a non-denominational religious legitimacy. This civil religion emerges from a groundswell of shared myths, ideas, and symbols that bind a people together and express reverence for a nation. This type of civil religion is most associated with modern America.

Top-down approaches to civil religion have been considered widely in political philosophy and see civil religion as something imposed by the state to enhance politics: religion mobilises patriotism, which in turn supports the political goals of the state. In these accounts, civil religion is a form of Erastianism. Religion has little or no independent authority apart from the state, to which it is subordinate. Civil religion is a solution to the 'problem' that religious authority poses to political authority and religious commitment poses to loyal citizenship. This 'problem' is defined neatly by Beiner: 'When religion asserts its own purposes, which are not those of politics, it poses an absolutely fundamental challenge to political authority, and politics cannot take such a radical challenge to its authority'.[23] According to Beiner, that challenge needs to be disarmed, and 'what to do about religion?' has been a perennial question in political philosophy.

Three solutions to the relationship between politics and religion have been proposed by political philosophy. The first, theocracy, combines politics and religion. Religion may be a bulwark of the political order, as in modern Iran, or faith leaders may have political authority and rule in the

---

[23] Ronald Beiner, *Civil Religion: A Dialogue in the History of Political Philosophy* (Cambridge, 2011), p. 1

name of and according to religion, as in Biblical Israel. Second, liberalism, the separation of politics and religion, in which religion is de-politised by restricting it to the realm of private belief rather than public faith. The formal separation of church and state might be hostile (an aggressive secularisation of public life) or respectful (a safeguarding of religious liberty and toleration of religion so long as it is removed from politics) – both neutralise the threat religious authority poses to political authority through the creation of distance between the two spheres. The third solution is civil religion, the domestication of religion by politics. Civil religion makes religion safer for the state by subordinating it to state power, controlled by politics for political ends.[24]

The articulation of civil religion in modern political philosophy has developed from Niccolò Machiavelli's comparison of Christianity and Roman religion in *The Prince* (1532) and the *Discourses on Livy* (1531).[25] Visions of civil religion by later early modern and Enlightenment thinkers – Francis Bacon, Thomas Hobbes, Baruch Spinoza, Jean-Jacques Rousseau, and others – are indebted to Machiavelli's framing of the problem.[26] Machiavelli is often seen as hostile to religion, but whether or not he rejected Christianity, merely critiqued contemporary iterations of it in Italian society, or saw its reform as a precondition of the fulfilment of the renewal of society and politics promised by republicanism is a matter of debate.[27]

Machiavelli's case for civil religion rested on two points. First, he argued that there was a tension between Christianity and republican politics. Christians were more concerned with the afterlife than with life on earth, with salvation rather than virtue, and this orientated their concerns away from the world and made them idle rather than active citizens. Their passivity was increased by the promotion of humility as the principal Christian virtue, which was incapable of cultivating the patriotism and zeal for war that had been fostered by the religions of ancient Rome.[28] Second, Machiavelli argued that despite the limitations of contemporary Christianity, religion had a *vital* role to play in civil society. A civil religion, exemplified in the religions of Rome, was politically advantageous for a republic and should be fomented and encouraged by a ruling elite to coerce

---

[24] *Ibid.*, pp. 1–8, 11–16, 307–8, 353–68, 409–20.
[25] Niccolò Machiavelli, *Discourses on Livy*, trans. Harvey C. Mansfield and Nathan Tarcov (Chicago, 1996), 1.11–15, 1.19, 2.2, and 3.1.
[26] See Timothy Sean Quinn, 'Machiavelli, Christianity, and Civil Religion', in *Civil Religion in Modern Political Thought: Machiavelli to Tocqueville*, eds Steven Frankel and Martin D. Yaffe (Pennsylvania, 2020), pp. 13–33, p. 15. See above note 00.
[27] For more positive readings of Machiavelli's position on Christianity and its influence on his politics see Sebastian de Grazia, *Machiavelli in Hell* (Princeton, 1989) and Maurizo Viroli, *Machiavelli's God* (Princeton, 2010).
[28] Machiavelli, *Discourses on Livy*, 1.2, 2.2 and 3.1.

the populace into being active, virtuous, and patriotic citizens.[29] The civic ceremonialism of Roman religion brought citizens together on regular occasions, reinforcing the citizenry's belief that the city was protected by the gods, exposing them to bloody sacrifices that readied them for war and cultivated the virtue necessary for a republic to thrive.

There is a tradition of thought in political philosophy that traces a line between Machiavelli's interpretation of Roman religion and equivalent statements of civil religion in Thomas Hobbes, Jean-Jacques Rousseau, and Enlightenment philosophy.[30] For Rousseau, civil religion fostered the citizenship necessary to consolidate the foundations of the state and cement the social contract.[31] Rousseau explained that although self-preservation and self-interest gave political society a purpose in the eyes of its citizens, it could not make those citizens love it.[32] A civil religion – a religion specific to a particular polity and people – would foment the patriotism that would bind citizens together. Rousseau's case for civil religion rested on two points. First, he argued that 'no state has been founded without religion serving as its base' – religion, by providing solidarity, was a necessary condition of politics; and second, that 'Christian law is at bottom more harmful than useful to a strong constitution of the state' – Christianity was incapable of being the base of politics because it was not a civil religion.[33] By asking citizens to follow two masters, their country and their church, Christianity was in tension with patriotism; and by celebrating meekness, it could not cultivate the active citizenship necessary for a republic to flourish.

Civil religion offered a solution. This religion, imposed on its citizens to convince them to submit to the state's authority, invested politics with a sacral understanding of the state necessary for civic republicanism to flourish. Where Christianity encouraged virtue in the private realm of personal piety, undoing the civic consciousness necessary to bind a republic together, Rousseau argued that a civil religion, by cultivating civic pride in a civic cult, would cultivate virtue in the public sphere and inspired citizens to defend and improve their polity in the belief that there was no good citizen or loyal subject outside the civil faith. Civil religion must be tolerant and restricted to a minimal creed. Citizens should believe in God and accept

---

[29] Ibid., 1.11–15, 2.2. On Machiavelli's views of religion (and his criticism of the Church) see *Machiavelli and Religion: A Reappraisal* special issue of *The Journal of the History of Ideas*, 60:4 (1999).

[30] On Hobbes, see below pp. 160–2, 210–12.

[31] Jean-Jacques Rousseau, *The Social Contract and Other Later Political Writings*, ed. Victor Gourevitch (Cambridge, 1997), book 8.

[32] For commentary, see Ronald Grimsley, *Rousseau and the Religious Quest* (Oxford, 1968); Roger D. Masters, *The Political Philosophy of Rousseau* (Princeton, 1968); A. Melzer, *The Natural Goodness of Man: On the System of Rousseau's Thought* (Chicago, 1990); John Ray, 'Rousseau's Civil Religion "Problem"' in Frankel and Yaffe (eds), *Civil Religion*, pp. 183–97.

[33] Rousseau, *The Social Contract*, pp. 146–9.

the reality of eternal justice (reward for the just and punishment for the wicked) in the life to come. Because all monotheisms could subscribe to these beliefs civil religion could exist alongside other faiths without imposing restrictions on them, ensuring the maintenance of political unity amidst religious diversity. Beyond imposing subscription to that simple creed, the state should not intervene in citizens' faith and ensure that the toleration of all creeds was protected by the state and prevent priests of any faith having political influence. Toleration was the surest way of maintaining peace and preventing the reoccurrence of the religious wars of previous centuries.[34]

The bottom-up understanding of civil religion is associated most closely with the sociologist Robert Bellah.[35] Bellah described the 'religious dimension' that was foundational to American civic life and imbued the US with a moral authority that gestured towards the sacred.[36] American civil religion was manifested in a set of ideas, symbols, and rituals that express the belief that America is a nation chosen by God to uphold God-given values. 'God' is loosely defined and is deliberately non-denominational in this civil religion. Although civil religion is indebted to America's Protestant heritage, it is not explicitly Christian but binds Americans of all faiths under God, fostering unity grounded in shared ideas and values, a civic faith in the transcendent authority of liberty, equality, and toleration.[37]

Bellah's civil religion fits Durkheim's conception of a moral community. Durkheim argued that there is a religious aspect to any human group that informs a system of 'sacred' beliefs, rituals, and symbols that appeal to moral values the group understands to be universal that serve as a unifying story of 'us', the moral identity of a people.[38] It was in rituals, symbols, and ideas that Bellah identified 'an elaborate and well institutionalised civil religion' woven into the fabric of American public life, sanctifying society by providing regular testimony of an obligation, individual and collective, to carry out God's work on earth.[39] That testimony can be found in the invocation of God and providence in the inaugural speeches of presidents, in the use of

---

[34] Rousseau, *The Social Contract*, pp 149–51. Rousseau's civil religion has been criticised as unworkable. See Beiner, *Civil Religion*, pp. 57–8, 215. See also Hilail Gildin, *Rousseau's Social Contract: The Design of an Argument* (Chicago, 1983), pp. 180–1.

[35] Robert Bellah, 'Civil Religion in America', *Daedalus, Journal of the American Academy of arts and Sciences*, 96 (1967), 1000–21. Bellah updated his concept in 'Religion and the Legitimation of the American Republic' in *Varieties of Civil Religion*, eds R. N. Bellah and P. E. Hammon (New York, 1980) and *The Broken Covenant: American Civil Religion in Time of Trial* (Chicago, 1992).

[36] Bellah, 'Civil Religion', p. 40.

[37] *Ibid.*, pp. 46, 50–1. My summary of American civil religion is indebted to Bellah and Philip Gorski, *American Covenant: A History of Civil Religion from the Puritans to the Present* (Princeton, 2017), pp. 13–14, 16–19.

[38] Emile Durkheim, *The Elementary Forms of Religious Life*, trans. Karen G. Fields (New York, 1995).

[39] Bellah, 'Civil Religion', p. 40.

religious terms on public occasions ('one nation under God' in the Pledge of Allegiance) or on public property ('in God we trust' on money), in the calendar of holidays, such as 4 July and Thanksgiving, that celebrate American ideals, and in the singing of the national anthem at public events, daily Pledges of Allegiance in schools, and display of the national flag on public holidays, and the respect accorded to the sacrifices of veterans to the nation and its ideals on Memorial Day that serve as patriotic rituals of the nation's moral authority under God.[40]

These symbols and rituals of civil religion, Bellah argued, suffused American life to create 'a genuine apprehension of universal and transcendental religious reality as seen in or, one could almost say, as revealed through the experience of the American people'.[41] The public history of America is suffused with religious language, a national history modelled on Exodus to plot the trial and redemption of a people.[42] In the seventeenth century, Puritans fled their Egypt (England) to build a New Jerusalem in America, John Winthrop's 'City On a Hill'. But like the Israelites, Americans suffered times of struggle and sacrifice – the Revolution (1775–83) and Civil War (1861–5) – in which their nation was purified and renewed to reconnect the nation with its mission and purpose. American civil religion has sacred *texts* – the Declaration, the Constitution, the Bill of Rights, and the Gettysburg Address. It has sacred *places* – the national cemeteries of Arlington and Gettysburg. It has *martyrs* – Abraham Lincoln and John Fitzgerald Kennedy. And it has *prophets* – the founding fathers.[43] But it was not the crude worshipping of the state.[44] Civil religion was a moral tradition emerging *from* a society not a civil creed imposed *on* a society by a government, from which it was somewhat apart. Bellah argued that because of this there was a prophetic element in civil religion that had been used throughout America's history as a source of judgement, holding the nation or its government to account when it fell short of its ideals.[45]

Bellah's thesis has been heavily criticised.[46] But it has also been hugely influential, inspiring social scientists to study equivalent 'civil religions'

---

[40] Ibid., pp. 42, 44–5, 46, 48–9.

[41] Ibid., pp. 40 (and see discussion on 41) and 49.

[42] For this aspect of Bellah's thought and American civil religion more generally, see Ray Haberski, *God and War: American Civil Religion Since 1945* (New Brunswick, 2012), pp. 77–81; Gorski, *American Covenant*, chapter 1.

[43] Bellah, 'Civil Religion', pp. 47–9, in particular.

[44] Bellah, 'Civil Religion in America', in *Beyond Belief*, p. 169.

[45] Bellah, 'Civil Religion', pp. 50–5. Gorski also stresses the element of renewal in *American Covenant*, passim.

[46] For a discussion see, R. E. Richy and D. G. Jones (eds), *American Civil Religion* (New York, 1974); Carolyn Marvin and David W. Ingle, 'Blood Sacrifice and the Nation: Revisiting Civil Religion', *Journal of the American Academy of Religion*, 64 (1996), 767–80; James Mathieson, 'Twenty Years After Bellah: Whatever Happened to American Civil Religion?', *Sociological Analysis*, 50 (1989), 129–46. The criticisms might be grouped as

in Australia, Chile, Denmark, France, Korea, Malaysia, North Africa, Norway, and the Soviet Union – the 'religious dimension' of public life is seen to be a core aspect of many national identities.[47] By underscoring the continued importance of religion in contemporary society, civil religions are often presented as a counterpoint to the secularisation thesis. They are also seen to bridge the gap between modern state and national identities. The rational-legal authority of modern bureaucratic states is often perceived to lack the emotional pull to bind a people into a nation. Civil religions can provided that pull, creating solidarity by 'abetting politics with transcendent sources of legitimacy'.[48]

Civil Religion and the Reformation

Both the top-down and bottom-up approaches to civil religion trace its origins to the age of Revolutions and Enlightenment. The American Revolution of 1776 is crucial to Bellah's account of civil religion as central to the idea of America; and Rousseau's outline of civil religion is the

---

follows. First, that Bellah's account of American history is selective and does not pay enough attention to the role of coercion, colonialism, and intolerance in America's past. See Leilah Danielson, 'Civil Religion as Myth, Not History', *Religions*, 10 (2019), 1–16. Second, the civil religion is not the only moral tradition in American society. It competes with religious nationalism and liberal secularism. See Steven M. Tipton, 'Civil Religion and Public Theology', in *The Anthem Companion to Robert Bellah*, ed. Matteo Bortolini (London, 2019), pp. 63–80; Marcela Cristi, *From Civil to Political Religion: The Intersection of Culture, Religion, and Politics* (Waterloo, ON, 2001); Marty, 'Two Kinds of Civil Religion', pp. 139–60; Robert Wuthnow, *The Restructuring of American Religion: Society and Faith since World War II* (Princeton, 1988), chapters 10–11; Will Herberg, 'America's Civil Religion: What it is and Whence in Comes', in Richey and Jones, *American Civil Religion*, pp. 76–9, 89. Third, that the concept 'civil religion' is imprecise, and perhaps too slippery to be useful. Separating it from political religion, protestant civil piety, and folk religion is hard. See Gorski, *American Covenant*, passim. See also Haberski, *God and War*.

[47] Pål Ketil Botvar, 'Civil Religion or Nationalism? The National Day Celebrations in Norway', *Religions*, 12 (2021), 1–15; Seong Hwan Cha, 'Korean Civil Religion and Modernity', *Social Compass*, 47 (2000), 467–85; Marcela Cristi and Lorne L. Dawson, 'Civil Religion in Comparative Perspective: Chile under Pinochet (1973–1989)', *Social Compass*, 43 (1996), 319–38; Grace Davie, 'Global Civil Religion: A European Perspective', *Sociology of Religion*, 62 (2001), 455–73; Jeffry R. Halverson, Scott W. Rushton, and Angela Tretherway, 'Mediated Martyrs of the Arab Spring: New Media, Civil Religion, and Narrative in Tunisia and Egypt', *Journal of Communication*, 63 (2013), 312–32; Niels Reeh, 'A Shining City on Another Hill: Danish Civil Religion as State Mythology', *Social Compass*, 58 (2011), 235–46; Daniel Regan, 'Islam, Intellectuals, and Civil Religion in Malaysia', *Sociological Analysis*, 37 (1976), 95–110; Margrit Warburg, 'The Danish Reformation Celebrations as Civil Religion', *Journal of Church and State*, 61 (2018), 222–41; Brad West, 'Enchanting Pasts: The Role of International Civil Religious Pilgrimage in Reimagining National Collective Memory', *Sociological Theory*, 26 (2008), 258–70.

[48] Williams and Fuist, 'Civil Religion and National Politics', p. 930.

yardstick for investigations of the concept's effects on political thought. But civil religion did not begin with or belong to the late eighteenth century. Although the term 'civil religion' did not appear in the period, English political thought in the late seventeenth century was crucial to the development of the concept, as work by Justin Champion, Jeffrey Collins, Mark Goldie, and Ashley Walsh has shown. Those historians have situated civil religion in the context of the English Enlightenment. For Champion, it proved vital as part of the attack on the Church of England by Republicans and Freethinkers and became crucial to the ways in which freethinkers reconsidered the role of religion in society. In an important study, Walsh has argued that the drive to reshape English Protestantism into something resembling a civil religion was much broader than radicalism. Anglicans and dissenters, Whigs and Tories, all wrestled with making religion 'civil' at the turn of the eighteenth century. This volume builds on the work of these historians to argue that the English Reformation and Revolution provide a crucial context for understanding the development of civil religion.

The English Reformation was Erastian – the authority of the church was swallowed by that of the state. The Tudor monarchs attached the church to the state and united both under the authority of the crown-in-parliament. The Royal Supremacy over the church claimed by Henry VIII in a series of laws passed between 1529 and 1536 not only separated England from the authority of the Roman Catholic Church but gave Henry (and all subsequent English monarchs) power over the doctrine and discipline of the Church of England. On paper, the results of the Henrician break from Rome – reiterated by Elizabeth I in 1559 – was a triumph of civil jurisdiction over ecclesiastical authority which denied any claims of independent authority for the church as a body apart from the commonwealth. In reality, the Tudor crown's amalgamation of civil and ecclesiastical jurisdiction left England's constitution ambiguous and strained.[49]

Royal Supremacy was a model of kingship that gestured towards the holy. The English monarch was reimagined as a godly magistrate with a God-given duty to ensure that true religion was preached to their subjects. Godly magistracy was exemplified by the magistrates of Biblical Israel and the early church. Tudor monarchs were presented as the heirs of the Old Testament kings of Israel – David, Hezekiah, and Josiah – who had crushed idolatry (reimagined here as popery) in their realms and propagated the word (Protestantism). Royal Supremacy was also presented as an emulation of the Christian emperors of Rome, who had united civil and ecclesiastical authority to ensure peace and unity in their commonwealths. In John Foxe's *Acts and Monuments* (1563) and John Jewel's *Apology* (1564), the Tudor monarchs were presented as Constantine, the emperor whose conversion

---

[49] Geoffrey Elton, *Tudor England*, 3rd edn (London, 1991), chapters 5–6.

to Christianity (AD312) had ended the persecution of the early church and whose godly magistracy had ensured the success of the gospel.[50]

Quashing the pretensions of priests was critical to the success of these godly magistrates. Protestant histories argued that it was necessary for princes to resist the claims of the church to autonomy, claims which, as the corruption of medieval Christianity by the Roman Church showed, led to persecution, false doctrine, and the usurpation of royal authority over the church in their realms by the papacy. These histories presented the English Reformation as the restoration of the pure church of Christ and the Apostles before papal corruption, plotting the past as a perennial battle of godly prince against over-mighty prelate finally resolved in the triumph of civil authority at the Reformation. Against critics who claimed Royal Supremacy was the exercise of civil tyranny over the church, Protestant histories argued that the supremacy of a godly magistrate was necessary to liberate Christianity from the tyranny of priests.

Anti-clerical positions such as these allowed the crown to present the English Reformation as moderate, a civil *via media* between the twin excesses of papal tyranny and Reformed Protestant anarchy that ensured peace, stability, and order in the commonwealth. Preventing those excesses gave the English state grounds for enforcing religious uniformity, insisting on all subjects attending the Church of England as a mark of political loyalty to the crown.[51] Attendance at its services was legislated in the 1559 Act of Uniformity, which imposed a heavy penal code to persecute dissent, and the establishment of oaths of obedience that made membership of the church a precondition of political officeholding.[52] The Erastian settlement made religious conformity and political loyalty one and the same: the godly magistrate had both a right to expect religious conformity and a god-given duty to enforce it.[53]

However, Royal Supremacy caused a series of headaches that ultimately destabilised English politics between the accession of Elizabeth I in 1558 and the Revolution of 1688. The first of these was the tension between the ideal of religious uniformity enshrined in the constitution and the impulse of Christian liberty innate in Protestantism. This tension was expressed in Puritanism, the hotter strain of Protestantism that emerged within the Church of England from the mid-1560s. Puritans claimed that the 1559 Religious Settlement had only half-Reformed the Church of

---

[50] Felicity Heal, *Reformation in Britain and Ireland* (Oxford, 2003), p. 388; V. Norskov Olsen, *John Foxe and the Elizabethan Church* (Berkeley, CA, 2022: original 1973), pp. 183–5.

[51] Ethan Shagan, *The Rule of Moderation: Violence, Religion, and the Politics of Restraint in Early Modern England* (Cambridge, 2011), chapters 1–3.

[52] Eliz. 1 c. 2.

[53] Alexandra Walsham, *Charitable Hatred: Tolerance and Intolerance in England 1500–1700* (Manchester, 2006), chapter 2.

INTRODUCTION

England and called for Elizabeth, as a godly magistrate, to implement a further Reformation of liturgy and discipline necessary to fully convert the English people.[54] That neither she nor her successor James I heeded these calls raised questions about civil control of religion in England – a godly magistrate was surely responsible for the edification of a godly people. Legal requirements to attend a half-reformed church or, in the case of ministers, to conduct worship according to the Book of Common Prayer they felt to be 'popish', bridled against puritan consciences and the belief that scripture, not the magistrate, should have the final word in matters of faith. By the end of Elizabeth's reign insistence on conformity to a church that remained unreformed smacked of tyranny to many of the godly.

The tension between Christian liberty and religious uniformity was closely related to the second headache that Erastianism caused the Tudor state: ecclesiology. The theology of the Church of England's structure, hierarchy, and authority was a source of continued debate and political strain from the mid-sixteenth century to the early eighteenth.[55] And the Erastian nature of the Reformation – the authority of the civil magistrate to determine what the church was when many reformers thought that scripture alone could determine that question – only added to the strain.

Soon after the 1559 Settlement, leading theologians like Thomas Cartwright, Lady Margaret Professor of Divinity at the University of Cambridge, claimed its episcopal structure was unscriptural, arguing that the Apostolic Church was Presbyterian – English law conflicted with the bible. In the early 1570s two radical *Admonitions* to parliament proposed that the religious settlement be rewritten along Presbyterian lines (abolishing bishops and their courts).[56] The crown's refusal to do so led many Puritans to see a tension between the authority of the magistrate and that of the word. Moreover, the bishop's defence of the 1559 settlement and clampdown on Presbyterians as 'seditious' voices in the church and state stirred-up anti-episcopal sentiments that became increasingly vehement in the 1580s.[57] This culminated in the Martin Marprelate tracts, a series of scabrous satires that indicted the Elizabethan bishops as 'petty popes and antichrists' who ruled over an unreformed church that remained a limb of the beast.[58] The persecution of Presbyterianism (and of Puritans more generally) in the 1590s

---

[54] Patrick Collinson, *The Elizabethan Puritan Movement* (London, 1967), parts 1, 2, and 4.
[55] On the eighteenth century, see Ingram, *Reformation without end*. On the long-Reformation more generally, see Nicholas Tyacke (ed.), *England's Long Reformation, 1500–1800* (London, 1996) and Patrick Collinson, *The Birthpangs of Protestant England: Religion and cultural change in the sixteenth and seventeenth centuries* (Basingstoke, 1988).
[56] W. H. Frere and C. E. Douglas (eds), *Puritan Manifestoes* (London, 1954).
[57] Collinson, *Puritan Movement*, parts 5 and 8; Patrick Collinson, *Richard Bancroft & Elizabethan Anti-Puritanism* (Cambridge, 2013); Polly Ha, *English Presbyterianism, 1590–1640* (Stanford, 2010).
[58] Joseph Black (ed.), *The Martin Marprelate Tracts* (Cambridge, 2008).

15

under Archbishop John Whitgift was severe, and saw bishops use the weight of the civil magistrate to enforce uniformity, partly under the auspices of protecting royal authority from sedition. Persecution was coupled with assertive defences of the Erastian settlement of 1559. Works of theology and history by Richard Bancroft, Whitgift, and Richard Hooker presented the ecclesiology of the Church of England as a matter determined by the civil authority under the Royal Supremacy. In his *Laws of Ecclesiastical Government* (1594-7), Hooker argued that all religious jurisdiction stemmed from the crown.[59] For Puritans who thought that ecclesiology unscriptural, English Reformation Erastianism enforced uniformity to a church that was at best impure and at worst tyrannical.

The relationship between Erastianism and ecclesiology caused friction elsewhere, too. Not all conformist churchmen were happy to accept that the authority of the church stemmed solely from the crown, and argued that the church was an independent body with authority grounded in scripture, the Church Fathers, and continuity with medieval Christianity. In the later sixteenth and early seventeenth centuries a growing body of ecclesiology added caveats to the Royal Supremacy. This work presented the Church of England as an episcopal church whose bishops had a *de jure divino* authority to govern independent of the civil magistrate.[60] From the mid-1620s this vision of the Church of England was associated most closely with the Archbishop of Canterbury William Laud. The church Laudianism created – characterised by heightened ceremonialism, the growing stature of the clergy, a growing authority for church courts, and a suspicion of Reformed Protestantism – upset the mainstream of English Protestantism, leading many to express concern that the Church of England was backsliding to popery in the hands of lordly prelates bent on usurping the authority of princes over their churches.[61]

The Tudor Reformations left a series of unresolved tensions between religion and politics that the Revolutions of the next century had to contend with: a clash of *de jure divino* and Erastian conceptions of authority in the constitution; the remit and limits of the Royal Supremacy; and the relationship between Christian liberty and the right of a godly magistrate to impose uniformity to a national church on its subjects. During the Civil War, those strains were reanimated in a new context, shaping debates about the constitution, royal authority, and the nature of religious and political

---

[59] Richard Hooker, *Of the Laws of Ecclesiastical Polity*, ed. Christopher Morris (London, 1954).

[60] Andrew Foster, 'The Clerical Estate Revitalised', in *The Early Stuart Church*, ed. Kenneth Fincham (Basingstoke, 1993), pp. 139-60; J. Sommerville, 'The Royal Supremacy & Episcopacy Jure Divino, 1603-40', *Journal of Ecclesiastical History*, 34:4 (1983), 548-58.

[61] See Nicholas Tyacke, *Anti-Calvinists: The Rise of English Arminianism 1590-1640* (Oxford, 1990).

liberty in important ways.⁶² And the uneasy alliance of what would become (after 1662) the High Church and the Erastian Royal Supremacy continued to destabilise politics into the early eighteenth century. Nonjuring after 1689, the Church in Danger campaign of the 1700s, and the Sacheverell Affair were all driven in part by the clash between the Erastian legacy of the Reformation and the *de jure divino* claims to independent authority by the Church of England.⁶³

Civil Religion and the British Revolution

The conflict between Charles I and his Parliament that led to personal rule, civil war, and regicide was both influenced by the religious conflicts sparked by the Reformation and in turn shaped religious divisions and tensions between church and state in important new directions. It is important to acknowledge, as several of the contributors to this volume do, that the term 'civil religion' was not one that was explicitly used by early modern thinkers. But several texts produced during the English Republic – in particular Thomas Hobbes's *Leviathan* (1651) and James Harrington's *Oceana* (1656) – reframed the relationship between church and state in ways that ultimately shaped the tradition of civil religion in subsequent centuries. Other texts not traditionally associated with the canon of civil religion responded to questions about the role of the magistrate in governing religion, the necessity of a national church, and the balance between individual Christian liberty and the public profession of religion in ways that also shaped political thinking on civil religion. Goldie has argued that a neo-Harringtonian tradition of English republicanism was vital to shaping Whig conceptions of civil religion and civil society later in the seventeenth century.⁶⁴

The Church of England's monopoly on religion collapsed in the 1640s and 1650s, and that collapse put strain on the Erastian nature of England's constitution as first Presbyterians and then Independents tried to find a workable settlement in England's increasingly diverse religious culture. For all their cries of persecution at the hands of the established church, the Presbyterians were as committed to uniformity as the bishops they had abolished. The Westminster Assembly of Divines, established in 1643 was tasked with restructuring the Church of England in a Presbyterian

---

⁶² See Michael J. Braddick, *God's Fury, England's fire: a new history of the English Civil Wars* (London, 2008), chapters 1, 6 and 16 in particular; Charles W. A. Prior and Glenn Burgess (eds), *England's wars of Religion, revisited* (Farnham, 2011). On the Restoration, see Jacqueline Rose, *Godly Kingship in Restoration England: The Politics of the Royal Supremacy, 1660–88* (Cambridge, 2011).
⁶³ Ingram, *Reformation Without End*; Geoffrey S. Holmes, *The Trial of Doctor Sacheverell* (London, 1973).
⁶⁴ See below, note 91.

mode, and in *A Holy Commonwealth* Richard Baxter offered his blueprint for a Christian Commonwealth modelled on that of the Hebrews. But the Presbyterian ideal of uniformity was shattered by the rise to prominence of the Independents for whom the key to peace was not uniformity but liberty of conscience.

As J. C. Davis emphasised, liberty of conscience needs to be understood in the context of the time, free from anachronistic assumptions.[65] Liberty of conscience denoted the freedom for each individual to seek knowledge of God and of the path to their own salvation for themselves. This was not incompatible with authority, submission, and discipline. What early modern advocates of liberty of conscience wanted was the freedom to submit to God's governance, as they understood it, rather than being dictated to in religious matters by any other authority, state or church. As Davis explained it, liberty of conscience and submission/discipline were two sides of the same coin: 'the mainstream spawned by the revolution, wanted submission to Christ and saw liberty as only a preliminary to that act'.[66] This meant that a commitment to liberty of conscience led to a wide array of different positions on ecclesiology, the constitution, and the relationship between church and state during the 1650s. These ranged from a godly commonwealth, via a broad Erastian settlement combined with toleration, through to the complete separation of church and state.

The Independents did not agree on what life after religious uniformity should look like. Opinions were myriad but might be lumped together as 'magisterial' and 'radical' independency for the sake of convenience. The programme of the 'magisterial independents' was laid out in *The Humble Proposals* presented to the Rump Parliament in early February 1652 by John Owen and his associates.[67] It sought to address the issue of how to ensure that all parishes in England were provided with 'able, godly, and orthodox Ministers', by setting up a system of Triers (to vet new ministers) and Ejectors (to remove unsuitable ones).[68] A mixed committee of respected ministers and laymen was to be established in each county to consider testimonials from potential ministers. Another committee comprising clergy and laity was to be appointed by Parliament to travel the nation 'to enquire after, examine, judge of, and eject' those who were found to be 'unfit for the Ministry, or

---

[65] J. C. Davis, 'Religion and the Struggle for Freedom in the English Revolution', *The Historical Journal*, 35:3 (1992), 507–30.

[66] *Ibid.*, 517 and 528.

[67] *The Humble Proposals of Mr. Owen, Mr. Tho. Goodwin, Mr. Nye, Mr. Sympson, and other ministers, who presented the petition to the Parliament, and other persons, Febr. 11 under debate by a committee this 31. of March, 1652 for the furtherance and Propagation of the Gospel in this Nation...* (London, 1652). On this see: Jeffrey R. Collins, *The Allegiance of Thomas Hobbes* (Oxford, 2005), pp. 167–9.

[68] *Ibid.*, p. 1.

teaching of Schooles'.⁶⁹ The *Humble Proposals* provoked much criticism, especially over the question of the magistrate's power in matters of religion. Yet, the Cromwellian religious settlement established in 1654 imposed a similar programme, the only difference being that in the Cromwellian system the Triers formed a central committee of clergy and laymen, while the Ejectors were organised at a local level and were all members of the laity. As Jeffrey Collins noted, 'Cromwell, though concerned to protect some free conscience outside the established church, was equally driven to protect the Erastian legacy of the Reformation within it.'⁷⁰

The more radical Independents overlapped, both in ideas and membership, with a cohort of 'godly republicans'. Yet just like the Independents, the republicans were divided. While Henry Vane, Henry Stubbe, and John Milton called for the separation of church and state, others – not least James Harrington – offered their own version of republican civil religion.⁷¹ Moreover in a further indication of the complexity of this debate, Harrington – on this issue at least – had much in common with Thomas Hobbes.

The works of Harrington and Hobbes must be seen not as stepping stones between Machiavelli and Rousseau in the development of a Civil Religion tradition of political philosophy, but as responses to the political problems of the 1650s outlined above. It might be thought that Hobbes the advocate of autocracy and Harrington the republican advocate of democracy would be worlds apart on the heated debate about the proper relationship between church and state in the 1650s, but their similarities on civil religion belie this. Those similarities result from them both responding to the same contemporary circumstances with regard to religion in Cromwellian England and the issues it raised. Indeed Harrington deliberately set up his position on ordination in direct opposition to both the Presbyterians (as represented by Lazarus Seaman) and orthodox Anglicans (epitomised by Henry Hammond) and in defence of Hobbes (whom Hammond had attacked).⁷² Moreover, both Hobbes and Harrington shared a discomfort at the divisions of the civil war, and a primary aim of both *Leviathan* and *Oceana* was to restore peace and harmony to a war-torn nation. In religious terms they both agreed that this could best be achieved through an Erastian settlement. This connection has also been noted by Jeffrey Collins, who suggests that it 'proves easier

---

⁶⁹ *Ibid.*, p. 4.
⁷⁰ *Ibid.*, p. 169.
⁷¹ On these divisions see Rachel Hammersley, 'Rethinking the Political Thought of James Harrington: Royalism, Republicanism and Democracy', *History of European Ideas*, 39:3 (2013), 357–70 and Martin Dzelzainis, 'Harrington and the Oligarchs: Milton, Vane, and Stubbe', in *Perspectives on English Revolutionary Republicanism*, eds Gaby Mahlberg and Dirk Wiemann (Farnham, 2014), pp. 15–33.
⁷² Henry Hammond, *A Letter of Resolution to Six Quaeres, of Present Use in the Church of England* (London, 1653). For the response to Hobbes see pp. 384–408.

to establish Thomas Hobbes's links with Interregnum republicans than to establish the extent of his royalist connections'.[73]

There were three key elements to Harrington's religious position. The first was Erastianism. Harrington insisted that both civil and religious matters should be firmly under state control. His sixth constitutional order in *The Commonwealth of Oceana* sets out the role of the Council of Religion. Its members are all Senators, and no ministers of religion are included among its membership, thereby ensuring civil control over religious affairs. Moreover, all ministers within the national system are educated at the public universities. In later works Harrington justified his reasons for adopting Erastianism, insisting on the need for 'public leading' in matters of religion.[74] Second, Harrington argued state control over a national church must be balanced with toleration for gathered congregations or Protestant sects. Not only could these congregations worship (and select their ministers) as they wished, but there was to be no disqualification from, or restrictions on, citizenship on the grounds of religion. As Goldie noted, Harrington's system constituted 'a judicious marriage of congregationalist Independency and Erastian centralism'.[75] National religion and liberty of conscience were mutually reinforcing in Harrington's mind. To have liberty of conscience it was necessary to have a national religion and to have a national religion required an endowed clergy. In this respect, Harrington's system was similar to that of the magisterial independents.[76]

The final element of Harrington's religious policy involved the election of ministers. This brought the practice of the Church of England in line with that of the primitive church, and mapped Harrington's religious policy onto his political system. In *Oceana* when a congregation required a new minister, it would apply to one of the universities which would send it a probationer to act as its minister for one year. At the end of the year the elders of the parish would put the probationer to the ballot. If he was approved by two thirds of the parishioners, he would be kept on. If not, he would be dismissed and an alternative probationer would be sent. Harrington justified this practice with reference to the primitive church. Engaging with the wider debate on ordination that was alive at the time, Harrington argued against both Anglicans and Presbyterians that within the primitive church elders had been elected by the raising of hands in the congregation (*chirotonia*) not the laying on of hands by a cleric (*chirothesia*), the apostles adopting the Graeco-Roman political practices in operation in the communities in which they lived. On this basis he insisted on ministers being elected by their

---

[73] Collins, 'Quentin Skinner's Hobbes', especially, 361–2. See also Collins, *The Allegiance of Thomas Hobbes*, pp. 159–205, quotation at p. 185.
[74] James Harrington, *The Art of Law-giving* (London, 1659), III, p. 678 in Pocock edition; James Harrington, *Aphorisms Political*, 2nd edn (London, 1659), p. 766 in Pocock edition.
[75] Goldie, 'The Civil Religion of James Harrington', p. 207.
[76] See John Coffey's chapter below, pp. 139–58.

congregations rather than being ordained by bishops. This, Harrington insisted, was the only way to banish priestcraft. As he asserted in *Pian Piano*, if it were acknowledged that ordination within the early church had been by the upholding not the laying on of hands – that is, by the power of the people not the clergy – and if ordination was then 'restored unto the People', Divines would lose that power and 'there is an end of Priest-craft'.[77]

The civil religion advocated by Hobbes differed from that recommended by Harrington in several important ways. Both adopted an Erastian position, insisting that both civil and religious matters should be firmly under state control. For Hobbes, the competing claims to authority between the civil and spiritual powers 'has of late... been the cause of civil wars in all places of Christendom' and England was no exception.[78] Hobbes therefore insisted on state control of religious matters, an argument that was set out in clear visual form in the frontispiece to *Leviathan*. Where Harrington thought that a democratic political system was best placed to ensure civil oversight of religion, however, Hobbes urged that it could only be achieved by a strong, autocratic magistrate. That magistrate, Hobbes argued, should enforce religious uniformity to quash schism and dissent to ensure that religious diversity did not lead to religious conflict. Where Harrington thought religious peace would be best secured by tolerating religious dissent, Hobbes saw dissent (if publicly expressed) as a threat to peace and sovereignty.

Hobbes's case for the magistrate's control over religion was based in part on his interpretation of the Apostolic Church. Hobbes drew a distinction between the period before the conversion of state powers to Christianity (when ecclesiastical power was held only by the apostles and those whom they ordained and operated purely by persuasion) and the situation after, when states adopted coercive measures with regard to religion. Once Christianity became the state religion, Hobbes explained, pastors in a Christian Commonwealth derived their right to teach and perform offices from the civil sovereign. This was because the ruler effectively took on the role of pastor, with power to ordain other pastors.[79] Whereas the sovereign's power was *iure divino*, coming direct from God, a pastor's power (including that of bishops) was *iure civili*, or derived from the sovereign. All ministers then, including bishops, were firmly under the civil state. Unlike Harrington, then, Hobbes did not interpret the method of electing ministers in the Apostolic Church as providing a model for his own time.

The Erastianism of Hobbes and Harrington was reflected in the Cromwellian religious settlement. Jeffrey Collins has argued that Hobbes found a hospitable environment for his political thought – and in particular his ecclesiological

---

[77] James Harrington, *Pian Piano*, in *The Political Works of James Harrington*, ed. J. G. A. Pocock (Cambridge, 1977), p. 384.
[78] Hobbes to Devonshire, 23 July 1641 as quoted in Collins, 'Quentin Skinner's Hobbes', 360-1.
[79] Thomas Hobbes, *Leviathan*, ed. Richard Tuck (Cambridge, 1991), p. 373.

principles – under the Cromwellian Protectorate, and has gone so far as to suggest that *Leviathan* was read as a Cromwellian text.[80] The same can be said of the religious provisions in *Oceana*. It too combined a national religion with liberty for tender consciences. The Triers performed the functions of Harrington's Council of Religion, while the role of the Ejectors was reflected in Harrington's Censors. It is, however, noteworthy that the democratic component of Harrington's system was again largely absent.

It is not surprising, then, that the Cromwellian religious settlement generated opposition from those who also opposed Harrington's religious proposals. Richard Baxter lamented the regime's encouragement of anarchy and licentiousness and welcomed Richard Cromwell's succession in late 1658 as a moment of hope and opportunity for the establishment of a holy commonwealth. At the same time, the radical independents and religious republicans condemned the regime for not granting sufficient toleration to the sects and decried the continued exercise of state power over religious matters as a betrayal of the Good Old Cause. As chapters by John Coffey and Connor Robinson in this volume show, the debate about the public role of religion under the commonwealth, the legitimacy of a national church, and the protection and fulfilment of Christian liberty, spanned the spectrum of religious and political positions during the 1650s. The civil religion of Hobbes and Harrington must be understood as part of much broader conversations about sovereignty, liberty of conscience, and the fulfilment of the Reformation that engulfed English politics in the mid-seventeenth century.

Understanding this should make us stress two points. First, as should be clear, it would be wrong to conclude that advocates of civil religion (or other forms of public religion) in the 1650s were 'Machiavellian' in the crude sense of subordinating religion to political ends. Most remained firmly grounded in the Christian faith and were engaged in genuine attempts to reconcile the tensions between church and state that had been generated by the recent religious and political conflicts, rather than to advance modern secularisation.

Second, we must see the emergence of civil religion in these decades as part of a complex picture. The Long Reformation compounded by the conflict between King and Parliament in the mid-seventeenth century raised a whole series of issues for the relationship between religion and politics, church and state. What we see in the writings of this period is, in Connor Robinson's words, a kaleidoscope of responses to these issues, and those that might be deemed 'civil religion' must be viewed as part of this wider dialogue and the complex alliances and divisions that it generated. Harrington's civil religion looks very similar to that adopted by Hobbes but the two men also departed from each other on certain key points. Conversely, in favouring the subordination of church to state rather than their separation, Harrington found himself at odds with godly republicans including Vane

---

[80] Collins, *The Allegiance of Thomas Hobbes*, pp. 160 and 173.

and Stubbe, but in line with both Cromwell and Penn. The debate, then, was complex, multifaceted and cannot simply be slotted into a narrative of the unfolding development of Civil Religion as a grand concept.

Civil Religion and the English Enlightenment

The civil religion of the Enlightenment was developed in response to the defining political problem of the seventeenth century – liberty. Political liberty was concerned with the relationship between monarchy and subject, the establishment of popular sovereignty, and the place of both in the constitution, matters that were central to the civil wars and 1688 Revolution. But religious liberty was equally important. Whether subjects had the right to believe and worship according to their conscience became a central problem of seventeenth-century politics, and had important ramifications for England's constitution, the structure of its state, and the role of the monarch and the established church in policing belief.[81] Since the Henrician Reformation of the 1530s, English monarchs had been duty bound to enforce religious uniformity in the form of conformity to the Church of England. Those Protestants who thought that the English Reformation was not reformed enough – Puritans in the late sixteenth century and a raft of heterodox Protestant non-conformists from the mid-seventeenth century – argued that their religious liberty was impeded by uniformity.[82] The prohibition on the public profession of faith for Protestants outside the established church, enforced conformity to a church they felt to be 'popish', and the use of the civil magistrate to impose a harsh penal code on dissent, made the church, its bishops, and its courts persecutory in their eyes.[83]

The fact that political citizenship, the right to hold office in parliament, local government, or the law, depended on conformity to the established church meant that constraints on religious liberty were constraints on political liberty. The civil wars of the 1640s, republican experiments of the 1650, succession crisis of 1678–83, and 1688 Revolution were all struggles about the twin heads of religious and political liberty. A battle between two conflicting Protestant tenets was an important dynamic of those struggles: the view that liberty was essential to being Christian (the Reformation had been a revolt against the spiritual tyranny of the papal church); and the view that the godly magistrate had a duty to impose true religion on its

---

[81] John Coffey, *Persecution and Toleration in Protestant England, 1558–1689* (Harlow, 2000), chapters 6–7; Walsham, *Charitable Hatred*.
[82] Peter Lake, *Anglicans and Puritans? Presbyterianism and English Conformist Thought from Whitgift to Hooker* (London, 1988).
[83] Mark Goldie, 'The Theory of Religious Intolerance in Restoration England', in *From Persecution to Toleration: The Glorious Revolution & Religion in England*, eds Ole Peter Grell, Jonathan Irvine, and Nicholas Tyacke (Oxford, 1991), pp. 331–68.

subjects (Reformation histories celebrated the crown as the surest protector of Protestant England from popish corruption).[84] The British Revolutions struggled with an insoluble problem – how to square the existence of a national church with a commitment to religious liberty.

The tension between liberty and uniformity became more acute at the Restoration. The Clarendon Code reasserted the political role of the Church of England, binding together monarchy and Anglicanism to make conformity to the church a precondition of loyalty to the crown in the wake of the puritan revolution of 1640–60 that had tried to destroy both.[85] For High Churchmen, any wavering on the strictures of conformity was a threat to order and an invitation to schism. From the early 1670s, those churchmen were vigorous in their commitment to doctrinal and ritual uniformity, suspicious of latitudinarian calls for comprehension or toleration as threats to its authority, and wedded to an anti-puritan ideology expressed in the formation of a persecuting society.[86] A coercive penal code prohibited Protestant non-conformists from public expressions of faith, subjected them to fines and imprisonments, and censored them in the press and pulpit. The church coupled this coercion with a vigorous defence of the *de jure divino* nature of the authority of the Church of England, its bishops, and the Royal Supremacy that protected both.[87] The campaign against political absolutism and religious uniformity were two sides of the same coin.

The relationship between church and crown was muddier after the 1688 Revolution. The Toleration Act of 1689 ended the Anglican monopoly of religion by extending toleration to most Protestant non-conformists.[88] The refusal of leading nonjuring Anglicans to takes oaths to the new monarchs, William and Mary, and the distaste of the High Church at those monarchs' commitment to Whiggery and appointment of a latitudinarian episcopate, led to the conservative core of the established church believing that there was a conspiracy of Whigs, non-conformists, and radicals to undermine the church. The Tory-High Church slogan 'the Church is in Danger' was a central part of British politics in the first decades of the eighteenth century.[89] Ecclesiology, the relationship between church and state, and tension between religious liberty and drive for Anglican hegemony was the 'axis for both religion and political disputes of the period'.[90]

One solution to those tensions was to limit the political authority of the clergy. Civil religion was one means of doing so and must be understood in a broader current of anti-clericalism that was fundamental to Whig politics

---

[84] Shagan, *Moderation*, chapters 1, 3 and 4; Walsham, *Charitable Hatred*, chapter 1.
[85] John Spurr, *The Restoration Church of England, 1646–89* (New Haven, 1991).
[86] Goldie, 'Theory of Religious Intolerance', *passim*.
[87] Cha II. C. 1; 16 Cha. 2. C 2; 25 Cha. 2. C. 2.
[88] Will & Mar c. 18.
[89] Julian Hoppit, *A Land of Liberty? England, 1689–1727* (Oxford, 2000).
[90] Champion, *Pillars of Priestcraft*, p. 6.

at the turn of the eighteenth century. Goldie has argued that religion was central to the Whig campaigns for liberty and parliamentary sovereignty that reshaped English politics from the 1680s.[91] The Whigs were as concerned to reframe the relationship between temporal and spiritual authority, *regnum* and *sacerdotium*, as they were to reshape the relationship between crown and parliament. Ending Anglican control over religion was at the core of calls for liberty. But as in the 1640s and 1650s, challenging religious uniformity involved reconsideration of what a church was and rethinking what its relationship with civil authority should be. Calls for civil religion appeared in this context.

The Whigs, republicans, and freethinkers, who made that case, were concerned above all with *sacerdos*: the claims of the clergy to a divinely appointed spiritual superiority over the laity.[92] Their case was anti-clerical, not anti-religious, with the clergy's control over religion, not with religion itself. They saw control as the product of priestcraft, the dogmatism and intolerance perpetrated by the clergy in all ages to maintain its sinister control of politics. 'Religion's safe, with priestcraft is the war,/ All friends to priestcraft, foes to mankind are', claimed John Toland, in what was no doubt a tongue-in-cheek quip to critics who thought him irreligious.[93] Gilbert Burnet, Bishop of Salisbury, remembered that 'priestcraft grew to be another word in fashion' during the 1690s when 'it became a common topic of discourse to treat all mysteries in religion as the contrivancies of priests to bring the world into a submission to them'.[94] Priestcraft was a three-pronged conspiracy for wealth and power. The clergy corrupted pure religion with mysteries that aped holiness, spellbinding the laity into submitting to their authority through the invention of superstitions, legends, and creeds that were a distraction from the simplicity of the gospel. They presented themselves as the sole interpreters of those mysteries, intermediaries with God on the laity's behalf. And they censored and persecuted to enforce lay submission to their invented creeds, manipulating the civil magistrate to punish those whom they declared heterodox or heretical to ensure their authority was unchallenged.[95]

---

[91] Mark Goldie, 'John Locke, the early Lockeans, and priestcraft', *Intellectual History Review*, 28 (2018), 125-44; Mark Goldie, 'Priestcraft & the birth of Whiggism', in *Political discourse in early modern Britain*, eds Nicholas T. Phillipson and Quentin Skinner (Cambridge, 1993), pp. 209-31; Goldie, 'The Civil Religion of James Harrington'; and Mark Goldie, 'Civil Religion & the English Enlightenment', in *Politics, politeness and patriotism*, eds Gordon J. Schochet, Patricia E. Tatspaugh and Carol Brobeck (Washington, DC, 1993), pp. 31-46. These ideas were developed by Champion, *Pillars of Priestcraft*, passim.

[92] Walsh, *Civil Religion*, pp. 16-17, 23-6, 34-5.

[93] John Toland, *Clito: A Poem on the Force of Eloquence* (1700), p. 26.

[94] Gilbert Burnet, *A History of his Own Times*, 2 vols (London, 1838), II, p. 649.

[95] See *The Folly of Priestcraft* (1690); *Priestcraft Expos'd* (1691); John Dennis, *The Danger of Priestcraft* (1702); Edmund Hickeringill, *The History of Priestcraft* (1705). The fullest

The term 'priestcraft' was first used in James Harrington's *Pian Piano* (1657), a defence of *Oceana* against the criticisms of Henry Ferne, the royalist archdeacon of Leicester. Ferne objected to much of *Oceana*, including 'what is said in relation to the church, or religion in the point of government, ordination, [and] excommunication'.[96] Ferne argued that the civil powers should not encroach on the *jure divino* authority of the church. For a commonwealth to be godly it was necessary to follow the model of the Apostolic Church, which Ferne argued had been governed by the clergy independently of the civil magistrate in the three centuries before the Roman emperors converted to Christianity. Harrington countered that this was a plea for priestly power, a power that history showed had curtailed liberties both Christian and civil. In all commonwealths that had been governed peacefully and effectively the civil authority had been supreme in both the temporal and spiritual spheres. Priests tried to disbar secular oversight of the church and lay discussion of religion because they wanted a monopoly on divinity, manipulating lay attachment to the supernatural to secure power and wealth. The Roman Church was the worst historical example of that conspiracy, Harrington argued, but priestcraft was a propensity of *all* churchmen. Securing peace and liberty in the commonwealth was dependent on the civil magistrate's preventing the clergy accumulating power. Civil oversight of religion was necessary if the English Republic was to shake the yoke of the priest.[97]

Priestcraft was also understood to be a prop of arbitrary government, twin conspiracies bent on corrupting the liberties of subjects. The premise here was simple. Priestcraft had allowed clergy of all stripes – Catholic, Protestant, and Presbyterian – to hold power over the minds of men; they used that power to support the civil tyranny of absolute monarchy; and in return the civil tyrant used the sword to protect the clergy's monopoly over religion.[98] The case was put forcefully by Robert Molesworth in his *Account of Denmark* (1694). Molesworth's history served to warn English society of the malign influence of the Anglican Church as a prop of tyranny by charting the extent to which the arbitrary authority of the Danish monarchy was facilitated by the hold of the clergy over its people's conscience that had allowed 'the passive obedience principle [to] ride triumphant in this

---

indictment of priestcraft can be found in Richard Baron's compilation, *Pillars of Priestcraft Shaken*, 4 vols (1768).
[96] James Harrington, *Pian Piano* (1657), 'Epistle to the Reader'. See Rachel Hammersley, *James Harrington: an Intellectual Biography* (Oxford, 2019), pp. 127–31; Rachel Hammersley, 'The Commonwealth of Oceana & the Republican Tradition', in *The Oxford Handbook of Literature and the English Revolution*, ed. Laura L. Knoppers (Oxford, 2012), pp. 534–50.
[97] *The Political Works of James Harrington*, ed. Pocock (Cambridge, 1977), pp. 371–83.
[98] See S. J. Barnett, *Idol Temples and Crafty Priests: The Origins of English Anti-clericalism* (New York, 1999).

INTRODUCTION

unhappy kingdom'.[99] The *Account* became a bestseller across Europe and warned Protestants who thought their Reformations had secured their liberties from corrupt priests. Although Catholic priests were 'the most exquisite' servants of tyranny, Protestant clergy, who depended on princes for their power and place in society, were quick to vouchsafe civil tyranny in support for the continuation of their tyranny over souls. Molesworth noted that 'the clergy, who always made such bargains, were…the instruments that first promoted, and now keep the people in a due temper of slavery'.[100] Blind obedience to priests fostered blind obedience to princes. Molesworth was far from alone in making this link. Thomas Pope Blount put it more bluntly. The 'chief business [of] these spiritual Machiavellians', he proclaimed, was 'to give a helping hand towards making princes arbitrary'.[101]

The war against priestcraft, then, was concerned with the restoration of political and religious liberties. Exposing the histories of priestly corruption was about the relationship between political authority and religious truth, and *who* had the authority to declare what was true in matters of religion and *on what grounds*. Champion showed that republican and radical counter-histories of Christianity sought to undermine the political authority of the Church of England by showing that authority to be conventional (the product of human history) rather than *de jure divino* (the grant of divine will): churches were invented by men, not decreed by God.[102] Anglican histories by clerics like Peter Heylyn grounded the moral and political authority of the Church of England, its spiritual supremacy over the laity, and its episcopal government, as a continuation of the Apostolic Church.[103] Radical counter-histories presented those claims as priestcraft, arguing that there was no case for the Anglican monopoly over religion on the grounds of either *de jure divino* or continuity with the Apostolic Church. The authority of priests was grounded in human machinations: the perversion of scripture and misuse of historical evidence to support priestly interest. Histories of religion exposed priestcraft at work.[104]

---

[99] Robert Molesworth, *An Account of Denmark* (1694), pp. 74. We are indebted here to Champion, *Pillars of Priestcraft*, pp. 178 and 182.
[100] *Ibid.*, sigs. B2r–b8v, pp. 55–75, quotation at p. 74. For similar accounts of priestcraft see William Stephens and John Dennis.
[101] Thomas Pope Blount, *Essays on Several Subjects* (1691), pp. 12, 52.
[102] Champion, *Pillars of Priestcraft*, chapters 4–6 in particular.
[103] See, for example, Peter Heylyn, *Ecclesia Restaurata: The History of the Reformation of the Church of England* (1661) and *A Help to English History* (1671). On Heylyn, see Anthony Milton, *Laudian & Royalist Polemic in seventeenth-century England: the career & writing of Peter Heylyn* (Manchester, 2007).
[104] Charles Blount, *The Oracles of Reason* (1693); E. Herbert, *The Antient Religion of the Gentiles* (1705); E. Herbert, *De Religione Laici*, ed. H. T. Hutcheson (Yale, 1944); John Trenchard, *A Natural History of Superstition* (1709); John Trenchard and Thomas Gordon, *Cato's Letters; Or Essays on Liberty, Civil and Religious*, 4 vols (1737).

This was the case made by Robert Howard in his *History of Religion* (1694). Howard, a privy councillor to William III, intended to show that 'religion has been corrupted, almost from the beginning, by priests' who had fooled the laity and civil authority to submit to their pretended power. That power was supported by two things – inventing creeds that were superfluous to Christianity and conning civil magistrates to persecute those who refused to subscribe to them – and gave priests a position in society that trod on the liberties of Christians and the magistrate. Howard pointed to the conversion of Constantine in the fourth century as critical to the origins of priestcraft in Christianity. For Howard, Constantine, the exemplar of a godly magistrate in much Protestant historiography, was a more complex figure. The emperor ended three centuries of persecution of Christians but showed himself to be biddable to a priesthood bent on shoring up its power over the church at the expense of the authority of the magistrate. From that point on priestcraft grew in Christendom as documented by Howard in the invention of creeds, the use of excommunication to enforce them and the enlistment of the magistrate to ensure the violent eradication of heretics who opposed the priests' curtailment of Christian liberty. Howard pointed to the invention of the Athanassian Creed at the Council of Nicaea in AD 325 as particularly significant in the enforcing of speculative theology in the church that was at odds with the 'plain and easy' teaching of the gospel. 'From this creed-making', Howard lamented, 'came persecution, almost equal to those of the heathen emperors', a cruel protection of priestcraft that was as 'violently pursued' by Catholics as it was 'among the most Reformed Christians'.[105]

If History exposed the corruptions of priestcraft, it also highlighted the civil possibilities of religion. An historical awareness of the role of non-Christian religions in past cultures was crucial in this regard, as *Pansebeia: Or, A View of All the Religions* (1653), by the Scottish-born Church of England clergyman Alexander Ross, demonstrated at length. Though thoroughly committed to the superiority of Christianity, Ross's efforts to produce his compendium of religious diversity in human history had underscored the saliency of faith to the social fabric and moral health of all societies:

> Religion is the pillar on which the great fabric of the microcosm standeth. All humane societies, and civil associations, are without Religion, but ropes of sand, and stones without mortar, or ships without pitch.[106]

---

[105] Robert Howard, *A History of Religion* (1696), pp. 69–88 in particular, quotations at iv, 5, and 85. We are indebted here to Goldie, 'Priestcraft & the birth of Whiggism', pp. 220–1.

[106] Alexander Ross, *Pansebia: Or a view of all Religions in the World*, 6th edn (1696), 'Dedication to the Worshipful Robert Abdy'. On Ross, see R. J. W. Mills, 'Alexander Ross's *Pansebia* (1653), religious compendia and the seventeenth-century study of religious diversity', *Seventeenth Century*, 31 (2016), 285–310.

INTRODUCTION

Even those who challenged the truth-claims of religion continued to underscore its necessity for a healthy commonwealth. From the mid-century, commonwealthmen and freethinkers wrote erudite studies of the Christian past to debunk the dominant clerical interpretation of that past – that Christianity was the only true religion, and the clergy were the only true interpreters of Christianity – and replaced them with broader histories that evaluated religion as a universal phenomenon of human society with particular forms that varied according to cultural and political context.[107] Works like John Toland's *Nazarenus* (1718) denied that Christianity was the only true religion by tracing its historical development alongside that of Judaism and Islam – religion developed with human history, not outside it.[108] The Christian faith was merely one faith among many. Histories that claimed to show it was the only true religion were priestcraft: distortions of the historical record bent on supporting the moral and political authority of priests in the present.

The ancient world provided models of what this reformed religion should be. The Roman Republic appealed for two reasons. First, it had curtailed clerical power through an Erastian constitution – both temporal and spiritual authority stemmed from civil power. Second, Rome had created a national religion that fostered solidarity among its people while also tolerating a diversity of religious belief in its population – a balance of political unity in the face of religious pluralism that had eluded seventeenth-century England. Republicans lauded Cicero, whose *De Natura Deorum* studied the forms and purpose of Rome's diverse religions. Cicero drew a distinction between *superstitio* (the worship of the gods out of fear, which had no useful purpose in the republic) and *religio* (the public adoration of the gods motivated by piety, which was useful in unifying the republic and cultivating patriotism). *Religio* bound the people, instilled a sense of providential purpose in their polity, and inspired virtue. That it had been invented by Rome's elites for the purpose of politics was incidental. *Religio* mattered not because its claims about the supernatural were true but because they bound citizens into a people, restraining the vices more persuasively than could on its own.[109] Auguries and divination were cases in point. Cicero believed that there was no basis in reason to accept the reality of either. But their influence on

---

[107] See, for example, Charles Blount, *Great is Diana of the Ephesians* (1680); Blount, *Oracles of Reason*; Dennis, *Danger of Priestcraft*; John Dennis, *Priestcraft Distinguished from Christianity* (1715); Matthew Tindal, *Christianity as Old as the Creation* (1731); John Toland, *Christianity Not Mysterious* (1696).

[108] John Toland, *Nazarenus Or, Jewish, Gentile, and Mahometan Christianity* (1718). See Justin Champion, *Republican Learning: John Toland and the crisis of Christian Culture, 1696–1722* (Manchester, 2003), pp. 40, 50, 169–73, 191.

[109] *De Natura Deorum* in C. D. Young (ed.), *The Treatises of Marcus Cicero* (1853), I, DND.2.72, chs xliii–vii; II, chs xxvii–v. See Champion, *Pillars of Priestcraft*, pp. 184–6.

public opinion was undeniable and for that reason the auguries were crucial tools of politics that must be publicly acknowledged and accepted.[110]

Walter Moyle's *Essay on the Roman Government* (1726) is a good example of how British Commonwealthmen used Roman civil religion to indict the church and state of their own society.[111] Moyle published translations of and commentaries on many classical texts, and praised ancient authors for their 'wonderful sense of religion', singling Numa Pompilius out for particular praise as the author of the 'wisest and most politic' civil religion that shaped the morality of Rome's citizens to benefit 'all the ends of civil society'.[112] Numa had found an ideal balance between the liberty of citizens and the needs of state, tolerating a diversity of private religious beliefs and practices while maintaining the profession of a public religion that was 'subservient to all the great ends of government and society'.[113]

Balance was only possible because Roman civil religion had a minimal creed, insisting only on the belief that the gods were authors of good and that it was necessary to worship them to receive that good. Moyle argued that the magistrate 'may venture to enjoin' these 'common principles of religion [that] all mankind agree in' because they would unify society, not divide it, and encourage acts of virtue and justice that would benefit society. But that magistrate 'must go no further if he means to preserve a uniformity in religion' and peace in the commonwealth – dogma and speculative theology sowed seeds of division and laid the foundations for persecution.[114] To ensure this did not happen, priests must be kept in check. In Rome, religion was part of the polity 'interwoven into the general interest of the state' and the clergy were part of the laity 'not a separate independent body from the rest of the commons' with their own interests and the motivation 'to act against the public good', like Christian priests. Because Rome chose its clergy from its nobility they had 'an interest in the civil state', not in an institution that claimed independence from that state like the Christian church.[115] And because Rome's clergy had no authority to sustain apart from the state they had no need to invent abstractions and mysteries to justify their positions or try to override the liberty of citizens by claiming the authority to supervise private beliefs or jurisdiction to coerce life and conduct. Roman civil religion was free of priestcraft; and Rome was therefore free of religious persecution.

---

[110] *De Divinatione* in Young (ed.), *Treatises*. On this topic, see Katherine A. East, '*Superstitionis Malleus*: John Toland, Cicero, & the war on priestcraft in early Enlightenment England', *History of European Ideas*, 40 (2014), 965–83.
[111] On Moyle we are indebted to Champion, *Pillars of Priestcraft*, pp. 188–91.
[112] C. Robbins (ed.), *Two Republican Tracts* (Cambridge, 1969), pp. 209–10, 215.
[113] *Ibid.*, pp. 210–11.
[114] *Ibid.*, p. 210.
[115] *Ibid.*, p. 216.

INTRODUCTION

Cicero's views (and those of the British Commonwealthmen who followed him) were open to the charge of cynicism – this was not 'real' religion motivated by faith and piety, but a manipulative tool of state. Champion argued that these charges were misplaced because republican engagement with religion in late seventeenth-century England involved a re-definition of what 'religion' meant along lines that were broader than the Christian understanding of the term. In Christianity, 'religion' was focused on the afterlife and on the inculcation of a set of beliefs in the laity by a clergy whose authority rested on their claimed authority to be able to guide the laity to that afterlife. In the ancient world, 'religion' was focused on this life and on the inculcation of virtues in the public that served the commonwealth by fostering unity and patriotism. Champion showed that far from wanting to eradicate religion from public life, English republicanism hoped to reframe its role in English society, replacing or remodelling the Anglican church with a national church 'devoted to the pursuit of virtue rather than mystery'.[116]

Civil religion was not the preserve of radicals alone. British political thought in the early eighteenth century remained committed to the public role of religion as an essential part of society. Ashley Walsh has shown that Whigs and Tories, and churchmen high, low, and dissenting, agreed on that role in principle, if not on the place of the church in the constitution in practice. Their debates, as Robert Ingram has shown, were about 'Reformation without end'. Eighteenth-century politics wrestled with the intellectual, political, and religious problems caused by the sixteenth-century Reformations in the aftermath of the English Revolution that had tried to solve them. Divisions about ecclesiology and the history of the church were forensic and fraught because religion continued to *matter*. Protestantism remained central to how eighteenth-century society conceived of itself, and in the wake of the 1688 Revolution continued to be a linchpin of its constitution. English national identity was wedded to the idea of a godly magistrate and a public life that was markedly Protestant, and remained committed to both as central to the maintenance of order. It duly celebrated its Reformation as a sea-change in the nation's history that had helped to secure the liberty of its people by wresting them from the superstition and tyranny of popery. But that celebration was balanced with a suspicion of the church's political power, its maltreatment of Protestant dissent, and, most concerningly, its tendency towards priestcraft. The model clergyman instilled in the laity a faith that was moderate and civil. They were an important part of civic life and civil society for that reason.

---

[116] Champion, *Pillars of Priestcraft*, p. 23.

ADAM MORTON AND RACHEL HAMMERSLEY

This Volume

The contributors to this volume show that the principal concerns of what would subsequently be called 'civil religion' developed as part of a variety of attempts to resolve political problems about the place of religion in English society, its role in supporting or subverting civic authority, and its relationship with liberty caused first by the Long Reformation and second by the civil wars and English commonwealth which attempted to resolve those problems. The volume argues that an appreciation of historical context is necessary to understand why models of civil religion developed as they did in seventeenth- and eighteenth-century England; and that appreciating the historical significance of those models allows us to see that civil religion did not belong to the Enlightenment in any straightforward sense. Rousseau's civil religion should not be seen as the bar against which to measure all others.

Mark Goldie's chapter provides a synoptic account of what he terms 'Christian civil religion' in early modern England. Goldie traces the emergence of this civil religion through the intertwining of several traditions which constituted it: the civil supremacy over the church established in the Henrician Reformation, Erastianism, providential readings of England's Reformation, and the emergence of anticlericalisms. The emphasis on '*Christian* civil religion' challenges conventional approaches to that topic. Political scientists have tended to interpret civil religion as hostile to Christianity. They argue that the civil religion developed during the Enlightenment in response to readings of Machiavelli, Hobbes, and Rousseau aimed to supersede Christianity with a new quasi-religion of civic patriotism. Christianity's other-worldliness, and the claims of priests to authority, were held to undermine the civic virtue expected of citizens in a secular state. On this reading, advocates of civil religion rejected Christianity and proposed a political system that rivalled secular liberalism, in which religion was separated from the state and relegated to the private sphere.

Goldie argues, conversely, that Christianity was crucial to the development of civil religion in England, stressing that it was grounded in the magisterial Reformation and in late medieval Catholic conciliarism, and hence belonged within the domain of Christian ecclesiology. Civil religion's anti-clericalism must be read as central to its Christianity. Advocates of a Christian civil religion in seventeenth-century England understood themselves to be godly reformers who sought the purification of Christianity by freeing it from priestly usurpation. The temporal state was to be an agent of godly reform and an instrument for restraining usurped church power. Since church hierarchies were inimical to Christian liberty, temporal supremacy over the church acted to support religious freedom, not to block it. Goldie argues that the Erastian subsuming of ecclesiastical under temporal authority was as important to the emergence of religious toleration as was the putative emergence of a doctrine of the separation of church and state. Civil religion was a product of the Reformation, not a rejection of it.

The Reformation is also crucial to the understanding of civil religion developed in Polly Ha's chapter. Ha shows that the sixteenth-century Protestants understood the English Reformation as a civil Reformation – religion benefitted the state by inspiring civil virtues in its subjects. The Church of England established by the Elizabethan state in the 1559 'Religious Settlement' was attached to the crown, legitimised by statute, and existed as a blend of civil and ecclesiastical jurisdictions. That Protestant settlement was presented as moderate and therefore civil, a *via media* between the zealous and uncivil alternatives Roman Catholic (tyrannous and persecutory) and Puritan (popular and seditious) which both threatened order by undermining ecclesiastical and monarchical authority. The Elizabethan state presented the Church of England's civility as necessary for maintaining order and peace in the commonwealth – the church curbed the excesses of over-zealous religion and therefore restricted the threat of religion to politics.

Ha shows how the case for moderation became unstuck in the late 1580s and 1590s in the face of the state's campaign against Puritan dissent from the Church of England, a campaign which culminated in 1593 with legislation that sentenced the most radical puritan sectarians to death. The debates between Puritans and conformists in the 1590s reconfigured the relationship between church and state established at the Reformation. Puritans claimed that the Church of England was a persecutory church, arguing that its prosecution of dissent in the pursuit of religious conformity amounted to a persecution of religious liberty. The state and the established church argued that Puritan dissent was a threat to order, and that enforcing conformity was a necessary safeguard of both from excessive zeal. Ha shows that the debate challenged core aspects of the relationship between church and state in England's Reformation – the Royal Supremacy, Erastianism, and the legitimacy and nature of episcopal authority – but at its root it was really a contest about the civil magistrate's role in determining the religion of its subjects. Richard Hooker's *Laws of Ecclesiastical Polity* (1594–) extended the magistrates' right to determine established religion considerably.

The debate was conducted within a shared language of civil religion. Both Puritans and conformists agreed that religion was vital to the commonwealth because it inspired civil virtues but positioned their opponent's model of civil religion as being a corruption of religion's capacity to do so. Both agreed that the balance of civil and ecclesiastical jurisdiction in any polity might easily slide into dominion but disagreed about where that boundary was. Puritans thought that English Reformation had exercised dominion of the state over the church, whereas conformists thought that godly republicanism promised to exercise dominion of the church over the state. But, crucially, in setting out their visions of civil/ecclesiastical jurisdiction, both Puritans and conformists shared a set of sources – the Roman republic, the Hebrew commonwealth, and scripture – and a commitment to the Reformation as a form of civil religion. Ha argues that understanding this means that we must place civil religion in a broader historical context than political scientists have traditionally allowed and see it as more varied and mutable than has hitherto been the case in scholarship.

Esther Counsell's chapter shows that the Reformation also shaped the civil religion proposed by Scottish minister and physician Alexander Leighton, who was censored by the Star Chamber for his critiques of the church under Charles I. Counsell argues that Leighton, like William Prynne and other puritan critics of the Jacobean and Caroline regimes, called for a renewal of an Erastian model of England's church and state that had been central to the constitution of the Tudor Reformation. Counsell argues Leighton's interpretation of that constitution, developed in his *Appeal to the Parliament* (1629), should be seen as the revival of an ancient form of civil religion. Henry VIII's break from Rome in 1533-6 established the Royal Supremacy over the church in a constitution which put the civic authority of the crown-in-parliament over religion, regulating the church and its clergy through statute law. As the principal temporal *and* spiritual authority in the realm, the godly magistrate was the keystone of the English state, and Protestant historians showed them to be a necessary bulwark against the pride and ambition of over-mighty priests from corrupting the commonwealth. Erastian Royal Supremacy was the safeguard of Protestant England. It protected England's church, state, and people from priestly corruption.

Leighton argued that the corruption of the English state during the 1620s was caused by Stuart kings' abandoning this tradition of Reformed civil religion. Their doing so had paved the way for the growth of vice, treason, and popery in the commonwealth. Civil religion had been undermined by two things: the ambitions of the bishops and the personal rule of Charles I. The case for a *jure divino* English episcopacy, developed by Archbishop John Whitgift in the 1580s and extended by Laudian churchmen in the early seventeenth century, posed a significant challenge to England's Erastian constitution by proposing a separate sphere of authority for bishops. In the Laudian model of the Royal Supremacy civil authority over the church was diluted, with the king's powers as Supreme Head of the church passing through the clergy, not parliament. Governing without parliament suggested that regulation of the national church was reserved for the king and the bishops. This reneged on a pivotal aspect of the Reformation constitution: parliamentary authority over the Church of England. In this context, Leighton's *Appeal* laid new emphasis on the civil supremacy of parliament over the church. The crown's abdication of its duties as godly magistrate made the intervention of parliament necessary to protect Protestant England (threatened by Laudian innovations in the church) and secure the peace, prosperity, and unity of the commonwealth (threatened by the decline of civil supremacy over the church). For Counsell, Leighton's works show that the puritan ecclesiology of the mid-seventeenth century was a reinterpretation of Tudor Erastianism. Puritan visions of a godly commonwealth were a form of civil religion in which the civil authority of the crown-in-parliament over the church was necessary to the health of the realm.

Advocates of civil religion are often presented as 'Machiavellian' in the crude sense of subordinating religion to political ends. However, as Charlotte McCallum shows us in her chapter, even those who were familiar with and drew on Machiavelli's ideas were not all 'Machiavellian' in the pejorative sense of that term; indeed some opposed priestcraft precisely because it constituted a threat to the true religion. McCallum considers a work of invention, Henry Neville's 'Nicholas Machiavel's Letter to Zanobius Buondelmontius in Vindication of Himself and His writing', which appeared in John Starkey's 1675 edition of Machiavelli's works. Neville's 'Machiavel' outlines a case for civil religion that is vehemently anti-clerical. But McCallum argues that Neville was not attacking Christianity but calling for it to be reformed via the eradication of priestcraft. Furthermore, McCallum even suggests that Neville's fictionalised 'Machiavel' in his spurious letter should give us pause for thought regarding the true nature of Machiavelli's own views on religion. Her chapter reminds us of the danger of tying civil religion too closely to narratives of rationalisation or secularisation. Most advocates of civil religion in seventeenth-century England remained firmly grounded in the Christian faith and were engaged in genuine attempts to reconcile the tensions between church and state that had been generated by the recent religious and political conflicts.

The next two chapters, by John Coffey and Connor Robinson, consider debates about the relationship between church and state in the 1650s, as the legacy of the Erastian Reformation crumbled. Both chapters show that English Republican positions on the public role of religion in the commonwealth were defined in relation to England's Long Reformation in general, and to Puritanism in particular. But both also question how useful the term 'civil religion', which was not native to that period, is in capturing articulations of public religion in Cromwellian England.

John Coffey argues that ideas of national religion in England's Interregnum (1649–60) were in tension with the Erastianism of classical civil religion. His chapter considers the position of two English Republicans, James Harrington (1611–77) and Marchamont Nedham (1620–78), on the idea of a national church. Although Harrington and Nedham's republican works are often seen to be in dialogue with the canon of early modern political thought (Machievelli, Hobbes, Locke, and Rousseau) Coffey shows that the religious debates of Cromwellian England shaped their thoughts about the relationship far more significantly. The remodelling of England's church and state by the Independents brought to power by the New Model Army in 1648–9 drew the Reformation's legacy of an Erastian national church to a close. Episcopacy was abolished, the church court system that policed conformity was dismantled, and the passage of the Toleration Act (1650) saw the abolition of compulsory attendance at the Church of England and with it the ideal of religious uniformity that had been enshrined in law since 1559. The Independents replaced a national church with a system of voluntary gathered congregations.

Coffey shows that Independents were contemptuous of any religion that was merely public or formal. They labelled such a faith 'state religion', the most equivalent term to 'civil religion' in this period. For Puritans, 'state religion' was superficial and offended Christ. Religion was defined by a sincere, voluntary conversion to Christ that led the believer to repentance and godliness. A national church enforced by the magistrate was in tension with this emphasis on sincerity – enforcing conformity only instilled a superficial faith. The magistrate's use of the sword to secure uniformity to a national church was also a persecution of tender conscience. For these reasons, Radical Independents argued that the absolute separation of church and state was necessary to the creation of a godly republic because liberty of conscience was the only route to sincerity in religion. Yet a national religion could not be abandoned entirely. Although Independents were unwilling to permit the magistrate authority over gathered congregations or the punishment of heresy many argued that civil authority must nurture religion through the provision of a non-compulsory public ministry because religion was good for the health of society and cultivated a sense that England's Republic had been blessed by providence. Independents also recognised the magistrates' role in safeguarding liberty of conscience, protecting the congregations from persecution or priestcraft. John Milton and Henry Vane both argued that minority godly rule backed by the army was the surest way to protect religious toleration.

Nedham and Harrington's works were written in the context of this debate about the relationship between national religion and a godly republic. They had to steer a course between Magisterial and Radical Independents when crafting their Republican positions on the relationship between church and state. Nedham initially resisted the existence of a national religion as inconsistent with a godly republic which tolerated different faiths among its subjects, but by 1657 argued that a non-coercive public faith would benefit the health of the republic. Harrington argued that even in a republic consisting of independent, gathered churches, a national religion was a necessity. The magistrate should have no power over doctrine, creed, or any aspect of a gathered church's ministry. But civil authority was necessary to protect liberty of conscience. Harrington argued that attacking this national religion was to risk the security of religious liberty in the republic.

INTRODUCTION

Connor Robinson's chapter, which analyses the debate between Henry Stubbe (1632–76) and Richard Baxter (1615–91) on the construction of a godly commonwealth, moves the discussion to the end of the 1650s and the period following Richard Cromwell's appointment as Protector. Stubbe is often regarded as an advocate of civil religion. But Robinson argues that the term does not capture his model for the relationship between church and state, which was intended to find a practical, peaceful solution to the immediate political problem of England's divisive, plural religious culture rather than to advocate a novel 'civil religion' that anticipated the Enlightenment. Robinson places Stubbe's ideas within the wider debate about civil and religious authority during the Protectorate that was triggered by frustrations about Oliver Cromwell's failure to fully realise a godly Reformation. His 'civil religion' was developed in two works published in 1659 – *An Essay in Defence of the Good Old Cause* and *A Light Shining out of Darkness* – in response to Baxter's *A Key for Catholicks* and *A Holy Commonwealth, or Political Aphorisms* of the same year.

For Baxter theocracy was the foundation of a godly society. A united godly magistrate and ministry would correct the antinomianism of the civil war sects, using the sword to discipline behaviour and ensure that religious practice was in keeping with God's will. For Stubbe, theocracy was a tyrannous imposition of civil authority on subjects' religious liberty. Discipline by the magistrate would not build the godly society Baxter promised because faith cannot be coerced. A godly commonwealth would be achieved through the protection of popular sovereignty and religious toleration, the twin liberties of the Good Old Cause. And those liberties would only be protected if civil and religious jurisdictions remained discrete rather than being united. The liberty to seek knowledge of God under the protection of religious toleration would not lead to the antinomianism that Baxter feared but would shore up civil authority. Because faith made people aware of their duties to God and humanity, once believers submitted their wills to God they would act for the benefit of society and submit themselves to legitimate civil authority. The civil and the religious complemented each other. The magistrate used its authority to protect religious liberty; and the pursuit of religious liberty would ensure that subjects recognised the authority of the magistrate.

Robinson argues that the views Stubbe developed in the debate with Baxter were refined a decade later in *An Account of the Rise and Progress of Mahometanism* (1671) and disagrees with other readings of that work as a radical statement of 'civil religion'. Stubbe has been presented as an early Enlightenment thinker sceptical about Christianity and committed to natural religion, but Robinson argues that *An Account* was more typical of mid-seventeenth-century debates in English Puritanism about maintaining peace in a plural Christian nation. Stubbe celebrated Islam not because he was sceptical about Christianity, but because it offered a model of how temporal and spiritual jurisdictions should be established to ensure civil peace. Mahomet attacked idolatry, practised toleration, and preached faith, a model of religion which Stubbe suggests had much in common with the Apostolic Church. The conversion of Constantine (AD 312) saw the corruption of Christianity through the ambitions of priests (who invented superstitions and creeds) and the union of spiritual and temporal authority in the godly magistrate (who persecuted those who would not follow those creeds). Christianity had become a religion of the sword, where Islam had remained a religion of faith. Stubbe argued that the magistrate had a duty to promote God's truth. But this was realised not by the sword, but by creating the civil conditions for individuals to pursue salvation as their conscience directed.

The role of civil religion in securing a godly society is also the theme of Andrew Murphy and Christie Maloyed's chapter, which considers civil religion in the thought of William Penn (1644-1718). They argue that Penn's plans for religion in the Quaker colony of Pennsylvania that he founded in 1682 was an example of what Beiner has termed 'liberal civil religion'[117]. Pennsylvania was to be a godly society. Yet godliness was defined not by the magistrate's pursuit of uniformity to a particular doctrine or liturgy, but by the promotion of virtue as both the true mark of a Christian *and* of a the common good. The term 'civil religion' did not appear in Penn's works. But Murphy and Maloyed show that something analogous to it was central to Penn's vision of a society in which religious toleration was essential to fulfilment and betterment. Penn designed a colony characterised by liberty of conscience and moral virtue.

Penn's emphasis of toleration was a reaction against the persecution of Protestant non-conformists in Restoration England. His civil religion reconceptualised *how* religion bound society together. In England, the ideal of religious uniformity that had existed since the Tudor Reformations made civil loyalty and religious difference incompatible – religious uniformity was the basis of civil unity. Penn disagreed. Uniformity was enforced by persecution. This caused division and undermined civil unity. Penn believed that social unity was best secured when a government safeguarded, rather than hindered, two things: civil interest (the rights, freedoms, and property of individuals) and a general religion (a broadly Christian commitment to charity and loving one's neighbour as oneself). The two were mutually supportive. A government which promoted civil interest would not threaten religious freedom. And the promotion of a general religion – one committed to the expression of the Sermon on the Mount and the 10 Commandments – secured civil interest by ensuring the moral health of society. For Penn the public profession of a non-sectarian vision of Christianity was the ethical foundation of citizenship. Virtues that enhanced civic interest (honesty,

---

[117] Beiner, *Civil Religion*, p. 418.

charity, humility, neighbourliness) were promoted, and vices that hindered it (drunkenness, fornication, licentiousness) were punished.

America is also a central part of John Marshall's chapter on John Locke. Marshall argues that at many points between the 1660s and the 1690s Locke's thought approached something like what would later be called 'civil religion'. He was committed to the public profession of faith, believed that a minimal creed was the surest foundation of a national church, and was committed to opposing enthusiasm (which caused schism) and priestcraft (which caused ignorance that led to violence) as the twin evils of a reasonable Christianity. To ensure civil peace, a national church must tolerate Protestants of all stripes. But toleration could not be extended to Catholics, who owed allegiance to foreign states, or atheists, whose unbelief undermined trust in oaths as a crucial social bond. In the *Two Treatises of Government* (1660), Locke argued that the magistrate's control over religion was necessary to the security of the commonwealth and the protection of a latitudinarian, comprehensive national Church of England. By the *Letter Concerning Toleration* (1689), however, Locke had departed from that Erastian position, arguing that toleration and Christian liberty were the surest foundations of civil peace.

Marshall shows that Locke's views on the relationship between church and state, the role of Christianity in promoting virtue and civility in the commonwealth, and his commitment to toleration helped to shape American political thought in the eighteenth century to the Revolution and beyond. But Locke's views on toleration were at odds with other aspects of his life and thought. Marshall shows that the commitment of Locke (and those who, like Thomas Jefferson, James Madison, and George Washington, were influenced by his ideas) to Christian liberty must be viewed alongside their support for colonialism and slavery. Locke believed that national churches must exercise more latitude in their creeds to allow a broader number of Christians to join their union and argued that Jews and Muslims should enjoy civil rights in a commonwealth. But he also argued that the liberty that the enslaved may enjoy as Christians did not alter their legal status as slaves. Tolerance and intolerance, liberty and slavery, existed side-by-side in his thought.

Jacqueline Rose considers the interpretation of Anglo-Saxon religious history from the Reformation to the early eighteenth century. Historians of political thought have long recognised that the Anglo-Saxon period was a usable past for early modern thinkers. The idea of the Norman Yoke – which posited that an ancient (Saxon) constitution had been usurped by the Normans, who imposed hereditary monarchy and a tyrannous priesthood on the English – played a significant role in the debates about sovereignty and liberty during the English Revolution, and in the Whig tradition that followed it. The ancient constitution was used to many ends by early modern thinkers. It could be used to support moderate ideas, like limited monarchy, or more radical positions, like theories of resistance or contract. Rose suggests that Anglo-Saxon ecclesiastical constitutionalism, which appeared to offer Protestants a vision of a pure British church free from priestly or popish corruptions, was equally adaptable. The period from the late sixth to the eleventh centuries was one in which church and 'state' appeared to be closely connected. Clergy sat on Anglo-Saxon councils, there was intermingling between civil and church law and courts, and membership of synods (church) and great councils (state) were indistinguishable. Rose suggests that the intertwined nature of religion and politics in the constitution should have made the Anglo-Saxon period ripe for considerations of the merits of civil religion.

Her chapter shows that such considerations did not come to fruition, however, and argues that this should warn us not to use the label 'civil religion' too loosely. Anglo-Saxon ecclesiastical constitutionalism was certainly useful to English Protestants. It discredited papal authority over England's church and therefore helped to legitimise the Reformation. Protestant historians like John Bale and John Foxe claimed that Christianity in England predated Augustine's papal mission of 597. There was thus a primitive, unpapal Christianity in Anglo-Saxon England which both Norman priestcraft and papal tyranny had corrupted and that the English crown restored at the Reformation. Rose shows that Protestant historians in the sixteenth and seventeenth centuries interpreted the intermingling of church and state in Anglo-Saxon ecclesiastical constitutionalism as a model for England's Reformation, using it to lend weight to Erastian conceptions of the constitution, the authority of parliament in deciding on religious matters, and the role of bishops in parliament. The Anglo-Saxon mixed constitution was also used to debate conflicting visions of England's Reformation, supporting both the puritan case for further Reformation and the conformist case against it. But at no point was the Anglo-Saxon constitution seen as a proto-civil religion.

Rose urges caution on claims for the Reformation origins of civil religion like those made in other chapters in this volume. She argues that although there were connections between Reformation languages of godly rule and the Royal Supremacy over the church on the one hand, and civil religion on the other, there were also marked differences. Under the Royal Supremacy the monarchy governed the church but deferred to the clergy's spiritual authority. Church and state were two complementary bodies united under the crown-in-parliament – the clergy were accorded space to interpret Christianity and had spiritual authority over crown and subjects. From the mid-seventeenth century, advocates of civil religion argued that the Royal Supremacy had not gone far enough in restricting clerical power, urging that the church should have no independence and become a part of the state. Royal Supremacy examined the Christian past to limit the authority of priests. Civil religion examined the pagan past to move beyond

INTRODUCTION

Christianity. That it did so by extending Protestant attacks on popery to the priesthood in its entirety shows that civil religion borrowed from the Reformation, *not* that it was an extension of it.

It is not claimed here that each of the thinkers or groups considered in this volume was an advocate of 'civil religion' – to do so would be anachronistic. But it is claimed here that these thinkers or groups, in whatever position on the formal relationship between church and state they advocated, made a case for the suffusion of politics with religion being necessary for the health of a polity. The way in which they made those cases was shaped by strains in England's constitution caused by the Erastian nature of its Reformation. The views on the thinkers considered here can only be understood fully in the context of the English Reformation and Revolution, and not as a precursor for the ideas of the Enlightenment of the late eighteenth century. Reading them in this way points to a more complicated gestation of what would become 'Civil Religion' and underlines the importance of the history of the church to the development of the history of political thought.[118]

---

[118] See Mark Goldie, 'The Ancient Constitution and the Languages of Political Thought', *Historical Journal*, 62, (2019), 3–34.

1

Civil Religion: Two Traditions

Mark Goldie

Post-secularism

In the middle decades of the twentieth century, intellectuals took for granted that God was dead. Atheists prophesied the day, soon, when religion would wither away, superseded by reason and science. Secularization was understood to be a necessary condition of modernity, the *telos* of history, and end point of the long march from the superstitious infancy of humankind. Following suit, historians of ideas either ignored the role of the divine in past thought, as of little intrinsic interest, or offered genealogies of secularism and unbelief in order to demonstrate the progressive disenchantment of the world. The Enlightenment, or one persuasive version of it, cast a long shadow over this enterprise, for many saw Enlightenment values as ranged against the darkness of the unregenerate religious mind. A classic of this treatment was Peter Gay's *Rise of Modern Paganism* (1966). It has present-day counterparts.[1]

Within intellectual history, the secularist paradigm produced such oddities as treatments of Thomas Hobbes's *Leviathan* which had nothing to say about the second half of that book, Book III, 'Of a Christian Commonwealth', and Book IV, 'Of the Kingdom of Darkness'; which regarded Isaac Newton's vast theological corpus as an aberration, even as evidence of mental derangement; which attempted to show that John Milton's *Paradise Lost* was secretly atheistical; and which regarded the young Karl Marx's engagement with post-Hegelian theology as merely adolescent.

But since about 1980 the secularization thesis has been in deep trouble and has begun to look threadbare.[2] Religion and its place in civil society

---

[1] Jonathan Israel, *Radical Enlightenment* (Oxford, 2001) and successor volumes; Anthony Pagden, *The Enlightenment and Why it Still Matters* (Oxford, 2015). See Antony La Vopa, 'A New Intellectual History? Jonathan Israel's Enlightenment', *Historical Journal*, 52 (2009), 717-38.

[2] John Milbank, *Theology and Social Theory: Beyond Secular Reason* (London, 1993); Peter Berger, *The Desecularization of the World* (Washington, DC, 1999); Jonathan Sheehan, 'Enlightenment, Religion, and the Enigma of Secularization', *American Historical Review*,

have once again taken centre stage, and concepts of political theology have returned.³ There are several reasons for this. One is the brute fact of the persistence of religion across large parts of the globe and the evidence of religious revivals. Another is the return of fundamentalisms and the weaponizing of religion in politics. An important contributor is the 'ethnicization' of religion. In the public domain it has become harder to criticize religion because to do so is now seen as an affront to a communal identity – and, in the case of Islam or Judaism, a species of racism. This has its counterpart in historical scholarship, where it has become fashionable to argue that 'religion', conceived of as doctrinal propositions, a species of metaphysics, is not a permanent aspect of faith and spirituality but an invention of the Christian Reformation and Counter-Reformation.⁴ Accordingly, medieval, and postmodern, spirituality are seen as more akin to the *pietas* of the classical world, comprising the ethical values, norms, habits, pieties, and rituals of particular societies and cultures. Thus to critique religion is no longer to challenge a creed but to affront a way of life. A recent doctoral thesis in jurisprudence argued that religion is an 'immutable characteristic' of persons.⁵

Some committed Christians are little short of triumphalist about the tide turning against the secularization thesis, and proclaim an era of post-secularism. Upending the atheists' teleology, post-secularists assert that

---

108 (2003), 1061–80; Jürgen Habermas and Joseph Ratzinger, *The Dialectics of Secularization* (San Francisco, 2006); Charles Taylor, *A Secular Age* (Cambridge, MA, 2007); J. C. D. Clark, 'Secularization and Modernization: The Failure of a Grand Narrative', *Historical Journal*, 55 (2012), 161–94. For a rearguard action: Steven Bruce, *Secularization: In Defence of an Unfashionable Theory* (Oxford, 2011). For secularism as a Christian construct: Larry Siedentop, *Inventing the Individual: The Origins of Western Liberalism* (London, 2014).

³ Michael Kirwan, *Political Theology: A New Introduction* (London, 2008); Peter Losonczi et al., (eds), *The Future of Political Theology* (Farnham, 2011); Jeffrey Robbins, *Radical Democracy and Political Theology* (New York, 2011); Craig Hovey and Elizabeth Phillips, (eds), *The Cambridge Companion to Christian Political Theology* (Cambridge, 2015).

⁴ Erika Rummel, *The Confessionalization of Humanism in Reformation Germany* (Oxford, 2000); Tomoko Masuzawa, *The Invention of World Religions* (Chicago, 2005); Guy Strousma, *A New Science: The Discovery of Religion* (Cambridge, MA, 2010); Brent Nongbri, *Before Religion: A History of a Modern Concept* (Cambridge, 2015); Thomas Bauer, *A Culture of Ambiguity: An Alternative History of Islam* (New York, 2021). For an anthropological perspective: Talal Asad, *Genealogies of Religion: Discipline and Reasons of Power in Christianity and Islam* (Baltimore, 1993); Talal Asad, *Formations of the Secular: Christianity, Islam, Modernity* (Stanford, 2003). A reviewer of these writes of their 'salutary and unsettling effect ... to make strange the "religion" of the West, as it is conceived by various tribes in the academy, and to make almost savage the concept of "the secular" that is so precious to natives of Western liberalism' (Kevin Seidel, *Iowa Journal of Cultural Studies*, 7 (2005), p. 113).

⁵ Mohamed Moussa, 'Divisive Rights: Constitutional Wrongs' (PhD, Cambridge, 2022). See also a powerful essay by Saba Mahmood, 'Religious Reason and Secular Affect: An Commensurable Divide?', *Critical Enquiry*, 35 (2009), 836–62.

the Enlightenment was a passing aberration in humanity's abiding encounter with the transcendent. With *schadenfreude* the religious pronounce that God survived the Enlightenment.[6]

Many post-secularists are post-liberals. That is to say, they form a perhaps unexpected alliance with postcolonialists, feminists, and Marxists, in pronouncing that liberalism's assumption of human universality and claim to neutrality in the face of human difference is fraudulent, a pretence that must be unmasked. Liberalism, they say, hides its structural biases, masks its hegemonies, and one of these is its negation of religion through exclusion and marginalization.[7] Where liberalism claims to construct a civil society and a public space that gives freedom to an indefinite plurality of religions, the charge now is that 'toleration', far from being a virtue, names the vice of inadequate recognition, and comes at the cost of religion's expulsion from the public square. Just as the postcolonialist holds that liberalism was entangled with imperialism at birth, so the postsecularist claims that liberalism was entangled with secularism at birth. Liberalism was not a courteous side-stepping of religion, but an aggressive crusade

---

[6] *Schadenfreude* aside, many studies now explore religious Enlightenments. Richard Sher, *Church and University in the Scottish Enlightenment* (Edinburgh, 1985); Mark Goldie, 'The Scottish Catholic Enlightenment', *Journal of British Studies*, 30 (1991), 20–62; B. W. Young, *Religion and Enlightenment in Eighteenth-Century England* (Oxford, 1998); Frederick Beiser, *The Sovereignty of Reason: The Defense of Rationality in the Early English Enlightenment* (Princeton, 1996); John Robertson, *The Case for the Enlightenment* (Cambridge, 2005); Jonathan Sheehan, *The Enlightenment Bible* (Princeton, 2007); Sarah Apetrei, *Women, Feminism, and Religion in Early Enlightenment England* (Cambridge, 2010); Jeffrey Burson and Ulrich Lehner (eds), *Enlightenment and Catholicism in Europe* (Notre Dame, 2014); William Bulman, *Anglican Enlightenment* (Cambridge, 2015); Lionel Laborie, *Enlightening Enthusiasm: Prophecy and Religious Experience in Early Eighteenth-Century England* (Manchester, 2015); William Bulman and Robert Ingram (eds), *God and the Enlightenment* (Oxford, 2016); Ulrich Lehner, *The Catholic Enlightenment* (Oxford, 2016); Robert Ingram, *Reformation without End: Religion, Politics, and the Past in Post-Revolutionary England* (Manchester, 2018); Joke Spaans and Jetze Touber (eds), *Enlightened Religion* (Leiden, 2019).

[7] Craig Martin, *Masking Hegemony: A Genealogy of Liberalism, Religion, and the Private Sphere* (London, 2010); Clayton Crockett, *Radical Political Theology: Religion and Politics after Liberalism* (New York, 2011); Miguel Vatter (ed.), *Crediting God: Sovereignty and Religion in the Age of Global Capitalism* (New York, 2011); Michael Kessler (ed.), *Political Theology for a Plural Age* (Oxford, 2013). Post-secularism also belongs to the case for 'provincializing' Europe and for restraining a liberal 'market' in religion. For a case that churches organic to a society merit protection against globalized free market religious pluralism see Chris Hann, 'Problems with the (De)privatization of Religion', *Anthropology Today*, 16 (2000), 14–20. For commentary on post-liberal Christianity, see Nicholas Wolterstorff, *The Might and the Almighty: An Essay in Political Theology* (Cambridge, 2012). I speak of an 'unexpected' alliance because many post-liberal Christians are conservative communitarians.

against religion.[8] The Anglosphere cannot exempt itself, as if the ferocity of French *laïcité* – from the Revolution's Civil Constitution of the Clergy, to the expulsion of Catholic religious orders in 1904, to the ban on the burka – was peculiar to Gallic liberalism. In Britain and North America anti-clericalism, and particularly anti-Catholicism, has been woven into the fabric of liberalism.

In the practice of intellectual history the conventional canon is being revisited.[9] Studies of the theology of Hobbes, Locke, Newton, Marx, and the young John Rawls abound.[10] New entrants to the canon, and revivals within it, are in evidence: Joseph de Maistre, architect of the nineteenth-century's religious counter-revolution against the Enlightenment;[11] J. N. Figgis, the early twentieth-century Anglican priest, who theorized contemporary politics in the light of medieval conciliarism and diagnosed the onslaught of liberal secularism against the churches in Liberal Britain and Third Republic France;[12] Jacques Maritain, the Catholic priest, who revived Thomism in the face of totalitarianism;[13] and Simone Weil, who transitioned from Marxism to Christianity and was always doubtful of liberal nostrums.[14] Meanwhile, in another part of the wood, it is *de rigueur* to invoke Carl Schmidt, the pathologist of Weimar democracy and abettor of Nazism, whose *Political Theology* (1922) argued that secular political concepts are transcriptions of medieval theological ones. His theme is reinforced in the work of Giorgio Agamben, which renews a theological – and liturgical – understanding of political power, as the temporal projection of the divine 'economy', God's conduct of his creation.[15] Within another domain, students of the history of scholarship are reminding us that central to early modern and Enlightenment concerns was 'sacred history', the investigation of Old Testament narratives as paradigmatic

---

[8] 'Hostility to the church was encoded within liberalism from its birth': Adrian Vermeule, qu. *Times Literary Supplement*, 2 Sept. 2022, p. 8.

[9] Alister Chapman, John Coffey, and Brad Gregory (eds), *Seeing Things Their Way: Intellectual History and the Return of Religion* (Notre Dame, 2009).

[10] For Newton see Rob Iliffe, *Priest of Nature: The Religious Worlds of Isaac Newton* (Oxford, 2017); for Marx: Gareth Stedman Jones, *Karl Marx* (London, 2016); for Rawls: Eric Gregory, 'Before the Original Position: the Neo-Orthodox Theology of the Young John Rawls', *Journal of Religious Ethics*, 35 (2007), 175–206.

[11] Carolina Armenteros, *The French Idea of History: Joseph de Maistre and his Heirs, 1794–1854* (Ithaca, 2011).

[12] Paul Avis (ed.), *Neville Figgis: His Life, Thought, and Significance* (Leiden, 2022).

[13] Samuel Moyn, 'Jacques Maritain, Christian New Order, and the Origins of Human Rights', in Luigi Bonanante et al. (eds), *Intercultural Dialogue and Human Rights* (Washington, DC, 2011).

[14] Eric Springsted, *Simone Weil for the Twenty-First Century* (South Bend, IN, 2021).

[15] Giorgio Agamben, *The Kingdom and the Glory: For a Theological Genealogy of Economy and Government* (Stanford, 2011). For political theology in the shadow of Schmitt see Graham Hamill and Julia Lupton (eds), *Political Theology and Early Modernity* (Chicago, 2012).

for the human condition, and as offering archetypes for understanding politics.[16] We begin to see the importance, for example, of such texts as Petrus Cunaeus's *De republica Hebraerum* (*The Commonwealth of the Hebrews*)[17] and John Selden's *De synedriis ... Ebraeorum* (*On the Councils of the Ancient Hebrews*).[18] Finally, there is a wave of scholarship which restores to our attention the politics of the early modern Bible and the presence of scripture in European political thought.[19]

Privatizing religion, nationalizing religion

For classical liberals, liberty involves, if not the suppression of religion, then its privatization, its separation from civic life. The patron saint of liberalism's privatization of religion is John Locke, or at least he remains so in standard accounts of him. It is an incessantly repeated claim that Locke removed belief to the domain of the inner self, broke asunder the Christian theocracy of the previous millennium, and decisively separated church and state. He turned churches into private associations within civil society and asserted that the state has no business with our salvation. For him, the notion of 'godly rule' was oxymoronic, a category error. He was, it is said, in favour of the disestablishment of the church.[20] There are reasons to question several of these claims and I shall return to Locke later. But I introduce him here

---

[16] J. P. Sommerville, 'Hobbes, Selden, Erastianism, and the History of the Jews', in *Hobbes and History*, eds G. A. J. Rogers and Tom Sorell (New York, 2000); Gordon Schochet et al. (eds), *Political Hebraism* (Jerusalem, 2008); Eric Nelson, *The Hebrew Republic: Jewish Sources and the Transformation of European Political Thought* (Cambridge, MA, 2010); Graham Hammill, *The Mosaic Constitution: Political Theology and Imagination from Machiavelli to Milton* (Chicago, 2012); Dmitri Levitin, 'From Sacred History to the History of Religion', *Historical Journal*, 55 (2012), 1117–60; Brian Cummings, *Mortal Thoughts: Religion, Secularity, and Identity in Shakespeare and Early Modern Culture* (Oxford, 2013); Charles Prior, 'Hebraism and the Problem of Church and State in England, 1642–1660', *The Seventeenth Century*, 28 (2013), 37–61; John Robertson, 'Sacred History and Political Theory', *Historical Journal*, 56 (2013), 1–29; Dmitri Levitin, *Ancient Wisdom in the Age of the New Science* (Cambridge, 2015); Philip Connell, *Secular Chains: Poetry and the Politics of Religion from Milton to Pope* (Oxford, 2016), chapter 1.

[17] Latin 1617; English 1653.

[18] Jason Rosenblatt, *Renaissance England's Chief Rabbi: John Selden* (Oxford, 2006); Gerald J. Toomer, *John Selden: A Life in Scholarship* (Oxford, 2009); Ofir Haivry, *John Selden and the Western Tradition* (Cambridge, 2017).

[19] Debora Shuger, *The Renaissance Bible* (Berkeley, 1994); Naomi Tadmor, *The Social Universe of the English Bible* (Cambridge, 2010); Kevin Killeen, *The Political Bible in Early Modern England* (Cambridge, 2017). More generally, we may note the increase of book titles using the phrase 'the politics of religion'. An early instance was Tim Harris, Paul Seaward, and Mark Goldie (eds), *The Politics of Religion in Restoration England* (Oxford, 1990).

[20] These are the standard readings of Locke, *A Letter Concerning Toleration* (1689).

because he remains the anchor-point in a standard liberal story in which, vis-a-vis religion, liberalism is defined, not as animus against religion, but as declaratory of the separateness of religion. Liberalism proclaimed itself, not the enemy of religion, but of theocracy, of the domination of the civil commonwealth by priests. Mark Lilla has called the seventeenth century the moment of the 'Great Separation' of religion and civil society (though he holds Locke to be merely the disciple of the chief progenitor, Hobbes).[21]

A number of scholars argue that in the emerging modern world there lay, at the opposite pole to liberal separation, an alternative, which might be called a rogue tradition, called 'civil religion'. In this argument, at some point between the Renaissance and the Enlightenment, the enemies of the Christian theocracy of medieval Europe reached a fork in the road towards modernity, and, whereas liberals opted for secular separation, others chose instead to advocate a new religion of the state. These proponents of civil religion sanctified the state and spiritualized citizenship, investing patriotism with the charisma of the sacred. They annulled ecclesiastical claims to autonomy, and rendered churches departments of state, thereby transfiguring the other-worldliness of religion, and overcoming its tendency to divide the loyalties of citizens between the competing claims of the city of God and the city of man. In 'civil religion', on this account, we find the alter ego of liberal modernity, a perverse manipulation of religion for the sake of enhancing patriotism, a development which could only have horrific outcomes in modern state-worship. Thus there are held to be two traditions emerging from the Enlightenment's assault on Christian theocracy: liberalism and civil religion.

Ronald Beiner tells this story in *Civil Religion: A Dialogue in the History of Political Philosophy* (2011). Here the presiding canon is Machiavelli, Hobbes, and Rousseau, the last of whom famously entitled the final chapter of his *Social Contract* 'Civil Religion', where he praised Hobbes for 'reuniting the two heads of the eagle' of spiritual and temporal power, and where he echoed Machiavelli's denigration of Christianity as enfeebling the prowess of the citizen.[22] For Beiner, civil religion is the polar opposite of liberalism, because of its perverse sacralization of the state and its neo-pagan subversion of Christianity.[23]

We have therefore an historical triad: the Christian theocracy of pre-modern times; liberalism's separation of religion from politics; and civil religion's manipulative inversion of Christianity. Both of the latter were programmes conceived to save civilization from the tyranny of priests and

---

[21] Mark Lilla, *The Stillborn God: Religion, Politics, and the Modern West* (New York, 2007).
[22] Jean-Jacques Rousseau, *The Social Contract*, ed. Victor Gourevitch (Cambridge, 1997), p. 146.
[23] In similar vein, a post-War tradition of intellectual history traced the origins of totalitarianism in the sacralization of the state: notably Jacob Talmon, *The Origins of Totalitarian Democracy* (London, 1952).

the violence of religious warfare and persecution. But while one programme produced the free societies of liberal modernity, the other created the new monster of the sanctified state, the ideological weapon of modern totalitarianism.

In pausing to consider an alternative line of argument, Beiner generously refers to my own writing. Of my essay on James Harrington's civil religion, he remarks that I 'see [civil religion] as a principled intellectual tradition, and as deserving of more intellectual sympathy'. And he notes that I find in Locke 'a significant civil religion dimension', though here, he says, I go 'too far'.[24] His remarks are rightly fleeting: he had only an essay to draw upon.[25] Here I attempt another short sketch of an alternative genealogy of civil religion, in which we find the idea of civil religion deeply embedded within the 'magisterial' or 'jurisdictional' tradition within Reformed Christianity.[26]

Christian civil religion

An alternative history stands upon two propositions. The first is that civil religion was deeply embedded *within* Christian political theology and was not the dissolution of it. It was a working out of the implications of a devout but anti-clerical tradition hostile to priestly claims to authority over the Christian believer: Christianity would be civil once the false pretensions of the *ecclesia* were removed. Liberalism was heir to the centuries' long struggle between *regnum* and *sacerdotium*, a quarrel within Christendom. The second is that, in this tradition, the ecclesiastical supremacy of the temporal state was a necessary instrument for liberating Christians from the tyranny of church jurisdiction. Here we turn the notion of separation on its head. If we wish to write a history of liberalism (though that is a doubtful enterprise) we shall find it not by seeking the origins of the separation of church and state but, on the contrary, in theories among Christian reformers which aimed to 'reunite the two heads of the eagle'. What we label liberalism began with an insistence that separation – dualism – was in fact the disastrous work of the medieval papacy and of its pseudo-Protestant, half-reformed heirs.[27] By asserting the autonomous authority and temporal jurisdiction of churchmen, the medieval church had set itself up as an insurgency against civil society

---

[24] Ronald Beiner, *Civil Religion* (Cambridge, 2011), pp. 2, 148.

[25] Mark Goldie, 'The Civil Religion of James Harrington', in *The Languages of Political Theory in Early Modern Europe*, ed. Anthony Pagden (Cambridge, 1987), pp. 197–224.

[26] I use the word 'Reformed' loosely, to refer to any who understood themselves to be engaged in the reformation of the Christian church: Protestant, but also, as we shall see, sometimes Catholic.

[27] This thought is well articulated by Patrick Deneen, 'The Great Combination', in Kessler (ed.), *Political Theology*, where he speaks of Augustine's 'Great Separation' and Hobbes's and Locke's 'Great Combination'.

and its rulers. Theologians had turned the 'church' into a separate body from the commonwealth of believers, a distinct and rival hierarchy and no longer a congregation of praying citizens. Overcoming this separation was conceived as essential to Reformed civil religion. As one (overly sanguine) Puritan author wrote in 1659, 'the Godliness of these times hath abolished the distinction of church and state, of civil and ecclesiastical jurisdiction, and taken away the distinction of clergy and laity'.[28] Put another way, civil religion was an extension of Luther's 'priesthood of all believers'.

Early modern civil religion was a reforming Christian project, and we need to seek it *within* theology, above all within ecclesiology. To dwell only on secular modes of argument, on natural law, legal constitutionalism, or classical republicanism, is to cleanse early modern political thought of its drastically providentialist character. At the junction of politics and religion lay ecclesiology, and it remains the hidden half of early modern political thought. (In the case of Hobbes's *Leviathan*, it is precisely one half, the second half). Consider how different the history of political thought would look if we gave as much weight to Hugo Grotius's immensely influential *De imperio summarum potestatum circa sacra* (*Of Sovereign Power in Sacred Matters*)[29] as we do to his *De jure belli ac pacis* (*Of the Law of War and Peace*), the latter so readily taken to be crucial in birthing modern political thought.

The protagonists of civil religion shared the common ambition of Christian reformers, in declaring that they sought *reformation*, the restoration of 'primitive' Christianity: the reconstitution of the pure religion of Christ, the Apostles, and the Fathers; freed from the false doctrines and dogmatizing of the Platonizing and Aristotelianizing theologians; freed from the inquisitions of heresy hunters; and from the accrual of power, jurisdiction, and property by clerical castes. The enemies were clergies and creeds, not Christ or Scripture. As John Toland put it in 1701, 'religion's safe, with priestcraft is the war'.[30]

To be sure, historians and political theorists ask of Enlightenment versions of these claims – and it must be asked – whether this stance of Christian reformation, the appeal *ad fontes*, which so obviously aligned with Erasmian and Protestant renewals of Christianity, was merely a protective manoeuvre, a mask of orthodoxy, in the face of charges of heresy. This

---

[28] Lewis Du Moulin, *Proposals, and Reasons ... Presented to the Parliament* (London, 1659), p. 37.

[29] Hugo Grotius, *De imperio summarum potestatum circa sacra*, ed. and trans. Harm-Jan van Dam, 2 vols (Leiden, 2001); the book was completed in 1617 and published posthumously in 1647. See Marco Barducci, 'Clement Barksdale, Translator of Grotius: Erastianism and Episcopacy in the English Church, 1651–1688', *The Seventeenth Century*, 25 (2010), 265–80.

[30] John Toland, *Clito* (London, 1700), p. 16. See Justin Champion, '"Religion's Safe, with Priestcraft is the War": Augustan Anticlericalism', *The European Legacy*, 5 (2000), 547–61.

question is asked of, say, Paulo Sarpi in the Venice of 1600, or Toland and the deists in the England of 1700. It is often argued, in the spirit of Leo Strauss, that Renaissance and early Enlightenment covert unbelievers adopted the doctrine of double truth, disguising their unbelief under the public face of Christian reform. Justin Champion has challenged this view, I think compellingly.[31] And my own inclination is not to engage in the hermeneutic of clandestinity, which assumes esoteric irreligion, but to accept that the intellectual resources of Christian thought provided the ubiquitous language of debate about the relationship between the spiritual and temporal realms. We need to heed the strictures of Dmitri Levitin in showing how many of the supposedly daringly radical intellectual pursuits of the Enlightenment were embedded in orthodox humanist enquiries into ancient philosophy, biblical philology, and sacred history. Much of what we call the Enlightenment is better characterized as the late Reformation or late Christian humanism.[32]

The domain of the study of civil religion entails sensitivity to the cultural resources and modes of reasoning that were brought to bear in constructing a vision of a Christian commonwealth made whole again. There were many. Above all, of course, the Bible. In particular, the invocation of the Hebrew commonwealth as an archetype of godly rule. Or the deployment of the Book of Revelation, which gave shape to providential readings of the history of the earthly commonwealth. John Foxe's *Book of Martyrs* (1563) was not only a martyrology but also a theodicy of an elect nation seeking to recast itself in the image of Christ.[33]

Equally, Christian Reformers were eclectic and syncretic in their cultural debts, so that we need to be alert to the moulding to Christian purposes of pre-Christian Greek but especially Roman conceptions of *religio*, *superstitio*, and *pietas*;[34] and to the ways in which the study of comparative religion, especially of Islam and Judaism, was brought to bear. The use of Stoic and Ciceronian resources was not a Trojan horse, an enemy within the gates of Christianity, any more than Aristotle was for Thomas Aquinas. Sarpi's circle, for example, mingled languages of Christian reform, classical republicanism, and imperial sovereignty in their assertion of the ecclesiastical autonomy of the Venetian republic against the arbitrary power of the papacy.[35]

---

[31] Justin Champion, *Republican Learning: John Toland and the Crisis of Christian Culture, 1696–1722* (Manchester, 2003).
[32] Levitin, *Ancient Wisdom in the Age of the New Science*.
[33] William Haller, *Foxe's Book of Martyrs and the Elect Nation* (London, 1963). The true title of Foxe's book was *The Acts and Monuments of … the Church*.
[34] Colin Kidd, 'Civil Theology and Church Establishments in Revolutionary America', *Historical Journal*, 42 (1999), 1007–26; Katharine East, '*Superstitionis Malleus*: John Toland, Cicero, and the War on Priestcraft', *History of European Ideas*, 40 (2014), 965–83.
[35] David Wootton, *Paulo Sarpi: Between Renaissance and Enlightenment* (Cambridge, 1983). See forthcoming work by Eloise Davies.

Christian authors were not embarrassed to invoke pagan exemplars. Thomas Elyot's *The Book Named the Governor* (1531) praised the quasi-mythic creator of Roman religion, Numa Pompilius, as a 'man of excellent wisdom and learning' who promoted temples, altars, and the public weal, and who 'with a wonderful wisdom and policy ... brought all the people of Rome to such a devotion'.[36] The Elizabethan Puritan George Whetstone, entreating the magistrate to 'suppress and chastise notorious vices', invoked the 'good laws and orders' of Numa.[37] Grotius cited Homer, Plato, Livy, and Horace on the public good of religion.[38]

A fundamental idiom of civil religion was its dependence on jurisprudence: the application of theories derived from civil or Roman law concerning *imperium*. Civil religion involved the re-assignment to the secular ruler of claims once made for the papal *imperium*. At the core of the 'magisterial' Reformation – of Reformations shaped by the state, by princes, by parliaments – was a view about jurisdiction. Armed with the Lutheran idea that all earthly rule, all external matters, including ecclesiastical, were temporal, and so belong to the prince, and combined with a Civil Law concept of *imperium*, what emerged was the doctrine of civil supremacy over the ecclesiastical sphere. In the famous formulation of the Henrician Act of Appeals of 1533, 'this realm of England is an empire', indicating the transference to the secular magistrate of claims made by the papacy. Central to the magisterial Reformation was the idealization of the 'Godly Prince'; central to Protestantism was spiritual liberation from popery. From this stemmed the assumed bond between religious freedom and the plenary authority of Godly Princes.

The jurisdictional concept of civil supremacy in matters ecclesiastical, as Jacqueline Rose shows, quickly fragmented into rival views about whether lay supremacy belonged with the prince, with parliament, or with the commonwealth at large, but these rival claimants agreed on the priority of the temporal.[39] Parallel work by Esther Counsell for the late Elizabethan and Jacobean period, and Ashley Walsh for eighteenth-century England explore the centrality of civil ecclesiastical supremacy as the jurisdictional core of Puritanism in the earlier period, and of Whig latitudinarianism in the later.[40]

---

[36] Quoted in Gregory Murry, 'Anti-Machiavellianism and Roman Civil Religion in the Princely Literature of Sixteenth-Century Europe', *Sixteenth-Century Journal*, 45 (2014), 331–50, at p. 344.

[37] George Whetstone, *A Mirour for Magestrates* (London, 1584), p. 12. See Mark Silk, 'Numa Pompilius and the Idea of Civil Religion', *Journal of the American Academy of Religion*, 72 (2004), 863–96.

[38] Hugo Grotius, *De imperio*, ed. van Dam, I, p. 175. With thanks to Esther Counsell for this.

[39] Jacqueline Rose, *Godly Kingship: The Politics of the Royal Supremacy* (Cambridge, 2011).

[40] Esther Counsell, 'Protestant Jurisdictionalism and the Nature of Puritanism, 1560–1642' (PhD, Cambridge, forthcoming); Ashley Walsh, *Civil Religion and the Enlightenment in England, 1707–1800* (Woodbridge, 2020). See also Justin Champion, *The*

The idea of the Godly Prince was reinforced by combining juridical claims about the supremacy of the magistrate with biblical and church-historical exemplars of Jewish and early Christian magistracy. In *De regno Christi* (1551) Martin Bucer provided an influential construal of the reforming Christian magistrate in the image of the fourth-century Emperor Constantine. By insisting that Constantine had convened the church Council of Nicaea, he made the emperor into a quasi-sacerdotal figure. For Bucer – who also invoked the Old Testament figures of David, Hezekiah, and Josiah – the Godly Prince should be a guide and support of a reforming, preaching clergy.[41] The image of Constantine as the archetype for godly rule became ubiquitous for those who sought to restrain the autonomous powers of the clergy and assert the pastoral role of princes. Constantine's rule was a motif in John Jewel's *Apology of the Church of England* (1564). The confessional state was constituted as an imperial church. Thomas Bilson urged that 'God in delivering the sword to princes, hath given this direct charge to provide that ... true religion be maintained in their realms'.[42] Peter Martyr, the Florentine reformer who settled in England, was no less thoroughgoing in the sacralization of civil power: 'the charge of religion belongeth to princes'. To Constantine was added the archetypes of the priest-king Melchizedek and the godly prophetess Deborah.[43] The theme was central to what we may call Foxean histories which pitted princes against prelates. Foxe quoted John Knox on Constantine, as 'a second Moses sent and set up of God, to deliver

---

Pillars of Priestcraft Shaken (Cambridge, 1992). The present essay does little more than summarize arguments found in the work of Champion, Counsell, Marshall, Rose, and Walsh. See also: S. J. Barnett, *Idol Temples and Crafty Priests: The Origins of Enlightenment Anticlericalism* (Basingstoke, 1999); Jeffrey Collins, 'Restoration Anti-Catholicism', in *England's Wars of Religion Revisited*, eds Glenn Burgess and Charles Prior (Farnham, 2011); Nelson, *Hebrew Republic*, chapter 3.

[41] Thomas Dandelet, 'Creating a Protestant Constantine: Martin Bucer's *De Regno Christi* and the Foundations of English Imperial Political Ideology', in *Politics and Reformations*, ed. Christopher Ocker (Leiden, 2007). See also Lewis Spitz, 'Luther's Ecclesiology and his Concept of the Prince as Notbischof', *Church History*, 22 (1953), 113–41.

[42] Thomas Bilson, *The True Difference between Christian Subjection and Unchristian Rebellion* (1585), p. 129.

[43] Torrance Kirby, *The Zurich Connection and Tudor Political Theology* (Leiden, 2007), at p. 59. Also: Martin Anderson, 'Royal Idolatry: Peter Martyr and the Reformed Tradition', *Archiv fur Reformationsgeschichte*, 69 (1978), 451–69; Torrance Kirby, 'Peter Martyr Vermigli on the Unity of Civil and Ecclesiastical Jurisdiction', *Archiv fur Reformationsgeschichte*, (2014), 161–93. On Deborah: Anne McLaren, 'Elizabeth I as Deborah: Biblical Typology, Prophecy, and Political Power', in *Gender, Power, and Privilege in Early Modern Europe*, eds Jessica Munns and Penny Richards (Harlow, 2003); Alexandra Walsham, '"A Very Deborah?": The Myth of Elizabeth I as a Providential Monarch', in *The Myth of Elizabeth*, eds Susan Doran and Thomas Freeman (Basingstoke, 2003).

his people out of their so miserable captivity into liberty'.[44] The shadow was long indeed. During the Civil War, Henry Parker declared that Constantine did more for Christianity 'than all the labours and endeavours of thousands of preachers'.[45] In the *Holy Commonwealth* (1659) of the Puritan Richard Baxter, and in the *Historical Essay Concerning General Councils, Creeds, and Impositions* (1676) of the poet and proto-Whig Andrew Marvell, we find that 'Christian Empire was at the heart of [their] political philosophy'. For them, historical judgement comprised a sorting of princes into those who fulfilled the Constantinian ideal and those 'who betrayed their imperial role'.[46]

A leitmotif of those who called for the dissolution of hierarchic church power was the insistence that the word 'church' derived from the secular Greek term *ecclesia*, denoting an assembly or congregation of the people. Thus a church, properly speaking, is nothing but the citizenry at worship: it is not a distinct institution that lies outside the *civitas*. Much hung upon whether English Bibles translated *ecclesia* as 'church' or 'congregation'. For the republican James Harrington, Pauline Christianity is a reconstruction of the Athenian polity, now infused with Christian faith.[47] Writing in 1612, the Congregationalist Henry Jacob remarked that Christ's church was a 'company of people joined together in a polity and signified by the Greek word *ecclesia*'.[48] For Richard Hooker, who provided the fullest systematization of the Elizabethan Reformation settlement in his *Ecclesiastical Polity* (1594), 'church' and 'commonwealth' were simply modal differences of the same body of people. 'Though properties and actions of one do cause the name of a commonwealth, qualities and functions of another sort give the name of a church to a multitude, yet one and the same multitude may be both'.[49]

---

[44] Quoted in A. P. Martinich, 'Interpreting the Religion of Thomas Hobbes', *Journal of the History of Ideas*, 70 (2009), 143-63, at 149. See Patrick Collinson, 'If Constantine, then also Theodosius: St Ambrose and the Integrity of the Elizabethan Ecclesia Anglicana', *Journal of Ecclesiastical History*, 30 (1979), 205-29.

[45] Henry Parker, *The True Grounds of Ecclesiastical Regiment* (London, 1641), p. 61: quoted in Charles Prior, *A Confusion of Tongues: Britain's War of Reformation, 1625-1642* (Oxford, 2012), p. 215.

[46] William Lamont, 'The Religion of Andrew Marvell', in *The Political Identity of Andrew Marvell*, eds Conal Condren and A. D. Cousins (Aldershot, 1990), qu. 142; Annabel Patterson et al (eds), *The Prose Works of Andrew Marvell*, 2 vols (New Haven, 2003), II, 115-76. See Annabel Patterson, *Marvell and the Civic Crown* (Princeton, 1978); Margarita Stocker, *Apocalyptic Marvell* (Brighton, 1986); Mark Goldie, 'Toleration and the Godly Prince in Restoration England', in Mark Goldie, *Contesting the English Polity, 1660-1688* (Woodbridge, 2023). For Puritan ecclesiological imperialism more generally see William Lamont, *Marginal Prynne* (London, 1963); William Lamont, *Godly Rule* (London, 1969); William Lamont, *Richard Baxter and the Millennium* (London, 1979); Jacqueline Rose, 'Roman *Imperium* and the Restoration Church', *Studies in Church History*, 54 (2018), 159-75.

[47] Goldie, 'Civil Religion of James Harrington'.

[48] Henry Jacob, *A Declaration* (Middleburg, 1612), pp. 18, 31.

[49] Quoted in Prior, *Confusion of Tongues*, p. 213.

Hooker's defence of the establishment and Jacob's separatist resistance to it, for all their profound differences, operated within the same paradigm. In the late seventeenth century, Locke's protégé Peter King insisted on the democratic congregationalism of the Apostolic church.[50]

The fusion of juridical theory and sacred history was a hallmark of early modern ecclesiology, and thereby the fusion of secular and sacred power. In Grotius's *De imperio* and Selden's *De synedriis* we find a commitment to establishing a *lack* of separation between the civil and ecclesiastical spheres, between the citizen and the Christian, using arguments which established the unitary nature of all jurisdiction, combined with historical accounts of the quasi-sacerdotal, or caesaropapal, role of Old Testament kings and early Christian emperors. The high priest Aaron was but the deputy and delegate of Moses. These texts offered a parade of emperors and monarchs who summoned synods, reformed churches, and set the laity at liberty from domineering prelates.

Not least of the keynote arguments in Christian civil religion was the insistence that forms of church government were *jure humano* (by human convention) and not *jure divino* (by divine right). Neither Christ nor the Apostles, nor the Fathers of the patristic age, prescribed any form of clerical hierarchy or authority as necessary to be upheld by Christians. The Petrine Commission – 'Thou are Peter and upon this rock I build my church'[51] – was not Christ's authorization of pope, bishop, or presbyter, but of the church universal and its believing members. Authority and hierarchy in the church are matters of human prudence and choice. This is the *adiaphorist* tradition, 'adiaphora' meaning 'indifferent things'. Belief in this or that ecclesiastical structure was held to be a 'matter indifferent' (that is, inessential) for salvation, not a 'matter necessary'.[52] Protestants railed against papal *jure divino* claims; Puritans railed against Anglican episcopal *jure divino* claims.[53] Thus, for the secular commonwealth to make whatever arrangements it chose for ecclesiastical governance could be no violation of Christ's requirements.

---

[50] Peter King, *An Enquiry into the Constitution ... of the Primitive Church* (1691).

[51] Matthew 16: 18.

[52] Bernard Verkamp, *The Indifferent Mean: Adiaphorism in the English Reformation* (Athens, OH, 1977); Jacqueline Rose, 'The Debate over Authority: Adiaphora, the Civil Magistrate, and the Settlement of Religion', in *Settling the Peace of the Church*, ed. N. H. Keeble (Oxford, 2014), pp. 29–56.

[53] W. Cargill Thompson, 'Sir Francis Knollys's Campaign against *Jure Divino* Episcopacy', in idem, *Studies in the Reformation* (London, 1980); J. P. Sommerville, 'The Royal Supremacy and Episcopacy *Jure Divino*', *Journal of Ecclesiastical History*, 34 (1983), 548–58; Jeffrey Collins, 'The Restoration Bishops and the Royal Supremacy', *Church History*, 68 (1999), 549–80.

Civil religion as anti-popery

All these strands of argument were rootedly anti-papal, although 'popery' came increasingly to be seen as paradigmatic of *any* sacerdotal claim to autonomous authority, Protestant as well as Catholic. In the critique of the autonomy of churches, repeatedly we find the Latin tag *imperium in imperio*, the charge that the church threatens to be a state within a state. In the English tradition there was incessant recourse also to the idea of *praemunire*, the crime of appealing to an authority beyond that of the civil sovereign. The English Reformation pivoted upon convicting the church of the guilt of *praemunire*.[54] Any ecclesiastical claim to authority bearing on the externals of life, which invoked a jurisdiction outwith that of temporal authority, was *ipso facto* an instance of *praemunire*.[55] At the birth of the English Reformation, William Tyndale, in *The Obedience of a Christian Man* (1528), spoke of a world turned upside down, because 'emperors and kings are nothing nowadays, but ... hangmen of the popes and bishops', whereas there should be 'one king, one law' in the commonwealth, and he called upon the king to enact 'a fully and godly reformation'.[56] The same message was articulated by Christopher St German, who inaugurated the common lawyers' long contest to suppress canon law.[57]

This critique was oriented towards annulling medieval Catholic claims. Yet it is an abiding feature of radical Protestant thought that it soon levelled a charge of crypto-popery against Protestant settlements that were but 'halfly' reformed.[58] Proponents of 'further reformation' came to believe that any pretension to autonomous ecclesiastical authority, such as that of Anglican prelates or Presbyterian elders, was a form, or remnant, of popery. Popery, construed as clerical usurpation, became the archetype of anti-clerical thought. And once radical Protestants began to discover a propensity to popery in *all* priestly religions, they produced a new term of art, 'priestcraft'. In England the word was coined in the 1650s and entered widespread use in the 1690s. The term would become a shibboleth of the Anglophone Enlightenment, but the structure of thought embodied in

---

[54] A. G. Dickens, *The English Reformation* (London, 1964), chapter 5.
[55] For the ubiquity of the appeal against *praemunire* among common lawyers see David Smith, 'Remembering Usurpation: The Common Lawyers, Reformation Narratives, and the Prerogative, 1578–1616', *Historical Research*, 86 (2013), 619–37.
[56] William Tyndale, *The Obedience of a Christen Man* (1528), pages unnumbered.
[57] Christopher St German, *Doctor and Student* (1528); *Treatise Concerning the Division between the Spirituality and Temporality* (1532). See Franklin Le Van Baumer, 'Christopher St German: The Political Philosophy of a Tudor Lawyer', *American Historical Review*, 42 (1937), 631–51.
[58] This charge was originally made in the 1580s against the Elizabethan settlement. See Mark Goldie, *Roger Morrice and the Puritan Whigs* (Woodbridge, 2007 and 2016), chapter 7.

the critique of 'priestcraft' derived from Protestant critiques of 'popery'.[59] 'Popery' was whatever alienated sanctity from citizenship. Reformation was thus a task of repatriation. In the rightly ordered commonwealth, wrote Robert Molesworth in 1694, 'the character of priest [will] give way to that of true patriot'.[60] In the eighteenth century we find the preoccupation with jurisdiction now accompanied by a theorem about Christian civility, which was the antithesis of the 'barbarism' of life under popery and crypto-popery, a life of oppression enacted by the ecclesiastically credentialed devout.

Thus the question of jurisdiction pointed not only to the powers of *regnum* as against *sacerdotium*, but to the degradation of the humanity and agency of every citizen under priestly rule. Broader analyses identified in the Catholic malformation of Christianity a wholesale accrual of earthly resources and powers to the sacerdotal caste, not least the vast property of the church, and its invasive authority over marriage, adultery, legitimation, and inheritance.[61] To use a later philosophical vocabulary, people were said, under 'popery', to live a life not of authentic selfhood but of alienation. The medieval world was one of 'externality', of religion embodied in idolatry and ecclesiastical domain, instead of internalized in the free spirituality of everyday life. The movement of reform aimed to return piety to the *civitas*, spirituality embodied in the life of the laity, the sacralization of worldliness. The reformed commonwealth was held to be 'secular', but in the sense of embodying Christianity in the *saeculum*, the temporal, the worldly.

The later philosophical formulation would find expression in Hegel's theology (and in the early thought of his disciple Marx), for whom the Reformation was a vital moment 'in opposition to Catholic externality'. To obliterate ecclesiastical 'externality' was to re-spiritualize civil society.

---

[59] Mark Goldie, 'Ideology', in *Political Innovation and Conceptual Change*, eds Terence Ball et al. (Cambridge, 1989), pp. 266–91; Mark Goldie, 'Priestcraft and the Birth of Whiggism', in *Political Discourse in Early Modern Britain*, eds Nicholas Philipson and Quentin Skinner (Cambridge, 1993), pp. 209–31; Mark Goldie, 'John Locke, the Early Lockeans, and Priestcraft', *Intellectual History Review*, 28 (2018), 125–44.

[60] Robert Molesworth, *An Account of Denmark* (1694), ed. Justin Champion (Indianapolis, 2011), p. 14. For the Leveller critique, in the 1640s, of clerical power as paradigmatic of all, and especially economic, oppression see J. F. Maclear, 'Popular Anticlericalism in the Puritan Revolution', *Journal of the History of Ideas*, 17 (1956), 443–70. Tithes and church landlordism were at the heart of a long, if often untheorized, tradition of popular hostility to clerical religion. See Christopher Hill, *The Economic Problems of the Church* (Oxford, 1956). Also: Nigel Aston and Matthew Cragoe (eds), *Anticlericalism in Britain, c.1500–1914* (Stroud, 2000). An influential text was John Selden's *History of Tithes* (1618), a sustained rejection of *jure divino* claims to church property.

[61] For the English common lawyers' drive to repatriate the domain of wills, marriage, and bastardy from their usurpation by canon law see, for example, Smith, 'Remembering Usurpation'; Mark Goldie, 'William Lawrence, the Law of Marriage, and the Case for King Monmouth', in Mark Goldie, *Contesting the English Polity, 1660–1688* (Woodbridge, 2023). Also John Halkett, *Milton and the Idea of Matrimony* (New Haven, 1970); Evivion Owen, 'Milton and Selden on Divorce', *Studies in Philology*, 43 (1946), 233–57.

Religion must be instantiated in civil society and be repatriated to it. For Hegel, the Greek ideal of human fulfilment in the *polis* was prototypical of the freedom promised by the Gospel. Hegel, so readily cast into the mould of a 'civil religion' quite alien to Christian theology, was heir to the traditions we have been sketching. 'In the Middle Ages', he wrote, 'the embodying of the divine in actual life was wanting'. Medieval religion was an 'externality' in multitudinous ways: in the idolatry of transubstantiation, 'bodying God in a particular material object'; in the church's monopoly of knowledge as 'the exclusive possession of a [priestly] class'; and in the clergy's 'acquisition of outward property'. These were calamities for selfhood and civil community. The Reformation consisted in the annulling of all this, the 'building up of the edifice of secular relations'. In England, he wrote, the Reformation and the Puritan Revolution were mounted 'in opposition to Catholic externality'.[62]

Dominus mundi

The medieval papacy claimed to be *dominus mundi*, lord of the world. The lawyer popes Hildebrand and Boniface used the Roman law conception of the *imperator* to invest the papacy as supreme emperors, suzerains over all earthly princes. This culminated in the papal claim to excommunicate and depose princes if they were heretics. The apogee was the Hildebrandine era – in the eleventh century Pope Gregory VII excommunicated the Emperor Henry IV three times – and Pope Innocent III's bull *Unam Sanctum* (1302), which declared the pope to be *dominus mundi*.[63] Protestants held that Catholicism was not only theologically idolatrous and superstitious, but also *ipso facto* antithetical to commonwealths, because of its claim to *temporal* supremacy. The papacy violated the *patria* by its claim to stand above it. Catholicism was, if committed to Hildebrandine papacy, simply incompatible with Christian magistracy: it placed a dagger at the breast of the prince, who ruled on sufferance, at the determination of his godliness in the eyes of the church.

In England, the memory of Pope Pius V's deposition of Queen Elizabeth in 1570, of the Gunpowder Plot (a Catholic terrorist scheme to destroy king and parliament), the Irish Massacre of Protestants in 1641, and the Popish Plot in 1678 (again to assassinate the king), provided a Protestant litany and evidence of the fragility of Christian liberty in the face of popish barbarity. The political theology of the Oath of Allegiance, imposed by James VI and

---

[62] G. F. Hegel, *The Philosophy of History*, ed. C. J. Friedrich (New York, 1956), pp. 343–4, 378–81, 422–4, 435; *The Philosophy of Right*, ed. T. M. Knox (Oxford, 1967), paragraphs 259–60, 270, 272, 285. See Laurence Dickey, *Hegel: Religion, Economics, and the Politics of Spirit, 1770–1807* (Cambridge, 1987).

[63] Walter Ullmann, *The Growth of Papal Government in the Middle Ages* (London, 1955).

I after the Gunpowder Plot, with its requirement to renounce the doctrine of the papal deposing power, ran through Protestant-Catholic debate for the next two centuries.[64] Francis Bacon called this 'the greatest duel which is in the Christian world; the duels and conflicts between the lawful authority of sovereign kings ... and the swelling pride and usurpation of the see of Rome *in temporalibus*'; 'these Roman soldiers do either thrust the spear into the sides of God's anointed [princes], or ... crown them with thorns'.[65] In the latter image, the prince becomes the suffering Christ, the victim of pharisaic papal pretenders to godliness, and emblem of oppressed Christian peoples. The memory of the papal interdict against King John – the theme of Shakespeare's play – was construed in the same light. The question of the papal deposing power still rankled in debates on Catholic Emancipation: in the 1790s Prime Minister William Pitt sought the opinion of European Catholic universities as to whether it was still a necessary doctrine of Catholicism.[66]

Protestant intellectuals were preoccupied with the conundrum of discerning if Catholicism could ever be compatible with temporal rule. The Catholic Church, it was repeatedly said, believed not only that the pope could depose heretic princes but also that a Catholic was not bound to 'keep faith with heretics'; in other words, that a Catholic could lie, or swear false oaths, with moral impunity, if done to heretics. This was the source of the obsession with 'casuistry' and 'Jesuitical' 'equivocation'.[67] If the deposing power licenced rebellion and assassination, the 'not keeping faith' dissolved the elemental bonds of civil society. The long history of Protestant anti-popery is not an aberration, an unfortunate prejudice staining Protestantism's alleged leaning towards liberty, but integral to the Reformed self-understanding about the integrity of civil society.[68]

The antithesis of priest and prince found an enduring metaphor, and visual image, in the drama of the foot upon the neck. The medieval popes were depicted setting their feet upon the necks of princes, or having emperors kiss their feet. A Lucas Cranach woodcut of c.1545 shows the emperor kissing the pope's foot. The Elizabethan lawyer Robert Gynes wrote that under the

---

[64] J. P. Sommerville, 'Jacobean Political Thought and the Controversy over the Oath of Allegiance' (PhD thesis, Cambridge, 1981).

[65] Francis Bacon, *The Charge ... whether the Doctrine ... Touching Deposing, and Killing, of Kings Excommunicated, were True, or No*, in *Resuscitatio* (1657), pp. 53, 55.

[66] Mary Sanderson, 'Limited Liberties: Catholics and the Policies of the Pitt Ministry', *Journal of British Studies*, 59 (2020), 737–63.

[67] Edmund Leites (ed.), *Conscience and Casuistry in Early Modern Europe* (Cambridge, 1988); Andrew Hadfield, *Lying in Early Modern English Culture: From the Oath of Supremacy to the Oath of Allegiance* (Oxford, 2017).

[68] I finish this essay the day after the coronation of Charles III, with its explicit affirmation of the Protestant character of English monarchy, as prescribed in legislation of 1689, passed in the wake of the deposition of the Catholic James II. From my Catholic childhood I recall an elderly Protestant gentleman saying to me, 'Ah, you're a Roman are you?', with a distinct implication that I was alien, not quite English.

regime of canon law 'the crown of the king was taken off his head and laid at the feet of the Holy Father'.[69] Foxe's woodcuts include one showing Pope Alexander treading on the neck of the emperor and another, converse image, of King Henry VIII trampling upon the pope.[70] A portrait of his son Edward VI likewise shows his youthful foot on the pope's neck.[71] The most famous icon of the right ordered civil religion is the frontispiece of Hobbes's *Leviathan* in which the symbols of the church are gathered in one hand of the sovereign and the symbols of temporal authority in the other – and in which the sovereign himself is no other than the combined congregation of the people.[72] In his *Ecclesiastical History* (c.1670) Hobbes, speaking of the medieval papacy, again evokes the image of foot and neck: 'on Caesar's neck, he domineering stood, / Waving his hands aloft, and vaunting, like a God'.[73]

The history of European political thought from 1300 to 1900 might be written as a story of 'political thought on the road from Canossa': a narrative conceived as a series of theories of the recovery of the sovereignty of the temporal state from its inversion, its archetypal opposite, in papal supremacy. Canossa was the quasi-mythic moment in 1077 when Hildebrand compelled the excommunicated emperor to kneel penitently in the snow before his castle. Bismarck, in his speech launching the *Kulturkampf* against German Catholics in 1872, pronounced that Germany shall never again 'go to Canossa'. He could take for granted that his audience understood the reference. Political thought 'on the road from Canossa' is ecclesiological thought, placed at the core of the emergence of the idea of the secular state liberated by Godly Princes and Godly citizens from ecclesiastical thraldom.[74]

Catholic jurisdictionalism

Civil religion has thus far been cast chiefly in English, Protestant terms. Yet, in some respects, there was little peculiarly English or even Protestant about it. The road from Canossa, from *Unam Sanctam*, begins before the Protestant era, for the political thought of Dante in *Monarchia* (1312) and

---

[69] Quoted in Smith, 'Remembering Usurpation', p. 629.
[70] Elizabeth Hageman, 'John Foxe's Henry VIII as *Justitia*', *Sixteenth Century Journal*, 10 (1979), 35–43, at 37. See John Foxe's Acts and Monuments Online.
[71] Artist unknown. https://www.npg.org.uk/collections/search/portrait/mw00459/King-Edward-VI-and-the-Pope
[72] Justin Champion, 'Decoding the *Leviathan*: Doing the History of Ideas through Images, 1651–1714', in *Printed Images in Early Modern Britain*, ed. Michael Hunter (Farnham, 2010).
[73] Thomas Hobbes, *A True Ecclesiastical History* (1722), p. 171. This is the translator's rendering of the Latin. The same image is in *Leviathan*, chapter 44.
[74] For two versions of such a history see J. Neville Figgis, *From Gerson to Grotius, 1414–1625* (Cambridge, 1907); Brian Tierney, *Religion, Law, and the Growth of Constitutional Thought, 1150–1650* (Cambridge, 1982).

Marsilius of Padua in *Defensor Pacis* (1324) was shaped in reaction to papal claims. They asserted the independence of empire, nation, and city state. Marsilius provided a sustained critique of priestly, and especially papal, encroachments on the civil realm, clerical 'disturbers of the polity'. He rejected any intrinsic coercive power in the church; asserted the power of the temporal ruler to make appointments to the ecclesiastical hierarchy; claimed that Constantine had granted the papacy its authority and not vice versa; asserted that the general council of the church and not the pope was supreme; advocated the presence of the laity in such councils; and urged the civil ruler to limit the proliferation of clergy.[75] Subtly adjusting the text, in 1535 William Marshall brought out an English translation attuned to the purposes of the Henrician Reformation.[76]

The late medieval conciliar movement was a rebellion by national states and national churches against the overweening claims of papal monarchy. The Council of Constance in 1415 deposed three popes and declared that supremacy lay with the representative body of the whole church and not with the pope personally.[77] A conciliarist tradition of Catholic anti-clericalism and *etatisme* can be traced through to the Enlightenment in Gallicanism, Jansenism, and Febronianism, and in the Italy of Pietro Giannone. In 1682 the Declaration of the French Church asserted the superiority of councils over popes and the liberty of sovereigns from ecclesiastical dominion. Sarpi's defence of Catholic Venice against the papal interdict in 1606 was an experiment in civil religion; so too was the Synod of Pistoia in 1780. Dale van Kley's work on the Gallican and Jansenist tradition shows how much was owed by the French Revolution's Civil Constitution of the Clergy to this prior tradition.[78] In Enlightenment Austria Febronius (Johann Nikolaus von Hontheim) shaped the reforms of

---

[75] Marsilius of Padua, *Defensor Pacis*, 2.3; 2.17.17; 2.19.9; 20.20.2; 2.20.8; 2.22.10. See Bettina Koch, 'Priestly Despotism: The Problem of Unruly Clerics in Marsilius of Padua's *Defensor Pacis*', *Journal of Religious History*, 36 (2012), 165–83. For Dante: C. T. Davis, *Dante and the Idea of Rome* (Oxford, 1957).

[76] Shelley Lockwood, 'Marsilius of Padua and the Case for the Royal Ecclesiastical Supremacy', *Transactions of the Royal Historical Society*, 1 (1991), 89–119. Marsilius also guided St German: Baumer, 'St German'.

[77] Brian Tierney, *Foundations of the Conciliar Theory* (Cambridge, 1955); Antony Black, *Council and Commune* (London, 1979); Francis Oakley, *The Conciliarist Tradition* (Cambridge, 2003). See also P. A. Sawada, 'Two Anonymous Tudor Treatises on the General Council', *Journal of Ecclesiastical History*, 12 (1961), 197–214.

[78] Dale van Kley, *The Religious Origins of the French Revolution* (New Haven, 1996); Dale van Kley, 'Piety and Politics in the Century of Lights', in *The Cambridge History of Eighteenth-Century Political Thought*, eds Mark Goldie and Robert Wokler (Cambridge, 2006). For Catholic conciliarism in America, see Michael Breidenbach, 'Conciliarism and the American Founding', *William and Mary Quarterly*, 73 (2016), 467–500; and Michael Breidenbach, *Our Dear-Bought Liberty: Catholics and Religious Toleration in Early America* (Cambridge, MA, 2021).

the Emperor Joseph II, drastically curtailing the powers of the church. This pan-European reforming Catholic movement culminated in the suppression of the Jesuit order across Catholic Europe between 1759 and 1773, the religious order held to be the papacy's praetorian guard. In England, among Catholics the question of jurisdiction caused vicious intramural divisions between conciliarists and papal 'curialists' from the time of James I's Oath of Allegiance through to debates on Emancipation, involving a long train of negotiations with the English state over draft oaths of allegiance, and, in turn, dividing views among Protestants as to the plausibility of the claim by some Catholics that to be of the 'church of Rome' was not to be committed to the political claims of the 'court of Rome'.[79]

Erastianism

It is tempting to bring all such movements, Protestant and Catholic, under the catch-all term Erastian, a slippery but useful shorthand. Thomas Erastus, writing in the 1580s, was preoccupied with delimiting the power of excommunication, by which popes and bishops cut heretics off from civil society. By the mid-seventeenth century the term Erastianism had broadened into a general assertion of temporal authority over churches.[80] Erastianism, committed to fusing church and state, was one of the dominant ideologies of the early modern period, and it might be more useful to study it, than proleptically to chase histories of the alleged separation of church and state. This claim has been compellingly argued by Eric Nelson.[81] He shows that it is a mistake to assume that Erastianism, because we think of it as theory of civil supremacy, the subordination of church to state, was a roadblock to religious toleration and pluralism. Quite the contrary. The Godly Prince, drawing to himself a power over churches and clergies, was able to make and enforce a *politique* judgement about the broad ambit that may be given to diverse religious groups, notwithstanding the contrary demands for 'orthodoxy' by hierarchies and by 'enthusiasts' (fanatics). It was by uniting the two heads of the eagle of spiritual and temporal that a space opened up

---

[79] Collins, 'Restoration Anti-Catholicism'; A. J. Brown, 'Anglo-Irish Gallicanism, 1635–1685' (PhD, Cambridge University, 2004); Joseph P. Chinnici, *The English Catholic Enlightenment: John Lingard and the Cisalpine Movement, 1780–1850* (Shepherdstown, WV, 1980).

[80] The classic account remains J. Neville Figgis, 'Erastus and Erastianism', *Journal of Theological Studies*, 2 (1900), 66–101.

[81] Nelson, *Hebrew Republic*, chapter 3. See also: Simone Zurbuchen, 'Republicanism and Toleration', in *Republicanism: A Shared European Heritage*, eds Martin van Gelderen and Quentin Skinner, 2 vols (Cambridge, 2002), II, pp. 47–72; Ian Hunter, *The Secularization of the Confessional State: The Political Thought of Christian Thomasius* (Cambridge, 2007); Goldie, 'Toleration and the Godly Prince'.

in early modern Europe for religious toleration. Civil liberty and the power of the state were not opposites, but the latter the handmaiden of the former, the guarantor against those who set themselves above or beyond the state. The 'turn toward toleration in Western Europe ... was primarily inspired ... not by creeping secularization ... [but] out of the Erastian effort to unify church and state, [and] not out of the desire to keep them separate'.[82] It is no paradox that Grotius and a phalanx of English Protestants and Whigs were committed to toleration while simultaneously upholding a national church and the civil supremacy.

Political science without history

Scholars sometimes find themselves saying things which are novel to one audience but entirely familiar to another. To sketch, as I have just done, the Reformation concept of the civil supremacy in matters ecclesiastical, is to describe what is perfectly routine to historians of early modern Europe. They will recognize it as the ideology of the 'magisterial' Reformation. But that dimension generally remains missing from accounts of the history of political thought offered by political scientists. Their 'civil religion' lacks grasp of Protestant – and Catholic conciliar – ecclesiology. If we address only the conventional great canon of philosophers and place them in conversation only with each other,[83] rather than embedding them in the thick texture of their intellectual environments, then we are apt to miss the traditions from which they emerged. Machiavelli-Hobbes-Rousseau is a non-existent beast, a snark. And the 'liberal' Locke is, by and large, a phantom too.[84] If we read the past through the wrong end of the telescope, and go searching for the roots of 'liberalism', or the origins of the American constitution's separation of church and state, or, alternatively, seek the philosophical sources of the twentieth century's perverted state-worship, then we miss something fundamental about the idea of civil religion in early modern European thought. If we persist in seeing civil religion as the alter ego of liberalism, rather than its progenitor, then we miss its ecclesiological character.

It is not that Machiavelli, Hobbes, and Rousseau are the wrong places to look, though they are limited places to look; rather that those authors expressed, albeit in stark and paradoxical form, some of the commonplaces of Christian civil religion. While I cannot begin here to adjudicate interpretations of those three figures, it is worth at least noting that a

---

[82] Nelson, *Hebrew Republic*, p. 89.
[83] The stated methodology in Beiner, *Civil Religion*.
[84] Duncan Bell, 'What is Liberalism?', *Political Theory*, 42 (2014), 682–715; Tim Stanton, 'John Locke and the Fable of Liberalism', *Historical Journal*, 61 (2018), 597–622.

number of scholars have identified the Christian political theologies to which their thought was indebted.

Machiavelli's pitting of the prowess of pagan Roman religion against the civic enfeeblement wrought by Christian other-worldliness was not dissimilar from a well-established tradition in which humanist Christian moralists synthesized a 'truer' Christianity with Roman religion. (We saw earlier instances of the invocation of Numa, as Machiavelli does). For Machiavelli, God intends a virtuous churchless republic established by philosopher-prophet-kings. Maurizio Viroli has proposed that 'Machiavelli's God is the God of Florentine republican Christianity'.[85] The republics of Renaissance Italy routinely, piously, recruited religion to sanctify the state. The seventeenth-century Genoese republic installed the Virgin Mary as its queen. Domenico Fiasella's painting 'La Madonna della Città' shows the Madonna with the Christ child in one hand and the civil sceptre in the other, while putti present to her the crown and keys of the city's sovereignty. The Madonna of Genoa reunites the two heads of the eagle.[86]

In Hobbes, as Jeffrey Collins has shown, we find a Reformation theologian who relied on a conventional view of the jurisdictional supremacy of temporal over ecclesiastical power, and was commonplace, if obsessive, in his anti-clericalism.[87] At the close of *Leviathan* Hobbes speaks of untying the knots of 'praeterpolitical church government in England': first, 'the power of the popes' was dissolved by Elizabeth; then the bishops, who dared to claim power *jure divino*, were dissolved, in the Civil War; then immediately thereafter upstart Presbyterian church power was overcome; so that we are now (under the English republic in 1651) 'reduced to the Independency of the Primitive Christians to follow Paul, or Cephas, or Apollos, everyman as he liketh best'.[88] Hobbes here speaks for a *politique* religious toleration under the ambit of an encompassing sovereign. A number of contemporary Puritans – as well as the Catholic followers of Thomas White, alias Blacklo – found affinity with Hobbes's claims. Several of his admirers were Erastian Independents, Puritans who sought toleration within a national church, the secular power holding the ring against prelates and fanatics alike.[89]

---

[85] Maurizio Viroli, *Machiavelli's God* (Princeton, 2010), p. 61. See also: Marcia Colish, 'Republicanism, Religion, and Machiavelli's Savonarolan Moment', *Journal of the History of Ideas*, 60 (1989), 597–616; Miguel Vatter, 'Machiavelli and the Republican Conception of Providence', *Review of Politics*, 75 (2013), 605–23; Vickie Sullivan, *Machiavelli's Three Romes* (Ithaca, 2020).

[86] Robert Oresko, 'The House of Savoy in Search for a Royal Crown', in *Royal and Republican Sovereignty*, eds Robert Oresko et al. (Cambridge, 1997), pp. 294–301. See also Gerald Parsons, *The Cult of St Catherine of Siena: A Study in Civil Religion* (London, 2017).

[87] Jeffrey Collins, *The Allegiance of Thomas Hobbes* (Oxford, 2005).

[88] Thomas Hobbes, *Leviathan*, ed. Richard Tuck (Cambridge, 1991), chapter 47, p. 479.

[89] Besides Collins see Leopold Damrosch, 'Hobbes as Reformation Theologian', *Journal of the History of Ideas*, 40 (1979), 339–52; Richard Tuck, 'The Civil Religion of Thomas Hobbes', in Phillipson and Skinner, eds, *Political Discourse*; Patricia Springborg, 'Thomas

In the case of Rousseau, it can be argued that his chapter on civil religion was 'much more about laicizing the state than it was about coercing belief'; that he nowhere suggests that government 'should replace Christianity with another religion'; and that he wanted government to ensure the 'excluding any antisocial – ... intolerant or fanatical – beliefs'.[90] He denounces Catholicism as 'giving men two legislations, two chiefs, two fatherlands, subjects them to contradictory duties and prevents them being at once devout and citizens'.[91] This is precisely the sentiment that has run all through the tradition I have sketched. Machiavelli, Hobbes, and Rousseau were not aberrations in the European tradition of Christian civil religion but offered a *reductio* of its logic.

The case of Locke

If a question mark may be placed against the conventional canon of 'civil religion', conceived as the sanctification of a post-Christian state, so, correspondingly, we may doubt Locke's role as the fountainhead of the alternative trajectory of modernity: liberal neutrality.[92] Given the constant iteration of the claim that he advocated the 'Great Separation', it is worth recording evidence that disrupts that account. We should be wary of distancing the tolerationist Locke from two Protestant norms: the exclusion of Catholicism, and the upholding of a national church. For brevity, I turn only to his unpublished treatise *The Nature of Churches* (1681).[93]

Hobbes and Cardinal Bellarmine: *Leviathan* and the Ghost of the Roman Empire', *History of Political Thought*, 16 (1995), 503–21; Jurgen Overhoff, 'The Lutheranism of Thomas Hobbes', *History of Political Thought*, 18 (1997), 604–23. For the Erastian Independents see James Jacob, *Henry Stubbe, Radical Protestantism, and the Early Enlightenment* (Cambridge, 1983), Collins, *Allegiance*, passim; J. P. Sommerville, 'Hobbes and Independency', *Rivista di storia della filosofia*, 59 (2004), 155–73. For the Blackloists, see Collins, 'Thomas Hobbes and the Blackloist Conspiracy of 1649', *Historical Journal*, 45 (2002), 305–31; Stefania Tutino, *Thomas White and the Blackloists* (Aldershot, 2008). For Anglican Hobbesian Erastians: John Marshall, 'The Ecclesiology of the Latitude Men, 1660–1689', *Journal of Ecclesiastical History*, 36 (1985), 407–27.

[90] Helena Rosenblatt, 'On the Intellectual Sources of Laïcité', *French Politics, Culture, and Society*, 25 (2007), 1–18, at 8–9. See also Antony Black, 'Christianity and Republicanism: from St Cyprian to Rousseau', *American Political Science Review*, 91 (1997), 647–56; Helena Rosenblatt, *Rousseau and Geneva* (Cambridge, 1997), pp. 58–68.

[91] Rousseau, *Social Contract*, pp. 146–7.

[92] The following account was written independently of John Marshall's far more capacious and compelling treatment in the present volume.

[93] Bodleian Library, MS Locke c. 34. Hitherto known as 'A Defence of Nonconformity' or 'Critical Notes on Stillingfleet'. An edition by Tim Stanton (the new title is his) is forthcoming (Oxford). I am indebted to him for access to his transcription. My interpretation is not necessarily his.

In *The Nature of Churches* Locke's anti-popery is vehement: the treatise breathes the spirit of the Whig campaign to expose the perpetrators of the Popish Plot. He is a perfervid believer in the Plot, and this is an urgent text for 'this conjuncture'. This is 'a time when popery so threatens and so nearly surrounds us and is ready by any way it can find open to enter upon us'. There are 'enemies in our bowels or spies amongst us, whilst their general and commanders, whom they blindly obey, declare war, and [have] an unalterable design to destroy us'. Papists are 'ready by blood, violence, and destruction to ruin our religion and government'. Locke speaks constantly of the 'superstitions', 'idolatries', 'fopperies', and 'corruptions' of the Church of Rome, but it is not absurdity of doctrine and practice that rule out popery; rather that to be subject to Rome is to live under foreign oppression. 'Nobody that is free would put himself under' papal tyranny. The papal practice of excommunicating entire societies is the height of 'arbitrary power' – he had in mind the Interdicts against King John in 1208 and Venice in 1606. Locke contends that his opponent's, Edward Stillingfleet's, crusade against Protestant nonconformity is a crass distraction when 'the Protestant religion required the united forces of all sorts of Protestants to make good their ground against the common enemy'. He takes very seriously the claim of 'canonists, Jesuits, and the popish party' that the pope is 'supreme prince and monarch of the Christian world', so that Catholicism is necessarily a rival *imperium* which challenges the integrity of English civil society. It is because of their sedition and treason that the laws should 'be strictly put in execution against papists'.[94] Locke's exclusion of Catholics from toleration in his *Letter Concerning Toleration* (1689) troubles modern readers as an eccentric oddity, a proto-liberal's unfortunate lapse. But his anti-popery, his belief that Catholicism represents a priestly *imperium* that nullifies the commonwealth, is integral to his vision of a free state.[95]

It does not follow that, for Locke, the liberal state (a term of course alien to him) must exclude established religions. The *Nature of Churches* is a plea for 'comprehension', inclusion within the church, as well as for toleration. It embraces a 'latitudinarian' position in the church politics of Restoration England, in holding that Puritan non-conformists should, if possible, be re-integrated into the national church, and, only if unwilling, tolerated outside the church. His argument takes for granted the existence and desirability of a national church. Locke wishes to see the Act of Uniformity of 1662 moderated. We should 'retrench' its requirements. Retaining unnecessary ceremonies is 'injurious to our church', and 'therefore the

---

[94] MS Locke c. 34, pp. 7, 11–12, 26, 30, 39, 90, 139, 158.
[95] For Locke and Catholicism, see John Marshall, *John Locke, Toleration, and Early Enlightenment Culture* (Cambridge, 2006), pp. 686–94; J. C. Walmsley and Felix Waldmann, 'John Locke and the Toleration of Catholics', *Historical Journal*, 62 (2019), 1093–1115; Jeffrey Collins, *In the Shadow of Leviathan: John Locke and the Politics of Conscience* (Cambridge, 2020).

taking away of as many as is possible' is a 'proper ... way now to bring the dissenters into the communion of our church'. Conformity is a virtue. 'Experience teaches that such a uniformity seldom fails to draw the ease of common charity closer and hold Christians firmer together'. Schism is a vice. It is 'without doubt every man's duty to preserve the peace and unity of the church as much as in him lies from the least rent or division whatsoever'. Locke avows his membership of the national church: 'I who am of the Church of England'. He did not himself share the dissenters' conscientious objections to contentious ceremonies. 'I readily agree' with Stillingfleet's position concerning kneeling before the eucharist and using of the sign of the cross in baptism. He praises contemporary Anglican clergy. 'I can truly say that I think there have never been ... so many learned and devout bishops anywhere in the world as in the Church of England'. He applauds 'those many excellent preachers we have in the Church of England whose lives as well as sermons I look upon and verily believe to be the most seriously Christian that are now in the world'. Furthermore, Locke shares a characteristic Anglican distaste for the aggressive and conceited displays of conscience among non-conformists. He refers to the 'indiscreet heats of dissenters'. He holds that there is 'weakness and perhaps mistakes of our dissenting brethren', and voices a standard Anglican charge that Presbyterians, when in power, did not themselves permit toleration, but domineered. In all this, Locke firmly positions himself as a latitudinarian within the Church of England.[96]

Locke's theoretical grounding lies in what we may call his catholic (small 'c') ecclesiology; or, rather, his sociology of religion. Although the pursuit of salvation is an 'intimate and peculiar concern' of each individual, nonetheless 'the actions of a private solitary life cannot reach to all the ... purposes of religion', so that when we embrace a religion we 'associate, and join in communion with some society'. Communal worship of the deity is an aspect of natural sociability. The Christian religion lays a duty on us to 'unite into societies for public worship, profession, and propagation of its doctrines, and edification of one another'. Locke further allows the idea of a *national* church. At the outset he declares 'I perfectly agree there may be a national church'. A national church is one to which the majority of a people belong. (The term 'established church' was not common until the eighteenth century.) Locke holds that a church cannot legitimately be the *creation* of the civil power, for it is a voluntary association, and our salvation is no part of the civil power's concern. Yet, in the spirit of catholicity, the people at large would do well voluntarily to associate within a united church that is not onerous to conscience.[97] (Its benefits include providing a bulwark against popery,

---

[96] MS Locke c. 34, pp. 8, 31, 96, 121, 143, 147, 154, 156–7.
[97] MS Locke c. 34, pp. 2, 19, 77.

and Locke again accepts a standard Anglican argument for uniformity: the duty of Protestant solidarity against the common enemy). Even though he rejects the 'Erastian' (he uses the term) doctrine of a state church, Locke concedes some idea of a 'godly magistrate' (he does not use the term), for a national church might also be defined as one which the civil magistrate 'countenances', or 'the state favours or maintains'. Locke means that a Christian ruler is entitled to provide an infrastructure of support for the church's pastoral and evangelical work. 'I think such a church might properly be called the legal, or political church', though he prefers 'national'. The state may endow a church with property, provide stipends or tithes, but all such things remain under the jurisdiction of the temporal government. Locke here seems far removed from the rigid separation of church and state which it is assumed he professed. He *does* avow a categorical distinction between church and state. But his position is that church and state are *analytically* or modally distinct – they are fundamentally different kinds of society with no intrinsic claims upon each other – but in practice they may and do overlap. It is tempting to see here the germ of the position that would be influentially argued by William Warburton in *The Alliance between Church and State* (1736): Lockean Anglicanism perfected.[98] While Locke is at pains to denounce the evils that, in history, arose from the 'complication of the civil and ecclesiastical power' – the appalling consequences of the spurious identification of those two distinct societies – he accepts a 'Church of England' that may be succoured by a civil magistrate who shares its persuasion.[99]

In *The Nature of Churches* there is a long excursus on early church history, and here Locke's ecclesiology cleaved to his contemporaries' preoccupation with the character of the Apostolic and Patristic, or 'primitive', church. He is emphatic that, in scripture, and the first post-Apostolic age, there was no hierarchical distinction between presbyters and bishops; that the institution of episcopacy emerged only gradually; that it was, at best, a convenient and practical form of organization, groups of pastors needing a convenor or president; or, at worst, a product of clerical ambition. He holds that in early surviving documents 'priest' and 'bishop' were terms 'promiscuously used'. The Apostles allowed 'latitude' in such matters. Church officers at the beginning 'were but presidents of the assemblies'; 'Christian churches at first had a kind of consistorial way of government'. The idea of the 'Apostolic succession', vaunted by believers in divine right ('*jure divino*') episcopacy, by which Christ's authority is handed down from bishop to bishop, through episcopal consecration, 'amounts to nothing'; it is arrant nonsense, and there is no such 'consecration' in scripture. If episcopacy is not *jure divino*, neither is rule by presbyters. Locke aligns

---

[98] Stephen Taylor, 'William Warburton and the Alliance of Church and State', *Journal of Ecclesiastical History*, 43 (1992), 271–86; Walsh, *Civil Religion*, chapter 3.
[99] MS Locke c. 34, pp. 103–4.

with a long-established moderate Puritan position, resistant to exorbitant claims to authority by bishops, but without objecting to *jure humano* episcopacy. Such Puritans insisted, plausibly enough, that their position stood in the mainstream of the English Reformation, and that only latterly, from around 1600, had a more ambitious *jure divino* episcopalian ecclesiology emerged, a neo-popish innovation.[100]

Locke replays this historical exploration of church history by restating the argument in naturalistic terms. All church government is secular government, in the sense that it has nothing essentially to do with scripture norms, for it is a matter of human convention. A church, in its external earthly forms, is like any other secular corporation, shaped by its members, as seems convenient to them in different times and places. 'Church ([like] all bodies politic) government ... [is] merely prudential', 'wholly within human prudence as the people themselves shall judge'. The words 'prudence' and 'prudential' recur. Having a presiding personage among clergy is prudent, for 'natural reason' suggests that governance is best managed with 'one to preside'.[101] To understand the manifold variegated forms of church government across the Christian world, we should look to cultural history, not to scripture. Locke is profoundly committed to the truth of scripture, but he does not think scripture prescribes forms of human association and jurisdiction, including those of the church itself. His assertion of the secular character of both church and state is the conceptual means of liberating both from theocracy and priestcraft. His deep piety coexisted with a lambent anti-clericalism.[102]

---

[100] MS Locke c. 34, pp. 72, 89–90, 100, 129.

[101] MS Locke c. 34, pp. 3–4, 95.

[102] For parallel readings of Locke see John Marshall, 'John Locke and Latitudinarianism', in *Philosophy, Science, and Religion in England, 1640–1700*, eds Richard Kroll et al. (Cambridge, 1992); John Marshall, *John Locke: Resistance, Religion, and Responsibility* (Cambridge, 1994); Richard Ashcraft, 'Anticlericalism and Authority in Lockean Political Thought', in *The Margins of Orthodoxy*, ed. Roger Lund (Cambridge, 1995); Sally Jenkinson, 'Two Concepts of Tolerance: Or why Bayle is not Locke', *Journal of Political Philosophy*, 4 (1996), 302–21; David MacCabe, 'John Locke and the Argument against Strict Separation', *Review of Politics*, 59 (1997), 233–58; Michael Zuckert, *Launching Liberalism: On Lockean Political Philosophy* (Lawrence, KS, 2002); Nelson, *Hebrew Republic*, pp. 135–7; John Perry, *The Pretences of Loyalty: Locke, Liberal Theory, and American Political Theology* (Oxford, 2011); Jack Turner, 'John Locke, Christian Mission, and Colonial America', *Modern Intellectual History*, 8 (2011), 267–97; Aaron Herold, 'John Locke's Theology of Toleration and his Case for Civil Religion', *Review of Politics*, 76 (2014), 195–221; Elizabeth Pritchard, *Religion in Public: Locke's Political Theology* (Stanford, 2014); Collins, *Shadow of Leviathan*. See also Christie Maloyed, 'A Liberal Civil Religion: William Penn's Holy Experiment', *Journal of Church and State*, 55 (2013), 669–89. A striking instance of the high tide of the mid-twentieth-century secularization thesis to which I referred at the outset is John Dunn's pronouncement in 1969 that, because Locke's theories were rooted in religious premises, Dunn 'cannot conceive of constructing an analysis of any issue in contemporary political theory around

CIVIL RELIGION: TWO TRADITIONS

Those whom we may think of as post-Lockean Whigs, putatively committed to liberal toleration, remained 'statist' in their conception of public religion. Toland, readily labelled a 'deist' and certainly a deep enemy of 'priestcraft', asserted that there should be a 'national religion, or some public and orderly way of worshipping God, under the allowance, involvement, and inspection of the civil magistrate'. He echoed Cicero in holding that sceptical doubt about religious creeds should not amount to rejection of public religion.[103] Matthew Tindal's *Rights of the Christian Church* (1706) is a 'blend of Erastianism and Lockean tolerationism', hostile to 'an independent clerical *sacerdos*', and indebted to a version of the Protestant magisterial tradition which placed ecclesiastical supremacy in crown-in-parliament, a tradition that ran from St German in the 1530s through Selden and Matthew Hale in the seventeenth century.[104] In John Trenchard and Thomas Gordon's *The Independent Whig* (1720) and *Cato's Letters* (1720–3) a Ciceronian purge of *superstitio* in the name of *religio* is married to an appreciation of public institutional Christianity in the Whig commonwealth.[105] In Whig America John Witherspoon forswore established churches and upheld toleration, yet held that 'the magistrate ought to make public provision for the worship of God' and that 'magistrates are called to use their authority for the glory of God' and to 'reform and restrain impiety'.[106]

In the tradition of civil religion we have been examining, it was high church theologians who were the proponents of the *separation* of church and state, by insisting upon the autonomous rights of the church and the indefeasible powers of ecclesiastics; and it was their enemies – many of whom liberal modernity has claimed as their ancestors – who sought the *union* of religion and civil society. Priests were the archetypes of incivility; their critics sought instead 'the synthesis of civility and piety'.[107]

---

the affirmation or negation of anything which Locke says about political matters': *The Political Thought of John Locke* (Cambridge, 1969), p. x. The claim was partially retracted in 'What is Living and What is Dead in the Political Theory of John Locke?', in Dunn, *Interpreting Political Responsibility* (Princeton, 1990). It is ironic that in 1969 Dunn initiated a return to placing Locke in theological context while repudiating Locke's relevance thereby.

[103] John Toland, *Anglia Libera* (1701), pp. 95–6; quoted in East, 'Superstitionis Malleus', 981.

[104] Dmitri Levitin, 'Matthew Tindal's *Rights of the Christian Church* (1706) and the Church-State Relationship', *Historical Journal*, 54 (2011), 717–40, at 718–19. Levitin rejects an alternative genealogy of Tindal from Harringtonian or Hobbesian civil religion; but I have argued here that these latter are not an 'alternative' tradition but themselves rooted in Protestant jurisdictionalism. On Hale: Alan Cromartie, *Sir Matthew Hale, 1609–1676* (Cambridge, 1995).

[105] Kidd, 'Civil Theology', p. 1013; Walsh, *Civil Religion*, chapter 2.

[106] Quoted in Jeffrey Morrison, 'John Witherspoon and the Public Interest of Religion', *Journal of Church and State*, 41 (1999), 551–73, at p. 566.

[107] Walsh, *Civil Religion*, p. 4.

Coda: Sarah Cowper

I close with a vignette. Between 1701 and 1716, Lady Sarah Cowper kept a diary, which is full of her spiritual meditations. It is a record of devout Anglicanism, committed to pious preparation for the sacrament, and rich in reflections on sermons and devotional reading. Yet equally it is savagely anti-clerical and assertively tolerationist. She writes: 'The reading of history doth teach us that the politic government of priests is unfortunate and fatal'. Priests are men 'who have coloured their passions with the name of the church'.[108] Cowper's diary epitomizes sentiments which dominated Whig latitudinarianism: the paradox of intense spirituality coupled with loathing of priestcraft. It would be a travesty to take her anti-clericalism out of context and to doubt her Protestant piety and love of the communal worship of the established Church of England. Her diary is a testament to what English civil religion had become by 1700.[109]

---

[108] Hertfordshire Record Office, DE/P/F31, pp. 125, 153. See Mark Goldie, 'Sarah Cowper's "Character" of John Locke', *Locke Studies*, 21 (2021), 1–25.

[109] For commenting on a draft of this chapter I am grateful to Jeffrey Collins, Esther Counsell, and the editors.

2

A Mutable Wall of Separation? Reconfiguring Ecclesiastical Civility, Mixed Polity, and Civil and Sacred Matter in Late Elizabethan England

Polly Ha

Reformation in England was in many respects a civil Reformation. However ambiguous the confessional character of the Church of England, it was unquestionably attached to the crown, legitimized by parliamentary statute, and created by an amalgamation of civil and ecclesiastical jurisdictions.[1] Civility itself became emblematic of the later Tudor Reformation under Queen Elizabeth's moderate religious settlement. Merely requiring outward conformity, the queen was emphatic that she was not interested in persecuting subjects over matters of conscience and making windows into men's souls.[2] The Elizabethan Church defined itself against the caricature of the uncivil and persecutory Roman Catholic regime of Queen Mary who sent hundreds of Protestants to the flames. The 'via media' of the Church of England was also useful for creating political stability by countering the opposite threat of puritan popularity and zeal. The godly, who agitated for the introduction of continental Calvinist models of church government in the later sixteenth century, threatened to plunge England into political chaos by toppling ecclesiastical hierarchy, inciting sedition, and reducing the country to political anarchy. By bridling the excesses of both Roman Catholic and puritan zealotry, the Church of England presented the most

---

[1] A classic account of the jurisdictional and legal implications of Henry's break with Rome can be found in G. R. Elton, *Reform and Reformation: England, 1509-1558* (London, 1977). See also *The Reign of Henry VIII: Politics, Policy and Piety*, ed. Diarmaid MacCulloch (New York, 1995).
[2] This familiar paraphrase is originally derived from J. Spedding, R. L. Ellis, and D. D. Heath (eds), *The Works of Francis Bacon* (London, 1861), I, p. 178.

viable option for bridging religious division and securing political stability.[3] It offered a model of ecclesiastical civility that was designed to ensure peace and stability in the church and commonwealth.

However, by the second half of Elizabeth's reign, that picture was beginning to fade. The civility of the Elizabethan Settlement appeared to be dissipating under a civil domination over religion, subjecting matters of conscience to the dictate of the state.[4] The late Elizabethan regime brutally exploited indifferent matters in the church over which the crown claimed authority to suppress dissent. The 1580s marked the height of Catholic prosecutions for treason in response to the growing number of Catholic conspiracies to replace Elizabeth I on the throne with her Catholic cousin, Mary Queen of Scots.[5] For many English Catholics the security of state was a mere guise for the persecution of consciences. The onslaught of anti-Catholic legislation became a blunt instrument to wield against a diverse English Catholic community who were not all complicit in conspiratorial activity.[6] The Church of England's attack against puritan nonconformity culminated in 1593. New statutory enforcement of conformity sentenced the most radical puritan sectarians to death.[7] Alongside the aggressive legislative response to puritan dissent in the late sixteenth century was a literary campaign to expose the political threat posed by puritanism. The 1590s, as Patrick Collinson put it, were 'nasty'. These years were rife with incivility, discord, and dissension. Such ecclesiastical controversy had not only erupted into the public sphere through uncivil speeches and 'paper bullets' but amounted to what contemporaries such as Richard Bancroft called the late 'jarrs and disorder' over religion.[8]

---

[3] Norman Jones, *Faith by Statute: Parliament and the Settlement of Religion, 1559* (London, 1982); Peter Lake, *Anglicans and Puritans? Presbyterianism and English Conformist Thought from Whitgift to Hooker* (London, 1988).

[4] Lake, *Anglicans and Puritans?*, chapters 3–4. Ethan Shagan, *The Rule of Moderation: Violence, Religion and the Politics of Restraint in Early Modern England* (Cambridge, 2011), chapter 3.

[5] In defense of the Elizabethan regime, apologists denied persecuting over matters of conscience. Since the Pope had excommunicated the Queen in 1570, and Catholic powers across Europe had declared war on Elizabeth, they argued that the regime had little choice but to reluctantly take action against religious nonconformists whose convictions led to civil disobedience. Far from quietly protecting their own individual conscience, Catholic recusants and radical separatists overtly dissuaded subjects from obeying the Queen. For an example of this rationale, see William Cecil's confessional politics in Stephen Alford, 'The Political Creed of William Cecil', in *The Monarchical Republic of Early Modern England*, ed. John McDiarmid (Aldershot, 2007), pp. 75–90.

[6] Patrick McGrath, *Papists and Puritans under Elizabeth I* (London, 1967), pp. 177–204.

[7] McGrath, *Papists and Puritans*, pp. 309–15.

[8] Patrick Collinson, 'Ecclesiastical Vitriol: Religious Satire in the 1590s and the Invention of Puritanism', in *The Reign of Elizabeth I: Court and Culture in the Last Decade*, ed. John Guy (Cambridge, 1995), pp. 159–64. Historians have argued that these religious conflicts in the 1590s coincided with wider changes in the Elizabethan regime with absolutist and authoritarian tendencies replacing consensual politics. Coercion of conscience now began

At the heart of all this contention was disagreement between conformists and puritans over the nature of the Church of England and the relationship between civil and ecclesiastical jurisdiction. It is therefore no surprise that the nasty nineties generated fresh debate over 'civil religion', the precise relationship between the church and state, and nature of civil and sacred matter. Two competing theories about clerical domination emerged amidst the late Elizabethan war over religion.[9] It was in the final decade of the sixteenth century that puritans began to raise the pitch of their plea for liberty of conscience against an oppressive regime dominated by bishops. In the eyes of the godly, conformists were guilty of subsuming ecclesiastical matters under civil jurisdiction and royal supremacy. Richard Hooker's *Lawes of Ecclesiastical Polity* went the furthest in justifying the civil magistrate's authority over spiritual matters by arguing for the Church of England as a civil religion. 'All jurisdiction ecclesiastical within this realme is now annexed to the Imperiall Crown'.[10] The puritans justified their civil disobedience, and circumvented the law, by appealing to Scripture as the supreme authority. This, according to conformist critics, was merely a ploy to seize power and eventually erect a godly theocracy over the state. Further seeking to secure a culture domination over society, the godly were also guilty of manipulating the masses by appealing to emotion over reason.[11]

Implicit, and at times explicit, in these two competing narratives of domination was the use of ancient Rome as a model for utilizing religion as a means of inculcating civic virtues. Developing into a virtue contest, conformist and puritan divines both claimed that their ecclesiastical polity promised to be the most judicious and beneficial to society. Historians have long noted the social benefits that conformists and puritans promised in their rival ecclesiastical models.[12] Yet they have seldom linked such

---

to force subjects into religious compliance beyond mere outward conformity. The crown formally suppressed leading puritan dissenters. It effectively silenced puritan discourse over ecclesiastical matters. John Guy, *The Reign of Elizabeth I: Court and Culture in the Last Decade* (Cambridge, 1995), pp. 126–49. For the rhetoric of religious war in the final decade of Elizabeth's reign, see Polly Ha, 'The Elizabethan Wars of Religion', in *Reformed Government*, eds Polly Ha, Jonathan D. Moore, and Edda Frankot (Oxford, 2022), pp. xiii–xxii. For early modern notions of civility see Teresa Bejan, *Mere Civility: Disagreement and the Limits of Toleration* (Cambridge, MA, 2017).

[9] For the binary division and dichotomy between conformist and puritan anti-types, see Peter Lake's argument for mutually exclusive conspiracy theories in the early seventeenth century in his 'Anti-Popery: The Structure of a Prejudice', in *Conflict in Early Stuart England*, eds Richard Cust and Ann Hughes (London, 1989), pp. 72–106.

[10] Richard Hooker, *The Folger Library Edition of the Works of Richard Hooker*, vols 1–5 (Cambridge, MA, 1977–90), vol. VI (New York, 1993), vol. III, p. 468 [hereafter cited as FLE].

[11] Hooker, *FLE*, I, pp. 18–21.

[12] A. F. Scott Pearson, *Church and State: Political Aspects of Sixteenth Century Puritanism* (Cambridge, 1928), p. 22.

discourses to a longer tradition stretching back to the antiquity of Roman civil religion. Indeed, reference to Roman civil religion raises the question of how far divines were willing to reduce the substance of true religion or co-opt it into a mere vehicle of the state. Additionally, it raises the question of how they distinguished between indifferent and essential matters of faith. It is therefore unsurprising that alongside the ancient Roman model of religion as a cultivator of civic virtue was a more sinister Machiavellian account of insincere religion serving as a mere means for seizing worldly power.[13] Crucial to Hooker's account of civil religion was the indifferent nature of ecclesiastical matters. By stressing silence on indifferent religious matters for the sake of civil peace, conformists anticipated later seventeenth-century arguments for civil silence.[14] However, as the discussion over civil religion continued to advance in the late sixteenth century, the category of adiaphora itself threatened to break down. If ecclesiology became associated with civil obedience, could civil obedience begin to constitute true religion itself? Why did Hooker suggest the godly could fall under the category of atheism and those of no religion? The puritans in turn developed their own Machiavellian line by associating the episcopal grasp for power with anti-Christian or pagan idolatry.

From this perspective, the 1590s appeared to mark a hardening of lines with increasingly inflammatory representations of episcopal and presbyterian incivility and worldly guile. Yet, it was precisely during this time that both godly and conformist divines modified their positions and introduced one of the most striking ideas in early modern discussions about civil religion: its multivalent and even mutable nature. More than one, or even two, ways of reading into the political implications of puritanism were possible. There was of course no straightforward connection between puritan appeals to liberty of conscience and later libertarian arguments for the separation between religion and politics. Neither did the godly covenantal vision of society straightforwardly equate to theocracy. As Philip Gorski has argued, the godly who migrated to the new world developed nuanced configurations of the relationship between the church and state as 'distinct but interrelated enterprises' which coalesced around the idea of a 'prophetic republicanism'.[15] Indeed, far from the impression of a single monolithic model, multiple

---

[13] Cf. Charlotte McCallum in this volume, pp. 119–38.

[14] See George Downame's argument for collective conscience holding a higher claim over individual conscience in indifferent matters. George Downame, *A Treatise Vpon John 8.36. Concerning Christian Libertie* (London, 1609), p. 114.

[15] Philip Gorski, *American Covenant* (Princeton, 2017), p. 46. For a recent discussion of the 'distinction' and 'collaboration' between civil magistracy and the church in the Dutch Republic see Polly Ha, 'Discovering Orthodoxy? Rethinking the Purpose and Impact of the Synod of Dordt' in *The Synod of Dordt: A Landmark in Turbulent Times*, eds Henk van den Belt, Willem van Vlastuin, and Klaas-Willem de Jong (Göttingen, 2022), p. 45.

visions of how to establish new civil and ecclesiastical society existed among early colonists in the new world, including Roger Williams' iconic insistence on a strict wall of separation between church and state.[16] Decades before the mass puritan migration to the new world in the early seventeenth century, puritan divines began entertaining nuanced configurations of mixed polity in the 1590s. Their flexible accounts of the relationship between civil and ecclesiastical society challenge the picture presented in the polemical literature by their contemporaries. While the godly played up the distinction between civil and ecclesiastical jurisdiction to disarm accusations of political sedition, they also stressed the compatibility of godly ecclesiastical alternatives with a diversity of constitutional models that could be mutually reinforcing. This included their own version of royal supremacy and a hybrid model of presbyterian government which fused the crown's authority with godly republicanism.

Conformist thought was also, even crucially, fluid. Hooker did not simply chart a pathway for a Royal Supremacist version of civil religion. As noted above, he conscripted certain republican principles, using ancient Roman, Jewish, and even Machiavellian accounts of civil religion in Book V of his *Lawes*. He further reconfigured mixed monarchy by basing royal supremacy on common consent, presenting a limited, legal supremacy in contrast to rival absolutist models.[17] In addition to appealing to ancient Roman and Machiavellian versions of civil religion alongside their competing configurations of royal supremacy, Hooker and his puritan contemporaries further turned to early English and ancient Jewish precedent to explore the boundaries between civil and ecclesiastical jurisdiction. While hurling accusations of domination against each other, they nonetheless found common ground in certain legal precedents where there were overlapping jurisdictions. However, it was also here, in the ambiguous overlap, that they differed and developed a crucial strand of thought within early modern deliberations on the nature of civil religion. Conforming puritans in late Elizabethan England argued for the fixed nature of sacred and civil matter and tended to turn to Hebrew examples to stress the continuity of ecclesiastical jurisdiction.[18] Hooker instead broadened the discussion of civil religion by building an intellectual framework for justifying the movement of jurisdictional boundaries. Instead of highlighting continuities across the

---

[16] For the Dutch influence on toleration in the early colonies see Evan Haefeli, *New Netherland and the Dutch Origins of American Religious Liberty* (Philadelphia, 2012). In addition to the well-documented dissent of Roger Williams, Presbyterian critics in the New England colonies challenged the prevailing ecclesiastical views of New England congregational divines. Polly Ha, *English Presbyterianism 1590-1640* (Stanford, 2010), chapters 4-5.

[17] See pp. 76-7, 84-5 below.

[18] See Polly Ha, 'Who Owns the Hebrew Doctors?' *Journal of Medieval and Renaissance Studies*, 53:1 (January 2023), 55-85.

Old and New Testament spiritual discipline, he drew from Hebrew example and Rabbinic literature to stress the mutable nature of civil and ecclesiastical matters and their commutation between different courts. Hooker's emphasis on the union between church and state is more familiar than his insisting on 'walles of partition between temporall jurisdiction and spirituall'.[19] Yet Hooker is to be credited for constructing a technically advanced, innovative wall, which was not only permeable, but also designed to be mutable in suiting the particular needs of its time and wider context.

The Virtue Contest over Ecclesiastical Civility and Distributive Justice

Puritan criticism (of prelacy and the Book of Common Prayer among other things) was in many respects an attack on the relationship between civil and ecclesiastical society in England. Probing the ambiguous mix of spiritual and temporal jurisdiction, they questioned the precise nature of civil and ecclesiastical cases. Which matters were sacred? Which were civil? What happened when there were overlapping jurisdictions? On what basis could bishops use civil power against spiritual offences? Such questions were off limits insofar as they touched the crown's authority over the Church of England. The queen made it clear that she was not interested in engaging in discussion about her supremacy and further reformation. One way around implicating the Queen was to redirect criticism against episcopacy and the Book of Common Prayer. Challenging the statutory form of public worship established in England, the puritans directed their constitutional assault on prelacy and the Prayer Book to Parliament. It was no coincidence that the godly campaign for further reformation unleashed by the petition for a presbyterian church polity in the *Admonition to Parliament* in 1572 positioned itself as a movement for legislative reform.

It was in Hooker's defense of the Book of Common Prayer in Book V that he engaged most explicitly in his defense of the Church of England as a civil religion. He opened with the general premise that religion, whether inspired by natural or special revelation, served to inculcate civic virtues. 'Let politie acknowledge it selfe indebted to religion, godlines beinge the chiefest top and welspringe of all true virtues.'[20] Gregory Murry has noted the tendency to withdraw from the positive example of ancient Roman civil religion following the anti-Machiavellian tracts that began to circulate in the late sixteenth century.[21] Yet, Hooker turned to the example of civil religion in ancient Rome to argue that however superstitious and misplaced their

---

[19] Hooker, *FLE*, III, p. 483.
[20] Hooker, *FLE*, II, pp. 16–17.
[21] Gregory Murry, 'Anti-Machiavellianism and Roman Civil Religion in the Princely Literature of Sixteenth Century Europe', *The Sixteenth Century Journal*, 45:2 (2014), 331–50.

faith, the Romans' hope, fear of perjury, and persuasion of the 'irresistible force of divine power' nonetheless became an asset and instrumental to their success.[22] However intermingled with error, any 'sparkes of the light of truth' were responsible for 'all true virtues' and should 'honor true religion as theire parente, and all well ordered common weales...to love her as theire cheifest state.'[23] The ancient Jews were another chief example of 'magnanimitie' that was motivated by 'meere Religion'.[24] Religion served to make 'all sortes of men' more publicly serviceable, whether governments 'the apter to rule with conscience' or subjects 'for conscience sake the wilinger to obay.'[25] Any commonwealth ought to regard religion as the 'highest of all cares apperteyninge to publique regiment'.[26]

Despite drawing from republican examples of civil religion, Hooker challenged the puritan insistence on ministerial parity, which lay at the heart of their agitation for a 'godly republican' alternative to episcopacy. A chief way to discredit puritanism and disarm its assault on episcopacy was to play up the danger godly reform posed to the commonwealth.[27] Over the course of Elizabeth's reign, conformists began to amplify their claim that the puritans' disciplinarian platform would lead to the destruction of civil society by subjecting the sovereign and all matters of the state to an inflexible reading of scripture. Hooker's *Laws of Ecclesiastical Polity* began by attacking godly scriptural epistemology. Here Hooker has been said to 'deliberately exaggerate the biblicism of the orthodox disciplinarians, making it out to be more extreme than was, in fact, the case.'[28] But however exaggerated, his point was to highlight the incivility that would follow from the puritans' theocratic usurpation of authority. The puritans threatened 'the destruction of the Queen's Supremacy, "the overthrow of all learning," the decay of the universities, and even, he suggests, without a shred of evidence, the abolition of the common law and its replacement by Scripture as "the only law whereby to determine all our civil controversies"'.[29]

---

[22] Hooker, FLE, II, pp. 20–2.
[23] Hooker, FLE, II, p. 22.
[24] Hooker, FLE, II, p. 18.
[25] Hooker, FLE, II, pp. 16–17.
[26] Hooker, FLE, II, p. 16.
[27] Peter Lake, *Anglicans and Puritans*, pp. 197–213 and Scott Pearson, *Church and State*, chapter 2. For variations in conformist anti-puritan discourse and the dangers of its popularity see also Peter Lake, '"Anti-Puritanism": The Structure of a Prejudice', in *Religious Politics in Post-Reformation England*, eds Kenneth Fincham and Peter Lake (Woodbridge, 2006), pp. 80–97; Peter Lake, 'Puritanism, (Monarchical) Republicanism, and Monarchy: or John Whitgift, Puritanism and the "Invention" of Popularity,' *Journal of Medieval and Early Modern Studies*, 40:3 (2010), 463–95.
[28] W. D. J. Cargill Thompson, 'The Philosopher of the 'Politic society': Richard Hooker as a Political Thinker', in *Studies in Richard Hooker*, ed. W. Speed Hill (Cleveland, 1972), p. 142.
[29] *Ibid*.

It is noteworthy that Hooker inscribed this line of argument against puritanism as an uncivil religion in his earlier redefinition of justice before the publication of his *Lawes*. Hooker's posthumously printed 'A Learned Sermon on the Nature of Pride' appeared to be originally delivered alongside his other sermons on Habakkuk on 'Certaintie' and 'Justification' in the mid-1580s. This dating of Hooker's sermons places them directly in the heat of his controversy with Travers as they clashed over their ministry at the Temple Church which climaxed in their famous pulpit battle that prompted Hooker to write his extended defense of the Church of England.[30] Indeed, it is possible to go further by identifying the 'Learned Sermon' as engaging with the puritan challenge more globally through its overall construction and aims. Hooker highlighted a distinction between immutable, natural law and positive law that was 'subject unto change'.[31] However, he also directly challenged godly republican ideas about ministerial parity by appealing to distributive justice. According to Hooker, ministerial parity did not align with equity if each person were to have 'which is due according to the difference of their quality.'[32]

Inverting the puritans' impassioned rhetoric for ecclesiastical reform, Hooker's sermon redefined the nature of pride to undermine the legal assault on episcopacy while exposing the public danger posed by puritanism to the commonwealth. Instead of associating episcopal hierarchy as a symbol of worldly ambition and spiritual usurpation of temporal power, he identified puritan hubris, along with its insistence on equality, as destructive to the commonwealth. Defending episcopal honor, he pointed out that the mere possession of virtue by bishops could not possibly amount to pride without contradicting the idea of virtue itself. Furthermore, distinction of rank and title were not misliked by Christ, but useful 'for orders sake unto authority whether it be ecclesiastical or civil'.[33] However imperfect the Church of England, it was relatively straight and rectified in comparison with those who 'bendeth so that it swerveth either to the right hand or the left by excessive or defect form'.[34] Indeed, incremental movement in a godly direction was superior 'in comparison of them which run cleen another waie'.[35] The Church of England was also virtuous in its general 'moderate and sober' character, which allowed it to be governed by reason. Travers

---

[30] His early biographer Kebel suggested that the sermon arose out of his controversy at the Temple Church by pointing to the internal content of the sermon, such as an emphasis on the mutability of positive law. Egil Grislis has argued that the sermon can be seen to have followed from their pulpit battle. Whereas Travers had made a public appeal in defense of his ordination and ministry, Hooker stressed public order and submission to ecclesiastical authority. Hooker, *FLE*, V, p. 299.

[31] Hooker, *FLE*, V, p. 335.
[32] Hooker, *FLE*, V, p. 347.
[33] Hooker, *FLE*, V, p. 318.
[34] Hooker, *FLE*, V, p. 312.
[35] Hooker, *FLE*, V, p. 314.

had complained against Hooker's leniency towards the Church of Rome, a 'Babylon', which held the people of God in captivity to idolatry. Hooker reversed the puritan use of 'Babilonianism', turning it against puritan vanity, conceit, and 'blindness', which were dominated by willful tyranny and 'brutish sensuality'.[36] He further condemned puritan pride by using the example of rebellion against Moses by Korah, Dathan and Abiram who threatened the destruction of civil order through their swelling of pride and 'mutinous repining at lawful authority'.[37] The implications were clear. The 'inordinate elation [of] the mind' represented by godly ambition could only result in the 'overthrow' of government and 'disturb the peace of the world'.[38] Puritan pride was the antithesis of godly government, justice, and order.

What is striking about Hooker's discussion of pride in his 'Learned Sermon' is his integration of civil virtues with spiritual ones under the general category of 'Justice'. He strung together civil virtues such as 'harmlesnes and sincerity in speech' and 'pursuit of peace' with pious virtues, placing special emphasis on *'continuance in praier, contrition of hart'*.[39] Further establishing the union between civility and piety, Hooker developed his argument for the rule of collective justice overweighing individual scruples over conscience. Hooker argued that man was created relationally and therefore ought to weigh justice communally.[40] Thus, those laws that protected against the 'most publique harm' could hold a higher claim above personal subjectivity in administering justice.[41] Hooker therefore curbed the excesses of popular government and appeals to liberty of conscience by arguing for mutual subjection to the state.

It was in response to the charge of theocratic usurpation of civil authority that puritans tended to stress the distinction between civil and ecclesiastical jurisdiction. The notion of constitutional relativity, or the permissibility of altering of civil polities, had surfaced within the resistance literature of monarchmachs. Distancing themselves from these earlier examples, puritans across the spectrum from the later sixteenth century onwards redirected constitutional relativity to argue for the compatibility of reformed ecclesiology with different civil polities. The varying constitutions in the

---

[36] Hooker, *FLE*, V, p. 314. For Travers's insistence on 'go[ing] out of Babylon', see Hooker, *FLE*, V, pp. 271–92.
[37] Hooker, *FLE*, V, p. 319. Although Hooker here emphasizes the political implications of their rebellion (Numbers 16:1–25), Travers later used the example to condemn ecclesiastical rebellion against a national church by congregational autonomy, Polly Ha, Jonathan D. Moore, and Edda Frankot (eds), *The Puritans on Independence* (Oxford, 2017), p. 126.
[38] Hooker, *FLE*, V, p. 320.
[39] Hooker, *FLE*, V, p. 332.
[40] Hooker, *FLE*, V, p. 333.
[41] Hooker, *FLE*, V, p. 337.

Old Testament scriptures and across history challenged the equation of self-governing congregations with inherent political sedition.[42]

One of the lengthiest responses to Hooker's *Lawes*, the 'Reformed Government', circulated in manuscript as a scribal publication in the mid-1590s.[43] In addition to stressing the relativity of civil constitutions, one of the main strategies was to invert the conspiratorial narrative against episcopacy itself. The puritans had long characterized bishops as evil councillors who deliberately mislead the prince to serve their own personal interests. Continuing this line of argument, the puritans argued that episcopal corruption was institutionally embedded into their office because of the partiality of their judgement clouded by their vested interest. Bishops had usurped temporal power and invested themselves with a higher social status. Episcopacy was a politic religion, which was inherently corrupt and flawed. It was non-existent in the Anglo-Saxon church.[44] Episcopal wealth and status was an innovation introduced after the Norman Conquest:

> [In the] 9th yeare of his raigne A Councell holden at London did decree... that Bishops should remove their seates 'from townes and villages into cityes': whereupon the Bishops removed from townes to cityes, as the Bishopprick of Selese was removed to *Chichester*, from *Cornewall* to *Exeter*, from *Wells* to *Bath*, from *Shirburne* to *Salisbury*, from *Dorcester* to *Lincolne*, from *Lichfield* to *Chester*...[45]

The temporal power enjoyed by prelates was 'but new in respect of the ould Bishops of England'. It had been 'hatched...by the Earles, Barons, and other nobles of this Realme' which was 'tolerated and suffered by the Princes'.[46] Since this encroachment, bishops proved themselves to be guilty of the politique use of religion, using Machiavellian deception and coercion to maintain their status and power. They were singlehandedly responsible for all the social ills which existed in later Tudor society from the increase in ungodliness, poverty, and crime, due to their preoccupation with their own aggrandizement, to the dearth and economic drain as a result of divine judgement, and the general decline of civil society itself through the neglect of the universities and decay in manners.[47]

Aside from charging episcopacy with inherent incivility, the 'Reformed Government' further argued for the wider civic virtues that would follow from instituting reformed religion. Conformist culture was too generic and unsuited to meet the diverse needs of a particular locale, congregation,

---

[42] Ha, Moore, and Frankot (eds), *Reformed Government*, pp. xxv–xxvii.
[43] *Ibid.*
[44] Cf. Jacqueline Rose's chapter in this volume, pp. 223–42.
[45] Ha, Moore, and Frankot (eds), *Reformed Government*, pp. 132–3.
[46] *Ibid.*, p. 133.
[47] For a fuller discussion of this line of argument and the paragraph below see the introductory sections to *Reformed Government*.

or individual. It bred a culture of complacency that reinforced clerical corruption. Furthermore, it encouraged members to be satisfied with a bare minimum religion, stunting growth, resulting in spiritual stagnation, and the decay of the commonwealth. In contrast to such minimal conformist religion, reformed religion positioned itself as offering a maximal vision of ecclesiastical reform, education and edification. Defending the particularization of personal sins, both publicly and privately, based on Acts 20:18-20, it argued for private instruction of families in addition to the public proclamation of the gospel in the pulpit.[48] Ministers were 'to instruct their flock...thorough every house: to warne every one, night and day, without ceasinge'.[49] This severity was seen as part and parcel of the highly customisable nature of the reformed alternative that was modular in its implementation. Teaching elders, for instance, would remedy widespread ignorance among the masses.

While Hooker used pagan Roman religion to extol the virtues of civil religion, the puritans also drew ecclesiastical analogies to Roman republican self-governance inculcating civility. The responsibility of lay governing elders was to 'marke, ouersee and obserue all mens manners' like the 'Censors off Rome who exacted and examined euery citezens life according to the lawes'.[50] Their collective bodies of church officers were organised as stationary courts which contributed to its flexibility and adaptability to various situations. '[L]ocal disciplie- by justices or by presbyteries – was cheap, acquainted with local circumstances and flexible'.[51] In short, the godly argued that the ecclesiastical discipline they desired promised nothing short of providing solutions for England's moral and social problems. For church reform would induce increased piety and this promised to elicit men and women across the spectrum and society into active engagement with the church, which would ignite moral and social reform locally. Moral and social reform would in turn strengthen the state through more efficient poor relief and the reduction of crime. On a national level, it would cause the commonwealth more generally to 'flourish' in peace and prosperity, from greater industry and economic development, to educational improvement and civility. So, the 'Reformed Government' cast ecclesiastical reform as the sinews that helped the commonwealth hold together by playing up the social benefits of local jurisdiction by elders, church discipline, and the efficient regulation of life and doctrine.[52]

---

[48] William Fulke, *A briefe and plaine declaration...a learned discourse* (1574), pp. 5-53.
[49] Ha, Moore, and Frankot (eds), *Reformed Government*, p. 111.
[50] Walter Travers, *A full and plaine declaration of Ecclesiasticall Discipline owt off the word off God* (Heidelberg, 1574), p. 156.
[51] Ronald A. Marchant, *The Church under the Law: Justice, Administration, and Discipline in the Diocese of York, 1560-1640* (Cambridge, 1969), p. 242.
[52] Polly Ha, 'Leveraging Historical Contingency: Christian Antiquity and Late Elizabethan Society' in *Reformed Government*, pp. xxxix-liii.

From Incivility to Machiavellian Insincerity

More was at stake in the virtue contest between puritan and conformist divines than merely making campaign promises and scoring polemical points. Indeed, Hooker went even further by reconstructing the relationship between true religion, the civil sphere, and royal authority. If Hooker argued that the puritan discipline threatened to subsume the entire civil sphere and all temporal matters under a theocracy, he also warned of another danger that puritanism posed: it threatened the destruction of true religion itself. Their mutation of religion mutilated it and could transform its very substance. Firstly, the puritans had violated civil religion by making the 'rule of mens private spirits' the judge and final arbiter in religious matters. For only those learned and experienced in the law could deliberate, determine, and exercise coercive jurisdiction in ecclesiastical affairs. Secondly, the puritans introduced incivility into religious discourse through the publication of their satirical Marprelate tracts which mercilessly lampooned bishops. Printed as a series of scurrilous attacks on prelacy from a secret press (1588-9), the Marprelate controversy broke conventional decorum by promiscuously mixing the stage play with sacred matter.[53] Marprelate had in effect invented a 'new method of turning things that are serious into mockerie'. The puritan manner of discourse appealed to emotional manipulation over reason. It failed to try 'what the most religious are able to say in defense of the highest points whereupon all religion dependeth.' Thirdly, the puritans were in danger of reducing religion to a mere political tool. Their 'politique use of religion', he argued, made 'religion itself...a meere politique devise, forged purposely to serve for that use'. Finally, as a 'false and fradulent means', this irreligion threatened to overthrow Princes and their states. Their end, which was political disloyalty, exposed their conversion of religion into a mere means. This hermeneutic of suspicion linked puritan popularity explicitly with political sedition and Machiavellian politics.[54] By turning to worldly means, the puritans were guilty of desacralization by stripping true religion of its substance.

Like Hooker, the 'Reformed Government' further argued that episcopacy was not simply guilty of confusing the boundaries between civil and ecclesiastical jurisdiction. By abandoning scripture as the basis for spiritual concord, it threatened to construct religion around a false unity that was prone to error or becoming devoid of any substantive faith:

> If unity simply without any further regard, had beene sufficient, there was as much unity as might be, in thos that made the *Golden Calfe*: and no lesse Unity in thos that joyntly with one voice cryed against our Saviour Christ, 'crucify him'; but such unity is but an unity in error, and no

---

[53] Joseph L. Black (ed.), *The Martin Marprelate Tracts* (Cambridge, 2008).
[54] For recent discussion of puritan popularity see note 83 below.

better in deede then a plaine Conspiracy agaisnt the truth, which is a thinge as much to be detested, as Unity in the truth is to be reverenced & embraced.[55]

The danger of equating piety with civil obedience was that it could relinquish matters of conscience, and possibly even true religion itself, to the state. In the hands of power-hungry bishops, it was only a matter of time before the demise of all piety and true religion. In the eyes of the godly, Hooker could be seen to be making a significant move. He was commuting the nature of true religion by moving it away from private conscience into the religion of the institutional establishment, and in turn imputing religion with a condition of civil obedience. For the root of superstition and false religion, according to Hooker, was not mindless attachment to tradition which allegedly departed from the primitive church. It was 'fear induced observance which [was] counter to reason'. Instead of measuring true religion by a rigid biblicism that turned scripture into a wax nose, Hooker argued that false religion was not only ill-informed and irrational but manifested by its political dissent. It was within this context that he equated particular manifestations of puritanism with the subversion of true religion, and even located them within the context of his discussion of atheism and those of no religion. In doing so, Hooker began to imply that there was a closer connection between the substance of true religion itself and conformity and civil obedience.

From one perspective, the final decade in Elizabeth's reign appears to have fed into two self-fulfilling prophecies. Hooker characterized the relationship between the church and state by its close union. He appeared increasingly to subsume religion under the state, especially in his defense of episcopacy and royal supremacy. In Book VII of the *Laws*, Hooker doubled his efforts to argue that bishops rightly participated in civil affairs and held seats in the House of Lords.[56] Alongside making the case for episcopal civil office, Hooker made it clear that he ultimately placed supreme authority in the crown as sovereign over the church.[57] In contrast to Hooker's emphasis on civil and ecclesiastical unity, the puritans stressed their distinction. To combine ecclesiastical and temporal power was unnatural; it united what God had severed. Even if ministers and magistrates could cooperate and

---

[55] Trinity College Dublin MS 140, fol. 67r.
[56] Hooker, *FLE*, III, pp. 231, 237. Book VII remained unpublished until later in the seventeenth century and was the last to appear. For a recent discussion of Hooker's defense of episcopacy see Rudolph Almasy, 'The "Public" of Richard Hooker's Book 7 of the *Laws*: Stitching Together the Unjoined', *Renaissance and Reformation*, 41:1 (2018), 131-61, and Ha, Moore, and Frankot (eds), *Reformed Government*, pp. xxxiv–xxxvi.
[57] 1. Eliz 2. Hooker, *FLE*, III, p. 468. For a recent discussion of the reception of Hooker's defence of royal supremacy in later civil religious discourse see Ashley Walsh, *Civil Religion and the Enlightenment in England, 1707-1800* (Woodbridge, 2020), p. 7.

move toward the same goal, to intermix them in a single person was likened to the hermaphrodite of two sexes.[58]

However, neither conformists nor puritans were simply reverting to the same arguments that they had made in the 1570s and 80s. Pushing their adversaries to their extreme implications appears to have had a dual effect of both amplifying disagreement while also nudging both parties closer to a middle ground. Counter-intuitively, both Hooker and his godly adversaries reconfigured the notion of mixed monarchy, drawing back from extreme imperial and populist representations. Hooker, quite significantly, curbed the excesses of state coercion over conscience by his reconfiguration of the mixed monarchy, basing its authority on collective consent. Instead of advocating an absolutist version of supremacy, he instead argued for a limited, legal supremacy, which restrained royal authority.[59] The godly similarly modified royal supremacy. Rather than suggesting a complete separation of church and state to discredit prelacy and debunk the caricature of a puritan theocracy, the godly entertained more nuanced models of mutually supportive civil and ecclesiastical jurisdictions. In response to the caricature of puritan theocratic usurpation of authority, the 'Reformed Government' went further than any other presbyterian treatise in fusing royal supremacy with reformed ecclesiastical polity. Arguing for the simple substitution of bishops with ministers and lay governing elders, it left the crown's authority over spirituals 'untouched and unblemished'. This hybrid 'presbyterian-royal supremacy' model applied the title of bishop to all ministers while allowing the Queen room to appoint a nominal bishop who would temporarily exercise some added responsibilities akin to a moderator over a synod or assembly. It thus argued for a limited supremacy, where the crown was not simply bound by divine law, but also human positive law. True, this reconfiguration of the crown's authority over spirituals reduced its authority to the point of almost nominalizing its role altogether. However, it nonetheless marked movement in the reformed vision. Furthermore, it stretched beyond a purely biblicist argument. The 'Reformed Government' was saturated in statues, drawing heavily from the year books, and from Fitzherbert.[60]

These reconfigurations of mixed monarchy are a striking reminder of how at the height of polemical incivility, both parties could nonetheless rescale the popular and monarchical dimensions in their version of mixed

---

[58] Ha, Moore, and Frankot (eds), *Reformed Government*, p. 116.
[59] W. D. J. Cargill Thompson, 'The Philosopher of the Politic Society: Richard Hooker as a Political Thinker' in *Studies in the Reformation*, ed. C. W. Dugmore (London, 1980), and Robert Eccleshall, *Order and Reason in Politics: Theories of Absolute and Limited Monarchy in Early Modern England* (Oxford, 1978).
[60] Ha, Moore, and Frankot (eds), *Reformed Government*, pp. 129–40. Sir Anthony Fitzherbert (c.1470–1538) was a prominent judge and jurist under Henry VIII who wrote one of the chief reference texts for writs.

polity. Whether directly or indirectly as a response to the exaggerated representations portrayed by their adversaries, both conformist and puritan divines modified their positions. The movement and flexibility in these competing visions of royal supremacy also offers a crucial point of entry into the nuanced views over civil religion that could assimilate republican and monarchical elements of government. Of course, both conformist and puritan modifications were open to accusations of paying mere lip service to popular or monarchical elements in their mixed polity. But there was nonetheless a set of assumptions and a common ground that they shared, even if inclined in different directions. Those matters that overlapped between civil and ecclesiastical jurisdiction both highlighted common ground while also exposing their differences. It was on the question of the nature of civil and ecclesiastical matters that Hooker made a major contribution to the discourse surrounding civil religion; here he introduced the idea of commutative justice as a means to justify the movement between civil and ecclesiastical matters and jurisdictions. In short, he erected a wall of separation; but instead of remaining a fixed barrier, he constructed a mutable wall that was permeable and capable of translating the nature of civil and sacred matter.

The Mutability of Civil and Sacred Matter and Commutative Justice

The prosecution of the puritans in the 1590s heightened contention over the relationship between civil and ecclesiastical jurisdiction. Hauled before the Court of High Commission, the main presbyterian leaders refused to incriminate themselves by complying with the oath *ex officio mero*. In their defense, the lawyer James Morice argued that it was unconstitutional to force suspects to swear oath to answer questions before any formal charges were presented. According to Richard Cosin, some 'grave, wise, and learned' men were sympathetic to these objections'.[61] This posed a serious enough threat to demand his vigorous defense of the ex officio oath in *An Apologie for sundrie proceedings by jurisdiction ecclesiastical* in 1593. Ethan Shagan has argued that Cosin's *Apologie* extended the boundaries of state control by justifying the use of coercion against conscience. Cosin exploited 'oaths as a liminal event between human and divine', placing them in the 'sphere of ceremonial observance' and thus under the government's jurisdiction. In effect, Cosin was arguing for the diversity, compatibility, and even mutability, of ecclesiastical and common law. This meant that legally, oaths could be *sacralized* by locating them within the sphere of indifferent ecclesiastical matters. But according to Cosin's critics,

---

[61] John Cosin, *An apologie for svndrie proceedings by iurisdiction ecclesiasticall* (London, 1593), A2v.

he was not simply expanding ecclesiastical jurisdiction. He was also in effect justifying the use of temporal punishments against spiritual offences. In the eyes of his puritan critics, this was to introduce a barbarous incivility and unjustified use of force akin to the Spanish Inquisition, against law, scripture, and English custom.[62]

It is worth returning to Hooker's fragments to find clues about how he argued for the mutable nature of matter to defend its movement between ecclesiastical and civil jurisdiction. He importantly builds a case for this relationship by acknowledging the distinction between spiritual jurisdiction and temporal power. Long before Roger Williams called for a 'wall of separation' between the church and state, Hooker introduced the language of a partitioning wall to preface his argument about the nature of civil and ecclesiastical jurisdiction.[63] For their safety it was 'requisite...to uphold and to keepe intier the walles of partition between temporall jurisdiction and spirituall'. Historically, temporal power encroached upon spiritual jurisdiction, and the liberty of the church should be protected.[64]

But this was not to erect an impermeable or immutable wall of separation. Hooker used the diversity and distinctions within each sphere to refute the idea of entirely distinct and separate temporal and spiritual jurisdictions, excluding any overlap between them. I have highlighted elsewhere how Hooker created a space for matters that had an overlapping and more ambiguous nature.[65] It is worth revisiting these particular cases here. Stressing the '*equal and indifferent mixture*' of particular cases, Hooker argued that it was possible to try them in either or both courts.[66] The 'laying of violent handes on a Clark hath sufficient remedie at the Common lawe as touching the bodilie harme he suffereth, and in regard of the Canon which maketh men for such disorders excommunicable the Court Ecclesiastical taketh likewise notice thereof. Artic. Cler. c. 6'. Secondly, Hooker argued that some cases, such as usury, simony and perjury, could overlap in their jurisdiction since they held a dual '*mixed and intermingled*' nature.[67] However, Hooker raised a crucial concept in a third possibility relating to the law of commutation and commerce: the movement of matter from a spiritual to a temporal nature. Although a particular case might come

---

[62] Ethan Shagan, 'The English Inquisition', pp. 551–63.

[63] In addition to arguing for a wall of separation between church and state in his famous letter, Williams also identified additional walls which protected the church's liberty. Roger Williams, *The Complete Writings of Roger Williams*, 7 vols (New York: 1963) III, p. 286. For examples of other independent divines using the idea of enclosed security through walls of ecclesiastical separation see John Rogers, *Ohel of Beth-shemesh, A tabernacle for the sun* (1653), p. 42 and Paul Hobson, *A Garden Enclosed* (1647), p. 38.

[64] Hooker, FLE, III, p. 483.

[65] The next few paragraphs draw from my previous discussion of Hooker and his puritan critics in *Reformed Government*, pp. xxxii–xxxiii.

[66] Hooker, FLE, III, p. 489.

[67] Hooker, FLE, III, p. 489.

under the jurisdiction of an ecclesiastical court, 'through commutation' it could change in its nature and fall under a lay court. Pecuniary transactions such as a cleric selling his 'tithes…to another man for money' initiated the commutation from a spiritual to lay court 'because by sale things spiritual become temporal, and tithes become chattels'.[68] The law of commutation was not only useful for delineating the finer points of civil and ecclesiastical jurisdiction, but of course supported Hooker's more general argument for the mutability of laws.

The 'Reformed Government' offers a striking rebuttal of Cosin's and Hooker's defense of civil religion. On the one hand, it agreed with its conformist adversaries that certain overlapping matters could be 'punishable both in the Ecclesiasticall Consistory, & likewise in the Temporall Courts', using the same case as Hooker of a clergyman who is beaten.[69] However, the 'Reformed Government' disagreed with Hooker on the nature of the case. Whereas the example for Hooker fell under the category of adiaphora, the 'Reformed Government' instead argued for their punishable nature 'in a divers sort & respect'. Defamation was triable in the consistory, but also in a temporal court to recover damages. Usury was only punishable in both courts 'in divers respectes' rather than having a mixed or intermingled nature.[70] These matters involved distinct actions in separate courts which were neither indifferent nor intermixed.[71] However, despite their disagreement on the nature of such overlapping cases, Hooker and the 'Reformed Government' shared the same interpretation of testament and wills. They both cited 11 Henry 7 f. 12 to make the point that probate of will entered into spiritual courts by custom that became its basis in contemporary law.[72] Just as Hooker and his puritan adversaries had counter-intuitively inched closer together by emphasizing the constitutional qualifications of royal supremacy, so they agreed on the gradual transference of testaments and wills to ecclesiastical courts in history, even while they disagreed over the commutative nature of those cases.

If commutative justice was useful for Hooker in defending the transference of matters from ecclesiastical to civil courts, it was also used in the reverse order to argue for the commutation of communal property to sacred ends. Public places of worship were a chief example of communal space that could be designated 'especiallie for mutual conference and as it were commerce to be had between God and us'.[73] Here in the context of public worship Hooker further defended the commutation of the civil to the sacred, including the consecration of time as well as space to sacred ends. Such matters had of

[68] Hooker, FLE, III, p. 484.
[69] Reformed Government, p. 130.
[70] Ibid.
[71] Ibid.
[72] Reformed Government, pp. 133-4.
[73] Hooker, FLE, II, pp. 362-3.

course come under fierce attack in the *Admonition Controversy* that appealed to divine prescriptions for regulating public worship. The puritans implicitly and explicitly challenged ecclesiastical and royal prerogative for consecrating communal spaces or assigning additional days for public festivals and fasts.

On one level, the debate over sacred space and days grew out of disagreement over how far scripture permitted human discretion over indifferent matters. On the one hand, the godly appealed to *jure divino* arguments to demand a stricter observance of the Sabbath while arguing that this freed men and women from *jure humano* traditions associated with remnants of Roman Catholic tradition which encroached on the remaining six working days. The thrust of Hooker's defense of the Book of Common Prayer and the Church of England's worship services stressed their nature as indifferent matters which simply concerned the 'convenient' public ordering of church affairs.[74] The church held discretion over adiaphora, those 'lawes touchinge mater of order are changeable, by the power of the Church' whereas 'articles concerninge doctrine not so'.[75] If the 'Quene or Soveraigne' as 'commandresse over other virtues' had wisdom to govern the commonwealth at large, then it was her peculiar prerogative to 'prescribe the order of doinge in all thinges', including public worship.[76]

However, instead of simply arguing for the discretionary power of the Queen and the church over indifferent matters, Hooker also made a case for the particular order of public worship in England. The 'vaine traditions' criticized by the puritans were rightly reflective of the 'Greatenes and dignity' that was 'measured by the worthines of the subject' comparable unto the publique duties of religion.[77] Religion was therefore not simply an ancillary aspect of public life, but the height of public duty by the supremacy of its subject. It was within this context that Hooker engaged in some of his lengthiest defenses for the continuity of Jewish practices in the Christian church. For instance, Hooker turned to the example of the Israelites to defend the consecration and hallowing of places for public worship.[78] The worship for the Israelites, from tabernacle and tent to temple, revealed their changing historical contexts.[79] The 'onlie things that maketh anie place publique is the publique assignment thereof unto such duties. The solemn dedication of a church, like the Temple, sanctified the place, sanctification of churches was essentially to 'make them places of publique resort'.[80] Likewise, the Jewish church supported the ecclesiastical power to dedicate commemorative days beyond the Mosaic law, such as Esther and Mordechai

---

[74] Hooker, *FLE*, II, p. 33.
[75] Hooker, *FLE*, II, p. 38.
[76] Hooker, *FLE*, II, p. 38.
[77] Hooker, *FLE*, II, p. 33.
[78] Hooker, *FLE*, II, p. 47.
[79] Hooker, *FLE*, II, pp. 47, 49.
[80] Hooker, *FLE*, II, pp. 50–3.

in the 'feast of lottes'.[81] That Hooker felt compelled to make a case for the consecration of communal space and time for sacred ends again points to his bridging the Church of England's worship with a wider tradition beyond Roman Catholic precedent.[82]

Yet, the debate returned to questions surrounding civil religion. Rather than rehearse puritan complaint literature on saints' days and popular festivals here, it suffices to underscore godly contempt for their wastefulness and public disservice.[83] Hooker, in turn, defended the sanctification of public property and time in terms of the civil virtues of obedience that could be inculcated through habit. Hooker stressed the public utility of festivals for 'refresh[ing] those poore and needie'. Their relaxation enabled them to collectively participate in a higher calling, inclining themselves 'more religiouslie [to] blesse God'.[84] Needless to the say, the godly were highly skeptical of any sanctity or pretended piety in such public festivals. In their view, popular customs had their roots in pagan culture. The Pope later co-opted such public revelry as an opiate of the masses.[85] It is worth noting that Hooker again moved these festivals away from Roman Catholic tradition, pointing to celebration both by the Jews in the Old Testament, and even public rest that was 'evident to the heathens by nature'.[86]

Stressing the distinction between civil and ecclesiastical matters enabled the godly to argue that it was not they who threatened to impose a theocracy on civil society. Instead, it was the overreaching power of prelates

---

[81] Hooker, *FLE*, II, p. 366.

[82] Jewel's early controversy with the Catholic apologist Thomas Harding raised the question of whether the Church of England 'teache men to Faste for policie, not for Religion.' John Jewel, *Defence of the Apologie of the Churche of England* (London, 1567), p. 15. Hooker's materiality, along with his language of commerce between the spiritual and temporal, could further challenge the 'simple bifurcation between sacramental –centered worship and word-centered worship and between conformist and nonconformist.' Rudolph Almasy, 'Richard Hooker and places of Worship – 'In due season they are all pleasaunt and good'", *Anglican and Episcopal History*, 85:3 (2016), 327. For pre-Reformation lay Catholic notions of sacred time, see Eamon Duffy, *The Stripping of the Altars: Traditional Religion in England, 1400–1580* (New Haven, 1992), pp. 37–47.

[83] Rather than taking puritan complaint literature at face value, Patrick Collinson and others have explored the broader social tensions within puritan texts. For example, see Patrick Collinson, *The Religion of Protestants: The Church in English Society 1559–1625* (Oxford, 1982), chapter 5, and Eamon Duffy, 'The Godly and the Multitude in Stuart England', *The Seventeenth Century*, 1:1 (1986), 31–55; Alexandra Walsham, 'The godly and popular culture', in *The Cambridge Companion to Puritanism*, eds John Coffey and Paul C. H. Lim (Cambridge, 2008), pp. 277–93; and Peter Lake, 'Deeds against nature: cheap print, Protestantism and murder in early seventeenth century England', in *Culture and politics in early Stuart England*, eds Kevin M. Sharpe and Peter Lake (London, 1994), pp. 257–83.

[84] Hooker, *FLE*, II, p. 364.

[85] Walsham, 'The godly and popular culture', pp. 277–93.

[86] Hooker, *FLE*, II, p. 365.

who encroached on civil life by making an unfounded claim over communal property, time, and space. The church had no business 'sacralizing' communal property or declaring particular times and dates in the calendar to be kept holy by calling public festivals and fasts. Jewish practices were either divinely prescribed or no longer binding. While Hebrew examples highlighted continuity in the spiritual discipline of excommunication, this did not grant the church license to impose additional days of rest.[87] If the godly later made exceptions for days of thanksgiving and fasting, they placed an emphasis on divine initiation and providence.[88] In contrast, Hooker further located the sanctifying of time and place within a broader discussion, challenging the danger of puritan liberty and its relation to wider political society. Puritan insistence on individual arbitration over six days 'shaketh universallie the fabric of government, tendeth to anarchie and meere confusion, dissolveth families, dissipateth colleges, corporations, armies, overthroweth kingdoms Churches and whatsoever is now through the providence of God by authority and power upheld'.[89]

Given the tendency for such polemical accounts to represent counterviews at their most extreme, it would be remiss to overlook how Hooker and his later puritan critics overlapped in their arguments. Even here in the argument over the sacralization of public space and time, they shared common ground. While Hooker and his puritan critics disagreed over ritual fasts, they both agreed that in exceptional circumstances, during 'times of publique calamity', it was appropriate to publicly assemble to fast and pray.[90] Amidst the extraordinary upheavals of the mid-seventeenth century, The Westminster Assembly agreed upon detailed prescriptions for the public observance of days set apart for thanksgiving and humiliation. New England divines not only observed days of thanksgiving and fasting, but further set apart days of civil religion, marking the election of civil magistrates, militia days, and the delivery of sermons as a deterrent against crime before public executions.[91] Regardless of whether such days were prescribed by the authority of the state or by the church, civil religion and holy days bore a remarkable resemblance in Old and New England.

What is striking, in addition to Hooker's concept of a mutable partition between civil and ecclesiastical jurisdiction, is the mutation of the arguments themselves. Drawing from diverse models of civil religion, Hooker and his puritan adversaries appropriated a range of sources for civil religion from pagan Roman religion to Jewish tradition which not only drew from Mosaic

---

[87] Cf. Ha, 'Who Owns the Hebrew Doctors?'.

[88] For puritan arguments against the church's authority to appoint holy days see John Primus, *Holy Time: Moderate Puritanism and the Sabbath* (Macon 1989), pp. 75-7.

[89] Hooker, *FLE*, II, p. 374.

[90] Hooker, *FLE*, II, p. 374.

[91] Cf Horton Davies, *The Worship of the American Puritans, 1629-1730* (London/New York, 1990), chapter 4.

law but Rabbinic literature.[92] They reconfigured the parameters of mixed monarchy and royal supremacy in the final decade of the sixteenth century. They both presented a vision of a limited royal supremacy, appealed to the role of collective consent as a basis for civil and ecclesiastical society, and turned to legal precedents to define the parameters of spiritual and ecclesiastical jurisdiction. They cast competing visions over which form of ecclesiastical polity lent itself to the greatest civil justice and stability. They were at odds over the movement of ecclesiastical and civil matters. They even suggested that their opponents might be in danger of altogether abandoning true religion by grasping after civil power. But the outcome was far from a straightforwardly polarized view over civil religion. In the midst of their exchanges, they entertained layered accounts of the overlap between civil and ecclesiastical jurisdictions, which could be mutually reinforcing and overlapping, rather than inherently dominating, in nature. Rather than simply subsuming religion under the state or seeking to establish theocratic godly rule over the state, they each refined their vision of how ecclesiastical polity could better inculcate both piety and civic virtue. Even as they disagreed over many things, they demonstrated mutability, and even a degree of civility, as they reconceptualised and introduced new ways of configuring the relationship between civil and ecclesiastical society.

---

[92] For a fuller discussion of Hooker's use of Moses Maimonides and the reception of rabbinic sources in puritan and conformist thought see, Ha, 'Who Owns the Hebrew Doctors?'.

3

Alexander Leighton and the Erastian fabric of early Stuart Puritanism

Esther Counsell

A key focus when investigating civil religion in the early modern period must be the attempt of European reformers to construct their own reinvigorated Christian commonwealths – whether these were city-state republics, princely territories, or sovereign kingdoms.[1] How early modern reformers conceived of the ideal relationship between religion and the civil state, and from where and whom they drew their inspiration, reveals much about the nature and trajectory of civil religion leading into the Enlightenment. This chapter considers the writing of a little-known Scottish minister and physician with the aim of articulating his notion of civil religion in the context of pre-Civil War England. Alexander Leighton's *An Appeal to the Parliament* (1629) was a prime expression of puritan dissent against the government of Charles I.[2] Leighton treated disorders of the Caroline church and state as the result of a shared affliction, a resurgent lordly clericalism in the royal courts and church.[3] Alongside William Prynne, he was later praised by the

---

[1] Generally, the term 'civil religion' has been much more readily applied to puritan political thought across the Atlantic than in the original context of early Stuart England. See as only one example, C. L. Maloy, 'A Liberal Civil Religion: William Penn's Holy Experiment', *Journal of Church and State*, 55 (2013). It has also been hitherto more utilized as a descriptor of post-1640s political thought in England (see for example M. Goldie, 'The Civil Religion of James Harrington' in *The Languages of Political Theory in Early Modern Europe*, ed. A. Pagden (Cambridge, 1987), pp. 197-222, and T. J. Koontz, 'Religion and Political Cohesion: John Locke and Jean-Jacques Rousseau', *Journal of Church and State*, 23 (1981), 95-115).

[2] A. Leighton, *An Appeal to the Parliament; or Sions Plea against the Prelacie* (Amsterdam, 1629). Hereafter the *Appeal*.

[3] For context on the *avante-garde* conformist and Laudian visions of clerical rule, see J. McGovern, 'The Political Sermons of Lancelot Andrewes', *Seventeenth Century*, 34:1 (2019), 3-23, and Andrew Foster's excellent anti-revisionist chapter 'Church Policies of the 1630s', in *Conflict in Early Stuart England: Studies in Religion and Politics, 1603–1642*, eds Richard Cust and Ann Hughes (Harlow, 1989), pp. 193-223.

Long Parliament for exposing at an early stage the theocratic ambitions of Archbishop William Laud, and for assembling the legal, biblical, political, historical, and reasoned case against 'Lordly Prelacy'. Both authors shared a reforming zeal and envisioned a flourishing and godly commonwealth during their lifetimes, and it was with this shared goal in mind that they both reconfigured the relationship between England's crown, parliament, and church.[4] Prynne has received far greater scholarly attention than his predecessor Leighton despite these similarities, and so this chapter will focus on the latter while highlighting the close ideological links between them.

Leighton's *Appeal* was an intellectual critique of Charles I's government based on the premise that the Stuart king's regime had departed from the political tradition of Reformed civil religion and was therefore set on a perilous path towards popery, treason, and moral decline. Here Leighton, alongside Prynne, can be described *prima facie* as Erastian in the general sense, for he believed, in line with the royal ecclesiastical supremacy, that the English Crown held supreme power over the doctrine and discipline of the Church of England, and that the ordering of religion was a foremost and God-given duty bestowed on princes and civil magistrates.[5] Leighton, when on trial before the Star Chamber in 1630, confessed his belief that Charles I possessed as much ecclesiastical sovereignty 'over all of his dominions, and therein over all his subjects and causes, as any of the Kings of Judah or Israel'.[6] Jeffrey Collins has noted that the inspiration for early modern Erastianism was in fact the ancient idea of civil religion, most famously depicted in the ancient kingdom of Israel, as well as the imperial policies of ancient Rome which integrated religious doctrine and ritual observance with civic duties, or the religious and civic laws in founding constitutions of Greek city-states, intermingled for the furtherance of civil unity, peace, and

---

[4] See further William Lamont, *Godly Rule: Politics and Religion, 1603–1660* (London, 1969), William Lamont, *Richard Baxter and the Millennium: Protestant Imperialism and the English Revolution* (Washington, DC, 1979), and S. McGee, *The Godly Man in Stuart England, Anglicans, Puritans, and the Two Tables, 1620–1670* (New Haven, 1976).

[5] See D. Alan Orr, *Treason and the State: Law, Politics and Ideology in the English Civil War* (Cambridge, 2002), pp. 102–3; Eric Nelson, *Hebrew Republic: Jewish Sources and the Transformation of European Political Thought* (Cambridge, MA, 2010), p. 92; S. Blackburn, 'Erastianism', in *The Oxford Dictionary of Philosophy*, 3rd edn (Oxford, 2016), p. 119. Neither Prynne nor Leighton were 'Erastian' during this period in the more specific sense which originates from the Heidelberg church discipline controversy of 1568, which implies support for Thomas Erastus' *Explicatio Gravissimae Quaestionis* (London, 1589) and his belief arising from biblical exegesis that excommunication was primarily a civil rather than spiritual censure. (See further C. Gunnoe, *Thomas Erastus and the Palatinate* (Leiden, 2010), pp. 163–209).

[6] S. R. Gardiner (ed.), 'Speech of Sir Robert Heath, Attorney-General, in the case of Alexander Leighton in the Star Chamber, June 4, 1630', *Camden New Series*, Vol. 14, p. xviii.

prosperity.⁷ Collins has written perceptively that the Henrician Reformation augmented England's 'long... experiment with Erastianism' by uniting the spheres of civil and ecclesiastical authority in the Tudor monarchy.⁸

This Erastian model dwindled rapidly with the advent of royally patronised *jure divino* theories of English episcopacy in the late Elizabethan and early Stuart Churches, touting an original episcopal right to order religion in a state or commonwealth.⁹ England's experiment with Erastian church government was, however, far from over, as recent scholarly work has proved with regards to the opening sessions of the Long Parliament and ensuing Interregnum years. Anthony Milton has recently noted that even in the commissioning of the Westminster Assembly can be displayed the dominance of Erastian ecclesiology in mid-seventeenth-century Protestant thought, with divines only permitted to discuss matters proposed by the English Parliament. Milton's persuasive thesis on England's 'Second Reformation' shows that the parliament-led and Erastian approach to England's church and religion during this period was no 'abberant, "foreign", and essentially destructive process', but one deeply engrained within the experience and memory of English Protestantism.¹⁰ The time is ripe for revisiting pre-civil war puritan ecclesiology and reconsidering, in a more nuanced sense than previously, its relationship with an historic Tudor Erastian mindset.¹¹

---

⁷ Jeffrey R. Collins, *The Allegiance of Thomas Hobbes* (Oxford, 2005), pp. 171, 14. On the Old Testament model of Erastianism, see Nelson, *The Hebrew Republic*, and G. Bartolucci, 'The Hebrew Republic in Sixteenth-century Political Debate: The Struggle for Jurisdiction', in *Ancient Models in the Early Modern Republican Imagination*, eds W. Velema and A. Weststeijn (Leiden, 2017), pp. 214–33.

⁸ J. R. Collins, 'The Restoration Bishops and the Royal Supremacy', *Church History: Studies in Christianity and Culture*, 68:3 (1999), 549–80; idem, 'The Church Settlement of Oliver Cromwell', *History*, 87 (2002), 18–40.

⁹ See J. Sommerville, 'The Royal Supremacy and Episcopacy *Jure Divino*, 1603–1640', *Journal of Ecclesiastical History*, 34:4 (1983), 548–58; W. D. J. Cargill Thompson, 'Sir Francis Knollys' Campaign Against the *Jure Divino* Theory of Episcopacy', in *The Dissenting Tradition: Essays for Leland H. Carlson*, eds C. R. Cole and M. Moodie (Ohio, 1975), pp. 39–69; and, Andrew Foster, 'The Clerical Estate Revitalized', in *The Early Stuart Church, 1603–1642*, ed. Kenneth Fincham (Basingstoke, 1993), pp. 139–60.

¹⁰ Anthony Milton, *England's Second Reformation: The Battle for the Church of England 1625–1662* (Cambridge, 2021), p. 218.

¹¹ This chapter seeks to move past a dominant scholarly paradigm which has judged English puritanism and Erastianism to be intrinsically opposed, which is based on two highly problematic assumptions: first, that it was high Anglican and conformist forces in Elizabethan and early Stuart England that were upholding the Erastian nature of the Tudor settlements, purely by paying lip-service to the royal supremacy and being allied closely with the monarchy; and, that Elizabethan and early Stuart puritans were the natural progenitors of post-1640s presbyterianism and radical non-conformity, rather than a more comprehensive and Erastian style of churchmanship. For the latter, see

This chapter traces sixteenth-century reformed Erastian ideas in Leighton's *Appeal*. The fiery treatise attests that a drastic intervention by Parliament on the question of religion and morals (*in lieu* of the Crown) was essential for the survival of England's royal supremacy and Protestant identity. The tradition of Reformed civil religion, which Leighton drew upon, highlighted amongst other things the supreme authority of monarchs and magistrates over the ecclesiastical sphere; the wisdom of regulating and enforcing clerical offices and behaviour through statutory law; and the continual vigilance required of Protestant rulers to protect true religion and the state from the corrupting influence of lordly prelates.

Leighton's *Appeal* sits alongside other puritan treatises censored by Charles I's Star Chamber, such as Prynne's *Historio-mastrix, the player's scourge* (1633), in being largely overlooked by historians of English political thought due to its overt religious zeal to see 'evil counsellors' damned for idolatrous subversions; while religious historians have tended simply to observe that such critiques of the early Stuart Church sought to revive English presbyterianism.[12] This is in keeping with their official reception by the Star Chamber during Charles I's Personal Rule: Attorney-General Sir Robert Heath described Leighton's *Appeal* as a libellous work that struck 'at the roote to destroy and roote out all the Bishops and bishopricks', an example of an ancient attempt to introduce parity, and therefore anarchy, in church government. Despite it boasting 344 pages, Heath confessed to not being able to find 'one discreet and temperate page in it'.[13] Laud, then bishop of London, condemned Leighton as a schismatic who 'would obtrude upon the Church a new Government, affirming that only, to be lawfull'.[14] By contrast, Leighton considered Laud's hierarchical theory of bishops' absolute dominion over other clergy and laity as a staggering departure from Protestant orthodoxy, just as it was contrary to all the 'Lawes Divine, Humane, as Civil-Law, Canon-Law, the Lawes of England, Statute, and

---

especially Mark Goldie, *Roger Morrice and the Puritan Whigs, The Entring Book 1677–1691* (Woodbridge, 2016), pp. 225–68.

[12] William Prynne, *Histrio-mastix, or, the player's scourge* (London, 1633). See especially Mark Kishlansky, 'A whipper whipped: the sedition of William Prynne', *Historical Journal*, 56:3 (2013), 603–27; and idem, 'Martyrs' Tales', *Journal of British Studies*, 53:2 (2014), 334–55. Based on a cursory reading of the anti-prelatical *Appeal*, Leighton has been historically sidelined as a hardline presbyterian, and this largely explains his subsequent neglect by historians of political thought, see William Lamont, *Marginal Prynne* (London, 1963), p. 45; Charles Prior, *A Confusion of Tongues* (Oxford, 2012), p. 41. Stephen Foster has noted that this categorization was also founded on Leighton's 'general notoriety, and probably, his Scottish birth' rather than serious analysis of his writings on church and state. See S. Foster, *Notes from the Caroline Underground: Alexander Leighton, the Puritan Triumvirate, and the Laudian Reaction to Nonconformity* (Hamden, CT, 1979), p. 19.

[13] Gardiner ed.,'The Speech of Sir Robert Heath', p. 1.

[14] A. Leighton, *An Epitome or Brief Discoverie, from the beginning to the ending, of the many and great troubles Dr. Leighton suffered in his body, estate, and family* (London, 1646), p. 70.

Common'.[15] Leighton and Prynne fervently believed that a foreign form of church polity had been constructed within the Church of England, and that what had been lost across the vicissitudes of the English Reformation was far superior: this being closest to the Erastian revision of church government under Edward VI, which had held (in keeping with wider Reformed churches) that discipline was an essential mark of a true church, and described a collegial and reformed model of episcopacy, that recommended the involvement of lay elders and congregations in any disciplinary procedures.[16]

Such past approaches too readily follow the lead of Charles I's key advisors in attaching the label 'presbyterian' to Leighton and Prynne's arguments. Unless to be anti-prelatical is to be presbyterian (in which case most sixteenth-century European reformers would meet this criterion), such a label only serves to impoverish the wider purpose and scope of both thinkers, as well as transplant their popular visions for pre-Civil War England to a future context of church polity debate which only took fuller flight during the Westminster Assembly Debates (1643-53). Both Leighton and Prynne were judged by the Long Parliament to have taken inspiration from a far wider and shared intellectual tradition of Protestant jurisdictionalism, or the fear of prelatical tyranny, which was deeply rooted in Tudor Protestant history and culture. Both took pains to seat themselves in the orthodox wing of magisterial Protestantism, assembling sources including reformed authors, English statute and common law, the sacred history of Christendom and the ancient world, scripture, church fathers, Roman civil and canon law, and classical political philosophy, to construct a conservative vision of the purpose and calling of the English Church's chief officials. Their case for a rebirth of civil religion on English soil, which necessitated the removal of lordly prelacy and the restoration of godly magistracy in its place, took confidence from the Erastian tendencies of the Henrician and Edwardian reformations, and yet, also drew upon an eclectic range of sources fit for an early modern commonwealth, making their political thought worthy of the ancient tradition of civil religion.

---

[15] *Ibid.*, p. 73, and see further the *Appeal*, pp. 129–35.

[16] J. C. Spalding, *The Reformation of the Ecclesiastical Laws of England, 1552* (Kirksville, MO, 1992), Sixteenth Century Essays & Studies Vol. XIX, pp. 33, 41, 43. See further on the Erastian nature of these revisions in Kirby, 'Lay Supremacy', pp. 360–1; J. C. Spalding, 'The *Reformatio Legum Ecclesiasticarum* of 1552 and the Furthering of Discipline in England', *Church History*, 39:2 (1970), 162–71; and Leslie R. Sachs, 'Thomas Cranmer's *Reformatio legum ecclesiasticarum* of 1553 in the context of English church law from the later Middle Ages to the canons of 1603' (JCD thesis, Catholic University of America, 1982), p. 154; and E. Cardwell, *The Reformation of the Ecclesiastical Laws as attempted in the Reigns of King Henry VIII, King Edward VI, and Queen Elizabeth* (Oxford, 1850), pp. 93ff.

Alexander Leighton, Puritanism, and pre-Civil War England

Between 1625 and 1640, over thirty books were suppressed or altered at the press, ringing alarm bells for Sir Edward Dering's parliamentary committee on religious innovations, which drew up a list of the purged books.[17] Leighton's unlicensed works, alongside those of Prynne, Henry Burton, and John Bastwick, featured prominently throughout the 1630s.[18] Indeed, it is hard to disassemble the polemical creature 'anti-puritanism' from the divisive reputation of Leighton himself; shortly before his arrest in February 1630 for writing the *Appeal*, Leighton was apportioned almost all blame for puritan opinions amongst the general populace in a letter to William Laud. Master of Trinity College, Cambridge, Samuel Brooke described puritanism to Laud as 'the roote of all rebellions and disobedient intractablenesse in Parliament', and of all 'Schisme and Saucinesse in the Country, nay in the Church it selfe'.[19] In short, it was making 'many thousands of our people, and to[o] great a part of the Gentlemen of the Land Laytons [Leightons] in their hearts'.[20] A more middle-of-the-road opinion on Leighton, by the post-Restoration biographer David Lloyd, lists Sir John Eliot, Sir Robert Cotton, John Hampden, and Dudley Digges as the 'wisemen' of the Parliament's puritan party, who held the very same beliefs 'covertly' as those which Leighton had aired publicly. To Lloyd, Leighton was the one amongst these 'to break the Ice, and feel the pulse of the times'.[21] This opinion places him in similar company to such Erastian-minded parliamentarians, concerned for the fate of reformed Protestant religion, the royal supremacy, and the ancient constitution, which as this chapter suggests, holds truer as the nature and context of Leighton's *Appeal* is re-assessed. Leighton would later be remembered as the father of the archbishop of Glasgow and principal of the University of Edinburgh, Robert Leighton, whose commitment to (and practice of) a reformed model of episcopacy under an Erastian government, as against Robert Baillie's Scottish presbyterianism, is perhaps less surprising than it has previously appeared.[22]

---

[17] Anthony Milton, 'Licensing, Censorship, and Religious Orthodoxy in early Stuart England', *The Historical Journal*, 41:3 (1998), 644.
[18] *Ibid*.
[19] William Prynne, *Canterburies Doome* (London, 1646), p. 167. This letter is cited more favourably by Peter Heylyn in G. Vernon (ed.), *Historical and Miscellaneous Tracts* (1681), p. 539.
[20] Prynne, *Canterburies Doome*, p. 167.
[21] David Lloyd, *Cabala, or, The mystery of conventicles unvail'd in an historical account of the principles and practices of the nonconformists, against church and state* (London, 1664).
[22] H. Ouston, 'Robert Leighton (bap. 1612, d. 1684)', *ODNB*; Walter Thornbury, 'New Palace Yard and Westminster Hall', *Old and New London: Volume 3* (London, 1878), pp. 536–44; and, 'A Letter from Robert to his father Alexander Leighton, doctor of medicine, on May 6 from Edinburgh' in J. Bruce (ed.), *Calendar of State Papers Domestic: Charles I, 1628–29* (London, 1859), pp. 97–112.

Alexander Leighton graduated with an MA from St. Andrews in 1587 and was ordained by 1603, working as a lecturer in churches in Newcastle upon Tyne until 1612. He possessed an extensive theological, classical, and scientific library demonstrating his familiarity with Latin, Greek, Hebrew, and French.[23] In 1617 he enrolled in medicine at Leiden, where he lodged with the publisher Thomas Brewer. Here he also befriended John Bastwick, before graduating in 1619, and moving to London to work as an unlicensed physician.[24] He attended Henry Jacob's Blackfriars congregation, and this connection may explain why his first three books were all published by the press associated with 'the Ancient (separatist) church of Amsterdam' owned by Sabine Staresmore, a member of Jacob's congregation.[25] He spoke out against the Spanish match in 1622, and again in his military treatise *Speculum belli sacri* (1624).[26] Thomas Webster has noted that the most 'vociferous protest' at plans for Prince Charles' marriage came from the sermons of Thomas Scott and Leighton. This led James I to issue proclamations, in particular the Declaration for Preachers in 1622, forbidding preachers to discuss matters of state.[27] Allegedly, William Laud believed that the *Speculum* alone should have condemned Leighton for high treason, and hanging, but for James I's intervention on the author's behalf after reading the work.[28]

Leighton's *Appeal* was written in Amsterdam in October 1628 with the connivance of a politicking puritan in London who had already amassed 500 signatures agreeing that Parliament must abolish lordly prelacy. Leighton commenced the work as a legal brief of a puritan collective. He drew up

---

[23] G. Davidson, 'Robert Leighton, his family and his library', *Transactions of the Society of the Friends of Dunblane Cathedral* (Dunblane, 1959), VIII, pp. 44–9.

[24] Charles Goodall, *The Royal College of Physicians of London, founded and established by law...* (London, 1684), p. 401. Leighton was not licensed to practice medicine on the grounds that he was an ordained minister.

[25] Foster, *Caroline Underground*, p. 13; George Yule, *The Independents in the Civil War* (Cambridge, 1958), pp. 8–17. Stephen Brachlow, 'The Elizabethan Roots of Henry Jacob's Churchmanship: Refocusing the Historiographical Lens', *Journal of Ecclesiastical History*, 36:2 (1985), 228–54 gives further reason to reject Leighton's presbyterian reputation, and to consider Jacobs' non-separatist congregationalism as rooted in mainstream Elizabethan puritan ecclesiology.

[26] Alexander Leighton, *Speculum belli sacri, or, The Looking Glass of the Holy War* (Amsterdam, printed by the successors of Giles Thorp, 1624).

[27] See G. W. Prothero, *Select Statutes and other Constitutional Documents illustrative of the reigns of Elizabeth and James I*, 4th edn (Oxford, 1964), pp. 422–4; Tom Webster, 'Early Stuart Puritanism', in *The Cambridge Companion to Puritanism*, eds John Coffey and Paul C. H. Lim (Cambridge, 2008), p. 50. See also Thomas Cogswell, 'England and the Spanish Match', in *Conflict in Early Stuart England*, eds Richard Cust and Ann Hughes (Harlow, 1989), pp. 107–33 and Peter Lake, 'Constitutional consensus and Puritan opposition in the 1620s: Thomas Scott and the Spanish Match', *Historical Journal*, 25 (1982), 805–25.

[28] Leighton, *An Epitome*, p. 68.

its ten positions after a gathering of the 'Godliest, Learnedst, and most judicious of the Land, both Ministers, and others ... some whereof were Parliament-men' at his house at Blackfriars.[29] The text itself was composed quickly, instigated by the fall of La Rochelle and in preparation for the 1628 Parliament, and only published in January or February 1629.[30] The Duke of Buckingham had suffered a heavy failure in losing that impregnable port city to French Catholic forces, spelling woe for the Protestant cause across Europe and fresh fodder for those suspicious of Charles I's key advisors. Leighton sent manuscript copies of the *Appeal* to every sitting member of the Commons, writing to his wife on 4 March 1629 from Utrecht that he hoped the House had 'the thing' by the time the letter reached her, little knowing that Charles I had closed Parliament two days earlier, largely due to the actions of Eliot, Hampden, and Digges, and effectively commenced his Personal Rule.[31] The first editions of the *Appeal* number over 600 copies, an enduringly significant mass of which fifty-four are preserved across forty-three separate libraries in the English speaking world. Its satirical engravings also took on a life of their own in pre-civil war English culture.[32]

Parliament, Star Chamber, and the Personal Rule

Soon after Brooke's ominous warning to Laud in 1630, Leighton was arrested for sedition with a warrant from the High Commission. His *Appeal* had declared the office and calling of lordly prelates, including their dependents and ceremonies, 'unlawful and Antichristian'.[33] To Leighton, present-day English bishops were not ashamed to call their powers *jure divino*, to use force and 'beare the multitude in hand', and

---

[29] Ibid., p. 2.
[30] There are in fact two 'first' editions of the *Appeal* printed in early 1629, as recorded in the English Short Title Catalogue. Leighton first commissioned the tract to be published by his printer Sabine Staresmore (ESTC S108410), but because time was of the essence, arranged for an improved second edition simultaneously with the Dutch printer J. F. Stam (ESTC S108409). The Stam edition is superior. See further Foster, *Caroline Underground*, p. 23, n. 45 and A. F. Johnson, 'The Exiled English Church at Amsterdam and its Press', *The Library*, Fifth Series, 5:4 (March 1951), 240.
[31] *Calendar of State Papers, Domestic: Charles I, 1628-29*, pp. 485-95, and Foster, *Caroline Underground*, p. 23, n. 46.
[32] Helen Pierce, *Unseemly Pictures: Graphic Satire and Politics in Early Modern England* (New Haven, 2008), pp. 124-6, 169. See also the Catalogue of Prints, British Museum, which contains reprints based on two separate copies of the 1628 Thorp edition of the *Appeal* from the Wren Library, Trinity College (*Political and Personal Satires*, Vol. 1, pp. 64-6 and Johnson, 'The Exiled English Church', p. 240). The *Appeal's* huge print-run of 600 copies, rare information in the context of this period, is owing to the own Star Chamber's findings (Gardiner (ed.), 'Speech of Sir Robert Heath', p. 2).
[33] Leighton, *Appeal*, p. 3.

making English laws of no effect, by 'changing, adding & taking away at their pleasure' what liberties owing to free subjects under the Crown.[34] The *Appeal* is carefully theoretical, with the Star Chamber readily acknowledging that it consistently lambasts bishops' lordly seats of power rather than episcopacy in particular.[35] He speaks respectfully of the King although not of the Duke of Buckingham, nor of Queen Henrietta Maria, his French Catholic wife.[36] Leighton contrasts her disadvantageously with Elizabeth I, and of their nuptials as even less suitable to England's interest than the failed Spanish match.[37] For writing and publishing the anti-prelatical work, Leighton was found guilty of sedition and libel in Star Chamber in June 1630, and sentenced by Attorney-General Sir Robert Heath to life imprisonment, a £10,000 fine, and to be whipped in Westminster before the Star Chamber, and to have one of his ears cut off, one side of his nose slit, and to be branded on his forehead with a double S, for 'Sower of Sedition'.[38] The true reason for the unprecedented extent of Leighton's corporal punishments lay in the authors' refusal to reveal who were his main supporters in writing and publishing: for, Leighton spoke of 'large numbers behind his back', over 500 gentlemen as signatories.[39] Heath readily believed that this act was 'more than enough to poison all a whole kingdom', which led to his dismembering fate, which Whig historian Samuel Gardiner surmised 'did as much to shake the throne of Charles as the exaction of ship-money'.[40]

Heath would become notorious during the Personal Rule for similar state prosecutions in Star Chamber against Sir John Eliot, the earl of Bedford, and Sir Robert Cotton.[41] Leighton's cause was said to unite the King and the Duke of Buckingham against the Commons, with puritan members of the House believing that 'the main end of his book was truth' (namely the charges of prelatical tyranny).[42] Leighton momentarily escaped the Fleet Prison on 11 November 1630, dressed as a tailor, from which tale we can gather further evidence about public sympathy towards his cause: multitudes rejoiced at his escape 'because he writ a book against them [lordly bishops],

---

[34] *Ibid.*, p. 4.
[35] Gardiner (ed.), 'Speech of Sir Robert Heath', p. 1.
[36] Leighton, *Appeal*, pp. 88, 179; 'The Speech of Sir Robert Heath on 4 June 1630' in J. Bruce (ed.), *Calendar of State Papers Domestic: Charles I, 1629-31* (London, 1860), pp. iv–v.
[37] Leighton, *Appeal*, pp. 92–5.
[38] Further punishments are detailed in G. Benson, *A Collection of Tracts* (London, 1748), pp. 220–1; Bruce (ed.), 'The Speech of Sir Robert Heath on 4 June 1630', pp. 273–84.
[39] Gardiner ed., 'The Speech of Sir Robert Heath', pp. xix–xx.
[40] *Ibid.*, p. xx.
[41] H. E. I. Phillips, 'The Last Years of the Court of Star Chamber 1630–41: (The Alexander Prize Essay)', *Transactions of the Royal Historical Society*, 21 (1939), 103–31.
[42] Bruce (ed.), *Calendar of State Papers Domestic: Charles I*, Vol. 175, p. 383.

and not one of a thousand dislikes him for it'.[43] Leighton's fate was further observed in tandem with the incarcerations of Eliot, Selden, and Cotton for their roles in the 1629 Parliament. These men were also accused by Heath of seditiously conspiring against the government of Charles I, having arranged for Eliot's reading of three Resolutions on Religion on 2 March that condemned innovating prelates in the English Church as capital enemies of the King and state.[44] Eliot's Resolutions, crafted with the advice of Cotton and Selden, demanded that the King remove papistical and Arminian bishops and clergymen, in accordance with existing English laws against papistry.[45] Henry Bouchier, the fifth earl of Bath, would marvel in a letter to James Ussher in June 1630 on both Selden's and Cotton's fates, before noting that in Leighton's case both Laud and Neile had given 'sentence as Judges', despite being bishops, and furthermore, 'declared partyes' against him: as he wrote, it all seemed 'strange to me [Bouchier] but that I wonder at nothing'.[46] In other words, it went against principles of civil and canon law for bishops to pronounce sentences of corporal punishment in the King's courts, let alone to do so in a case for which they themselves were declared parties.

Leighton would later make the same observation regarding this offence against canon and civil law in his retrospective *Epitome*, recounting that Laud had justified his presence throughout the trial and sentencing as an ecclesiastic by choosing to be overly literal: there would be no 'losse of life, or member', as the canon law required, for 'to take away the Ear is not losse of hearing, and so no member lost; neither is the slitting of the Nose losse of smelling, and so no member lost'.[47] Laud's presence in the civil proceedings evidently astonished Bouchier, a seasoned observer of London politics, but even more so, the new climate of acceptance attending it. Royal absolutism was in full swing with the closure of Parliament and access to Cotton's parliamentary library being tightly restricted. Therefore, there remained little hope of raising the banner for a reformed and limited episcopacy through Parliament or the courts. The

---

[43] Bruce (ed.), *Calendar of State Papers Domestic: Charles I, 1629–31*, p. 383. There was considerable public outrage at the cruelty of the sentence: see further *A brief account of Archbishop Lauds cruel treatment of Doctor Leighton*, cited from Phillips, 'The Last Years', p. 1.

[44] W. Notestein and F. H. Relf (eds), *Commons Debates for 1629* (Minneapolis, 1921), pp. 103–6; Harold Hulme, *The Life of Sir John Eliot, 1592–1632: The struggle for parliamentary freedom* (London, 1957), p. 316. The other members put into custody were William Coryton, Sir Denzil Holles, Benjamin Valentine, Sir Miles Hobart, Sir Peter Hayman, Sir William Strode, and Walter Long.

[45] S. R. Gardiner (ed.), *Constitutional Documents of the Puritan Revolution, 1625–1660* (Oxford, 1906), pp. 80–1; Notestein and Relf (eds), *Commons Debates for 1629*, pp. 103–6.

[46] Henry Bouchier to James Ussher, 12 June 1630 [Bodl. MS Lett. 89, f. 119v-r], in Elizabethanne Boran (ed.), *The Correspondence of James Ussher*, 3 vols (Dublin, 2015), II, pp. 527–8 (quotation on p. 527).

[47] Leighton, *An Epitome*, pp. 73ff. For Leighton's legal evidence indicting clergymen involved in cases of civil judicature, see the *Appeal*, pp. 129–35.

Commons' revolt in March 1629 had spoken of a perceived rise in prelatical tyranny that was not only causing the subversion of legally established Calvinist doctrine and liturgy but stepping into crypto-papistical territory by usurping the supreme authority of the Crown and Parliament over religion. Cotton suspected an episcopal plot to change England's religion through Convocation and advised Eliot to pass his Resolutions as a preventative measure.[48] Both viewed England's civil supremacy over religion, practically modelled through Parliament, as a timely cure against tyranny in church and state.

Censored puritans such as Leighton and Prynne, who viewed the English Parliament as an essential component of the royal supremacy, were emblematic of a broader ideological divide in James I's court and parliament, well-described by Conrad Russell: one worldview existed where 'the ecclesiastical was a separate sphere of authority, in which the king's powers as supreme head of the church descended only through clerical channels', and the other belief that 'ecclesiastical authority was subject to the same rule of law as everything else'.[49] These diverging episcopal and parliamentarian models of the royal supremacy have been surveyed elsewhere, and for the purposes of this chapter, give context to the *Appeal*'s exaltation of parliamentary statute as higher in authority than bishops in terms of the orthodox church doctrine.[50] However, Leighton was not advocating a new idea of parliamentary supremacy – despite this later triumphing on its own terms – so much as insisting on a Tudor Protestant distinction between the temporal and spiritual jurisdictions, which classified church affairs as temporal rather than spiritual, and therefore rightly handled by civil magistrates and judges rather than clergymen. Leighton believed that Parliament had been divinely intended to protect those 'silver streames of divine and humane Lawes', welling beneath England's ancient constitution and established ecclesiastical laws, and to 'bar and abandon all the pitchie waters of the Babilonish Lake', denouncing extra-statutory canons and *avant-garde*, popish customs.[51] Leighton cared deeply about the declining influence of civil authority over the control of national religion and this belief drove his institutional loyalty to Parliament, which was emblematic of the importance of the rule of law in national life.

---

[48] A. B. Grosart (ed.), *De jure maiestatis, or, Political treatise of government (1629–30) and the Letter-Book of John Eliot (1625–1632)* (London, 1882), pp. 37–8.

[49] Conrad Russell, *King James VI and I and His English Parliaments: The Trevelyan Lectures Delivered at the University of Cambridge, 1995*, eds Richard Cust and Andrew Thrush (Oxford, 2011), p. 147.

[50] See further Conrad Russell, 'Whose Supremacy? King, Parliament and the Church, 1530–1640', *Lambeth Palace Library Annual Review* (1995), 53–64 and 'Parliament, the Royal Supremacy and the Church', *Parliamentary History*, 19 (2000), 27–37; Jacqueline Rose, *Godly Kingship in Restoration England* (Cambridge, 2011), chapter 1; Alexandra Gajda, 'The Elizabethan Church and the Antiquity of Parliament', in *Writing the History of Parliament in Tudor and early Stuart England*, eds Paul Cavill and Alexandra Gajda (Manchester, 2018), pp. 77–105.

[51] Leighton, *Appeal*, 'An Epistle to the High Court of Parliament'.

Prynne received a similar sentence for sedition and libel to that of Leighton before Star Chamber in 1634, for his 1000-page tome *Histrio-mastix*: life imprisonment, a £5,000 pound fine, and having his ears cropped for sedition. It was only in 1637 that both Leighton's and Prynne's mutilations would cease to be exceptional, being dealt out once again against the 'puritan triumvirate': Prynne, Henry Burton, and John Bastwick.[52] One incriminating element in Prynne's *Histrio-mastix* case in 1634 was his decision to cite one of Leighton's unlicensed works against stage-plays with approbation multiple times.[53] Both authors were on friendly terms, with Leighton's wife Isobel delivering to Prynne the gift of a beaver hat in the Tower of London when he was on trial for sedition for the second time in 1637.[54] The incriminating features of Prynne's *Histrio-mastix* were held by the then Attorney-General William Noy to be contempt for the Crown and its government, through characterizing princes or magistrates who did not suppress stage-plays, or conversely choose even to attend them, as partakers in seditious activity.[55] The King and Queen's known attendance at, and even performances in stage-plays, assisted in Noy's arguments for Prynne's sedition, for Prynne must have known he was dangerously implicating the royal family: to quote Noy, 'he teaches the people as if there were a just occasion to lay their violent hands upon Princes'.[56] However, Noy's portrayal of the *Historio-Mastix* must be set alongside the backdrop of a literary anti-theatre tradition in reformed Protestant theology, which before Leighton's text in 1625 had included English treatises by John Rainolds, Thomas Beard, and Dudley Fenner.[57]

---

[52] Primary reports of these Star Chamber proceedings can be found in W. Cobbett (ed.), *Cobbett's Complete Collection of State Trials*, 34 vols (1808–28), III, pp. 711–70, and William Prynne, *A New Discovery of the Prelates Tyranny* (London, 1641). See further William Lamont, *Marginal Prynne, 1600–1669* (Toronto, 1963), pp. 28–50; Foster, *Notes from the Caroline Underground*, pp. 47–71; Kevin Sharpe, *Personal Rule of Charles I* (New Haven, 1992), pp. 758–65; Kishlansky, 'A Whipper Whipped', and 'Martyrs' Tales'; and David Cressy, 'Puritan Martyrs in Island Prisons', *Journal of British Studies*, 57:4 (2018), 736–54, esp. p. 736, n. 3 (for a helpful list of the most salient historiography).

[53] This is Leighton's *A shorte treatise against stage-playes* (Amsterdam, 1625), which Prynne notes was 'tendred to the Parliament' in 1625, as part of a copious list of works by church fathers and Protestant reformers against men putting on women's apparel and other effeminate practises in stage plays (Prynne, *Historio-mastix*, p. 198, Leighton, *A shorte treatise*, pp. 17, 26–28). For Prynne's other references to Leighton see *Historio-mastix*, pp. 179, 488, 559, 562, 588, 698.

[54] F. Condick, 'Alexander Leighton (c. 1570–1649)', *Oxford Dictionary of National Biography*; TNA:PRO, letters to Isobel Leighton (SP 16/103/39; SP 16/138/10, 23, 90; SP 16/142/114).

[55] See Kishlansky, 'Whipper whipped', p. 615.

[56] Ibid., p. 619. For Prynne's own account of this trial, see Henry Burton's *A Divine Tragedy* (London, 1636), and William Prynne's *New Discovery of Free-State Tyranny* (London, 1655).

[57] John Rainolds, *Th'Overthrow of Stage-Playes, by the Way of Controversie betwixt D. Gager and D. Rainoldes* (Middelburg, 1599, reprinted in Oxford, 1629); Thomas Beard,

Mark Kishlansky has retrodden the Crown's proceedings against Leighton and Prynne, seeking to debunk the Foxean martyrological myth and litany of woes attached to what were, in his view, clear-cut cases of dangerous sedition.[58] He argued that both Leighton and Prynne had committed premeditated and full-frontal attacks on Charles I's ecclesiastical government which posed a serious challenge to church and state.[59] Kishlansky appears to accept the Lord Keeper Coventry's words in Star Chamber, 'We sit not here to meddle with matters of religion', at face value, while dismissing Prynne's appeals of loyalty to the English Crown as little other than a premeditated act of 'shrewd protection' to avoid criminal prosecution in the common law courts for treason.[60] Yet the reality is less clear-cut: this was a political climate in which the Star Chamber was inclined to interpret Prynne's panegyrics on Elizabeth I's reign as personal criticism of Charles I.[61] Kishlansky's approach has done little to explain the popular outrage attending Leighton's or Prynne's punishments, nor to elucidate the deliberately anti-Laudian nature of their arguments in the context of the Personal Rule. There is no question that the charge of sedition was established on a technical point, *stricto jure*. But it is hardly revelatory to condemn Leighton and Prynne as seditious libellers on the same grounds as that of the Star Chamber's judgment.[62] It is doubtful that either thought it seditious to wish for a re-enactment of Christendom in England – with its aggressive displays of Christian state power fondled lovingly by papist and Protestant antiquary alike – and for the supreme authority of King-in-Parliament to condemn libertine morality and false religion. Here, historians must not forget the extraordinary context of Prynne's case, in which Charles I's decision to govern without parliaments sent a conclusive message to its members that church government was reserved for the King and his clergy. This was the first time that a Protestant monarch in England

---

The theatre of Gods judgements (London, 1597), and Dudley Fenner, *A short and profitable treatise, of lawfull and unlawfull recreations* (Middelburg, 1590). See further Jonas Barish, *The Antitheatrical Prejudice* (Berkeley, 1981), Margot Heinemann, *Puritanism and Theatre: Thomas Middleton and Opposition Drama under the Early Stuarts* (Cambridge, 1980), and Huston Diehl, *Staging Reform, Reforming the State: Protestantism and Popular Theatre in Early Modern England* (Cornell, 1997).

[58] Kishlansky, 'Martyrs' Tales', esp. pp. 340–3. See also Kishlansky, 'Whipper whipped', pp. 613, 624.

[59] Kishlansky, 'Martyrs' Tales', pp. 343–4.

[60] William Prynne, *A Brief Relation of Certain Special and Most Material Passages* [E. 162 (2)], p. 139, quoted by Kishlansky, 'Martyrs' Tales', p. 343.

[61] Lamont, *Marginal Prynne*, p. 32; Bodleian Library Douce MSS. 173, f. 6 6v; TNA., SP. 16/534, f. 152; Prynne, *Histrio-mastrix*, p. 834.

[62] Kishlansky makes no attempt to explain Prynne's motivations in writing *Histrio-mastrix*. He only notes that even with the fuller manuscript record of the legal proceedings, 'it is difficult to assess Prynne's intentions', and that simply, 'you cannot look into another man's heart'. He does reference Prynne's own accounts to be found in Burton's *A Divine Tragedy* (London, 1636) and Prynne's *New discovery of free-state tyranny* (1655) but calls them 'self-serving' and inadequate for a proper assessment of his trial (p. 627).

had disposed, very publicly, with a living remnant of Henry VIII's reformation statutes, which was a parliament-legislated (civil) religion overseeing the clerical sphere.[63] The repeated focus of Prynne's condemnatory weight of sources spoke to the need for governance over the clergy, their proper subordination along with the laity to the superior moral authority of the civil power, given the clergy's inherent tendency to mislead the people into the 'most pernicious Corruptions'.[64] Prynne's exaltation of civil governors as supremely authoritative in religion was his most seditious act.

Both Leighton and Prynne would enjoy better fortunes following their rapid acquittals and release by April 1641. One of the first actions of the Long Parliament, after hearing Leighton's petition read twice on 9 November 1640, had been to order his removal from the Fleet Prison to a more comfortable abode, with freedom to travel abroad.[65] Leighton's and Prynne's detailed accounts of their sufferings in prison before the House were also immediately published for public consumption.[66] In the meantime, a committee heavy with puritan members such as John Hampden, William Strode, Denzil Holles, Oliver St John, John Pym, William Bagshaw, Francis Rous, and Harbottle Grimston examined his case finding multiple

---

[63] Prynne saw this as a point of Elizabethan Protestant orthodoxy. See, for example, Thomas Harding's accusation of John Jewel that his *Apologia Ecclesiae Anglicanae* (1563) defended a 'parliament-religion' or 'parliament-faith' alike to pagan Rome (given that the English Parliament legislated for doctrine and liturgy without the assent of bishops or clergy). Jewel's reply was to defend the right of the Parliament to confirm and ratify ecclesiastical bills without clerical assent: Jewel favoured King Canute and other 'godly catholic princes in old times [who] thought it their duty, before all other affairs of the common weal, first to determine matters of religion, and that even by the parliaments of this realm' (John Jewel, *The works of John Jewel, Vol. IV*, ed. J. Ayre (Cambridge, 1850), pp. 902–5, quote on p. 905).

[64] Prynne, *Histrio-mastix*, p. 1.

[65] On the resolution of Leighton's case by the Commons see 'House of Commons Journal Volume 2: 21 April 1641', in *Journal of the House of Commons: Volume 2, 1640–1643* (London, 1802), pp. 124–5. Concerning Prynne, see 'House of Commons Journal Volume 2: 14 April 1641', in *Journal of the House of Commons: Volume 2, 1640–1643* (London, 1802), p. 120. Apparently, when Leighton's petition and detail of his sufferings was read aloud in the chamber, the House had been moved to tears (See Benson, *Collection of Tracts*, p. 224, and Phillips, 'The Last Years', p. 121). Leighton's Petition and case report, standing alongside those of Lilburne, Prynne, Bastwick, and Burton, can be found in John Rushworth (ed.), *Historical Collections of Private Passages of State: Volume 4, 1640–42* (London, 1721), pp. 20, 228–9.

[66] See Alexander Leighton, *A decade of grievances, presented and approved to the right honourable and High Court of Parliament* (London, 1641), later expanded into *An Epitome or Briefe Discoverie* (1646), and W. Prynne, *The humble petition of Mr. Prynne, late exile, and close prisoner in the Ile of Jersey* (London, 1641), which is the republished second part of *The humble petitions of Mr. Burton, Dr. Bastwicke, Mr Prynne, presented to the honorable knights, citizens, and burgesses of the Commons* (London, 1641).

miscarriages of justice.[67] Leighton served as the namesake of this committee charged with examining cases of episcopal overreach in the name of state safety, with similar cases such as that of John Lilburne referred to it also.[68]

Leighton's *Appeal* and English Protestant orthodoxy

Leighton's unlicensed medical practice between 1619 and 1626 poised him to treat the condition of England's church and state as delicately balanced, and according to quotidian practice, tending either towards healthful nourishment or lethal disease.[69] Leighton's philosophy of state is best described as a theologically integrated one, placing his vast reading of 'the Statutes… [and] the best Common-Lawyers, and Civilians, and some Canonists' within an all-encompassing vision of godly rule, and characteristically Reformed and Erastian in the connection drawn between lordly prelacy, and the meddling of clergymen in civil judicature, with a diseased corruption of the state.[70] Leighton's own commitment to a Foxean prince is first evident in his *Speculum belli sacri* (1624), dedicated to Prince Charles, Prince Frederick of Bohemia, and the Lady Elizabeth. He expresses his hope that Charles' future reign will provide for the merciful rescue of God's people in the Palatinate, and, in a biblical allusion to God's own kingdom, be the tree 'from whose shade the Saints doe looke for shelter, & refreshing'.[71] He also alludes to Haman's anti-Semitic conspiracy against God's people in the court of the Persian king Xerxes, in order to emphasize that a 'Princely resolution and irrevocable word' was God's chosen form of rescue.[72] Haman is compared to English prelates and royal advisors in the court of Charles I for seeking personal advancement through defaming faithful servants of God as seditious conspirators, and attempting to usurp the royal prerogative for the purpose of their destruction. The whole of

---

[67] 'House of Commons Journal Volume 2: 9 November 1640', in *Journal of the House of Commons: Volume 2, 1640–1643* (London, 1802), pp. 22–5. For the detailed list of illegalities, see J. Rushworth, *Historical Collections of Private Passages of State: Volume 4, 1640–42*, pp. 228–9.

[68] See further on 'Dr Leighton's Committee' in Rushworth, *Historical Collections of Private Passages of State: Volume 4, 1640–42*, pp. 45–68.

[69] See M. Pelling and F. White, 'Leighton, Alexander', in *Physicians and Irregular Medical Practitioners in London 1550–1640 Database* (London, 2004), British History Online http://www.british-history.ac.uk/no-series/london-physicians/1550-1640 [accessed 13 July 2023]. See also Leighton's political belief expressed in his *Epitome*, that checks and balances ensured a well-tempered civil state, 'kept as it were in an equall balance', just as Roman tribunes kept the consuls and the state in equilibrium, achieving 'concordia discors, that keepeth the state in tune and temper' (Leighton, *An Epitome*, p. 54).

[70] Leighton, *An Epitome*, pp. 66, 72.

[71] See Ezekiel 31.6, Mark 4.32.

[72] Leighton, *Speculum belli sacri*, 'An Epistle'. See Esther 4.14.

scripture taught that both pagan and Christian princes were gods on earth, and the supremacy of the 'Princelie name' eventually proved essential for the safety of the Jews through the timely intervention of Queen Esther. Leighton urges the English Parliament to do likewise, and 'interpose her selfe for her Countrey' against 'the overtopping growth' of treasonous advisors who sought to subvert first the state of religion, and then the state itself.[73] The 'Prelacie' currently 'smelleth vildlie of Popelike pride' and are 'a terror to all' except those who 'stand too nigh to them in a contiguitie of profitt'. Leighton urges English parliamentarians to, like the Roman patriots or Athenian kings, withstand these 'enemies of God, and the State' and be 'willing to dye that the glorie of their nation might live'. They must be faithfully plain with Charles I, 'his royall Majestie', and identify the threat to his safety arising from both 'eminent and imminent' places.[74]

The *Appeal* spans over three hundred pages and systematically attacks lordly prelacy according to Reformed doctrine, English law, and the ecclesiastical history of Christendom. It seeks to harness a magisterial tradition which saw England's royal supremacy, rather than episcopal government, as the beating heart of English Protestantism. The removing of English bishops from their positions of political authority and influence, or as he terms them, 'the Hierarchicall government' – due to the key claim of English archbishops from John Whitgift onwards to possessing a *jure divino* superiority over ordinary ministers – could correct the disease infecting the commonwealth at present: where religion and state were not co-operating handmaidens, but the church was 'overlording' itself above secular rulers.[75] Leighton's *Appeal* surveys England's sacred history as an exercise in anti-clerical vigilance. In Leighton's anti-clerical account of English history, there is an eternal tussle between England's royal throne and priestly attempts to circumvent or usurp its exclusive claim to govern the clergy and laity. Key examples of this high-priest motif in Saxon times are Archbishops Theodorus, Lambright, Dunstan (known as a sorcerer), and Thurstane, until Leighton arrives at that 'proud Popeling' Thomas Beckett, who 'would not suffer... [clergy] to be tried by the Laws of the Land', using the Roman laws of sanctuary to protect them from secular justice.[76] The Norman Conquest is also depicted by Leighton as ultimately the failure of Saxon prelates: it was the 'idleness, avarice, dissolute life, and overlording of the clergie' which brought about impiety amongst the laity and ultimately subjection to 'the intollerable tyrannie of the Normans'. The enslavement encompassed church as well as state as William the Conqueror's cleric Stigandus corruptly

---

[73] Leighton, *Speculum belli sacri*, 'An Epistle'.
[74] Ibid.
[75] Leighton, *Appeal*, pp. 4, 13, 36, 54, 189, 262.
[76] Ibid., p. 56.

assumed the place of archbishop, thinking 'he should make a Conquest of the English clergy as his Master had made a conquest of the Kingdome'.[77]

Leighton identifies two pillars which make English prelacy discordant with England's commonwealth of laws and royal supremacy: (i) the *jure divino* superiority over other ministers that derived church hierarchy apart from the King's name, and (ii) the tyrannous consequence, of bishops exercising ecclesiastical jurisdiction belonging to the Crown, but in the name of their own independent clerical office. In this way, English prelates sinned against noblemen and gentry, 'for besides their sinning against their soules, in keeping out a powerfull ministrie, they intrude upon secular offices due to the nobility and gentry, and that against the law of God, the nature of callings, the Cannon law, and the very law of nations'.[78] He outlines the areas and practices by which this imbalance was reaching papal proportions, from using 'their own names and their own seales' rather than the King's when issuing writs for exercise of the King's ecclesiastical jurisdiction, to forcing ministers to swear the oath *ex officio*, which Leighton describes as 'against all laws of Heaven and Earth'.[79] The unlawfulness of the *ex officio* oath in church court proceedings was a long-standing puritan criticism dating back to its use to enforce Archbishop Whitgift's subscription test between 1583 and 1585.[80] Leighton lists its history as being a 'tricke of imprisonment' by Pope Eugene II in AD 824, and dates its introduction on English soil to a popish act introduced during Henry IV's reign, enabling English prelates to imprison and execute English Lollards such as John Badby and Sir John Oldcastle.[81] Leighton describes this 'selfe-accusing oath', used against such 'professors of the Gospell', as 'against the Law of God, the Honour of the King, the law of the Land, the nature of Ecclesiasticke jurisdiction, and the right of the Subject'.[82] Leighton's language describing the oath's ability to force truthful confessions of private belief from ministers and laypeople, by which many are 'vexed and insnared', purposely resurrects the impassioned language of the Reformation Parliament's *Supplication of the Commons* (1532), addressed to the Convocation, on the very same misuse of spiritual jurisdiction.[83]

Leighton's main argument with regards to the use of the *ex officio* oath in church courts was that it contravened Roman civilian principles of judicial

---

[77] *Ibid.*, p. 55.
[78] *Ibid.*, p. 129.
[79] *Ibid.*, pp. 32, 39.
[80] Leighton attacks Archbishop Whitgift's justification for reviving the *ex officio* oath on p. 34. See Patrick Collinson, *The Elizabethan Puritan Movement* (London, 1967), pp. 243–88.
[81] Leighton, *Appeal*, pp. 32–3. This statute was 2 Henry 4, cap. 15.
[82] *Ibid.*, and further, pp. 49–50
[83] *Ibid.*, p. 47. See further 'The Supplication of the Commons, 1532' in Gerald Bray (ed.), *Documents of the English Reformation*, pp. 51–6, and Stanford E. Lehmberg, *Reformation Parliament 1529–36* (Cambridge, 1970), pp. 139–41.

procedure, as well as English common law, by denying English subjects the right to remain silent.[84] Leighton impresses that Henry IV's statute permitting the use of the *ex officio* oath, originating in Roman canon law, was not enforceable, for it had been passed without the consent of the House of Commons, and was conclusively abrogated by Henry VIII's Reformation Parliament for its clear detraction from the Tudor royal supremacy in its attribution of coercive power to ordinary bishops by right of their office alone. Leighton lauds the supreme unity of civil and ecclesiastical jurisdiction within the English Crown from this significant juncture, 'leaving not the least impression of any such power to the *Ordinary*', and utilizing the sweeping language of the *Act for the Submission of the Clergy* (1534), 'making utterlie void, and of none effect' past ecclesiastical statutes which stated the contrary.[85] Asserting the primacy of English statute law above episcopal tradition, Leighton quotes Sir Francis Bacon, Lord Chancellor of England between 1618 and 1621, declaring the self-accusation oath as contrary 'to the laws of the Land, and custome of the Kingdome'. He also lists Marian martyr John Lambert's recorded opposition, Nicholas Fuller's arguments on the liberty of the subject, the law of nature 'registred in the Civill law... [that] a man must not betray another, much lesse himself', Gratian's canon laws, and finally, its rejection by Catholic city-states of the *regnum Italicum* including Venice.[86] He also quotes Trajan in Pliny's Letters on the injustice of proceeding to examine someone without third party accusation, which the Roman senator termed 'an evill example (saith he) and not heard of in our age'.[87]

Leighton calls on English parliamentarians, to whom his *Appeal* is addressed, to behave like 'the Romane Patriots, or the Athenian Kings', and to boldly acknowledge lordly prelates 'to be enemies to God, and the State'.[88] Such classical allusions had not been atypical in the English Parliament itself, with the keen Tacitean Eliot imprisoned in the Tower in 1626 for comparing the Duke of Buckingham to the traitor Sejanus, thus inopportunely comparing Charles I with the Roman Emperor Tiberius. Eliot viewed Buckingham as privy to a papal plot within the royal court, using 'shadows and pretences' to cover his evil design against the Protestant cause in Europe, and permitting through gross negligence the fall of La

---

[84] See further M. H. Macguire, 'Attack of the Common Lawyers on the Oath *Ex Officio* as Administered in the Ecclesiastical Courts of England', in *Essays in History and Political Theory in Honour of Charles Howard McIlwain*, ed. C. F. Wittke (Cambridge, MA, 1936), pp. 199–229, and R. H. Helmholz, 'Origins of the Privilege Against Self-Incrimination: The Role of the European *Ius Commune*', *New York University Law Review*, 65:4 (1990), 962–91.

[85] Leighton, *Appeal*, pp. 33–4, and see further on the *Submission*'s significance, p. 39.

[86] Ibid., pp. 48–50. See further on the state of Venice's church polity in Leighton, *An Epitome*, p. 74.

[87] Ibid., p. 48 citing Apud. Plin. Lib. 10. Epist. 98.

[88] Ibid., 'The Epistle to the Reader', sig. A2r.

Rochelle to French Catholic forces.[89] Likewise, Leighton consistently ties the fate of English religion to the state: describing bishops as an 'overtopping growth' seeking to subvert the church first, and then the state itself. In the 'suppressing, or advancing' of their power 'standeth the ruine, or reviving' of the King's authority.[90] Their tyranny over the Church threatened the ancient English constitution, which taught an aristocratic form of government under a supreme monarchical head; while the English commonwealth was 'by common consent... a free commonaltie', it was in its choice of political governors 'an Aristocracie' like those noble city-states, rather than in absolute subjection 'as that of the Assyrians, Persians, or the like'.[91] Likewise, the English Church was from Christ's initial teachings in Matthew 18 an aristocratic polity, with 'such Bishops as God ordained together with ruling Elders', citing in support the Reformed theologians Sibrandus Lubbertus, Franciscus Junius, dean of Exeter Matthew Sutcliffe, and William Whittaker.[92] The root of prelatical tyranny lay not in *jure divino* claims to ecclesiastical power, but one step below this, in the heterodox assertion that there existed a *jure divino* distinction between the offices of bishops and ministers, rather than a merely *jure humano* one: as the church fathers Augustine, Jerome, and Ambrose attested, bishops held distinction in the New Testament alike to aristocratic senators, and yet they were 'no other than Ministers or teaching Elders' alike to their fellow ordained clergymen.[93] The pinnacle of Leighton's evidence against any *jure divino* distinction between bishops and ministers, which was in his view the fertile seeding ground for clerical overlording, comes from the Elizabethan Church establishment, a letter from the President of Corpus Christi, Oxford, John Rainolds to the Erastian counsellor Sir Francis Knollys, confirming that 'God never made, nor doth the scripture witness anie such distinction, but that Bishop and Minister were all one'.[94] Rainolds' contemporary at Oxford, the theologian and biblical translator for the Authorized Version, Dr Thomas Holland, is also quoted by Leighton for additional support as

---

[89] Conrad Russell, *Parliaments and English Politics, 1621–29* (Oxford, 1979), pp. 260–322;John Eliot, *The Monarchie of Men*, ed. A. B. Grosart (London, 1879), II, p. 35; M. F. Tenney, 'Tacitus in the politics of early Stuart England', *Classical Journal*, 37:3 (1941), 156, 159. On the reinvention of the Roman discourse of treason in pre-Civil War England, see further Orr, *Treason and the State*, pp. 22–5.

[90] Leighton, *Appeal*, sig. A4v, A3v.

[91] *Ibid.*, p. 7.

[92] *Ibid.*, p. 7, n. 23.

[93] *Ibid.*, p. 7. Leighton uses the term *jure positivo* rather than *jure humano*, but his meaning is the same: 'it is not of Gods appointment' (p. 7). Leighton also cites on this point Titus 1.3, 7 and Peter Lombard's *Sentences*, Bk. 4, Dist. 24, and Gratian, Dit. 95, Duarer. *De sacris Ecc. Minist.* C. 7, Sect. 9.

[94] *Ibid.*, p. 8.

saying in July 1608 that a bishop was no distinct order from a minister, nor superior to him by divine institution.[95]

Leighton considered prelatical claims to an independent authority over inferior clergy as a direct attack on the reformed Protestant orthodoxy of the English Church, encompassing authorities from the wide net of Augustine, Anselm, Gratian, David Pareus, Archbishop Cranmer, Hugh Latimer, Martin Bucer, Thomas Bilson, to William Fulke and William Whitaker.[96] Cranmer's 'De Divinis Officiis' section in the *Reformatio legum Ecclesiasticarum* (1551–3) had treated parish ministers as commensurate to bishops in ecclesiastical authority by assuming that they could pronounce the sentence of excommunication in their own congregations, having received consent to do so from their diocesan bishop, and this (to quote Cranmer) 'so that by all means we may reintroduce the ancient discipline into the church as much as possible'.[97] For evidence of novel appeals to a *jure divino* authority over fellow clergy, derived from God's commandments rather than the King's prerogative, Leighton singles out polemical works by Archbishops Whitgift, and Bancroft, and Bishops George Downham, Thomas Morton, Alexander Lindsay, and James Spottiswood.[98] As Bishop of Winchester under James I, Bilson was not so foolhardy, careful to attribute the episcopal office to *principis-praerogativam* (the King's prerogative), so much so that Bilson proceeded to charge the King with any failure of theirs: 'let it be laid upon the Magistrate, and not upon the Bishops'.[99] To Leighton, when English prelates chose rather to emulate their papal forebears and 'play the Rex', they impersonate 'Romes right hand' and seek to dismantle England's lawful governors.[100] Leighton also assembles the proto-Protestant authorities of Jan Huss and John Wycliffe, as well as Martin Luther, Huldrych Zwingli, alongside Latimer and Cranmer as 'learned witnesses' for the case against *jure divino* episcopacy in both English law and orthodox Protestant divinity.[101]

Leighton's key litmus test for English Protestant orthodoxy on the nature of episcopacy, Cranmer's *Reformatio*, was in fact Edward VI's committee-led revision of English church offices.[102] The royal commission charged with

---

[95] *Ibid.*, p. 8. See further on Holland and *jure divino* episcopacy, Goldie, *Roger Morrice and the Puritan Whigs*, p. 295.

[96] *Ibid.*, p. 21.

[97] *Ibid.*, p. 27; G. Bray (ed.), *Tudor Church Reform: The Henrician Canons of 1535 and the 'Reformatio Legum Ecclesiasticarum'*, Church of England Record Society 8 (Woodbridge, 2000), pp. 342–3.

[98] Leighton, *Appeal*, p. 28.

[99] *Ibid.*, pp. 26–7, quoting from Thomas Bilson, *De perpetua Ecclesiae Christi gubernatione* (London, 1611), cap. 15, pp. 402–3.

[100] *Ibid.*, pp. 21, 53.

[101] *Ibid.*, p. 27.

[102] Bray (ed.), *Reformatio in Tudor Church Reform*; Torrance Kirby, 'Lay Supremacy: Reform of the canon law of England from Henry VIII to Elizabeth I (1529–1571)', *Reformation and Renaissance Review: Journal of the Society for Reformation Studies*, 8:3 (2006),

revising the English ecclesiastical constitution was spear-headed by Cranmer and also included Latimer, John Hooper, Peter Martyr Vermigli, John à Lasco, Nicholas Ridley, and civilians Walter Haddon and William Petre, the latter of whom had presided over Thomas Cromwell's vicegerential court and favoured an Erastian overhaul of church court jurisdiction.[103] Although the resulting *Reformatio* never achieved statutory status, it was published with Archbishop Matthew Parker's approval and an attempt was made to pass it in the Parliament of 1571–2.[104]

Leighton's *Appeal* and the sacred purpose of civil law

Mark Goldie has observed that early modern proponents of civil religion took pride in throwing out 'Priestianity' – the canons, litanies, ceremonies, priestly garb, signs of the cross – without discarding the doctrines of their reformed faith, sourced from their prime authorities on religion: Christ and scripture.[105] We see this clear distinction throughout Leighton's *Appeal* but chiefly in his estimation of legal opinions concerning English statute and common law which he places higher in authority to church customs and traditions, which he terms with the popish tagline 'mens inventions'.[106] He considered human constitutions to be supremely authoritative over that of priestly custom and practice, in a mirroring of God's written laws in the Decalogue which were to guard generations of Israelites from idolatry.[107] To Leighton's mind, therefore, chapter 29 of 'the great Charter of England', or Magna Carta, stood clearly in the way of English bishops asserting a *jure divino* right to deprive inferior ministers from their livelihoods on account of being 'Disciplinarians' or 'Schismaticks'. English governors could not remove any subject from his freehold without clear evidence of a crime being committed against parliamentary statute, and only then when proved

---

349–370; and Sachs, 'Thomas Cranmer's *Reformatio legum ecclesiasticarum* of 1553', pp. 37–64.
[103] Geoffrey Elton, *Reform and Renewal* (Cambridge, 1973), pp. 134–5.
[104] Kirby, 'Lay Supremacy', p. 349; Thomas Freeman, '"The Reformation of the Church in this Parliament": Thomas Norton, John Foxe and the Parliament of 1571', *Parliamentary History*, 16:2 (1997), 131–47; Spalding, 'The *Reformatio Legum Ecclesiasticarum* of 1552', 162–71.
[105] See Goldie's chapter in this volume, and his 'John Locke, the early Lockeans, and priestcraft', *Intellectual History Review*, 28:1 (2018), 129–30, 133.
[106] Leighton, *Appeal*, p. 94. This was an increasingly popular pejorative in puritan theological works in pre-Civil War England, perhaps most significantly being used by William Ames in his printed debate with Bishop Thomas Morton (see William Ames, *A reply to Dr. Mortons generall Defence of three innocent ceremonies* (Amsterdam, 1622), and *A fresh suit against human ceremonies in God's worship* (Amsterdam, 1633)).
[107] Leighton, *Appeal*, pp. 94–5.

'by the verdict of 12 men'.[108] Nevertheless, ministers who refused to swear the *ex officio* oath before church courts were 'thrust from their benefices by the bare and peremptorie command of the Bishops'.[109] The result had been four hundred ministers silenced or suspended by virtue of the 1604 canons, enforced by the ecclesiastical hierarchy despite their status as clerical canons, or new impositions, never passed by Parliament. Without the sanctifying sanction of civil authority, these canons urging subscription to the statement that the English Prayer Book was entirely biblical, could only be regarded in the Reformed tradition as 'men's inventions'. While Parliament did not, in Leighton's view, have an absolute power to declare what was religious orthodoxy, it did have the right to outlaw clerical legislation that was being imposed against English subjects in denial of their natural rights according to England's ancient constitution. He therefore lauds the 1610 Parliament's passing of an act declaring that 'where the [1604] Canons would charge body goods and Lands of the subject, that charge shall be of no force, except it were confirmed by act of Parliament'.[110]

The assent of Parliament was symbolic to Leighton of the supreme power that the civil government entire – including the Crown, Parliament, and the law courts – possessed in England over the external affairs and ordering of religion. Concerning the fines, deprivations, and imprisonments of puritan ministers, Leighton recalls Martin Bucer's *De Censura*, or 'censure of the English Liturgie', listing the Romish errors remaining in the Edwardian Prayer Book (1547). This was establishment opinion from the Edwardian era attesting to the wounds inflicted on the consciences of Protestant clergy who followed the Prayer Book's orders and ceremonies.[111] Seen through this guise, Leighton views parliamentarians as akin to 'Elders of Israell', with an advisory share in the Crown's ecclesiastical supremacy, to condemn such inquisitions which offended Protestant consciences as well as the laws of the land. Quoting Thomas Smith's *De Republica Anglorum*, he describes Parliament as the highest court of judicature, with power to probe the proceedings of church courts and investigate internal diocesan matters: it was the 'supream Court' able to call 'any place, or person to an account', with 'the power of the whole Kingdome, yea both of the head and of the body'.[112] Leighton's *Appeal* further demonstrates how London MPs in the 1572 Parliament attempted to reform Sabbath-keeping laws and reformation of abuses, only for bishops in the House of Lords to question Parliament's role in legislating on this issue. The undergirding reformed influence to Leighton's assertions here regarding

---

[108] Ibid., pp. 257, 31. See further on the revival of chapter 29 in Elizabethan and early Stuart political thought in John Baker, *The Reinvention of Magna Carta 1216–1616* (Cambridge, 2017), pp. 249–75, 463–6, 500–10.
[109] Leighton, *Appeal*, p. 32.
[110] Ibid.
[111] Ibid., p. 93, n. 125.
[112] Ibid., p. 174, n. 230.

state-sanctioned morality and obedience to divine law is the Old Testament juridical principle repeatedly cited by reformed commentators in the context of political theology or statecraft: a godly magistrate is to be '*Custos Utriusque Tabulae*', a keeper of both the tables of the Mosaic law, and charged with the law of God to see it kept by those under his authority.[113] Leighton cites the hugely popular Heidelberg Catechism that Moses' Ten Commandments – neatly divided into laws of doctrine and worship, and latterly of morality and civility – puts the duty on magistrates to legislate accordingly in both spheres for the sake of their people's flourishing.[114] In his view, religion and the state must go together: for 'as to the strict keeping of the first table, bindeth on the duties of the second table, so remissness or mixture in the first, maketh us loose in the duties of the second', and so, the state is more likely to sink. Religion was a necessary handmaiden of the state because it taught the civic and moral virtues.

In a tactic spear-headed by Sir Edward Coke, the Magna Carta had been put to polemical use in the 1604 and 1610 Parliaments against the jurisdiction of church courts, with a 1604 draft bill called for 'Due Observation of the Great Charter of England', insisting that canons passed in Convocation had no legal validity unless confirmed by act of parliament.[115] Significantly, Leighton also quotes Coke's parliamentary report *De Jure Regis Ecclesiastico* (1605) for evidence that English bishops' exercise of ecclesiastical jurisdiction in their dioceses is a bestowal of the King's royal prerogative, which can be removed 'at his pleasure'.[116] Coke's *De Jure* was a defense of the royal supremacy and contains a full account of the struggles between the pope and the English Crown culminating in Edward III's reign, and presents the common law punishment of treason as 'the essential bulwark against the renewal of Catholic encroachment'.[117] A prominent critic of the High Commission's authority to fine and imprison ministers, Coke held that the charge of *praemunire* was still available against ecclesiastical courts that derived their authority from the Crown, because Henry VIII had continued to utilize the charge after he had established his royal supremacy over Convocation.[118]

---

[113] This is a ubiquitous motif in early modern English reformed political thought. See Jonathan Willis, *The Reformation of the Decalogue* (Cambridge, 2017), and A. A. Gazal, '"A Christian prince hath the charge of both tables": John Jewel's biblical doctrine of the royal supremacy', in *Reformation faith: exegesis and theology in the Protestant reformations*, ed. Michael Parsons (Exeter, 2014), pp. 57–70.

[114] See further Anthony Milton, 'A Missing Dimension of European Influence on English Protestantism: The Heidelberg Catechism and the Church of England, 1563–1663', *Reformation & Renaissance Review*, 20:3 (2018), 235–48.

[115] See Christopher Brooks, *Law, Politics and Society in Early Modern England* (Cambridge, 2009), p. 113.

[116] Leighton, *Appeal*, p. 27.

[117] David Chan Smith, 'Remembering Usurpation: the common lawyers, Reformation narratives, and the prerogative, 1578–1616', *Historical Research*, 86 (2013), 619–37 at 634.

[118] Rose, *Godly Kingship*, p. 70.

Ecclesiastical courts could nevertheless operate 'flatlie opposite' to the King's prerogative in post-Reformation England, such as when bishops delegated their ecclesiastical authority to chancellory officials and archdeacons, as if it were theirs to delegate. In the act of signing 'in their owne names, and with their own seales' to imprison ministers, such bishops 'eat up and consume the power of the Laws of the Land'.[119]

Leighton argues in the *Appeal* that supreme ecclesiastical jurisdiction belonged solely to the English throne, and that the Caroline episcopate, in asserting an independent *jure divino* right to impose ceremonial innovations, was behaving 'opposite to King and his Lawes'.[120] He quotes from Nicholas Sanders' *De origine ac progressu schismatis anglicani* (1585), the official royal edict of Edward VI written to Archbishop Cranmer, which states that 'from the King all power and jurisdiction proceedeth &c. We give thee [Cranmer] power within thy Diocese, ... at our pleasure'.[121] Leighton impresses that from the first year of Edward VI's reign onwards, it was unlawful for bishops to exercise civil jurisdiction in their dioceses, nor send out writs 'but in the Kings name, and under the Kings seale'.[122] This statute, though abrogated by Mary I, was reenacted by Elizabeth I and James I. Leighton then writes in a knowing tone that English parliamentarians knew many of Charles I's bishops to be, by virtue of their lordly offices, 'all over head and eares in a *Praemunire*' of the same sort that saw others dependent on the King's mercy in Edwardian England.[123] Significantly, this Edwardian statute singled out by Leighton had already been Sir Edward Coke's statute of choice to question the legality of various Jacobean bishops using their own episcopal seals and styles for judicial proceedings. In the Parliament of 1608-9, Coke had argued that Edward VI's statute had been made to ensure that 'all summons, citations, and process in ecclesiastical courts, shall be made in the name and the style of the King, and that their seals shall be engraven with the King's arms'. The sitting committee of Lords and Commons, anxious to move that such bishops as used their own form of seals 'were not lawful Bishops', was however disappointed to learn on the authority of Coke and Sir John Popham that this same statute was, however regrettably to all, 'not now in force', as it had not been explicitly revived by Elizabeth I, who had revived one of her father's conservative statutes on bishops' styles and proceedings over that of her more reformed and Erastian brother's.[124]

---

[119] Leighton, *Appeal*, pp. 39-40, 36.
[120] *Ibid.*, p. 25.
[121] *Ibid.*, p. 26. This statute is 1 Ed. VI, cap. 2.
[122] *Ibid.*, p. 26.
[123] *Ibid.*, p. 26.
[124] Edward Coke, 'A Case at a Committee concerning Bishops', in *The Reports of Sir Edward Coke, knt. (1572-1617) in English, in thirteen parts complete*, ed. G. Wilson (London, 1777), VII, sig. B3v-r.

Leighton's opinion stood hopefully with that of the 1608–9 committee on religion, which certainly encompassed Coke's own anti-prelatical sympathies.[125] Coke himself believed that 'the Power of Princes' in religious matters had been 'greatly decayed, and been but little regarded' throughout James I's reign.[126] While the Tudor reformation statutes had clearly stated that the Church of England belonged within the Crown's dominion, English prelates were increasingly recapturing essential markers of ecclesiastical sovereignty with the Crown's approval; yet, in challenging the right of Parliament and the law courts to intervene to correct abuses of church power, Leighton viewed the royal supremacy as being severely undermined.[127] The Tudor royal supremacy had been built on the authority of parliamentary statute, upon the right of Parliament to debate and pass legislation concerning religion, and upon the reformed Protestant notion of godly rule which laid the control of religion with magistrates and justices as well as royal princes. Jonathan Willis has accurately concluded that the royal supremacy was seen by late Elizabethan and early Stuart thinkers as not only 'an exercise in theocratic kingship', but a theocratic exercise that incorporated the entire civil and administrative state, 'through religious endorsements of and justifications for the exercise of civil governance and justice'.[128]

Conclusion

Although it was a retrospective account aimed at an Erastian-dominated Long Parliament, Leighton's *An Epitome* resurrects the same chorus lines on civil supremacy over religion that consistently populated the pages of his seditious 1628 text. Neither epitomic nor brief, it is a philosophical and theological pronouncement on the primacy of the laws of God in civil and ecclesiastical life, and on the incumbent duty of the King and Parliament to legislate them above and before any church authorities, and further, to see these laws observed by ministers in the Church of England. Against the measure of his own strict Erastian separation of clergymen from political power, Leighton criticizes Laud and other bishops for manufacturing misinformation about the true contents of the *Appeal*, and for masquerading as civil justices rather than spiritual preachers of God's word.[129] He also

---

[125] See further Smith, 'Remembering Usurpation', pp. 620, 633–5.

[126] University of Oxford, Queen's College MS. 215 f. 24v, cited from Smith, 'Remembering Usurpation', p. 635.

[127] For context surrounding Leighton's fears, see Andrew Foster, 'The Clerical Estate Revitalised', in *The Early Stuart Church, 1603–1642*, ed. Kenneth Fincham (Basingstoke, 1993), pp. 139–60; Orr, *Treason and the State*, pp. 206, 478, and D. Alan Orr, 'Sovereignty, Supremacy and the Origins of the English Civil War', *History*, 87:288 (2002), 479–82.

[128] Willis, *The Reformation of the Decalogue*, pp. 16–17.

[129] Leighton, *An Epitome*, p. 53.

takes a leaf from John Foxe's *Acts and Monuments* (1563) in detailing in precise terms the physical sufferings endured by religious dissidents, with the express aim that the Parliament would never again let bishops 'trample on their Estates, their Necks, Bodies, and Soules', turning Englishmen into their 'Artificiall slaves'.[130] Citing Tacitus and Jean Bodin, Leighton asserts that the bishops' factional warring against the Commons in the heart of the King's court overthrew the state and was tantamount to conspiracy, which end is the destruction of 'the stern of Government'. Tacitus remarked on those from 'base and poore' backgrounds – in Leighton's view, this included Laud and other high-rising churchmen who had 'no hope to raise themselves' other than through clericalist ideologies – as deriving chief benefit from the multiplying of 'dissentions within the Publique State'. Their asserted right to rule thwarting 'the joynt priviledg of all good Subjects', namely the right of the King and Parliament in all matters including religion (above that of clergy), was the cancer causing 'the very open and publike Diseases of the Church and State'.[131]

It is within a broader post-Reformation context that we can begin to understand Leighton's demand that the English Parliament take charge of religion. Leighton consistently posited that Laud's sedition derived from his rejection of a reduced episcopacy according to Reformed lines, thus rendering early Stuart England into a pre-Reformation historical paradigm once again, with 'Prelates overtopping of Kings, and States, and manifest Treasons against both' the political drama set on endless repeat.[132] Leighton condemns both bishops and judges of the Caroline regime who failed in this God-given duty by distributing corrupt and nefarious religious teachings to the people.[133] He refers to Roman civilians – champions of the authority of the civil state over religion – such as Baldus de Ubaldis and Emperor Justinian, whom Leighton praises as zealots for the conservation of the laws, both civil and ecclesiastical, rather than their innovation. The history of the Roman Empire taught that the conservation or innovation of the Laws, and thus of religion, sprang from the integrity or corruption of the *Custodes Legum* ('Minsters of the Laws').[134]

Puritans such as Leighton and Prynne were devoutly religious, vociferous readers and humanist book collectors, and relentlessly eager to see a diminished England once more occupy a celebrated place within the European Reformed community. The *Appeal*, and Prynne's similarly censored *Historio-Mastix*, have been largely overlooked by historians of political thought, not least because both engage in diatribes of prophetic damnation with a lyrical ease that can only jar with the modern reader.

[130] *Ibid.*, p. 76.
[131] *Ibid.*, pp. 55–6.
[132] *Ibid.*, p. 70.
[133] *Ibid.*, p. 52.
[134] *Ibid.*, p. 51.

However, both texts were later lauded by the Long Parliament as early prognoses as to the tyrannous endpoint of Laudian clericalism, seemingly hiding in plain sight. Both puritan authors drew upon a shared reformed tradition of legal, biblical, political, historical, and reasoned arguments against a corrupted form of episcopacy, 'Lordly Prelacy', which was raising its spectre over English courts, parliament, and royal court as well as church spaces and dioceses. They boasted a reformed religion not solely tied to moral and virtuous pursuits but mandating the jurisdictional supremacy of the civil power over the administration of religion, in a way which would drastically transform mid-seventeenth-century Britain.[135]

We must begin to state their political thought in a more positive sense than anti-clerical, anti-episcopal, or even that much-misunderstood category of 'puritan': Leighton was an Erastian theorist for an ancient kind of civil religion which located the authority to order religion squarely with lay magistrates, rather than high churchmen or an independent assembly of priests. Civil princes, lawmakers, and judges were to govern the Church of England as part of God's endowment to them of supreme civil and ecclesiastical power, and to protect it from clerical usurpation. A positive way to state Prynne's and Leighton's anti-prelatical discourses would be to state that both authors lamented the neglect of state-sponsored clerical regulation and discipline, imposed with the authority of English statutory law, in the Constantinian model of imperial legal codes that applied to both church and state. This was a failure of Christian imperial rule on the part of England's post-Reformation monarchs and their advisors. However rooted these ideas were in Old Testament and Roman imperial forms of juridical theocracy, they provided crucial stepping-stones for the defeat of extra-legal church powers, and the triumph of a supremely authoritative – and in this sense, entirely modern – civil state.

---

[135] Willis, *The Reformation of the Decalogue*, pp. 345–54.

4

Reading Machiavellian Civil Religion in Early Modern Britain

Charlotte McCallum

Religion is of central importance to Machiavelli's political thought, but he has long been believed to have considered it a political tool rather than a matter of genuine belief. In early modern Britain, he was regularly accused of instrumentalising religion, of making piety into 'meerely a matter of policie' and of seeing religion as a 'politicke devise' designed 'to keepe men in awe' rather than an end in itself.[1] His name alone became a shorthand for this political use of religion and in most cases became little more than a political insult.

Modern scholars have tended to read Machiavelli's civil religion along similar lines. For example, in Justin Champion's view, 'Machiavelli insisted on the value of religion as a tool of political manipulation'.[2] Many still consider him to be a critic of the failure of Christianity to support the state. Robert Black argues that he believed Christianity inhibited the qualities demonstrated by good citizens and good rulers, claiming that 'in the *Discourses* Machiavelli did no less than identify Christianity as the greatest foe of *virtù*'.[3] It is for this reason that Machiavelli is often believed to have preferred paganism to Christianity. Leszek Kolakowski, for example, argued that:

> *although it was both false and expounded insincerely*, Roman paganism nonetheless deserved praise. Machiavelli was not so much a sincere pagan as he was an advocate of paganism considered as a noble lie. Christianity,

---

[1] John Randall, *Twenty Nine Lectures of the Church* (London, 1631), p. 179; William Perkins, *A Treatise of Mans Imaginations* (Cambridge, 1607), p. 62.
[2] Justin Champion, *The Pillars of Priestcraft Shaken: The Church of England and Its Enemies, 1660–1730* (Cambridge, 1992), p. 196.
[3] Robert Black, *Machiavelli: From Radical to Reactionary* (London, 2022), p. 109.

meanwhile, might and often did frustrate state power, and for that it was to be blamed.[4]

It is in this form that Ronald Beiner presents Machiavelli in his study of civil religion. In proposing a solution to the problems posed by Christianity, Machiavelli is often believed to have been trying to, as Beiner puts it, 'paganize' Christianity.[5] In Beiner's view, Machiavelli and subsequent civil religionists including Thomas Hobbes, James Harrington, and Baruch Spinoza aimed 'to reduce Christianity to a kind of civil cult instrumentalized to the needs of the commonwealth no less than the pagan cults had been'.[6] This does not necessarily mean that they did not believe that Christianity was the correct form of religion, but only that Christianity should be twisted to the needs of the state, as the Romans had adapted their religion for political ends. Machiavelli, of course praises some Christians, such as the Swiss 'who are today the only people who, in respect to both religion and military usages, live as did the ancients'.[7] Yet this still arguably requires that the demands of politics rather than the dictates of God determine how religion is practised and thus entails the privileging of politics over religion.

The question of religious truth rarely emerges in such studies of Machiavelli's civil religion, understandably as it is elusive in Machiavelli's work. Notwithstanding several touches of fervour, in chapter twenty-six of *The Prince* and his 'Exhortation to Penitence', Machiavelli's discussion of religion tends to dwell on its political benefits with very little consideration of its veracity.[8] He even compares the religion of his contemporaries unfavourably with that of the ancients, though as is often the case with Machiavelli, this material is more nuanced than it might initially seem. As a result, Machiavelli is often understood as a secular thinker, and he has played a key role in the secularisation thesis. Friedrich Meinecke and Felix Raab read the reception of his ideas as integral to the undermining of Christianity in politics in mainland Europe and England respectively, while John Pocock tied the reception of Machiavelli's republican thought to the

---

[4] Leszek Kolakowski, *Modernity on Endless Trial* (Chicago, 1990), p. 63. Italics original.
[5] See Ronald Beiner, *Civil Religion: A Dialogue in the History of Political Philosophy* (Cambridge, 2011), pp. 17-28.
[6] *Ibid.*, p. 308. For similar interpretations of Machiavelli and his reception as involving the instrumentalisation of religion, see Kolakowski, *Modernity on Endless Trial*, pp. 60-3; Champion, *The Pillars of Priestcraft Shaken*, pp. 196-7.
[7] Niccolò Machiavelli, 'Discourses', in *The Chief Works and Others*, vol. I, trans. Allan H. Gilbert (Durham, NC, 1965), p. 229.
[8] On the 'Exhortation', see Cary J. Nederman and Nelly Lahoud, '"This Is the Way I Pray": Precatory Language in the Writings of Niccolò Machiavelli', *Intellectual History Review*, 31 (2021), 1-22.

realisation that politics and history were governed by individual action and not by God.[9]

Although Machiavelli's works have lent themselves to secular and even anti-Christian readings so well that criticisms of 'atheists and Machiavels' became a refrain in polemic in early modern Britain, he was highly valued in certain circles. Of particular note for our purposes is the high esteem in which he was held by republican civil religionists of the late seventeenth century, including James Harrington, Henry Neville, John Starkey, Algernon Sidney, and to some extent, John Milton.[10] All of these figures were critics of monarchy and the clergy and in this respect could be considered to reinforce Pocock's argument about the interrelation of Machiavellian secular values and republican thought.

More recently, other scholars have demonstrated that these republican civil religionists certainly did not wish to extricate religion from statecraft or even to use it for political ends. They opposed priestcraft, precisely because they considered priests to be a threat to true religion. As Blair Worden points out, this was 'not a refutation of religion but an impulse to rescue it from clericalism, from priestcraft, from dogmatism, from superstition, from fanaticism'.[11] Their concerns here were both religious and political. As Mark Goldie points out, for the civil religionists of the seventeenth century (in this case, Harrington, Hobbes, and John Locke), 'true religion had a necessary relationship with the right ordering of the commonwealth'.[12] As he argues, '[a]ll these philosophers agreed that a religion which sunders a person's existence as a citizen is false religion, it is popery, or priestcraft'.[13] To excise the political influence of priests on the state was a political and a religious duty, then, and the good of the state could not be fully extricated from that of the soul.

---

[9] Friedrich Meinecke, *Machiavellism: The Doctrine of Raison d'État and its Place in Modern History*, trans. Douglas Scott (London, 1957); Felix Raab, *The English Face of Machiavelli: A Changing Interpretation, 1500–1700* (London, 1964); J. G. A. Pocock, *The Machiavellian Moment: Florentine Political Thought and the Atlantic Republican Tradition* (Princeton, 1975), p. 350.

[10] On Harrington, see Rachel Hammersley, *James Harrington: An Intellectual Biography* (Oxford, 2019), pp. 16–21. On Starkey and Neville, see Mark Knights, 'John Starkey and Ideological Networks in Late Seventeenth-Century England', *Media History*, 11:1/2 (2005), 127–45; Gaby Mahlberg, 'Machiavelli, Neville and the Seventeenth-Century English Republican Attack on Priestcraft', *Intellectual History Review*, 28:1 (2018), 79–99. On Sidney, see Jonathan Scott, *Algernon Sidney and the English Republic 1623–1677* (Cambridge, 2005), pp. 30–35. Milton demonstrated great interest in Machiavelli's *Discourses* in his commonplace book. See Maurice Kelley, 'Milton and Machiavelli's "Discorsi"', *Studies in Bibliography*, 4 (1951), 123–7.

[11] Blair Worden, 'The Question of Secularisation', in *A Nation Transformed: England after the Restoration*, eds Alan Houston and Steve Pincus (Cambridge, 2001), p. 28.

[12] Mark Goldie, 'The Civil Religion of James Harrington', in *The Languages of Political Theory in Early-Modern Europe*, ed. Anthony Pagden (Cambridge, 1987), p. 201.

[13] Ibid., 202.

Bearing all this in mind, what did these republican civil religionists get from Machiavelli? How could Machiavelli be, in the words of Henry Neville one of his most passionate devotees, 'divine'? Neville is one figure who used to fit quite neatly into the secularisation thesis. As a civil religionist, he was repeatedly labelled an atheist by his political opponents.[14] He reportedly claimed that 'nothing could be said for the Scripture which could not be said for the Alcoran' and he praised the 'divine Machiavel' when many of his contemporaries were using his name synonymously with atheism.[15] The presbyterian Richard Baxter argued that he and Harrington, his friend and collaborator, seemed to be pagans, stating that they appeared to be 'of the old religion, I meane that of old Rome, though something as if they were Christians be intersperst'.[16] In 1675, Neville produced one of the most extensive and on the surface, most surprising, engagements with Machiavelli's civil religion, 'Nicholas Machiavel's Letter to Zanobius Buondelmontius in Vindication of Himself and His Writings' which appeared in John Starkey's 1675 edition of Machiavelli's works. The 'Letter' serves as a defence of Machiavelli and as an overview of Neville's views that probably could not safely be printed under his own name. In his preface to the 'Letter', Starkey provides the flimsiest of fictions to attribute it to Machiavelli with a convoluted account of its coming to him by way of an English gentleman who, like Neville, returned to England from Florence in 1645.[17] He never claims to have seen the original. In order to undermine any suspicions that it might be authentic, the 'Letter' is dated the first of April (i.e. April Fool's Day), 1537, ten years after Machiavelli's death. Although Neville never admits to any involvement with the book at all, the overlap between this work and Neville's own writing is substantial as Gaby Mahlberg and Vickie B. Sullivan demonstrate in detail.[18]

The 'Letter' bears many of the characteristics of republican civil religion as outlined by Goldie and Worden. In the 'Letter', 'Machiavel'

---

[14] Neville's purported atheism was even discussed in parliament. See Thomas Burton, *The Diary of Thomas Burton*, ed. John Towill Rutt (London, 1828), pp. 296–305.

[15] Oxford, Bodleian Library, Clarendon MS 60, fols 152–3; Henry Neville, *Plato Redivivus: Or, A Dialogue Concerning Government* (London, 1681), p. 117.

[16] Richard Baxter, quoted in William Montgomerie Lamont, *Richard Baxter and the Millennium: Protestant Imperialism and the English Revolution* (Washington, DC, 1979), p. 189.

[17] John Starkey, 'The Publisher to the Reader Concerning the Following Letter', in *The Works of the Famous Nicolas Machiavel, Citizen and Secretary of Florence* (London, 1675), sig. *v; Piero Innocenti and Marielisa Rossi, 'Introduzione', in *Bibliografia Delle Edizioni Di Niccolò Machiavelli* (Rome, 2015), III, p. xxxiii.

[18] Gaby Mahlberg, *Henry Neville and English Republican Culture in the Seventeenth Century: Dreaming of Another Game* (Manchester, 2009), pp. 211–15; Vickie B. Sullivan, *Machiavelli, Hobbes, and the Formation of a Liberal Republicanism in England* (Cambridge, 2004), pp. 188–96.

presents himself as an ally to the Protestants, expressing admiration for 'that Famous Reformer, fled some years since out of Picardy, to Geneva'.[19] This is clearly meant to refer to John Calvin who published his *Institutes of the Christian Religion* in 1536, by which point, the real Machiavelli was of course already long dead. The 'Letter' is utterly anticlerical. It interprets priestcraft as a remnant of Catholicism and a poison to the state, priests are presented as 'the causers of all the Soloecisms and immoralities in Government, and of all the impieties and abominations in Religion, and by consequence of all the disorder, villany, and coruption we suffer under in this detestable Age'.[20] As 'Machiavel' tells us, if Calvin fails to 'wholly extirpate this sort of men [i.e. clergy]', then there will be 'a diffusive Papacy in every Diocess, perhaps in every Parish... to diffuse new corruption and putrifaction through the body of Christ, which is his Holy Church, nor to vitiate and infect the good order and true policy of Government'.[21] As Goldie points out, anticlerical thinkers like Neville and Harrington hoped 'to fulfil the priesthood of all believers'.[22] To entirely abolish the clergy was a more extreme interpretation of Martin Luther's idea of bridging the gap between spiritual and secular life than most Protestants now upheld, but 'Machiavel' considers this to be the logical fulfilment of the Bible's instructions and Luther and Calvin's reforms. In other words, while the priesthood remained, the Reformation was unfinished and the state would continue to be stifled by the imperium of priests.

Given what we know about Machiavelli and his reputation for irreligion and the suspicious date, we might be left wondering how seriously we should take Neville's reading of Machiavelli as a pious proto-Protestant. Neville had a background in satirical literature with his *A Parliament of Ladies* (1647) and *The Isle of Pines* (1688).[23] Indeed, Paul A. Rahe has called the 'Letter' a 'gentle mockery of those who could not stomach *The Prince*', suggesting that it is an intentionally absurd attempt to demonstrate that politics is not compatible with religious and moral concerns.[24] However, as scholars now recognise, Neville was also a Protestant who did believe that the business of statecraft was compatible with religious concerns.[25]

---

[19] Henry Neville, 'Nicholas Machiavel's Letter to Zanobius Buondelmontius in Vindication of Himself and His Writings', in *The Works of the Famous Nicolas Machiavel, Citizen and Secretary of Florence* (London, 1675), sig. ****r.
[20] Ibid., sig. **2r.
[21] Ibid.
[22] Goldie, 'The civil religion of James Harrington', p. 203.
[23] See Gaby Mahlberg, 'Historical and Political Contexts of The Isle of Pines', *Utopian Studies*, 17:1 (2006), 111–29.
[24] Paul Anthony Rahe, *Against Throne and Altar: Machiavelli and Political Theory under the English Republic* (Cambridge, 2008), p. 7.
[25] On Neville's religion, see Mahlberg, *Henry Neville*, pp. 188–90.

If we do not interpret Neville's assertions of Machiavelli's divinity and his rewriting of him as a proto-Protestant prophet as an insult to the Christian faith or a parody, how can we understand it? This chapter will address this question with particular reference to this most brazen and provocative of seventeenth-century republicans, with consideration of his broader context as well as the other figures associated with the volume, the publisher, John Starkey, and the translator known only as J. B. In doing so, it will demonstrate that Machiavelli's civil religion, and its reception, are rather more complex than previous studies have suggested. When we address the context in which Machiavelli was read, with all its variations and contradictions, Neville's 'Letter' no longer appears an outlier in responses to his work. As I shall argue here, the 'Letter' deserves to be read as a genuine interpretation of Machiavelli's civil religion.

Religion in the *Discourses*

In order to address how Machiavelli's readers confronted the problems his works posed, it is first necessary to explore in detail what they were. This is a complex matter as his works present no clear answers as to what he really believed. As a result of this ambiguity Machiavelli has variously been described as an atheist, a pagan, and a Christian, and modern scholars remain divided on the question of his religious views.[26] This diversity of opinion highlights the fact that his works are highly ambiguous and they presented great difficulties to early modern readers as they do to readers today. While *The Prince* has typically received the most attention for arguing that princes should sometimes feign virtues including piety, rather than practise them, it is the *Discourses* that was often considered most offensive in its treatment of civil religion and it is this text that I will focus on here.

Religion is of central importance in the *Discourses*. Throughout the text, Machiavelli notes how necessary it is to the welfare of the state. In I.11 He uses the example of Rome to demonstrate that 'where there is religion, it is easy to bring in arms; but where there are arms and not religion, only with difficulty can the latter be brought in'.[27] In I.12, he notes that the health of religion is paramount for the good of the state, arguing that '[t]hose princes or those republics that wish to keep themselves uncorrupted must above everything else keep the ceremonies of their religion uncorrupted and hold

---

[26] See Leo Strauss, *Thoughts on Machiavelli* (Chicago, 1995), p. 12 for Machiavelli's role as a source of evil; Anthony Parel, *The Machiavellian Cosmos* (New Haven, 1992), pp. 61–2 for an account of him as a pagan and Maurizio Viroli, *Machiavelli's God*, trans. Antony Shugaar (Princeton, 2010) for an argument that Machiavelli was a Christian.
[27] Machiavelli, 'Discourses', pp. 224–5.

them always in respect, because one can have no better indication of the ruin of a country than to see divine worship little valued'.[28]

Machiavelli argued that Rome owed more to its legendary second king, Numa Pompilius, for the piety he fostered in the state, than to Romulus. He notes (echoing his source, Titus Livy's *Ab Urbe Condita*) that Numa made the Romans so religious that 'he who will go over countless actions both of the people of Rome altogether and of many of the Romans for themselves, will see that these citizens feared much more to break an oath than to break the laws, since they respected the power of God more than that of men'.[29] As he elaborates, 'he who examines Roman history well sees how helpful religion was in controlling the armies, in inspiring the people, in keeping men good, in making the wicked ashamed'.[30] In Machiavelli's account, religion gives oaths meaning, but is also instrumental in inculcating good civic virtues.

Machiavelli's critics argued that he did not give due importance to true religion, suggesting that lies could be even more useful than the truth. As his sixteenth-century translator, John Leuytt put it, Machiavelli does not appear to 'distinguish' between religions or 'prefer[...] the true and good, before the false and fained as though he would hold religion but a meere ciuill intention to hold the world in reuerence & feare'.[31] This is evident even in Machiavelli's discussion of Numa. Numa nurtured Rome's religion through falsehood, an eventuality that Machiavelli recounts with great admiration. Numa encouraged religious belief through a 'noble lie' in the form of a fictitious conversation with a nymph. On the basis of this lie he created various religious institutions through which the people could direct their worship to the gods. As Livy notes, Numa's intention was to 'civilise' the 'rough and ignorant' Romans.[32] According to him, Numa recognised that the need to worship the gods 'was unlikely to touch them unless he first prepared them by inventing some sort of marvellous tale'.[33] As Machiavelli summarises the matter, Numa, 'finding a very savage people and wishing to bring it to obey the laws by means of the arts of peace, turned to religion as something altogether necessary if he wished to maintain a well ordered state'.[34]

Machiavelli demonstrates once again that states should use falsehood to encourage piety, recommending in I.12 that 'whatever comes up in favour of

---

[28] Ibid., p. 226.
[29] Ibid., p. 224. Also see Titus Livy, *The Early History of Rome*, trans. Aubrey De Sélincourt (London, 2002), p. 54.
[30] Machiavelli, 'Discourses', p. 224.
[31] London, British Library, Additional MS 41162, fol. 1r. Thomas Burton, *The Diary of Thomas Burton*, ed. John Towill Rutt (London, 1828), pp. 296–305.
[32] Livy, *The Early History of Rome*, p. 52.
[33] Ibid., p. 53.
[34] Machiavelli, 'Discourses', p. 223.

religion, even though they think it false, [rulers of republics and kingdoms] are to accept and magnify'.[35] In Machiavelli's view, this falsehood should only be used in the service of religion and the state. He objected to the idea that religion be manipulated towards the service of private interest, arguing that 'when these [oracles] turned to speaking so as to please the powerful, and their falsehood was discovered by the people, men became unbelieving and ready to upset any good custom whatever'.[36] Yet he still argued that religion could benefit from lies.

Machiavelli's claim that religion could be nourished by falsehood was widely condemned. Edward Dacres, translator of the 1636 edition of the *Discourses* objected that 'true Religion hath no neede of helpe from falsehood, nor can get any strength from lyes'.[37] While Dacres acknowledges that the Roman religion was indeed false, he argues that 'the Romans were deceiv'd here-in, which cannot be deny'd, yet without doubt they never did this thinking to deceive themselves or with intention to deceive others'.[38] In other words, they did not deliberately build their religion upon deceit as Machiavelli claims, because any truth in that religion would not benefit from such dishonesty.

Machiavelli provided ample material to offend early modern Christians, then, but the passage most often cited as evidence for Machiavelli's preference for paganism over Christianity is his discussion of religion and warfare in II.2. It is worth quoting in full:

> Pondering, then, why it can be that in those ancient times people were greater lovers of freedom than in these, I conclude it came from the same cause that makes men now less hardy. That I believe is the difference between our religion and the ancient. Ours, because it shows us the truth and the true way, makes us esteem less the honor of the world; whereas the pagans, greatly esteeming such honor and believing it their greatest good, were fiercer in their actions... Ancient religion, besides this, attributed blessedness only to men abounding in worldly glory, such as generals of armies and princes of states. Our religion has glorified humble and contemplative men rather than active ones. It has, then, set up as the greatest good humility, abjectness and contempt for human things; the other put it in grandeur of mind, in strength of body, and in all the other things apt to make men exceedingly vigorous. Though our religion asks that you have fortitude within you, it prefers that you be adapted to suffering rather than to doing something vigorous. This way of living, then, has made the world weak and turned it over as prey to wicked men, who can in security control it, since the generality of men,

---

[35] *Ibid.*, p. 227.
[36] *Ibid.*
[37] Edward Dacres, 'Animadversion', in *Machiavel's Discourses upon the First Decade of T. Livius* (London, 1636), p. 68.
[38] *Ibid.*, p. 67.

in order to go to Heaven, think more about enduring their injuries than about avenging them.[39]

Scholars have traditionally read this passage as a criticism of the Christian religion itself. Beiner, for example, argues that this passage demonstrates that 'Christianity has celebrated slavishness and encouraged human beings to despise liberty, or the harsh politics required for the defense of liberty'.[40] According to this interpretation, Machiavelli understands Christianity as a peaceful religion which impedes, rather than encourages, military success.

There is another interpretation of this passage, however. Marcia L. Colish reads it as a criticism of the version of Christianity practised by Machiavelli's contemporaries and not the Christian religion as a whole. As she points out, 'the claim that Christianity induces pacifism would have raised eyebrows in Machiavelli's day. For throughout the Middle Ages religious wars had been fought on the authority of Christian leaders'.[41] The passivity Machiavelli criticises here can therefore be better understood, as Colish argues, as a criticism of the church of his time rather than anti-Christianity. Indeed, Machiavelli does go on to suggest that Christianity can allow warlike behaviour, stating:

> This way of living, then, has made the world weak and turned it over as prey to wicked men, who can in security control it, since the generality of men, in order to go to Heaven, think more about enduring their injuries than about avenging them. Though it may appear that the world has grown effeminate, and Heaven has laid aside her arms, this without doubt comes chiefly from the worthlessness of men, who have interpreted our religion according to sloth and not according to vigor. For if they would consider that it allows us the betterment and the defense of our country, they would see that it intends that we love and honor her and prepare ourselves to be such that we can defend her.[42]

Thus, these are in fact 'false interpretations' that lead to such laziness and idleness and, as Machiavelli states, 'our religion' indeed 'allows us the betterment and the defense of our country'. This is where we see the clearest statement of his civil religion and the idea that the good of the state might even be a religious pursuit.

---

[39] Machiavelli, 'Discourses', pp. 330–1.
[40] Beiner, *Civil Religion*, p. 18; also see Gregory Murry, 'The Best Possible Use of Christianity: The Rhetorical Stance of Machiavelli's Christian Passages', *History of Political Thought*, 36:2 (2015), 264.
[41] Marcia L. Colish, 'Republicanism, Religion, and Machiavelli's Savonarolan Moment', *Journal of the History of Ideas*, 60:4 (1999), 601.
[42] Machiavelli, 'Discourses', p. 331.

Like Machiavelli's contemporaries studied by Colish, Machiavelli's early modern English readers believed Christianity to be compatible with and even conducive towards war. As a result, they rarely censured him on the basis of being anti-Christian for opposing passivity, but instead for the notion that Christianity made men unwarlike which would have made it wholly inadequate as a civil religion. John Boys, Dean of Canterbury, for example, argued that '[i]t doth not follow, which is obiected by some Polititians, that because the religion of Christ teacheth peace, therefore it is vnfit for warre, and because it perswadeth patience, therefore it makes men cowards'.[43] 'Machiavel' is cited in the margin. This same criticism was repeated throughout early modern Britain.

There is some variation in how even this passage was read, however, which points to the diversity of early modern reading practices. Barnabe Barnes, for example, quoted this passage at length to criticise those who 'in hope of beatitude, and towards the fruition of a second comfortable life, deuise in these days how to tollerate and not to reuenge injuries: as if that no saluation can come from aboue, but by keeping of their swordes and armes rustely sheathed and cased'.[44] Although such charitable interpretations were rare, Barnes's comments are an important reminder of the ambiguity of Machiavelli's works which affected his reception in the early modern world just as it troubles scholars today.

Defending Machiavelli's Religion in early modern Britain

I have presented some of the most common criticisms of Machiavelli's civil religion, but the overall picture is rather more complex. The *Discourses* was also the source of some of the positive responses to Machiavelli in this period as it is in this text that we find many of Machiavelli's criticisms of the church of his day as well as his argument that religion brings political benefits. As the author Thomas Fuller noted, '[s]ure he who is a devil in this book [i.e. *The Prince*], is a Saint in all the rest... His notes on Livy, but especially his Florentine History savours of Religion'.[45]

Machiavelli's discussion of the importance of religion in politics was overwhelmingly well-received. Virtually all would argue that widespread piety made for good governance and good people and so these parts of the text were of course received positively in the seventeenth century. The nonconformist scholar Joseph Hall noted in *The Interest of These United Provinces* that:

---

[43] John Boys, *Remaines of That Reverend and Famous Postiller, Iohn Boys, Doctor in Divinitie, and Late Deane of Canterburie* (London, 1631), p. 189.
[44] Barnabe Barnes, *Foure Bookes of Offices* (London, 1606), p. 173.
[45] Thomas Fuller, *The Holy State* (Cambridge, 1642), p. 387.

[e]ven Machiavel, as wicked as his writings are in many things; yet asserts (as a Politician) that true Religion must above all things be regarded by those that desire to preserve themselves, and that there is no certius indicium de reip[ublica] ruina [i.e. no more certain indication of the fall of a republic] than the contempt of Religion.[46]

Machiavelli's words were therefore more valuable because of his reputation for irreligion; even someone as allegedly irreligious as himself could see that religion brought political benefits. The notion that 'even Machiavel himself could say, that the giving God his due, is the cause of the greatness of any State' was repeated throughout the seventeenth century in various forms.[47]

It was of little consequence that in these passages, Machiavelli was concerned with paganism and not Christianity because even false religions were believed to be conducive to political success. The usual explanation for this was that all religions contained some truth. As Nicholas of Cusa noted in the fifteenth century, 'all diversity' of religious practice was 'located more in rites than cultivation of the one God, whom everyone in every culture has presupposed and worshipped'.[48] In this respect, the form of worship did not matter as much as the object, which was God. This position persisted to the early modern period. Notably, in Livy's account, Numa did not invent the Roman belief system, but rather encouraged veneration towards the gods, thus although the practices were false, the belief was true and at the heart of it was perhaps a genuine attempt to engage with the deity. This explained the veneration for religion even in pagan literature. Indeed, the theologian Richard Hooker argued in his fifth book of *Ecclesiastical Polity* that 'whatsoever good effects do grow out of their Religion, who embrace instead of the true a false, the Roots thereof are certain sparks of the Light of Truth, intermingled with the darkness of Error; because no religion can wholly and onely consist of untruths', or in other words, even false religions have political benefits, because all religions contain some truth.[49]

There were two main explanations for the truth found even in pagan religions and consequently the benefits they brought. The first derives

---

[46] Joseph Hill, *The Interest of These United Provinces* (Middleburg, 1673), sig. C2r.
[47] John Hewit, *Repentance and Conversion, the Fabrick of Salvation* (London, 1658), p. 212; Hugh Blair, *Gods Soveraignity, His Sacred Majesties Supremacy, the Subjects Duty* (Glasgow, 1661), p. 9; Thomas Jackson, 'A Treatise Concerning the Singes of the Time, or Gods Forewarnings', in *Diverse Sermons: With a Short Treatise Befitting These Present Times* (Oxford, 1637), p. 11.
[48] Nicholas of Cusa, *Nicholas of Cusa on Interreligious Harmony: Text, Concordance and Translation of De Pace Fidei*, ed. and trans. James E. Biechler (Lewiston, NY, 1991), p. 62.
[49] Richard Hooker, 'Of the Laws of Ecclesiastical Polity', in *The Works of Mr. Richard Hooker* (London, 1666), p. 131.

from the long tradition of *prisca theologia* that held that the original revelation became dispersed and made its way to the pagans who received a partial and distorted version of it. The second which, as Dimitri Levitin notes became much more common in the seventeenth century, was that pagans were able to access certain aspects of religion through reason.[50] As a result, the similarities between Christianity and paganism were believed to arise from a form of natural religion, through which observers could grasp the *effects* of God, and mistakenly worshipped those. Hooker subscribed to this view of Roman religion. Describing the pagans, Hooker notes that:

> whereas we read so many of them so much commended, some for their milde and merciful disposition, some for their vertuous severity, some for integrity of life, all these were the fruits of true and infallible principles delivered unto us in the word of God, as the Axioms of our Religion, which being imprinted by the God of Nature in their hearts also, and taking better root in some them in most others, grew, though not from, yet with and amidst the heaps of manifold repugnant Errors; which Errors of corrupt Religion, had also their suitable effects in the lives of the self-same parties. Without all controversie, the purer and perfecter our Religion is, the worthier effects it hath in them, who stedfastly and sincerely embrace it, in others not.[51]

As Hooker explains here, the best qualities of virtuous pagans derive ultimately from the Christian God. Hooker's contemporaries gained this knowledge from the Word, or the Bible, while the pagans still had access to the more partial and limited form of revelation detectable in the natural world otherwise known as the 'Book of Nature'. As Hooker notes, this partial revelation is certainly not as effective as true religion, given that it is interspersed with error. However, it does explain civic virtues exhibited by certain pagans. If all goodness comes from the true God, then these virtuous pagans must have some access to the true God also.

Machiavelli's treatment of paganism was sometimes, albeit rarely, interpreted along similar lines. Leuytt defended Machiavelli, and his translation on this basis, arguing that Machiavelli praised paganism because 'as a bad government is to be preferred before licentiousness... so superstition is better than Atheisme, for there is no gouernment but holdeth somewhat of good order, so there is no religion that participateth somewhat of truth'.[52]

---

[50] See Dmitri Levitin, 'From Sacred History to the History of Religion: Paganism, Judaism, and Christianity in European Historiography from Reformation to "Enlightenment"', *The Historical Journal*, 55:4 (2012), 1117–60.
[51] Hooker, 'Of the Laws of Ecclesiastical Polity', p. 131.
[52] BL Additional MS 41162, fol. 1v.

Such an argument, Leuytt maintains, 'most part of the wiser sorte haue always affirmed' and this is certainly true of Hooker.[53]

Such an interpretation of pagan religion did not necessarily release Machiavelli from blame. Crucially, Hooker distinguishes his position from the advocates of 'politick use of religion', objecting that 'when they should define what means are best for that purpose, behold, they extol the wisdom of Paganism'.[54] Hooker appears to be referring to Machiavelli here, objecting that 'they give it out as a mystical precept of great importance, that Princes, and such as are under them in most authority or credit with the people, should take all occasions of rare events, and from what cause soever the same do proceed' and to 'for the strengthening of their States, to maintain Religion, and for the maintenance of Religion, not to make choice of that which is true', both of which have a parallel in the *Discourses*.[55]

To some extent, Hooker's criticism are fair; as I have demonstrated above, Machiavelli does extoll the benefits of the 'noble lie' and he makes no concession to the notion that the truth of a religion might add to the political benefits that it brings. Yet there is room even in Machiavelli's work for the notion that the benefits of pagan religion come from God. Machiavelli also refers to the pagans as if they too venerated the one true God even if their religious practices were misguided. Indeed, he noted that Numa 'established [Roman religious practices] in such a way that for many ages there was never so much fear of God [Dio] as in that republic'.[56] As he argues, also in relation to Numa, 'truly no one who did not have recourse to God [Dio] ever gave to a people unusual laws, because without that they would not be accepted'.[57] Although his pagan example feigned a religious experience, Machiavelli still treats him as if he turned to God in order to innovate in the state.

Whether or not readers were alive to the nuances of Machiavelli's religion, he helpfully provided ample criticism of the church of his day. Without doubt, he considered the church of his time to be woefully inadequate for political, and perhaps even religious reasons too. I.12 points to this fact in its very title: 'how important it is to take account of religion, and how Italy, having been without it because of the Roman Church, is ruined'.[58] As Machiavelli states, 'those peoples who are nearest to the Roman Church,

---

[53] *Ibid.*
[54] Hooker, 'Of the Laws of Ecclesiastical Polity', p. 133. Also see Machiavelli, 'Discourses', p. 227.
[55] *Ibid.*, p. 133.
[56] Machiavelli, 'Discourses', p. 224.
[57] *Ibid.*, p. 225.
[58] *Ibid.*, p. 226.

the head of our religion, have least religion'.[59] It is clear that despite the religious ceremonies and institutions the contemporary Roman Church upheld, what it lacked was the veneration towards God, (although in a misguided way) that was central to Rome's success.

This material was a gift to Protestant readers who were able to turn Machiavelli's criticism of the church of his day into condemnation of the Catholic Church of their own time. For example, clergyman Robert South argued in a sermon printed in 1660 that:

> Machiavel himself, in his Animadversions upon Livy, makes it appear, that the Weaknesse of Italy, which was once so strong, was caused by the corrupt practises of the Papacy, in depraving, and misusing Religion to that purpose, which he, though himself a Papist, sayes could not have hapned, had the Christian Religion been kept in its first, and native simplicity.[60]

This argument came straight out of Machiavelli's argument in I.12 that princes must maintain their religion. As he goes on to say, 'he who considers its [i.e. Christianity's] foundations and sees how different its present habit is from them, will conclude that near at hand, beyond doubt, is its fall or its punishment'.[61] Machiavelli, of course, had nothing to say on Protestantism, having written the text between 1513 and 1518. In this passage, he merely addressed the practices of the church of his time rather than matters of doctrine. Yet as an English churchman, wishing to demonstrate the superiority of his faith over Catholicism, South used Machiavelli to argue that Catholics had distorted Christianity and that this was responsible for Italy's military and political failings. Even Machiavelli, who South maintained was still a Catholic, could see this. In this reading, the 'religion of this sort... in the form in which its giver founded it' that would keep 'Christian states and republics... more united, much more happy than they are' was the original form of Christianity which Protestants harked back to and from which they believed Catholicism to be a gross distortion. South thereby attributes the cause of Italy's weakness not to Christianity as a whole, but to Catholicism.

South insisted that 'the safety of Government is founded upon the truth of religion' and yet he himself uses Numa's approach to religion as a positive example elsewhere.[62] The implication here is that, as in Machiavelli's account, the Catholics were less pious than the Romans and that their religious practices lacked the political benefits and perhaps even

---

[59] Ibid., p. 228.
[60] Robert South, *Interest Deposed, and Truth Restored, or, A Word in Season, Delivered in Two Sermons* (Oxford, 1660), p. 10.
[61] Machiavelli, 'Discourses', pp. 226, 228.
[62] South, *Interest Deposed*, pp. 12, 20.

the modicum of truth that Roman paganism possessed. Catholicism, in this account, simply weakens the state by harming religion.

Machiavelli, republicanism, and civil religion:
Nicholas Machiavel's Letter to Zanobius Buondelmontius in Vindication of himself and His Writings

Having explored some of the ways in which readers responded to Machiavelli's civil religion, it now remains to address Neville's spurious letter. Unlike the authors already discussed, Neville was not hostile to Catholics, though he agreed that Catholicism was a false religion and wholly unsuited to the business of statecraft.[63] As I have indicated in the introduction, his main concern was the clergy, which he considered a remnant of Catholic and even Jewish superstition. It was they who prevented effective republican government. Following Harrington, who wrote of the 'Antipathy, which is between a Clergy and a Popular Government, and of that simpathy which is between the Mitre and the Crown', the 'Letter' argues that the clergy have an interest in supporting monarchy and preventing republicanism, that 'these men by the Bishop of Rome's help, have crept into all the Governments in Christendom, where there is any mixture of Monarchy, and made themselves a third estate'.[64]

The 'Letter' provides the kind of account of Machiavelli's own personal political views and his thoughts on salvation that is missing from his works, albeit an entirely false one. For those who, despite all the evidence to the contrary, were convinced of its authenticity, it silenced doubts as to Machiavelli's piety. Neville's 'Machiavel' exemplifies the doctrine of *sola scriptura*, providing the kind of exegesis of which many a protestant anticlericalist would be proud. As he states, eschewing Catholic tradition, he is 'fully persuaded, that all Divine verities, which God then designed to teach the world, are contained in the Books of Holy Scripture, as they are now extant and received amongst us'.[65] For this reason, he rejects purgatory, the veneration of saints' icons, prayers to the cross, the Inquisition, the authority of the pope, and fish days, and crucially, the 'most Hellish of all the innovations brought in by the Popes, which is the Clergy'.[66] He provides a Biblical reason for republicanism, arguing that 'God himself never made but one Government for men, that this Government was a Common-wealth

---

[63] On Neville's attitude to Catholics and Catholicism, see Gaby Mahlberg, 'Henry Neville and the Toleration of Catholics during the Exclusion Crisis', *Historical Research*, 83:222 (2010), 617–34.
[64] James Harrington, *The Prerogative of Popular Government*, book II (London, 1658), p. 83. Neville, 'Letter', sig. **2r.
[65] Neville, 'Letter', sig. **r.
[66] *Ibid.*, sig. **r.

(wherein the Sanhadrim or Senate, and the Congregation or popular Assembly had their share) and that he manifested his high displeasure when the rebellious people would turn it into a Monarchy'.[67]

Neville invented a great deal in the 'Letter', then, but other aspects derive heavily upon and refer back to Machiavelli's works. Neville has 'Machiavel' argue that the Catholic Church threatened both good government and true religion, making him state that 'I have very frequently in my Writings, laid the blame upon the Church of Rome, not only for all the misgovernment of Christendom; but even for the depravation and almost total destruction of Christian Religion'.[68] As I have already demonstrated, there was a great deal of material in Machiavelli's works and the *Discourses* in particular that could be, and was, read as evidence against the Catholic Church.

Other parts of the 'Letter' draw on more specific parts of the *Discourses*. Like the real Machiavelli, in the 'Letter', 'Machiavel' contrasts the version of Christianity practised by his contemporaries unfavourably with the religion of the pagans, noting that:

> whereas all other false worships have been set up by some politick Legislators, for the support and preservation of Government, this false, this spurious Religion brought in upon the ruines of Christianity by the Popes, hath deformed the face of Government in Europe, destroying all the good principles, and Morality left us by the Heathens themselves, and introduced instead thereof, Sordid, Cowardly, and impolitick Notions, whereby they have subjected Mankind, and even great Princes and States, to their own Empire, and never suffered any Orders of Maxims to take place where they have power, that might make a Nation Wise, Honest, Great or Wealthy.[69]

This passage interprets Machiavelli's criticisms to refer specifically to the actions of the papacy and the priests they inspired. According to this account, Catholicism is an exception to the notion that even false religion brings some good, because it does precisely the opposite, harming the state instead of supporting it by pursuing the interest of the papacy instead of the common good. The popes have therefore not, according to 'Machiavel' used their power to reinforce good behaviour, as these false religions did, but only their own empire. They are the atheists who use religion for their personal benefit. Whereas these pagans had set up false religions for the benefit of the state, the Catholics had destroyed everything good that they left them, a heinous crime indeed when one considers the early modern veneration of Rome. This has left princes and states weak. Neville implies that the papacy has kept princes and states cowardly in order that it can subjugate

[67] *Ibid.*, sig. *2v.
[68] *Ibid.*, sig. **r.
[69] *Ibid.*, sig. **r.

them. This recalls I.12 of the *Discourses* where Machiavelli discusses how the church's domination has caused Italy's divisions, that '[s]ince the Church has not been powerful enough to take possession of Italy and has not permitted any other to possess it, she is the cause why the land has been unable to unite under one head' as well as chapter three of *The Prince* where Machiavelli discusses how the King of France was ruined by the church, and that 'the French know nothing of politics, because if they knew anything, they would not let the Church attain such strength'.[70] In this respect, it vindicates him from accusations that he was anti-Christian. According to the 'Letter', his target was much more specific.

The reference to these 'Cowardly' notions also recalls Machiavelli's criticism of Christian passivity in II.2. The 'Letter' thereby interprets Machiavelli's criticisms of the church as criticisms of the papacy. The translator of the rest of the book, a figure known only as J. B., makes his views on II.2 much more explicit than Neville. His translation of the passage from II.2 quoted above is as follows:

> So that it seems to me, this way of living, so contrary to the ancients; has rendred the Christians more weak and effeminate; and left them as a prey to those who are more wicked, and may order them as they please, the most part of them thinking more of Paradise than Preferment, and of enduring than revenging of injuries; as if Heaven was to be won rather by idleness than arms: but that explication of our Religion is erroneous, and they who made it were poor and pusillanimous, and more given to their case than any thing that was great: for if the Christian Religion allows us to defend and exalt our Country, it allows us certainly to love it, and honour it, and prepare our selves so as we may be able to defend it.[71]

It is quite clear from this that J. B.'s version of Machiavelli blames the church of his time for the problems faced by Christian states rather than the religion itself. The criticism of those that behave 'as if Heaven was to be won rather by idleness than arms' suggests that heaven can indeed be won militarily. The comment that 'that explication of our Religion is erroneous' is J. B.'s addition and drives home the point that Christianity is indeed a militaristic religion and not a passive one much more explicitly than in the original. Machiavelli blames the 'worthlessness of men' for this eventuality, suggesting that men are prone to such a lazy interpretation of their religion, but J. B.'s translation implies that it was particular men who made this interpretation that others now follow. This passage is indicative of the way in which the translation obliterates much of the ambiguity of Machiavelli's

---

[70] Machiavelli, 'Discourses', p. 229; Niccolò Machiavelli, 'Prince', in *The Chief Works*, vol. I, p. 20.
[71] Machiavelli, 'Discourses upon Livy', in *The Works of the Famous Nicolas Machiavel, Citizen and Secretary of Florence*, trans. J. B. (London, 1675), p. 365.

writing. If one only knew Machiavelli from this translation, there would be little doubt that he is a Christian.

'Machiavel' associates pagan vigour with piety once again when he argues that in order to do good, one must 'extirpate this cursed and apostate race [i.e. priests] out of the world' and thereby 'restore the good policy (I had almost said with my Author Livy the sanctity too) of the Heathens, with all their valour, and other glorious endowments'.[72] He thereby implies that priests stifle the civic virtues of the pagans, including their veneration towards God.

Reinforcing Machiavelli's status as a proto-Protestant in favour of reform, 'Machiavel' even suggests that the Reformation was inevitable, expressing admiration of 'that bold Fryer, who the very same year in which I prophesied that the Scourge of the Church was not far off, began to thunder against their Indulgences, and since hath question'd many Tenents long received and impos'd upon the World'.[73] This is evidently intended to refer to Martin Luther who produced his *Ninety-five Theses* in 1517, when Machiavelli may have written the *Discourses*. The 'Letter' thereby implies that Machiavelli predicted the Reformation in that text. Machiavelli did indeed state in I.12 of that book the Church was so corrupt that 'he who considers its foundations and sees how different its present habit is from them, will conclude that near at hand, beyond doubt, is its fall or its punishment'.[74] In any case, the interpretation of this ruin or punishment as the Reformation was one reading that was relatively believable. Indeed, even Machiavelli's eighteenth-century translator, Ellis Farneworth, who otherwise thought little of Neville's *Letter* and J. B.'s translation, agreed with it. As he noted on the same passage in his translation of the *Discourses*, 'Machiavel seems here to have had the Spirit of prophecy upon him, and to have foretold the Reformation which happened not long after in Christendom'.[75] The fact that Machiavelli appeared to be correct in this prophecy might lead one to consider his other 'prophesies': in particular, his argument that failure to extirpate the clergy will allow them to spread their corruption.[76] Not only was the clergy responsible for Italy's weakness, then, according to this reading, but priests had actually brought the Reformation upon themselves as a form of divine punishment.

Whereas English churchmen used Machiavelli to bolster their criticisms of foreign politics and religion, 'Machiavel' directs the readers to think about the clergy rather than an external enemy or oppressed minority. This was

---

[72] Neville, 'Letter', sig. **2v.
[73] Ibid., sig. **2r.
[74] Machiavelli, 'Discourses', p. 228.
[75] Elias Farneworth, note on Discourses in *The Works of Nicholas Machiavel, Secretary of State to the Republic of Florence*, ed. and trans. by Elias Farneworth (London, 1762), II, p. 42.
[76] *Letter*, sig. **3r.

because unlike these other authors, Neville's objection was not the Catholic faith, but rather the meddling of the church in state matters. Neville and his coreligionists held that no one should be elevated to a position of superiority in religion because the truth should be apparent to all, thus there should be no priests to meddle in state affairs, but rather, all magistrates should make their decisions on the basis of religious truth. That was the way to ensure true religion and thus effective governance.

Conclusion

When viewed in the context of Machiavelli's reception in Britain, then, the 'Letter' is not quite so absurd as it might initially seem but belongs to a long tradition of reading Machiavelli as a critic of the Catholic Church. Certain aspects of the text remain rather dubious. The real Machiavelli never showed as much attention to the Bible in his writing as the fictional 'Machiavel' and the kind of exegesis Neville attributes to him here is entirely fanciful, as is the effusive praise of Cosimo de' Medici that we find at the end of the text.[77] Most of Neville's predecessors took a far more nuanced approach to Machiavelli and even Harrington, who rivalled Neville in his admiration for Machiavelli, acknowledged that in places Machiavelli was 'justly reprovable'.[78]

Yet it is still possible that Neville and Starkey considered this reading to be consistent with Machiavelli's thinking. As I have shown here, Neville does indeed draw heavily upon Machiavelli's writing within the 'Letter' to make the point that priests had distorted religion to the detriment of both the soul and the state. In addition, many of its arguments are consistent with Neville's own interpretation of Machiavelli expressed elsewhere. Neville spoke of Machiavelli in the highest possible terms, as 'Divine' in his other work too and despite his own exceptional sympathy for Catholics themselves, he showed that religion to have some of the same problems that he describes in the 'Letter', noting that the Catholic 'is not yet *Master* of his own *Faith*, having given it up to his *Church*'.[79]

The 'Letter' was indeed considered to be a believable interpretation of Machiavelli's work in the seventeenth century and as a result contributed to interpretations of Machiavelli's civil religion. While the text certainly met with a mixed reception, it was in some quarters read as genuine. The London-based French bibliophile, Jean Cornand de Lacroze notes that a friend of his 'extreamly wonder'd at [de Lacroze's] Asserting the Truth of this Paper [the *Letter*], adding withal, that there hardly was any Man

---

[77] Neville, 'Letter', sig. **4r.
[78] James Harrington, *The Common-Wealth of Oceana* (London, 1656), p. 143.
[79] Neville, 'Letter', p. 107; Neville, *Plato Redivivus*, pp. 21, 46, 124.

of Sense, but held it for a Forgery', but he himself believed it to be the Florentine's own work, marvelling that 'so great a Man as *Machiavel* should have defended the Protestant Faith at the same time as *Luther*', though de Lacroze's focus was on its criticism of Catholicism, as it was for many of its readers.[80] Elsewhere, it was cited as if it had indeed been written by Machiavelli. John Robertson, a Quaker, wrote in his objection to priests that '(as Machiavel tells us) they have been now for more than a thousand years forming and setting up an interest, distinct and separate from all the rest of Mankind'.[81] The real Machiavelli never mentioned priestcraft; this came straight from the *Letter*.

The 'Letter' reflects common readings of Machiavelli's works, then, but it is also symptomatic of the diversity of responses to Machiavelli in early modern Britain. To many of his readers, Machiavelli was at once an atheist and a proponent of the idea that religion was good for the state. These views are even sometimes found in the same works. Yet as I have shown here, the reception of Machiavelli's civil religion in early modern Britain was therefore a complex matter, depending almost as much on the political stance of the reader as on the content of the texts.

---

[80] Jean Cornand de Lacroze, 'Book Review', *The Works of the Learned: Or, An Historical Accounted and Impartial Judgment of Books Newly Printed, Both Foreign and Domestick, as Also the State of Learning in the World* 7 (February 1692), p. 282.

[81] John Robertson, *Rusticus Ad Clericum, or, The Plow-Man Rebuking the Priest* (Aberdeen, 1694), 6 paraphrasing 'Letter' sig. **2r.

5

Republicans and Independents: Debating 'National Religion' in Cromwellian England

John Coffey

In the political debates of the 1650s, the term 'civil religion' is conspicuous by its absence. On the few occasions when the phrase was used, it stood for a superficial, formal religion, the opposite of godly, heart religion. In a posthumously published sermon by the early Stuart Puritan, Samuel Crook, Roman 'civil Religion' was contrasted with Christianity:

> Saint *Augustine* sheweth out of *Varro*, that among the ancient *Romans* there was a *civil theologie*, that is, a Religion accommodate to the *City*, and to which the Citizens were to conform themselves; so where there is good government, it produceth in the greatest number a kinde of *civil Religion*, or *Religion of civility*, which being entertained without the power of godlinesse, giveth definition to our *Civil* hypocrite.[1]

Puritans, 'the hotter sort of Protestant', were not content with 'civil Religion' of this kind, 'having a form of godliness, but denying the power thereof'.[2] They were wary of a 'heathen' or 'pagan' politics 'fetch'd from Athens' or from Rome and based on 'meerly Natural' principles.[3] Their own ideal of civic reformation drew on both the Christian civic humanism of Erasmus and the model of Reformed city states in Geneva and Zurich.[4] Most wanted the nation's public religion to be an earnest evangelical Protestantism, bolstered and enforced by godly magistrates.[5] But external enforcement was

---

[1] Samuel Crook, *Ta Diapheronta, or, Divine Characters* (1658). The original sermon was preached in 1615.
[2] The biblical reference was 2 Timothy 3:5, a key text in the case against 'formal', or 'external' religion.
[3] Note the godly critique of Harringtonian republicanism discussed in Ruth Mayer, *1659: The Crisis of the Commonwealth* (Woodbridge, 2004), pp. 219–23.
[4] See Margo Todd, *Christian Humanism and the Puritan Social Order* (Cambridge, 1988).
[5] On Puritan attempts to instantiate godly rule see Patrick Collinson, *The Religion of Protestants: The Church in English Society, 1559–1625* (Oxford, 1982), chapter 4:

in tension with the Puritan emphasis on personal, inward conversion.[6] The premium placed on sincerity and interiority fostered voluntary religion and produced what later came to be known as 'the voluntary principle', the idea that individuals should be free to choose their religion for themselves.[7] For radical Puritans (a distinct minority) this principle called into question the very concept of 'State Religion', a term they employed with contempt.

James Harrington did not write of 'civil religion', or of the 'national church', and he avoided the pejorative term 'state religion'. Instead, he talked in more neutral terms of 'national religion', participating in the heated debate about the nation's religious settlement. The classical republicans of the 1650s are often placed in dialogue with canonical figures in the history of early modern political thought: Niccolò Machiavelli and Jean-Jacques Rousseau, Thomas Hobbes, and John Locke. Yet during England's republican decade, Marchamont Nedham, and James Harrington had to define English republicanism in relation to English Puritanism, especially the political theologies of the Independents.

This chapter reexamines rival accounts of 'national religion' developed by Independents, republicans, and republican Independents in the English Revolution. It begins by explaining the deep divisions among religious Independents over the principle of religious establishment. The Presbyterian ideal of religious uniformity had been shattered by the triumph of the Independents in 1648–9. The Independents, however, were not of one mind. The dominant faction, close to Cromwell throughout the 1650s, were the 'magisterial' Independents, firm believers in the need for a 'public profession' of national religion. Their project was under almost constant fire from a loose grouping of radical Independents, who denied the magistrate's powers in matters of religion and advocated a separation of church and state. Some of these figures, notably John Milton and Sir Henry Vane the Younger, developed explicitly republican political theories, and are sometimes known as 'godly republicans'.[8]

'Magistracy and Ministry'; David Underdown, *Fire from Heaven: Life in an English Town in the Seventeenth Century* (London, 1992); Bernard Capp, *England's Culture Wars: Puritan Reformation and its Enemies in the Interregnum, 1649–1660* (Oxford, 2012).

[6] Augustine himself had sought to resolve this tension in his letters on the Donatist controversy, arguing that while religious coercion could not directly convert, it could force the recalcitrant to attend catholic worship, listen to sermons, and reconsider. See Mark Goldie, 'The Theory of Religious Intolerance in Restoration England', in *From Persecution to Toleration*, eds O. P. Grell, Jonathan Israel, and Nicholas Tyacke (Oxford, 1991), pp. 331–68.

[7] Collinson, *The Religion of Protestants*, chapter 6: 'Voluntary Religion'; Geoffrey Nuttall, *Visible Saints: The Congregational Way, 1640–1660* (Oxford, 1957), chapter 3.

[8] Twentieth-century scholars referred only occasionally to 'godly republicans', but the term has taken hold in the twenty-first century. See Michael Winship, 'Godly Republicanism and the Origins of the Massachusetts Polity', *William and Mary Quarterly*, 63 (2006), 427–62; Michael Winship, *Godly Republicanism: Puritans, Pilgrims and a City*

After surveying the views of religious Independents, the chapter will turn to Marchamont Nedham and James Harrington, showing how each sought in quite different ways to navigate between these rival Independent camps. The standoff between radical and magisterial Independents created openings and problems for these classical republicans. While they could exploit the internal tensions among Independents, neither faction was a natural partner. The conservative Independents were still wedded to the magisterial Reformation ideal of state-enforced religious orthodoxy, and this implied a continuing role for the clergy as arbiters of doctrinal correctness. Radical Independents, by contrast, questioned the very notion of a religious establishment: their demand that the link between church and state should be 'severd' ran against the classical republican ideal of civic religion and risked opening the door to further chaos and division. Intellectually and politically, Nedham and Harrington were caught on the horns of a dilemma in the 1650s. In positioning themselves vis-à-vis the magisterial and the radical factions, they took different approaches.

I

We will begin our discussion with the magisterial Independents, for it was these conservative Congregationalists who crafted the religious settlement of the 1650s. After Henry Jacob, the chief theoreticians of Congregational ecclesiology were Puritan clergy in exile: William Ames, Thomas Goodwin, and Philip Nye in the Netherlands; John Cotton in Massachusetts.[9] Goodwin and Nye returned to England in the early 1640s, and as 'Dissenting Brethren' in the Westminster Assembly fought a rearguard action against the Presbyterian majority.[10] Outside the Assembly, they were soon joined by the brilliant young theologian John Owen who became Cromwell's chaplain in 1649–50.[11]

---

on a Hill (Cambridge, MA, 2012); Feisal G. Mohammed, 'Milton, Sir Henry Vane, and the Brief but Significant Life of Godly Republicanism', *Huntington Library Quarterly*, 76 (2013), 83–104. Winship is primarily concerned with the magisterial Independents, Mohammed with the radical Independents.

[9] See Winship, *Godly Republicanism*. On Jacob, see Polly Ha, with Jonathan D. Moore and Edda Frankot (eds), *The Puritans on Independence* (Oxford, 2017); on Ames, see Keith Sprunger, *The Learned Doctor William Ames* (Urbana, IL, 1972); for Cotton, the best place to start is with Sargent Bush Jr. (ed.), *The Correspondence of John Cotton* (Chapel Hill, NC, 2001).

[10] See Hunter Powell, *The Crisis of British Protestantism: Church Power in the Puritan Revolution, 1638–44* (Manchester, 2015). Powell's emphasis on the complexity of ecclesiastical politics is reinforced in Elliot Vernon's major new study of the Presbyterians: *London Presbyterians and the British Revolutions, 1638-1664* (Manchester, 2021).

[11] There is now a large and growing literature on Owen. The best starting point is Crawford Gribben, *John Owen and English Puritanism: Experiences of Defeat* (New York,

In Massachusetts Bay, it became clear that Congregationalism was compatible with magisterial Reformation.[12] Access to the sacrament of communion was restricted to devout Puritans ('visible saints'), and the franchise restricted to church members, creating a distinct kind of 'godly rule'. Cotton advocated the implementation of elements of the Mosaic judicial law, and he endorsed the use of civil penalties against heretics and schismatics, such as the antinomians or Roger Williams, banished from the colony in the mid-1630s. Finally, Massachusetts preserved something akin to a system of parish churches: in many villages and towns, a single church functioned as the de facto parish church, with the whole population expected to attend public worship, though only a minority were communicant members. Unity and purity were held in tension as New England Puritans sought to proclaim the Calvinist gospel to the whole population while gathering a godly minority for eucharistic fellowship.

In England, under Commonwealth and Protectorate, the magisterial Independents sought to construct a different sort of religious establishment.[13] The so-called Toleration Act of 1650 had abolished compulsory attendance at parish churches, replacing an all-inclusive national church with a dual system of parish and gathered churches. Sunday worship was required, but it could be either at 'some public place' or 'some other place'.[14] Tithes were retained to support the parish ministry, but this provoked protests from various Baptists, Quakers, and Fifth Monarchists, complaints that rose to a crescendo during the Nominated Assembly (or 'Parliament of the Saints') in 1653.[15] The magisterial Independents resisted such clamours. Owen was appointed Vice-Chancellor of Oxford University in 1652 and – along with Goodwin and Nye – played a key role in forging the new religious settlement.[16] In March 1657, when Marchamont Nedham met

---

2016). For his conflicted views on toleration see John Coffey, 'John Owen and the Puritan Toleration Controversy, 1646–59', in *The Ashgate Research Companion to John Owen's Theology*, eds Kelly Kapic and Mark Jones (Farnham, 2012), chapter 14.

[12] For what follows see David D. Hall, *A Reforming People: Puritanism and the Transformation of Public Life in New England* (Chapel Hill, NC, 2012), chapter 3: 'Godly Rule'; and Francis Bremer, 'Dissent in New England', in *The Oxford History of Protestant Dissenting Traditions, vol. I: The Post-Reformation Era, c. 1559–1689*, ed. John Coffey (Oxford, 2020), chapter 7.

[13] See Sarah G. Cook, 'The Congregational Independents and the Cromwellian Constitutions', *Church History*, 46 (1977), 335–57.

[14] S. R. Gardiner (ed.), *The Constitutional Documents of the Puritan Revolution, 1625–1660* (Oxford, 1889), pp. 391–4.

[15] On tithes, see Margaret James, 'The Political Importance of the Tithes Controversy in the English Revolution, 1640–1660', *History*, 26 (1941), 1–18; Barry Reay, 'Quaker Opposition to Tithes, 1652–60', *Past and Present*, 86 (1980), 98–120.

[16] On Owen's troubled term as Vice-Chancellor, see the magisterial study of Cromwellian Oxford in Blair Worden, *God's Instruments: Political Conduct in the England of Oliver Cromwell* (Oxford, 2012), chapter 4.

Oliver Cromwell in Goodwin's lodgings at Whitehall, the journalist told the Protector the talk of the town: '*vox populi* said Mr. Nye should be Archbishop of Canterbury, and Dr. Owen of York'.[17]

In reality, as architects of the Cromwellian religious settlement, Owen and Nye were reluctant even to speak of a 'national church'. Historians have written confidently of 'the Cromwellian Church',[18] but as Matthew Bingham has emphasised, the Congregational Way was more radical in theory than is often recognised. It defined a church as a voluntary local congregation composed of 'visible saints' (i.e., the godly), and as self-governing and independent, not subject to the jurisdiction of Presbyterian assemblies, episcopal courts or the impositions of magistrates. This was a *jure divino* ecclesiology drawn from the New Testament, especially the pastoral epistles addressed to Timothy and Titus. And since church polity (on this view) was something prescribed by Scripture, it was not among the *adiaphora* (things indifferent) determined by Christian magistrates. Moreover, as Bingham observes, Congregational ecclesiology challenged 'not just the Church of England but the basic logic of Christendom itself'. By strictly defining a church as a self-governing congregation of visible saints it subverted the very idea of an all-inclusive 'national church' with authority over local churches. Congregationalists policed their language to remove references to 'national churches', which they saw as mere fictions.[19] Instead, the constitutional documents of the 1650s spoke of 'the public profession of these nations'. The magistrate could govern the public profession, acting as patron of the public (parish) ministry, but he had no such jurisdiction over gathered independent churches, who chose their own pastors and governed their own affairs.

Yet the magisterial Congregationalists were not willing to abandon Christendom altogether. Although the New Testament is as innocent of Christian magistrates as of national churches, Congregationalists found justifications for state religion elsewhere. The Old Testament, they noted, had not just praised godly kings and queens, it had prophesied that rulers would become 'your nursing fathers'.[20] And they suggested that the religious

---

[17] *Calendar of State Papers Domestic* (1656-57), p. 318.
[18] See for example, Clare Cross, 'The Church in England, 1646-1660', in *The Interregnum*, ed. Gerald Aylmer (London, 1972), pp. 99-120; Jeffrey Collins, 'The Church Settlement of Oliver Cromwell', *History*, 87 (2002), pp. 18-40; Ann Hughes, '"The Public Profession of these Nations": The National Church in Interregnum England', in *Religion in Revolutionary England*, eds Christopher Durston and Judith Maltby (Manchester, 2006), chapter 4. Anthony Milton provides a rationale for the term in his landmark study, *England's Second Reformation: The Battle for the Church of England, 1625-1662* (Cambridge, 2021), chapter 10.
[19] Matthew Bingham, 'On the Idea of a National Church: Reassessing Congregationalism in Cromwellian England', *Church History*, 88 (2019), 27-57 (quotation at 38). See also Nuttall, *Visible Saints*, pp. 64-5.
[20] The biblical proof text was Isaiah 49:23: 'kings shall be thy nursing fathers'. On Owen's endorsement and qualification of this principle see *The Works of John Owen*, 16

role of the magistrate was supported by the light of nature itself. In setting up a government, argued Philip Nye, the people had to consider 'the public weal and public good, and make a law for it, or give a power for it'.[21] Since 'religion' is of 'greatest public good and public concernment', it was legitimate for a people to 'sit down in a commonwealth to do what may be done in a lawful way for the preserving [of their religion]'.[22] The case for an established religion then, rested not only on Scripture but on natural law.

If we examine the constitutional texts of the 1650s, we can see how the Independents created a new kind of religious establishment. When Cromwell's Protectorate was created in December 1653, Independents sought to formalise a religious establishment in the new constitution, The Instrument of Government. It stipulated that 'the Christian religion' was to 'be held forth and recommended as the public profession of these nations', though to that 'public profession held forth none shall be compelled by penalties or otherwise'. There would be protection for 'such as profess faith in God by Jesus Christ', though this liberty would not be extended to 'Popery', 'Prelacy', or 'licentiousness'. 'Provision' and financial 'maintenance' would be made for a public ministry of 'able and painful teachers'.[23] A centralised body of Triers was set up to vet candidates for the parish ministry, one in which Cromwell himself was intimately involved, becoming the nation's leading ecclesiastical patron.[24]

While the establishment of the Triers was welcomed by magisterial Independents and Presbyterians, they worried about the doctrinal vagueness of the Instrument. Toleration for 'such as profess faith in Jesus Christ' seemed to open the door to anti-Trinitarians. John Owen laboured in vain to forge a national confession of faith and prescribe compulsory attendance at public worship (whether in gathered churches or parishes).[25] Conservative

---

vols (London, 1850–3), XIII, pp. 60, 401–2. It is worth noting that Owen opposed the offer of the crown to Cromwell in 1657 (see Gribben, *John Owen*, pp. 169–70).

[21] Gardiner (ed.), *Constitutional Documents*, p. 416.

[22] Philip Nye at the Whitehall Debates (December 1648) in *Puritanism and Liberty: Being the Army Debates (1647–49) from the Clarke Manuscripts*, ed. A. S. P. Woodhouse ([1938]: London, 1992), pp. 159–60. The original edition is *The Clarke Papers: Selections from the Papers of William Clarke, I-II*, ed. C. H. Firth ([1891, 1894], London, 1992), II, p. 119. Nye's thought has received much less attention than Owen's, and the main study focusses on his Restoration writings: D. Nobbs, 'Philip Nye on Church and State', *Cambridge Historical Journal*, 5 (1935), 41–59.

[23] Gardiner (ed.), *Constitutional Documents*, p. 416.

[24] On the Triers and Ejectors, see Collins, 'The Church Settlement of Oliver Cromwell'; and Rebecca Warren, 'The Ecclesiastical Patronage of Oliver Cromwell, c. 1654–1660', in *Church and People in Interregnum Britain*, ed. Fiona McCall (London, 2021), pp. 65–86.

[25] See Ryan Kelly, 'Reformed or Reforming? John Owen and the Complexity of Theological Codification for Mid-Seventeenth-Century England', in *The Ashgate Research Companion to John Owen's Theology*, eds Kapic and Jones, pp. 3–30; Manfred Svensson, 'John Owen and John Locke: Confessionalism, Doctrinal Minimalism, and Toleration', *History of European Ideas*, 43 (2017), 302–16; Hunter Powell, 'Cromwellian Calvinism:

Puritans agitated successfully for the prosecution of heretics: the Socinian John Biddle was exiled, and the Quaker James Nayler whipped, branded, and imprisoned – measures approved by conservative Independents as well as Presbyterians.[26] When a new constitution, The Humble Petition and Advice, was drawn up in 1657, it restricted toleration to 'such who profess faith in God the Father, and in Jesus Christ His eternal Son, and true God, and in the Holy Spirit, God co-equal with the Father and the Son, one God blessed for ever'.[27] Socinian critics detected the hand of 'Doctor *John Owen*' in 'the compiling and drawing up of this Proposal'.[28] The nation's religious establishment was (once again) officially Trinitarian. Cromwell, like the godly kings of Judah, was fulfilling his appointed role as a 'nursing father' to the church.

For Erastians and classical republicans, the conservative Congregationalist position was double-edged. On the one hand, Congregational divines drew clear limits to the magistrate's authority in matters of religion; it is misleading to think of the Independents as Erastians.[29] Conservative Independents were *jure divino* Congregationalists, who (like divine right Presbyterians) maintained a two-sphere theory of church and state. Churches were under the authority of Christ, and the magistrate had no right to interfere in their internal affairs or impose conformity in polity or worship. They offered magistrates a policy of 'live and let live'. As David Hall puts it, Cotton's thesis was this: 'never let the church assert any authority over the civil state, and never let the civil state dictate matters of doctrine or polity to the church'.[30] Self-governing congregations insisted on their right to excommunicate, even if the excommunicated member was a magistrate (the key point at issue for Erastus in sixteenth-century Zurich).[31] And Owen and his clerical colleagues expected Calvinist divines to have a major role in defining the 'fundamentals' or orthodox doctrine of the nation's religious settlement.

On the other hand, by redefining the visible, institutional church as local, private, voluntary, and select, the Congregationalists made the church

---

England's Church and the End of the Puritan Revolution', in *The Oxford Handbook of Calvin and Calvinism*, eds Bruce Gordon and Carl Trueman (Oxford, 2021), chapter 21.

[26] Aviku Zakai, 'Religious Toleration and its Enemies: the Independent Divines and the Issue of Toleration during the English Civil War', *Albion*, 21 (1989), 1–33; Leo Damrosch, *The Sorrows of the Quaker Jesus: James Nayler and the Puritan Crackdown on the Free Spirit* (Cambridge, MA, 1996).

[27] Gardiner (ed.), *Constitutional Documents*, p. 454.

[28] [John Croope?], *Panarmonia. Or the Agreement of the People* (1659), pp. 30–1.

[29] Contra Jeffrey R. Collins, *The Allegiance of Thomas Hobbes* (Oxford, 2005), chapters 3–6. On this point see Johann Sommerville, 'Hobbes and Independency', *Rivista di Storia della Filosofia*, 59 (2004), 155–73.

[30] Hall, *A Reforming People*, p. 110.

[31] See the classic article by J. N. Figgis, 'Erastus and Erastianism', *Journal of Theological Studies*, 2 (1900), 66–101.

less threatening to the state. Shrunk to the size of local congregations, the institutional church was no longer a national political body governed by authoritative ecclesiastical courts or an episcopal hierarchy. Congregational ecclesiology removed the menace conjured by *jure divino* Presbyterians and Prelatists: a national clericalist church to rival the state. The Triers were not church officers, but government officials. This, at least, was music to an Erastian's ears, and the magisterial Independents recognised the authority of rulers to establish and police the public profession of religion.

II

There was, of course, another wing of the Independent coalition, more iconoclastic in its approach to the question of state religion. In a series of provocative pamphlets in 1644, Roger Williams, Henry Robinson, John Goodwin, William Walwyn, Richard Overton, and John Milton confronted the magisterial Reformation conception of the magistrate as one who should wield the sword in defence of religious orthodoxy. In stark contrast to Cotton and the Dissenting Brethren, these writers ruled out the use of religious coercion against heretics.[32]

It is here that we begin to encounter the Independent critique of 'State Religion'. Williams, Robinson, and Goodwin each used the term in the 1640s, as they opposed Presbyterian plans for religious uniformity, and it was deployed again in the 1650s against magisterial Independency by Williams, Goodwin, George Fox, and ultimately Milton. According to Williams, 'State Religion' was 'a denyall of Christ', for it turned Christianity into something merely 'civill and Politicall'; indeed, it was a mark of Antichrist, for the early Christian martyrs had been persecuted by a 'Nationall or State Religion'.[33] 'State Religion' implied Machiavellianism.[34] It stole from the church and gave to the state. It was formal, external, enforced; the opposite of authentic true religion: sincere, personal, and free.

The radical Independents (and we can include the Levellers in this faction) were agreed that the magistrate had no authority to enforce orthodoxy or punish heresy.[35] Yet there was some confusion among them over the legitimacy of a religious establishment. All shared the Congregationalist belief that there was no such thing as a 'National Church'. Believers should

---

[32] See John Coffey, 'Puritanism and Liberty Revisited: The Case Toleration in the English Revolution', *Historical Journal*, 41 (1998), 961–85; Rainer Forst, *Toleration in Conflict: Past and Present* (Cambridge, 2003), pp. 175–86.

[33] Roger Williams, *The Bloudy Tenent of Persecution* (1644), pp. 18, 39, 57, 58; *The Bloudy Tenent Yet More Bloudy* (1652), pp. 7, 23, 90, 120, 131, 262.

[34] Williams, *The Bloudy Tenent Yet More Bloudy*, p. 189.

[35] See Rachel Foxley, *The Levellers: Radical Political Thought in the English Revolution* (Manchester, 2013), chapter 4.

be free to leave the parishes and join themselves with gathered churches. But what about a religious establishment that recognised liberty of conscience – was this permissible?

Roger Williams thought not. He launched a sustained polemic against state religion of any kind. The Reformers had called their nations 'new Israels', but Williams insisted that Old Testament Israel was 'no patterne nor precedent' for Christians. The enforcers of religious uniformity could not legitimate their practice by appeal to biblical kings. After Christ, there was only one new Israel – the Christian Church. As for civil states, 'all Nations are meerly civill'.[36] The magistrate had no religious function beyond protecting peaceable believers of different faiths. He was to protect the bodies and goods of men but had no responsibility for their souls.

The Levellers took inspiration from Williams, but in the first Agreement of the People (which was not a purely Leveller document), 'the publike way of instructing the Nation (so it be not compulsive)' was 'referred' to the 'discretion' of the magistrates.[37] This was reinforced in the second Agreement: 'the instruction or directing of the Nation in a public way, for the matters of Faith, Worship or Discipline (so it be not compulsive, or expresse Popery) is referred to their discretion'.[38] By contrast, the third 'Agreement of the Free People of England' (1649), the most Leveller of the three texts, issued in the name of John Lilburne, William Walwyn, Thomas Prince, and Richard Overton, included no reference to 'public' or 'national' religion, thus raising the question of whether any such establishment was necessary or legitimate; the document repudiated tithes and devolved the choice and payment of pastors to 'the parishioners of every particular parish'.[39]

The radical Independents were less cohesive than the conservative or magisterial Independents. Although often dubbed 'sectarian', they were divided over ecclesiology: some were Congregationalists, others Baptists, others Seekers, and still others (like Walwyn) were close to the gathered churches without joining one. They were divided over theology: some were Calvinists, others Arminians, while others (like Milton and Overton) were attracted to the heterodox doctrine of mortalism and (in Milton's case) anti-Trinitarianism. They would divide over politics, especially over their attitudes to Oliver Cromwell. Nor were they unanimous on the limits of toleration – for Roger Williams it must be extended to 'the most *Jewish, Turkish, Paganish* and *Popish consciences* and *worships*'.[40] Milton, by contrast,

---

[36] [Roger Williams], *The Bloudy Tenent of Persecution* (1644), sig. a2v, pp. 80, 104, 184–85.
[37] *Leveller Manifestoes of the Puritan Revolution*, ed. Don M. Wolfe (New York, 1944), p. 227. On the different *Agreements* and their authorship, see *The Agreements of the People, the Levellers and the Constitutional Crisis of the English Revolution*, eds Philip Baker and Elliot Vernon (Basingstoke, 2012), pp. 2–9.
[38] *Leveller Manifestoes*, p. 300.
[39] *Leveller Manifestoes*, p. 408.
[40] [Williams], *Bloudy Tenent*, sig. a2r.

excluded Roman Catholics from toleration on three grounds: (i) 'poperie' was not so much a religion, as an allegiance to 'a Roman principalitie'; (ii) poperie was a religion of 'implicit faith' not individual conscience; and (iii) popish 'idolatrie' was 'an impietie' – 'a magistrate', thought Milton, 'can hardly err in prohibiting and quite removing at least the publick and scandalous use thereof'.[41]

Nevertheless, the battle lines between the magisterial and the radical Independents were clearly drawn, and the two factions faced off in a series of encounters. John Cotton and Roger Williams swapped polemical blows from the mid-1630s to the early 1650s, and Rhode Island (a somewhat anarchic haven for Quakers and other sects) offered a stark contrast to established order of Massachusetts Bay (where Quakers were hanged for sedition after violating banishment orders).[42] In England, the main set-piece piece debate between the rival camps took place in December 1648, on the eve of the trial of Charles I, when John Goodwin, John Wildman, and Overton took on Henry Ireton and Philip Nye before the New Model Army Council at Whitehall.[43] A further clash occurred in 1652, when John Owen's 'Humble Proposals' recommended that everyone 'be required to attend the publike Preaching of the Gospel every Lord's Day', that there be a centralised national system of examiners and ejectors for the parish ministry, and that those who opposed fundamental doctrines should be silenced. As 'nursing fathers', Christian magistrates had to foster the soteriological role of the church by patronising godly preachers and banning false teachers. Although this was a commonplace of the magisterial Reformation, it was now controversial. 'The Humble Proposals' provoked a storm of protest from radical Puritans like Sir Henry Vane, whom Milton praised for knowing 'the bounds' of 'spiritual power and civil, what each means/What severs each'.[44]

---

[41] John Milton, *A Treatise of Civil Power* (1659), in *Complete Prose Works of John Milton, VII: 1659–60* (New Haven, 1980), p. 254. See Thomas N. Corns, 'John Milton, Roger Williams, and the Limits of Toleration', and Andrew Hadfield, 'Milton and Catholicism', in *Milton and Toleration*, eds Sharon Achinstein and Elizabeth Sauer (Oxford, 2007), chapters 4 and 9.

[42] See Glenn A. Moots, 'John Cotton and Roger Williams', in *Great Christian Jurists in American History*, eds Daniel L. Dreisbach and Mark Hall (Cambridge, 2019), chapter 1.

[43] The debates were published in the 1890s in Firth (ed.), The *Clarke Papers*, II, pp. 71–132; and in a modernised version in Woodhouse (ed.), *Puritanism and Liberty*, pp. 125–78.

[44] John Milton, 'To Sir Henry Vane the Younger' (1652). See Carolyn Polizotto, 'The Campaign against The Humble Proposals of 1652', *Journal of Ecclesiastical History*, 38 (1987), 569–81.

III

Milton and Vane are often categorised with the godly republicans of the 1650s, a set of figures who emerged from the ranks of radical Independency.[45] Vane had jousted with conservative Congregationalists ever since he was ousted as governor of Massachusetts Bay during the Antinomian Controversy. In the 1650s, he was the most eminent statesman aligned with English republicanism.[46] As Blair Worden has noted, Milton, Algernon Sidney, and Edmund Ludlow revered Vane.[47] He was a personal friend of Williams and Milton. The godly republicans were divided by the events of 1653: some, such as Milton, had stuck with Cromwell and the Protectorate, while others (including Vane, Ludlow, Sidney and John Bradshaw) had broken with the new regime. By 1659, they were reunited in opposition to the resurgent Presbyterians.

Milton now wrote 'against Erastus, and state-tyrannie over the church'. The Jews had a 'national church' and 'their whole commonwealth was a church', but Christianity was 'delivered without the help of magistrates'. It was not part of the magistrate's role to 'settle religion' – that was up to 'particular churches'.[48] Milton lambasted the magisterial Independents for seeking 'to be Dependents on the magistrate for thir maintenance'. 'Independence and state-hire in religion', he wrote, 'can never subsist long

---

[45] For different perspectives on godly republicanism, see Jonathan Scott, *Commonwealth Principles: Republican Writing of the English Revolution* (Cambridge, 2004), chapter 2; Eric Nelson, *The Hebrew Republic: Jewish Sources and the Transformation of European Political Thought* (Cambridge, MA, 2010), chapter 1; Michael Winship, 'Algernon Sidney's Calvinist Republicanism', *Journal of British Studies*, 49 (2010), 753–73; Winship, *Godly Republicanism*; Mohammed, 'Milton, Sir Henry Vane, and the Brief but Significant Life of Godly Republicanism'; John Coffey, '"The Brand of Gentilism": Milton's Jesus and the Augustinian Critique of Pagan Kingship, 1649–71', *Milton Studies*, 48 (2014), 67–95.

[46] Scholars have written a great deal about Vane, but there is no definitive, well-rounded study of his life and thought, and among the major figures of the English Revolution, he remains one of the most elusive. On his troubled time in Massachusetts Bay, see Michael Winship, *Making Heretics: Militant Protestantism and Free Grace in Massachusetts, 1636–1641* (Princeton, NJ, 2002); for Vane's political career see Valerie Rowe, *Sir Henry Vane the Younger: A Study in Political and Administrative History* (London, 1970); on his constitutional thought, there is an older study by Margaret Judson, *The Political Thought of Sir Henry Vane the Younger* (Philadelphia, 1969); on his mystical theology, see David Parnham, *Sir Henry Vane, Theologian: A Study in Seventeenth-Century Religious and Political Discourse* (Cranberry, NJ, 1997); on his apocalypticism, see John Coffey, 'The Martyrdom of Sir Henry Vane the Younger: From Apocalyptic Witness to Heroic Whig' in *Martyrs and Martyrdom in England, c. 1400–1700*, ed. Thomas Freeman (Woodbridge, 2007), chapter 10.

[47] 'If there was a single hero of their time for Ludlow, for Sidney, for Milton, it was Vane': Blair Worden, *Roundhead Reputations: The English Civil Wars and the Passions of Posterity* (London, 2001), p. 197.

[48] Milton, *A Treatise of Civil Power*, in *Complete Prose Works*, VII, pp. 251–2, 270–1.

or certainly together'.[49] Parliament had responsibility for the 'civil only' not the 'ecclesiastical'. Under the Old Testament law, church and state had been 'one flesh'; under the New Testament, God had 'hath now severd them'.[50] Milton, notorious as defender of divorce and apologist for the regicide (when the king was 'put to death by the severing of his head from his body'),[51] was now advocating the divorce and severance of church and state.

Separating church and state was not a popular policy, and in seeking to secure it, Milton and Vane argued for a senate comprised of ideologically sound men who supported the good old cause of civil and religious liberty. As Henry Stubbe pointed out in 1659, 'Those who are for a free Toleration are the lesse numerous, beyond all proportion'. Opponents of toleration constituted the majority of the population, owned most of the land, and predominated in the ministry and the universities. Given arms and ammunition, Presbyterians and Episcopalians would surely destroy 'Sectarian-Toleration'.[52] Even conservative Independents would restrict it. Only a radical Independent oligarchy backed by the army could stop the return of religious uniformity.

Ironically, then, the enemies of 'State Religion' sought a rule of 'the Puritan illuminati' (as Pocock puts it).[53] In order to ensure 'liberty of conscience', its godly champions had to seize the helm of the state. Radical Independents and godly republicans continued to view politics in intensely providentialist terms – their political discourse acknowledged the hand of God in the victories of the New Model Army and the erection of the English republic. They did not doubt the legitimacy of public piety or days of fasting and thanksgiving.[54] And while denying the magistrate coercive power against heretics, the violators of revealed religion, they typically granted the magistrate coercive power against blasphemers and atheists, violators of natural religion. Milton praised the 1650 Blasphemy Act, directed against Ranters, as 'well deliberated'.[55] Blasphemy and licentiousness, unlike heterodox theology, was incompatible with social order. Few joined Walwyn in suggesting toleration even for misguided atheists. Godly republicans sought to dismantle the apparatus of 'State Religion', but they still envisaged a political culture suffused with piety and providentialism. Vane wanted to

---

[49] *Considerations touching the Likeliest Means to turn Hirelings out of the Church* (1659), in *Complete Prose Works*, VII, p. 318.
[50] See also Milton, *A Treatise of Civil Power*, in *Complete Prose Works*, VII, pp. 239, 260.
[51] Gardiner (ed.), *Constitutional Documents*, p. 380.
[52] Henry Stubbe, *An Essay in Defence of the Good Old Cause* (London, 1659), sig. **8v–**8r.
[53] *The Political Works of James Harrington*, ed. J. G. A. Pocock (Cambridge, 1977), p. 109.
[54] See Worden, *God's Instruments*, chapters 1–2.
[55] Milton, *A Treatise of Civil Power*, in *Complete Prose Works*, VII, p. 246.

make the English 'a holy as well as a free people'.[56] Rule by a godly minority would ensure the separation of church and state and give free rein to voluntary religion.

IV

The positions of these competing factions provide a context for the proposals of Marchamont Nedham and James Harrington. Neither man was an unequivocal Parliamentarian in the 1640s (Nedham had edited both Parliamentarian and Royalist newsbooks, while Harrington combined royal service with Parliamentarian allegiance).[57] Neither was a Puritan, and Nedham has been identified as part of a 'a libertine alliance', though he was a friend of godly republicans like Bradshaw and Milton.[58] In the 1650s, however, they operated in a political world dominated by Puritan Parliamentarians, especially by religious Independents. The standoff between radical and magisterial Independents created openings and problems for these classical republicans. While they could exploit the internal tensions among Independents, neither faction was a natural partner. Intellectually and politically, Nedham and Harrington were caught on the horns of a dilemma in the 1650s. In positioning themselves vis-à-vis the magisterial and the radical factions, they took different approaches.

Over the course of the 1650s, Nedham realigned himself, collaborating first with Milton (under the Commonwealth) and then with Nye (under the Protectorate). In *The Case of the Common-wealth of England* (1650), Nedham argued for a multiconfessional polity that tolerated different religions, and eschewed persecution; he cited the contemporary examples of multiconfessional states: Egypt, the Ottoman empire, Poland, Transylvania, and the Dutch republic.[59] These models had little appeal for John Owen, but Roger Williams had praised religious coexistence in 'the Cities of Holland, Poland, or Turkie'.[60] Nedham's editorials in *Mercurius Politicus*, written in 1651–2 under Milton's oversight, and republished in *The Excellencie of a Free State* (1656), reiterated this position. As Glenn Burgess observes,

[56] Henry Vane Jr., *A Needful Corrective of Ballance in Popular Government, Expressed in a Letter to James Harrington* (1660), p. 2.
[57] For an important reassessment of Harrington's Parliamentarianism and his royal service see Rachel Hammersley, *James Harrington: An Intellectual Biography* (Oxford, 2019), chapters 2–3.
[58] Paul Rahe, *Against Throne and Altar: Machiavelli and Political Theory under the English Republic* (Cambridge, 2008), pp. 205–11.
[59] Marchamont Nedham, *The Case of the Common-wealth of England stated* (1650), pp. 97–9.
[60] Williams, *The Bloudy Tenent*, p. 166. See John Coffey, 'European Multiconfessionalism and the English Toleration Controversy, 1640–1660', in *A Companion to Multiconfessionalism in the Early Modern World*, ed. Thomas Max Safley (Leiden, 2011), pp. 340–65.

Nedham's 'hostility to a national church' stood in contrast to Harrington's *Oceana*.[61] Against those who advocated 'a National way of Churching', Nedham advanced the dispensational argument developed by Williams and Milton, drawing a stark contrast between the Jewish and the Christian dispensations. Christ had come

> to set an end to that Pompous Administration of the Jewish Form...that as his Church and People were formerly confined within the Narrow Pale of a particular Nation, so now the Pale should be broken down, and all Nations taken into the Church: Not all Nations in a lump; nor any whole Nations, or National Bodies to be formed into Churches; for his Church or People, now under the gospel, are not to be a Body Political, but Spiritual and Mystical...a picking and chusing of such as are called and sanctified; and not a company of men forced in, by Commands and Constitutions of Worldly Powers and Prudence.[62]

This was arguably a statement that all Congregationalists could agree with – the Church (in the Christian era) was no longer national, but particular; no longer compulsory, but voluntary.[63] But Nedham went further. Antichrist 'hath twisted the Spiritual Power...with the worldly and secular interest of the State', particularly after Constantine, and the Protestant Reformers had maintained 'a State Ecclesiastical united with the Civil'. The enforcement of orthodoxy and the punishment of heresy was a lamentable feature of this regime.[64] This critique of the magisterial Reformation challenged the position of the conservative Independents, and it coheres with Nedham's participation in the campaign against the *Humble Proposals* in 1652, when his editorials in *Mercurius Politicus* were 'plainly accommodated to sectarian opinion', and drew on a sermon by Vane's friend, Peter Sterry.[65]

With the establishment of the Protectorate, however, Nedham changed his tune. In his apology for the new regime, *A True State of Case of the Commonwealth* (1654), he complained of those who 'professed fully against the Magistrates power in any matters of Religion', and sought to abolish tithes and a public ministry. Against this extreme position, Nedham endorsed the Instrument of Government, including the Protector's authority to maintain 'a Godly Ministry' funding by a system of tithes.[66] As Philip Connell notes, Nedham and his fellow republican John Hall were reacting against the Fifth

---

[61] Glenn Burgess, *British Political Thought, 1500–1660* (New York, 2009), pp. 345–6.
[62] Marchamont Nedham, *The Excellencie of a Free State* (1656), p. 148.
[63] The claim that it was no longer political, but spiritual, was more debateable; it could be read as a denial of the existence of ecclesiastical *polities* independent of the state's jurisdiction.
[64] Nedham, *Excellencie of a Free State*, pp. 148–52.
[65] See Philip Connell, *Secular Chains: Poetry and the Politics of Religion from Milton to Pope* (Oxford, 2016), p. 30.
[66] [Marchamont Nedham], *A True State of the Case of the Common-wealth* (1654), pp. 14–17.

Monarchists, who denounced tithes and 'state religion' while demanding a rule of the saints. But he was also breaking with the radical Independents and adopting a distinctly Hobbesian position on the magistrate's power in matters of religion. Nedham's relationship to Milton, Connel suggests, 'must have been sorely tested by the uncompromising terms in which Nedham framed his public endorsement of the Cromwellian church'.[67]

By 1657, Nedham had joined forces with Nye to defend the religious establishment against another radical Independent, John Goodwin. Goodwin had written a sharp attack on 'State Religion', particularly the institution of the Triers, which (according to Goodwin) was dominated by anti-Arminians. Goodwin argued that this centralised system for vetting the parish ministry should be dismantled.[68] It was at this point that Nedham stepped in, with *The Great Accuser Cast Down: Or A Publick Trial of Mr John Goodwin*. It is a neglected tract, but a revealing one, and behind it Goodwin himself detected the hand of Nye, his old Congregationalist adversary at the Whitehall Debates a decade earlier.[69] Certainly, the work seems like a hybrid, combining a Calvinist concern for orthodoxy with an Erastian republican concern for state religion.

Nedham was keen to stress that the Cromwellian establishment was not a clericalist affair. The Triers were deputies of the civil magistrate and were appointed for 'a civil end and purpose, *Viz*. to see that the publick State-Maintenance' was distributed 'according to the Magistrate's own appointment and direction'.[70] In fact, some of the Triers (notably the Baptist army officer William Packer) were laymen, not clergymen. The religious 'Establishment' of the Protectorate was a matter of civil power, not church power. All it involved, as Cromwell himself had noted in his 1654 speech, was the magistrate exercising his own liberty of conscience while recognising the liberty of conscience of others.[71] Cromwell had every right to establish a state religion, universities as 'schools of the prophets', and 'state maintenance' for the ministry.[72] As long as this establishment was non-coercive, it was entirely compatible with the liberty of conscience of others.

This was very much in line with Harrington, but Nedham (or Nye) went on to abuse Goodwin for dissenting from Calvinist orthodoxy. He was 'a meer brat of Arminius', who had learned his errors from the ancient heretics and

---

[67] Connell, *Secular Chains*, pp. 32–4.
[68] John Goodwin, *Basanistai. Or the Triers or Tormentors Tried and Cast* (1657). On the pamphlet and ensuing controversy, see John Coffey, *John Goodwin and the Puritan Revolution* (Woodbridge, 2006), pp. 255–8.
[69] See John Goodwin, *Triumviri* (1658), sigs. A3v-a4.
[70] Marchamont Nedham, *The Great Accuser Cast Down, or A Publick Trial of Mr John Goodwin of Coleman-Street, London, at the Bar of Religion and Right Reason* (1657), p. 79.
[71] Nedham, *The Great Accuser Cast Down*, p. 25.
[72] Nedham, *The Great Accuser Cast Down*, p. 82. The phrase 'State-Maintenance' is used on pp. 16, 43, 56, 62, 79.

may well be drifting towards Arianism or even Socinianism.[73] Like his 'brother' Roger Williams he seemed to argue for 'a brave latitude' for all religions.[74] Nedham did not deny that Goodwin had a right to liberty of conscience, but the critique of Arminianism diverges from Harrington's much less dogmatic approach and echoes earlier Presbyterian polemics. It reveals the proximity (in 1657 at least) between Nye's Calvinist confessionalism and Nedham's republican civil religion. Despite his friendship with Nedham and his sympathies for Machiavelli, Nedham could lend his pen to the cause of Calvinist orthodoxy, while godly republicans repudiated the very idea of 'state religion'.

V

If we turn to Harrington's *Oceana*, we can see how he took a different approach, triangulating between magisterial and radical Independents. In considering 'the parties that are godly', he noted different factions: 'some for a national religion and others for liberty of conscience, with such animosity on both sides as if these two did not consist'. Here he referred to the polarised positions of Presbyterians (who favoured a system of national religious uniformity) and radical Independents (who argued that liberty of conscience required disestablishment). The 'most dangerous' faction, he added were those 'holding that the saints must govern' (a clear reference to the Fifth Monarchists, but possibly also to the party around Vane).[75] Harrington firmly opposed godly oligarchy, favouring 'good laws' over 'good men' as the guarantor of civil and religious liberty.[76]

In avoiding these twin extremes, Harrington joined forces with the magisterial Independents. He endorsed an argument advanced by Oliver Cromwell: that to strip the magistrate of power in religion was to rob him of liberty of conscience. Speaking to the First Protectorate Parliament in 1654, Cromwell had declared:

> Is not Liberty of Conscience in religion a fundamental? So long as there is liberty of conscience for the supreme magistrate to exercise his conscience in erecting what form of church-government he is satisfied he should set up, why should not he give it to others? Liberty of conscience is a natural right; and he that would have it ought to give it, having liberty to settle what he likes for the public.[77]

---

[73] Nedham, *The Great Accuser Cast Down*, pp. 54, 72.
[74] Nedham, *The Great Accuser Cast Down*, p. 124.
[75] *The Political Works of James Harrington*, p. 204
[76] See Martin Dzelzainis, 'Harrington and the Oligarchs: Milton, Vane and Stubbe', in *Perspectives on English Revolutionary Republicanism*, eds Dirk Wiemann and Gaby Mahlberg (Abingdon, 2014), chapter 1.
[77] *Writings and Speeches of Oliver Cromwell*, ed. W. C. Abbott, 4 vols (Cambridge, MA, 1937–47), III, p. 459

The speech was a seminal one, for Cromwell was the first to state (in plain English) that 'liberty of conscience is a natural right'.[78] In a single paragraph, the Lord Protector had managed to defend religious establishments while issuing a ringing affirmation of religious freedom. Harrington does not reiterate his phrase about 'natural right', but he does pick up on Cromwell's other distinctive claim: that magistrates too should enjoy liberty of conscience. By 'denying the magistrate to have any jurisdiction' in matters of religion, he suggests, sectaries make the same move as popes: 'the magistrate, losing the power of religion, loseth the liberty of conscience which in that case hath nothing to protect it'.[79] It was a judo-like move, turning the force of their own argument against the disestablishmentarians.

Harrington reiterated the point in later works. Minorities who attacked 'national religion' were assailing the 'liberty of conscience' of the majority. If the early Christians had tried to 'take away tithes and abolish the national religion' of the Jews, they would have 'endeavoured to violate the consciences of the unconverted Jews' and thus ensured that 'liberty of conscience' was 'taken away' from the Christian minority to boot. Such reflections yielded two aphorisms: 'That there may be liberty of conscience, there must be a national religion'; 'That there may be a national religion, there must be an endowed clergy'.[80]

As well as siding with the magisterial Independents on the establishment principle, Harrington also affirmed some of their points about the parish ministry. Like Owen and Nye, he wished to maintain the parochial system, staffed by a learned ministry trained in the universities. His defence of the universities (he noted that the Dutch, Venetians and Swiss republics were 'addicted' to them) was a rebuff to radical critics of Oxford and Cambridge, such as William Dell.[81] Harrington concurred with the magisterial Reformers that the parish ministry ought to 'have ancient languages and the knowledge of ancient times', and he wanted them to be supported by compulsory tithes (to ensure their 'comfortable subsistence').[82] At the same time, they were to be elected by 'the suffrage of the people' (a notable recognition of the Congregationalist insistence on popular consent and the voluntary principle).[83] Moreover, Harrington made a significant

---

[78] See John Coffey, 'How Religious Freedom became a Natural Right: The Case of Post-Reformation England', in *From Toleration to Religious Freedom: Cross-Disciplinary Perspectives*, eds Marietta van der Tol, Carys Brown, John Adenitire, and E. S. Kempson (Oxford, 2021), pp. 23–56.
[79] *The Political Works of James Harrington*, p. 186.
[80] *Aphorisms Political* (1659), in *The Political Works of James Harrington*, pp. 766–7.
[81] *The Political Works of James Harrington*, p. 305. On Dell, see Leo F. Solt, 'Anti-Intellectualism in the Puritan Revolution', *Church History*, 25 (1956), 306–16; Peter Burke, 'William Dell, the Universities and the Radical Tradition', in *Reviving the English Revolution*, eds Geoff Ely and William Hunt (London, 1988), pp. 181–9.
[82] *The Political Works of James Harrington*, pp. 306–9.
[83] *The Political Works of James Harrington*, pp. 385, 556. On Harrington's democratic theory of ordination see Hammersley, *James Harrington*, pp. 195–200.

concession to the two-sphere principle of the Congregationalists: gathered congregations would coexist alongside the parish assemblies in a dual system, and the gathered congregations would not be 'molested or interrupted in their way of worship...but vigilantly and vigorously protected'. A national 'council of religion' would 'have the care of the national religion and the protection of the liberty of conscience'.[84] Like the Congregationalists, Harrington did not speak of a national church (except the 'National Church' of the Jews); unlike the Congregationalists, he preferred to speak of 'gathered congregations', rather than 'gathered churches'.[85] By side-stepping normative ecclesiological language, he made it clear that his religious settlement was quite different to the *jure divino* systems of many contemporary theologians.

On the limits of toleration, Harrington took a mediating position between conservative and radical Independents. In contrast to Henry Ireton in 1648, he maintained that there was 'no coercive power in the matter of religion to be exercised in this nation'.[86] There should be 'liberty of conscience entire', so that Protestants of all stripes would enjoy not only 'free exercise' of their religion, but civic equality.[87] In Oceana, gathered congregations could not be 'Jewish', 'Popish' or 'idolatrous', but there was no bar on heterodox Protestants like the Socinians, whose emergence had so alarmed John Owen.[88] Harrington studiously avoided the concepts of 'orthodoxy' and 'heresy'; the only time he used the word 'heretic' was in relation to the French Wars of Religion, when he makes it clear that this is 'their word', not his.[89] Nor does he refer to a set of doctrinal 'fundamentals' to define the nation's Protestant faith. He steered clear of confessionalisation, and stretched liberty of conscience beyond the limits set out by Ireton, Owen, and Nye. Yet he did not go as far as Williams or Walwyn, who included Jews, Catholics, and pagans as beneficiaries of liberty of conscience.

Harrington also triangulated between conservative and radical Independents on the matter of Old Testament Israel. The former group had appealed to Hebrew kings to justify the magistrate's coercive power in matters of religion; the latter had insisted that the religious authority of the Old Testament magistrate had been abrogated by the coming of Christ. With the magisterial Independents, Harrington acknowledged the Hebrew republic as a model for a Christian religious establishment; alongside other antique republics it demonstrated the legitimacy and necessity of national religion. Yet as Eric Nelson has observed, Harrington was among those Hebraists who argued that

---

[84] *The Political Works of James Harrington*, p. 251.
[85] *The Political Works of James Harrington*, pp. 186, 217, 560.
[86] *The Political Works of James Harrington*, p. 251.
[87] *A System of Politics*, in *The Political Works of James Harrington*, p. 844. See also *Aphorisms Political* (1659), in *The Political Works of James Harrington*, p. 764.
[88] *The Political Works of James Harrington*, p. 217. See Sarah Mortimer, *Reason and Religion in the English Revolution: The Challenge of Socinianism* (Cambridge, 2010), chapters 7–8.
[89] *The Political Works of James Harrington*, p. 440.

biblical Israel allowed 'liberty of prophesying', and thus provided a model for a tolerant religious establishment.[90] This latitudinarian Hebraic Erastianism was not going to satisfy either Roger Williams or John Owen, even though Harrington had something to offer them both.

VI

We began by noting that our protagonists did not speak of 'civil religion'. But as Teresa Bejan and Keith Thomas have shown, contemporaries were preoccupied by the idea of civility.[91] The writings of Roger Williams, for example, were peppered with this vocabulary. He had first-hand knowledge of the hospitality of the Wampanoag and Narragansett, and challenged stereotypes of their barbarism: 'There is a savour of civilitie and *courtesie* even amongst these wild *Americans*, both amongst *themselves* and towards *strangers*.' Indeed, the civility of pagans put to shame the persecuting incivility of Christians: 'If Natures Sons both *wild* and *tame*./Humane and Courteous be:/How ill becomes it Sonnes of God/To want Humanity?'[92] To persecute was 'a breach of Civilitie it selfe'. Williams had no time for an established 'civil religion', but he argued that with a policy of religious equality 'true *civility* and *Christianity* may both flourish in a *State* or *Kingdome*'.[93] In a society free of religious persecution, confessional rivals would display 'the beauty of *civility* and *humanity*'.[94]

Proponents of religious uniformity, of course, argued that confessional pluralism was a recipe for internecine feuds, and pointed to the French Wars of Religion as a case in point.[95] In the wake of the English Civil Wars, argues William Bulman, Anglican conformists engaged in their own Enlightenment project, 'convinced that religious and public life finally needed to be organized in a manner that prevented the fires of zeal from laying waste to civil order'.[96] The prescriptions of Bulman's protagonists differed radically from those of Independents and republicans, though all sides shared a preoccupation with forging civil peace by taming religious passions. For some, the quest for religious civility led to a 'national religion' or an established church. For radical Protestants like Williams and Milton, it pointed beyond 'State Religion'.

---

[90] Nelson, *The Hebrew Republic*, pp. 117–22.
[91] Teresa Bejan, *Mere Civility: Disagreement and the Limits of Toleration* (Cambridge, MA, 2017); Keith Thomas, *In Pursuit of Civility: Manners and Civilization in Early Modern England* (New Haven, 2018).
[92] Roger Williams, *A Key into the Language of America* (1644), pp. 9–10.
[93] Williams, *The Bloudy Tenent*, p. 26, sig. a3v.
[94] Roger Williams, *The Hirelings Ministry None of Christ's* (1652), p. 29.
[95] Conrad Russell, 'Arguments for Religious Unity in England, 1530–1650', *Journal of Ecclesiastical History*, 18 (1967), 201–26.
[96] William Bulman, *Anglican Enlightenment: Orientalism, Religion and Politics in England and its Empire, 1648–1715* (Cambridge, 2015), p. xii.

The prospects of republicans and Independents were dashed by the restoration of episcopacy in 1660, but the positions they staked out would endure. Harrington's vision of a tolerant 'national religion' prefigures the Christian 'civil religion' championed by eighteenth-century Enlightenment thinkers: established, Erastian, tolerant, latitudinarian, and civic-minded.[97] The nostrums of radical Independents and godly republicans had a bright future in the United States, where the separation of church and state was combined with republican exclusivism, and evangelical sects burgeoned within a public culture steeped in Protestant providentialism.[98] The proposals of the magisterial Independents fared less well over the long term: the Congregational establishments in Connecticut and Massachusetts held out respectively to 1818 and 1833, but by the 1830s the heirs of the Puritans on both sides of the Atlantic were increasingly Miltonic in their commitment to disestablishment.[99] Fewer and fewer Protestants believed that the state had the authority to punish heresy or schism. Conceptions of religious civility that had once seemed avant garde were becoming commonplace.

This long argument among Anglophone Protestants about church-state relations provided openings for the idea of civil religion. As Ashley Walsh points out, historians have increasingly come to think of civil religion 'not as a concept that was ranged against Christian belief and practice but as one that emerged from within Christian contexts'. He suggests that 'future work would benefit from examining how political philosophers engaged with Christian intellectual culture, especially theology and ecclesiology, to reconcile the spiritual with the temporal and to have Christianity serve civil peace and flourishing'.[100] Harrington and Nedham provide case studies in such engagement, but they illustrate how theology and ecclesiology presented challenges as well as opportunities. Nedham's shifting positions and Harrington's triangulations remind us that political theorists would have trouble navigating the choppy waters of Protestant controversy.

---

[97] Ashley Walsh, *Civil Religion and the Enlightenment in England, c. 1707–1800* (Woodbridge, 2020).

[98] On the American fusion of republicanism with voluntarist evangelicalism see Mark Noll, *America's God: From Jonathan Edwards to Abraham Lincoln* (New York, 2002). See also George F. Sensabaugh, *Milton in Early America* (Princeton, 1964).

[99] See Timothy Larsen, *Friends of Religious Equality: Nonconformist Politics in Mid-Victorian England* (Woodbridge, 1999); John Coffey, 'Between Reformation and Enlightenment: Presbyterian Clergy, Religious Liberty and Intellectual Change, 1647 to 1788', in *Insular Christianity: Alternative Models of the Church in Britain and Ireland, c.1550-c.1750*, eds R. Armstrong and T. O'Hannrachain (Manchester, 2013), pp. 252–71.

[100] Ashley Walsh, review of Steven Frankel and Martin D. Yaffe (eds), *Civil Religion in Modern Political Philosophy: Machiavelli to Tocqueville* (University Park, PA, 2020), in *Eighteenth-Century Studies*, 56 (2023), 336–8.

6

Henry Stubbe and Civil Religion

Connor Robinson[1]

Henry Stubbe (1632–76), or Stubbs, was known to his contemporaries for his unparalleled gifts as a scholar of classical languages and for a compulsion to voice his opinions in so fanatical and unfiltered a manner that it frequently threatened to embroil him in episodes of physical violence.[2] Today he is known as a proponent of civil religion whose discretion was so deftly maintained that he was able to disguise the true character of his opinions for decades. This picture of Stubbe was first developed in James R. Jacob's monograph *Henry Stubbe, Radical Protestantism and the Early Enlightenment* (1983), which presented an arresting thesis which continues to inform scholarly interpretations of both Stubbe and early modern civil religion. Jacob argued that Stubbe consistently adhered to a 'radical civil religion' across his lifetime, one characterised by a 'vitalistic naturalism and his commitment to a primitive, natural religion which provided a historical foundation for his critique of clerical claims to separate spiritual authority, his Erastian tolerationism and his belief in universal charity to the poor and moderate economic levelling'. Stubbe's thought, Jacob suggested, was framed by a distinctively secular understanding of history, according to which '[t]here is no spiritual order governed by

---

[1] I wish to record my warmest thanks to Professor Tim Stanton and Dr Tim Stuart-Buttle for reading and commenting on earlier drafts of this essay. As ever, I owe much to their time and wisdom. A fortnight prior to the conference upon which this volume is based, my grandfather Denis Ostick passed away. His support was always absolute, unconditional and unwavering. I dedicate this essay to him in very loving memory.

[2] Anthony Wood, *Athenae Oxonienses: an exact history of all the writers and bishops who have had their education in the University of Oxford*, ed. Philip Bliss, 3 vols (London, 1813–20), III, cols 1067–73, esp. 1071–2: 'He was a very bold man, utter'd any thing that came into his mind, not only among his companions, but in public coffee-houses (of which he was a great frequenter) and would often speak his mind of particular persons, then accidentally present, without examining the company he was in, for which he was often reprimanded, and several times threatened to be kick'd and beaten'.

159

supernatural forces operating in either nature or history ... the spiritual and divine are conflated with the natural and historical'.[3]

For Jacob, the civil religion propounded by Stubbe was the product of his participation in a sort of Hegelian dialectic with Thomas Hobbes and James Harrington, in which Stubbe attempted to resolve the tension between Hobbes's conception of sovereignty and Harrington's republicanism, whilst retaining their shared Erastianism and anticlericalism. At the Restoration, Jacob argued, Stubbe turned to 'satire and subterfuge' to conceal his radicalism in response to a hostile culture of coercion and censorship, but it obtrudes, for those who know where to look, in his criticisms of the Royal Society and his justifications of war with the Netherlands in the 1670s.[4] It is in Stubbe's *Account of the Rise and Progress of Mahometanism*, however – written sometime in the early 1670s and disseminated in manuscript form, but not published until 1911)[5] – that the full implications of his anticlericalism for his political theory were laid bare. Stubbe's *Account* detailed the devastating effects of religious superstition on political life and envisaged the creation of a society that was de-Christianised and perhaps even wholly secular in its presuppositions. Jacob viewed the *Account* as the logical culmination and fullest expression of Stubbe's enduring commitment to natural religion, Erastian tolerationism, and anticlericalism. The *Account* is, it follows, the prism through which one must read all of Stubbe's other works. Jacob further inferred that Stubbe's consistent anti- or post-Christian civil religion was the missing link between the radical religious thought of the Puritan Revolution and the early Enlightenment deism of John Toland and other 'freethinkers'.[6]

---

[3] James R. Jacob, *Henry Stubbe, Radical Protestantism and the Early Enlightenment* (Cambridge, 1983), pp. 2–3.

[4] *Ibid.*, pp. 3, 42, 109. This treatment is indicative of sympathy for Leo Strauss's approach to intellectual history as outlined in *Persecution and the Art of the Writing* (Chicago, 1952).

[5] Henry Stubbe, *An Account of the Rise and Progress of Mahometanism*, ed. Hafiz Mahmud Khan Shairani (London, 1911). An updated and corrected edition of the text is Henry Stubbe, *Henry Stubbe and the Beginnings of Islam: The Originall & Progress of Mahometanism*, ed. Nabil Matar (New York, 2014). Throughout this essay, I refer to Matar's edition, but I cite it as *Account* as this is the title known to scholars.

[6] Jacob, *Henry Stubbe*, chapter 8. This interpretation built upon P. M. Holt, 'A Seventeenth-Century Defender of Islam: Henry Stubbe (1632–76) and his book', *Friends of Doctor Williams Library*, 26 (1972), 1–30, who argued Stubbe arrived at a view akin to Edward Gibbon's account of the triumph of 'barbarism and religion'. Jacob's interpretation was expanded upon in Justin A. I. Champion, 'Legislators, Impostors, and the Politic Origins of Religion: English Theories of 'Imposture' from Stubbe to Toland', in *Heterodoxy, Spinozism, and Free Thought in Early-Eighteenth-Century Europe*, eds Silvia Berti, Françoise Charles-Daubert, and Richard H. Popkin (Dordrecht, 1996), pp. 333–56; idem, '"I remember a Mahometan story of Ahmed ben Edris": freethinking uses of Islam from Stubbe to Toland', *Al-Qantara*, 31 (2010), pp. 443–80. Champion argued Stubbe and Toland's respective works on Islam formed part of the 'free-thinking

Recent scholarship has challenged this picture. Dmitri Levitin is particularly critical of Jacob's interpretation of Stubbe, referring to his attempts to shoehorn Stubbe into the category of 'radical' as bordering on conspiracy theory. More broadly, Levitin questions the entire concept of an 'early Enlightenment', observing that early modern European intellectuals (almost without exception) understood themselves not as iconoclasts, but as restorers of an original or true order of things.[7] Noel Malcolm's study of early modern Europe's engagement with Islamic political and religious thought complements these claims, by showing that the study of Islam by Christians aimed at bolstering and developing a deeper understanding of Christian truth. In passing, Malcolm casts doubt on Jacob's analysis, suggesting that little that is new or revealing can be gleaned about Stubbe's thoughts on the proper relationship between temporal power and religion from the *Account*: it was because Stubbe already held certain views on that relationship that he found the history of early Islam appealing, 'realizing that is could be used as grist to his mill'.[8]

The present chapter builds upon this revisionist scholarship, which has tended to treat Stubbe only in passing. It argues that we ought to interpret Stubbe's politico-religious thought as emerging out of the culture of 'spiritual reformation' and 'reforming the Reformation' which characterised the Puritan Revolution.[9] Positioning Stubbe in relation to Hobbes, Harrington, and Toland is not objectionable in itself, but doing so does little to illuminate how the Revolution was shaped largely by theological and ecclesiological questions, the urgency of which compelled Stubbe and his contemporaries to fundamentally rethink the nature of the true church, how its past ought to be understood, and how its purposes were to be realised.[10] The widespread concern to address these questions placed side-constraints on how the state and the authority of the civil magistrate were construed. The ecclesio-political thinking of the English Reformation from the beginning was much preoccupied with these questions.[11] To individuals of all political and Protestant persuasions, the Revolution offered a unique opportunity

---

early Enlightenment', with both analysing the role of the extraordinary human lawgiver composing religious ceremonies out of political prudence to reform corrupted religion and establish civil peace.

[7] Dmitri Levitin, *Ancient Wisdom in the Age of the New Science: Histories of Philosophy in England, c1640–1700* (Cambridge, 2015), pp. 307–13 and passim.

[8] Noel Malcolm, *Useful Enemies: Islam and The Ottoman Empire in Western Political Thought, 1450–1750* (Oxford, 2019), pp. 318–26, 411.

[9] Bernard Capp, *England's Culture Wars: Puritan Reformation and Its Enemies in the Interregnum, 1649–1660* (Oxford, 2012).

[10] Anthony Milton, *England's Second Reformation: The Battle for the Church of England, 1625–1662* (Cambridge, 2021).

[11] Karl Gunther, *Reformation Unbound: Protestant Visions of Reform in England, 1525–1590* (Cambridge, 2014); Anthony Milton, *Catholic and Reformed: The Roman and Protestant Churches in English Protestant Thought, 1600–1640* (Cambridge, 1995); Nicholas Tyacke,

to conclude the Reformation as a movement by realising its promise in full whilst necessarily adjusting to an unprecedented constitutional and ecclesiastical upheaval. Stubbe did not aim to tear down Christianity, but instead defended the Reformation as 'the greatest wonder God hath produced after the *Churches* being 1200. years in the *Wilderness*'.[12]

Throughout his life, Stubbe professed a commitment to formulating the proper relationship between civil and religious authority in terms commensurate with the Reformation, and consistent with the authority of tradition (especially early Church history), providential theology, liberty of conscience, and toleration. Rather than reading Stubbe proleptically, as Jacob does, it is more illuminating to consider Stubbe's thought as developing contingently in response to shifting circumstances and new challenges. It is argued here that the foundations of Stubbe's thought were laid in 1659 through his engagement and interaction with the thought of Richard Baxter and that these ideas were subject to refinement and development in Stubbe's later works.

Baxter's significance is often understated nowadays, both in relation to Stubbe[13] and in those studies of the political and religious thought of the 1650s which focus obsessively on Hobbes and his reception or on the republicanism Hobbes formally disavowed as a dangerous folly of 'democraticall gentlemen'.[14] In his day Baxter was a prominent figure, who developed striking arguments on jurisdictional and ecclesiological issues which, *ex negativo*, helped to set the terms of Stubbe's own inquiries.

The first section of this essay focuses on three key works by Stubbe, each published in 1659, and demonstrates how he developed his own views in contradistinction to those of Baxter. The second section shows how, after the Restoration, Stubbe remained broadly committed to the conclusions he had reached in 1659, but that these were adjusted in light of the political and religious circumstances of Restoration England, including in his study of Islam. The concluding section considers how, if at all, this alternative reading of Stubbe affects our understanding of early modern civil religion more generally.

'The Puritan Paradigm of English Politics, 1559–1642', *The Historical Journal*, 53 (2010), pp. 527–50.

[12] Henry Stubbe, *A Light Shining out of Darkness*, 2nd edn (London, 1659), p. 172. I refer to the second edition of this text throughout this essay.

[13] Jacob, *Henry Stubbe*, p. 31 consigns Baxter to a cameo appearance.

[14] Examples include Jeffrey R. Collins, *The Allegiance of Thomas Hobbes* (Oxford, 2005); Eric Nelson, *The Hebrew Republic: Jewish Sources and the Transformation of European Political Thought* (Cambridge, MA, 2010); Jonathan Scott, *Commonwealth Principles: Republican Writing of the English Revolution* (Cambridge, 2004).

Stubbe, Baxter, and the Good Old Cause

Stubbe's *An Essay in Defence of the Good Old Cause*, published in September 1659, provided the most sophisticated articulation of the principles of the Good Old Cause given during the revolutionary period. Its fundamental precepts were succinctly but powerfully asserted in the opening pages of the essay:

> LIBERTY, *civill*, and *spirituall*, were the GOOD *old cause*. And however some may say that it was none of The *Old cause* to assert any proper Sovereignty in the people: yet I must tell them that the *vindications of the Parliament against the papers of the King* then in being shew us, that such a *Sovereignety* was presupposed, and if it were not the *old cause*, it was the foundation thereof, and avowed for such.[15]

Several pages previously, in a premonition to the reader, Stubbe had asserted, seemingly incongruously, that he '*owne*[*d*] *entirely* Perkin's *doctrine in the* chaine of Salvation; *and if* I *differ from* Beza *about* punishing heretics, I *know not how* I *am bound up to call any man Master*'. Likewise, in anticipation of the charge that he advocated the licentious toleration of all opinions, Stubbe had asserted '*that there is no necessity* [of] *that, and my history of* Toleration *will envince it*'.[16] Stubbe wanted to make pellucidly clear that the Good Old Cause had been committed to popular sovereignty and civil and religious liberty from the beginning, and it had never aimed at tearing down the Reformation or unleashing religious anarchy. The ideals of the Cause coincided with those of the Reformed tradition.[17] The Cause was not a break with the past or a rejection of tradition: the clue was in the name. It was to be understood, rather, as an attempt to bring the Reformation to completion against a background of rapidly shifting practical realities.

Stubbe was not alone in purporting to speak on behalf of the Good Old Cause. From the late 1640s onwards, innumerable authors endeavoured to examine the principles for which Parliament had first taken up arms against the Crown and the Mitre. By 1659, the Good Old Cause had been associated with a range of positive positions, from republican exclusivism, the separation of church and state and liberty of conscience, to an end to a centralised and university-trained ministry. This literature offered far

---

[15] Henry Stubbe, *An Essay in Defence of the Good Old Cause* (London, 1659), Preface. For an excellent discussion of Stubbe's constitutionalism, which is beyond the scope of this essay, see Alan Cromartie, 'Democracy, Toleration, and the Interests of the People', in *Democracy and Anti-Democracy in Early Modern England 1603–1689*, eds Cesare Cuttica and Markku Peltonen (Leiden, 2019), pp. 45–65.

[16] Ibid., Premonition to the Reader, sig.*3.

[17] William Prynne, a prominent critic of the Good Old Cause, had denounced it as a front for a Jesuit plot to overthrow law, liberty, and the Protestant faith itself. See his *The Re-publicans and Others Spurious Good Old Cause ... Anatomized* (London, 1659), p. 1 and *The true good old cause rightly stated, and the false un-cased* ([London], [1659]), p. 1.

more than a 'passionate nostalgia for the earlier years of the revolution and an acute sense of betrayal'.[18] Those who subscribed to the Cause decried the rule of the Protectorate, the proposed resurrection of the ancient constitution outlined in the Humble Petition and Advice, the corrupted 'spirit' of members of Parliament, and the Cromwellian religious settlement which, they claimed, failed to grant sufficient toleration to sectarians who had contributed to the revolutionary movement. These frustrations were expressed in a millenarian theological language which cast the adherents of the Cause as an elect aristocracy of the godly and bewailed the political and religious direction the nation had taken since the regicide. The Cause's zealots invited comparisons with the Protestant martyrs, who had sacrificed themselves under Marian persecution to save the reformed English faith. The overthrow of the King and the established church, they argued, had created an opportunity to realise the Cause: to bring the struggle of the Reformation, the contestation between true Christians and corrupted papists, to a close and to reap the rewards of godliness, peace, and liberty.[19]

Stubbe did more than anyone to translate the melange of ideas that travelled under the banner of the Cause into a manifesto for the political and religious settlement for the nation. He did so, in a move which brilliantly showcased his acerbic and polemical talents, by deliberately inverting the image of the Cause depicted and decried by Richard Baxter in his *A Key for Catholicks* and *A Holy Commonwealth, or Political Aphorisms* of 1659. Stubbe took up all the charges levelled against the Cause by Baxter, turned them back against him, and reconstructed the Cause in positive terms that cast Baxter and his political and religious positions in a deeply unflattering light.

In early 1659, Baxter had as many reasons for optimism as did the adherents of the Good Old Cause. As a chaplain in the New Model Army during the late 1640s, he had been horrified by the theological licentiousness he witnessed. On his return to his Kidderminster ministry, he determined to restore spiritual discipline to his congregation and the nation. His *Aphorismes of Justification* (1649) attacked the Antinomian tendencies he detected in the Army, which he interpreted as attempting to deny the threat of divine penalties for worldly misbehaviour on the part of a self-declared elect, and postulated in their place a soteriological framework which emphasised the importance of the worldly conduct of the believer in their life-long path to justification. Baxter spent the next decade attempting to

---

[18] A. H. Woolrych, 'The Good Old Cause and the Fall of the Protectorate', *The Cambridge Historical Journal*, 13 (1957), pp. 133–61.
[19] Some of the key literature of the Good Old Cause includes John Bond, *Eschol, or Grapes (among) thorns* (London, 1648), esp. pp. 42–4; Thomas Saunders, John Okey, and Matthew Alured, *The Humble Petition of Several Colonels of the Army* (London, 1654); Sir Henry Vane, *A Healing Question Propounded* (London, 1656); Anon, *The Fifth Monarchy, or Kingdom of Christ, in Opposition to the Beast's, Asserted* (London, 1659), esp. pp. 52–3.

work out the political and religious conditions necessary to restore order to a world turned upside down.[20]

On Richard Cromwell's succession to the office of Lord Protector following Oliver's death in September 1658, Baxter rejoiced. The Protectorate and his Parliament briefly appeared to be free, or prospectively so, of the sectarian Army's poisonous politics and religion. For a brief moment, Baxter glimpsed the city on a hill, a theocratic commonwealth in which godly magistrates and ministers had been united providentially in a holy alliance to bring about discipline and nurture righteousness. The prospect of a truly lasting settlement seemed tantalisingly within reach. The *Political Aphorisms* of his *A Holy Commonwealth* explored the political implications of the reflections on soteriology and discipline arrayed in the *Aphorismes of Justification*. They were written to capitalise on this providential moment and to condemn those who would thwart its possibilities. Accordingly, Baxter fiercely attacked the Good Old Cause, seeing in it a resurgence of Antinomianism, arguing that its cardinal tenets of popular sovereignty and liberty of conscience demonstrated that the Cause's adherents were 'masked Papists' seeking to destroy the English commonwealth and the Protestant faith. Only seditious agents of the Bishop of Rome could advocate the recipe for anarchy and licentiousness its central tenets comprised:

> It tends to the destruction of the Commonwealth, if there be liberty for all to perswade the people to sedition and Rebellion: And therefore it must tend to the destruction of the Church, and of mens Souls, and consequently of the Commonwealth in the chief respects, if all have leave to do their worst to preach up Infidelity, Mahometanisme, Popery, or any false Doctrine or Worship, against the great and necessary Truths.[21]

The positive argument of *A Holy Commonwealth*, meanwhile, made clear that in 'a Divine Common-wealth the Honour and Pleasing of God, and the salvation of the people are the Principal Ends, and their corporal welfare but subordinate to these'.[22] A theocracy was the form of government without equal because it fulfilled the ends of society more perfectly than any other. Had it not been the pattern of the Hebrew Commonwealth? The realisation

---

[20] See William M. Lamont, *Richard Baxter and the Millennium: Protestant Imperialism and the English Revolution* (London, 1979), chapter 3. The reader can follow, broadly speaking, the development of Baxter's thought during the 1650s with reference to Richard Baxter, *Aphorismes of Justification* (London, 1649); idem, *The Saints Everlasting Rest* (London, 1650), Preface; Richard Baxter to Edward Harley, 15 September 1656, in *The Calendar of the Correspondence of Richard Baxter*, eds Geoffrey F. Nuttall and N. H. Keeble, 2 vols (Oxford, 1991), I, pp. 222–6; Richard Baxter, *A Key for Catholicks* (London, 1659), pp. 313–68.

[21] Richard Baxter, *A Holy Commonwealth, or Political Aphorisms* (London, 1659), An Addition to the Preface.

[22] *Ibid.*, p. 212.

of a Christian commonwealth on the same pattern was, Baxter intimated, the end for which the Reformation had been set in train in the first place.

Stubbe's understanding of civil and religious liberty issued in an altogether different view of the relationship between civil and ecclesiastical jurisdiction. Here Stubbe's declared debt to Perkins's 'chaine of Salvation' is especially relevant.

Perkins adhered to a supralapsarian conception of predestination which diluted the significance of the Fall in the scheme of Salvation: God has predestined some persons to election and others to damnation prior to the Fall. Nobody, however, can judge whether they, or any other individual, are among the elect or the reprobate.[23] God's will is inscrutable. The only signs are from the effects of election in the elect, the testimony of God's spirit and the works of sanctification.

This view of predestination informed Perkins's influential definition of Christian liberty. By virtue of Christ's sacrifice, faithful Christians were endowed with 'libertie to come out of the kingdome of darkness into the Kingdom of grace, and from the bondage of sinne into the glorious libertie of the sonnes of God'.[24] This, in turn, informed Perkins's account of the authority of the civil magistrate and the purposes of political society, whereby 'humane lawes binde not simply of themselues, but so farreforth as they are agreeable to Gods word, serue for the common good, stand with good order, and hinder not the libertie of conscience'.[25]

Liberty of conscience refers to the freedom to seek knowledge of God for oneself. The scope of this liberty raised questions about other liberties besides. Those who did not recognise their duty fully to submit their wills to God's will had no title to claim liberty of conscience, and they were similarly unlikely to use the civil liberties they enjoyed for the right ends: namely, serving God and the common good.[26] Perkins's view of predestination dictated that the will of man could only act in conformity with God's will through the assistance of His saving grace, which operated on the conscience via the Holy Spirit. On this matter, he joined hands with Luther and Calvin in making it clear that liberty of conscience was quite compatible with absolute civil subjection.[27] They endeavoured to refute the idea that freedom *from* sin meant freedom *to* sin. Liberty of conscience, or Christian liberty,

---

[23] Hence the title of one of Perkins's most popular works, *A Graine of Mustard-seed* (London, 1611), which seeks to reassure the faithful that even if they struggle to identify signs of election within themselves, they ought not to give up hope.

[24] William Perkins, *A Golden Chaine, or, The Description of Theologie* (London, 1621), p. 799.

[25] *Ibid.*, p. 855.

[26] Mark A. Hutchinson and Timothy Stanton, 'On liberalism, liberty of conscience, and toleration: some historical and theoretical reflections', in *Toleration and the Challenges to Liberalism*, eds Johannes Drerup and Gottfried Schweiger (London and New York, 2020), pp. 53–76.

[27] See *Luther and Calvin on Secular Authority*, ed. Harro Höpfl (Cambridge, 1991).

came to denote the freedom to believe and worship within the confines of Christian truth. Stubbe presupposed Perkins's predestination and accepted this view of Christian liberty and temporal subjection, but he owned an alternative understanding of the relationship between the magistrate and liberty of conscience via a semantic reformulation which paired 'civil' and 'religious' liberty without conflating them.[28]

For Stubbe, '*Magistracy* is the exercise of a *Morall power*: one of these is the root and measure of the other, which if it exceed it becomes *exorbitant*, and is no longer *Magistracy*, but a corruption thereof'. Magistracy is a human power designed to pursue worldly ends:

> things *Civil* and *Spiritual* being of a different nature, and not *subordinate*, so as he who is deputed to administer the *former*, is not thereby impowered to entermeddle with the *latter* any way ... [for] Men *embody* under *Magistrates* for upholding *civill commerce*, but they gather into *Churches* to maintain a *spirituall communion*.[29]

In other words, the civil and spiritual were discrete spheres of jurisdiction, not two aspects of one single jurisdiction. Civil jurisdiction arises from man's natural inclination to be sociable and from the rational recognition of necessities which he can only attain through mutual co-operation and collective force. Society can only be upheld by a power the principal end of which is the pursuit of the good of the community, securing each individual in the rights agreed on with their fellow men, and executing the trust placed in them by the political community. Everyone's 'conscience' provides sufficient knowledge of his duties to his fellow man and to God: it informs them both that magistracy is necessary, and that its authority is limited to the purposes for which it was initially instituted.

This conception of magistracy went hand-in-hand with Stubbe's claim that the marrow of the true Protestant faith consisted

> in a multitude of Propositions ... not [to] be proved by *natural reason* and *common principles*, but *pure Revelation*, which is delivered in the Scripture, in *Tongues disused*, and a *phrase peculiar thereunto*, and for the explanation whereof *Tradition* is no way conducible; but only the *Spirit* guiding those that are not reprobate unto all knowledge.[30]

However, because God had 'left the world no *infallible Judge* to expound the Scripture' and no 'common evidence in the delivery of *Spirituall* matters', it necessarily followed that the '*Spirit of God* in each Saint is the sole

---

[28] For the background to and the process of the pairing of 'civil' and 'religious' liberty, see Blair Worden, *God's Instruments: Political Conduct in the England of Oliver Cromwell* (Oxford, 2012), pp. 313-54.
[29] Stubbe, *An Essay in Defence*, pp. 1, 26.
[30] Ibid., p. 21.

Authentique Expositor of Scripture'.[31] True faith is the essence of belief and worship arrived at through the Spirit. This assumption lay behind Stubbe's claim that it is '*morally impossible*, as well as *unlawful*' for the magistrate to impose upon the conscience of his subjects, for to do so would be to encroach on the jurisdiction of Christ's governance over the individual. Moreover, as faith was arrived at by persuasion and through the Spirit alone, physical coercion via the magistrate's sword was useless: 'Force, and Terrour may bring men to an *outward complyance* but not alter their *judgements*'. An insincere outward profession of faith was condemnable: 'To believe, what appears untrue, seems to me *impossible*: To professe, what we believe untrue, I am sure, is *damnable*'.[32] This is not religious scepticism; the emphasis is placed on the sincerity and certainty with which one believes. These views combined to give the magistrate an almost entirely negative role in the economy of salvation: to maintain the worldly conditions under which individuals might pursue their own salvation as the spirit directed, and by this means fulfilling the scriptural duty to be 'a *Nursing Father* unto *Truth*'.[33]

At first glance, the combination of views Stubbe was advancing seem an odd mix: the insistence that he was continuing the theological orthodoxies of the leading reformers; the Hobbesian noises made about the magistrate's duty to secure civil peace; the un-Hobbesian stress on the separation of civil and ecclesiastical jurisdiction, and the pairing of civil and religious liberty. Stubbe's position, however, becomes more readily intelligible once we grasp that it systematically (and deliberately) controverted Baxter's vision of the relationship between civil and religious authority. Stubbe attacked Baxter directly in a pamphlet of June 1659; and the *Essay*, published three months later, further developed Stubbe's critical counterblast against Baxter.

The opening sections of the pamphlet rebuked Baxter's suggestion that Sir Henry Vane (Stubbe's patron) was a masked Papist and countered that it was Baxter himself who had long been propounding corrupt Romish opinions. Stubbe condemned Baxter's *Aphorismes of Justification* as fundamentally unsound and unorthodox 'in the great point of *Justification* by the righteousnesse and obedience of *Christ* as *Mediator*'.[34] 'Now', Stubbe continued archly, 'as *Luther* saith well, If a man be sound in this one Article of free Justification by the righteousnesse of Christ, it will minister light and direction to him in points of an inferiour and lesser consequence'. Conversely, if he is defective on this point, he is likely to be defective on every other point. So it was with Baxter: his views 'touching *Justification, Conversion*, the Nature of *Speciall Grace, Assurance, Perseverance*, the extent

---

[31] Ibid., pp. 39–40.

[32] Ibid., pp. 21, 32, 38.

[33] Ibid., p. 50, paraphrasing Isaiah 49:23.

[34] Henry Stubbe, *A vindication of that prudent and honourable knight, Sir Henry Vane, from the lyes and calumnies of Mr. Richard Baxter, minister of Kidderminster* (London, 1659), pp. 8–9, citing Baxter, *Aphorismes of Justification*, pp. 45, 70, 78, 82–3, 91.

and effects of the *death* of Christ'[35] aligned him with the Papists, not with the Reformers, and those views were carried into his political opinions, which were equally unsound.

Stubbe connected Baxter's *Aphorismes* directly to his political project: the structures Baxter advocated answered to the model of justification he was assuming and were designed to bring each conscience into alignment with God's will via the will of the magistrate. But, Stubbe observed, 'how far the *Magistrate* is to proceed in suppressing erroneous *Doctrines*, and where the *bounds* are to be set, beyond which he is not to go, I suppose a wiser man then Master *Baxter* cannot easily determine'. Stubbe cited the Polish scholar and Calvinist Bartholomew Keckerman's assertion that '*the bond between the Magistrate and his Subjects*, is essentially *Civil*', thereby affirming Hobbes's conclusion without mentioning his name.[36] 'It seems', Stubbe continued, that

> he was not of your opinion, that *Magistracy* is from Christ as *Mediator*: for if this were true, then every *Magistrate* that doth not submit to the *Mediatory* Kingdome of Christ, is a meer *Usurper*, and may be lawfully deposed; and so whilst you seem to attribute much to the *Christian* Magistrate, you destroy Magistracy in most Nations and Countries in the world, where neither *Magistrate* nor people acknowledge the Lord Jesus.[37]

By making Christ, or Christian Magistracy, the formal cause of government, Baxter had delegitimised most past and existing political orders and implied a duty to resist them on the part of subjects.

Countering Baxter's notion that the Christian magistrate should extirpate error and enforce discipline through the sword, Stubbe admonished him that the 'weapons of your warfare should be *spirituall* and heavenly, not *carnall* and *worldly*. Nor is the Gospel, in the power of it, planted or propagated by the *Civil* or *Martiall* Sword; but by the Spirit of God, in preaching, prayer, Christian conference, and a holy conversation'. What Baxter really wanted was to 'bring the *civil* Magistrate under your Girdle, to be at your Beck, and Command, that you may dispose of civil affairs as you please in *ordine ad spiritualia*'.[38] Stubbe implied in protest what he would affirm in the *Essay*: that civil and spiritual affairs were distinct, that the latter did not properly come under the jurisdiction of the civil magistrate, and that they ought to be free for individuals to contemplate and practice as they themselves determined. In other words, the notion of 'civil and religious liberty' – the fundamental precept of the Good Old Cause – put forth by Stubbe in his *Essay* was a direct repudiation of the ideal of the godly magistrate as the

---

[35] Stubbe, *A Vindication*, p. 9.
[36] Ibid., p. 14.
[37] Ibid.
[38] Ibid., p. 19.

active instrument of reformation and builder of a united godly society set out by Baxter.

One logical development which complemented this train of thought and was explored by Stubbe in his *Essay* was the question of toleration, which he treated as inextricably connected with the nature of Christian faith. To him, it was clear that

> where there is wanting an infallible Expositor of the minde of God (which being to be accepted upon *Revelation*, is not to be discussed by *Reason*) there is not onely cause for a *Toleration*, (why should any be forced from what he holds to be true, unto that which another can not evidence but it may be false?), but sufficient ground from former practices and usages to reestablish the like forbearance.[39]

No magistrate or pastor could claim definitive knowledge of revealed truth. Attempting to define religious truth was to define departures from it: that is to say, heresy and blasphemy. This was a prerogative falsely claimed by civil powers which gave justification for persecution. The sanctity of the Holy Scriptures was violated when employed to justify earthly tyranny. The natural reason of man was sufficient to enable them to grasp the dictates of nature and the will of God relating to the present life alone, and to live in tolerable conformity to both. What natural reason alone was *incapable* of providing was a definitive understanding of the Word and, by extension, truth. This is not to say that truth did not exist, but that truth could not be claimed as the sole possession of one particular magistrate or church, for neither was endowed with greater access to revealed truth than the laity. It followed that any attempts to define deviations from truth were both illegitimate and futile.[40]

In fact, said Stubbe, history confirmed as much. He endeavoured to show that a broad toleration was the policy of the early Church, at a time when it remained pure in doctrine and uncorrupted by Popish superstitions and coercive practices, a holy era which the Good Old Cause and the Reformation were attempting to restore.[41] For example, for several centuries after the conversion of the Western Roman Empire by Constantine, 'NO GODLY EMPEROUR EVER yet did choose to punish or afflict any infidell that he might force him to renounce his errour, and yet gentilisme of it self decayes and ceaseth; that you may learne the strength of truth, and the weaknesse of Errour'.[42] This model was gradually replaced over time by a

---

[39] Stubbe, *An Essay in Defence*, p. 42.
[40] *Ibid.*, pp. 113–29.
[41] For the turn to the primitive Church, see Jean-Louis Quantin, *The Church of England and Christian Antiquity: The Construction of a Confessional Identity in the 17th Century* (Oxford, 2009).
[42] Stubbe, *An Essay in Defence*, p. 55.

policy of coercion, causing men to 'not relinquish their Religion, but the Profession thereof'.[43]

These themes were explored further in a third work dating from 1659, *A Light Shining out of Darkness*, in which Stubbe went deeper into the history of the early Church.[44] He determined that in Christian antiquity the Church had existed as a series of individuated congregational assemblies, with each congregation electing one amongst their own to administer the sacraments. This person had a wholly pastoral role in the congregation: he was a guide, picked out from his fellow worshippers for the sake of order and mutual edification, who remained permanently accountable to the congregation of which he was a member. As the congregation's reading of Scripture together served as the means of grace, it was not necessary for a clergy who followed in a direct line of succession from Christ and the Apostles by administering sacraments in order to be a recipient of it.[45] This form of church was later corrupted by changes to the status and function of the ecclesiastical office of priests.

Once priests were invited into the courts of power and made civil servants at the behest of the civilian nobility, they acquired an office with civil jurisdiction and authority. Tithes were claimed and granted on the spurious basis of divine right, and the people were deprived of their rights and roles in church-governance. Stubbe, echoing Hobbes and Harrington, emphasised the human origins of the 'priesthood'. Significantly, however, he did not view the problem as they did, as the inherently despotic nature of 'priests', but rather as the corruption of the previously harmonious relationship between Empire and Church through the conflation of temporal and spiritual jurisdiction. The long-term stability of that enterprise rested upon each respecting the jurisdiction of the other and upon churches respecting the jurisdiction over their own beliefs and actions enjoyed by all their members equally, each being guided by the spirit in such matters.

These historical discoveries were put to work in a defence of the Quakers. It was commonplace for Quakers to be labelled incompatible with magistracy due to their understanding of the church as a purely spiritual and invisible body utterly separate from the temporal state, their refusal to recognise the authority of any human ecclesiastical power, and their opposition to taking oaths. That Stubbe should have come to their defence may seem surprising, at least until we remember that Baxter had argued that the Quakers were intolerable.[46] Unsurprisingly, Stubbe disagreed.

---

[43] *Ibid.*, pp. 91–2.
[44] The first edition was published in June 1659. The second edition, which was significantly expanded and included a defence of the Quakers, was published in November 1659.
[45] Stubbe, *A Light Shining*, pp. 1–18.
[46] Richard Baxter, *One Sheet against the Quakers* (Kidderminster, 1657).

He argued, liberally citing the authority of Luther, that there was no visible or outward priesthood under the New Testament. The only priesthood is Christ's, which is spiritual, and common to all Christians, removing the need for the priest to act as a mediator between the individual believer and God: 'as the *Priesthood* is a fiction, so is this *Ministery of the word fictitious, novell*, and *Sacrilegious*, the *true* and *onely Ministery of the word* being *common to all Christians*'.[47] Stubbe identifies the Quakers as the brethren of the '*primitive Ascetics*, who alone upheld *Christianity* of old', thereby implying that they were, in an unorthodox manner, 'Puritans' in their own right.[48] The Quakers' ministry of pure spirituality informed their mistrust of ecclesiastical authority and its claims to infallibility, to which Stubbe was wholly sympathetic: '[a]re the *Quakers fanaticall*, if they regard not the *expositions of fallible* men, *private, contradictions*, and *no way authentique*; since besides the *internall expositour*, an *external, visible, infallible, authentique, publique expositour* is as far from being needful, as he is from being *constituted by Christ*[?]'.[49] As for their refusal to take oaths, the Quakers, Stubbe wrote, 'do not transgresse [the basic rules of civility], onely upon another principle performe the same things ...They neither refuse to obey, or discharge *Magistracy*; they deny that any such thing is consequentiall to their *Tenets*'.[50] That is to say, their conduct was perfectly consistent with magistracy and they could perform the duties of a subject, even though in matters of salvation they took their own way to heaven and even if their principles were misliked. The refusal of the Quakers to take oaths in view of their conception of what Christ had commanded was beside the point, because 'I know not how Christ's commands do enterfere with *civill polity*'.[51]

Stubbe's distinction between the temporal and spiritual had been insisted upon in his *Essay* to the extent that he advocated the toleration of Roman Catholics, suggesting it was possible for them to submit to the civil magistrate under the same conditions as Protestant subjects and thereby 'enjoy a *Toleration* moderated according to the conveniency of the Republique'.[52] This was a highly unusual position to adopt, one that went beyond the toleration of John Milton and Stubbe's patron Sir Henry Vane.[53] Later in 1659, having experienced the Presbyterian-supported Booth Rising and the collapse of the alliance between Army and Parliament, Stubbe no longer considered the toleration of Roman Catholics viable. His reasons

---

[47] Stubbe, *A Light Shining*, p. 67.
[48] *Ibid.*, p. 81.
[49] *Ibid.*, p. 83.
[50] *Ibid.*, p. 89.
[51] *Ibid.*, p. 91.
[52] Stubbe, *An Essay in Defence*, p. 139.
[53] Martin Dzelzainis, 'Milton, Sir Henry Vane the Younger, and the Toleration of Catholics', in *Milton and Catholicism*, eds Ronald Corthell and Thomas N. Corns (Notre Dame, IN, 2017), pp. 65–83.

for thinking it impossible were similar to those of Milton, Vane, and his Christ Church colleague John Locke: namely that allegiance to the Pope for Roman Catholics must always supersede all other oaths and obligations. The Pope was supreme in all matters, civil and ecclesiastical, which meant the distinction between the temporal and the spiritual upon which Stubbe insisted was rejected by Roman Catholics – their faith was inseparable from their political obligations.[54] These considerations led Stubbe to reflect in October 1659 that '[t]here is no *religion* which can lead a man to renounce the performances of *such actions,* as render him capable of *civil* or *political Society*'.[55]

As so often with Stubbe, this was more than abstract speculation. It had a target and the target was Baxter and his supposed Presbyterian allies.[56] They deplored the Quakers' refusal to take oaths. Stubbe retorted that if '[t]he *Quakers* take no *Oaths,* the other [the Presbyterians] never keeps them'.[57] The Quakers and other potential allies of the Good Old Cause were shown to be compatible with magistracy because of their commitment to liberty of conscience, their belief in true religion as a spiritual affair based purely on revelation, and their scepticism towards clergy. It was the Presbyterians, on account of their demands for religious uniformity abetted by the coercive action of the godly magistrate, not the Quakers that were intolerable. They, not the Quakers, evinced a persecuting spirit. *Their* demands confused the offices of the magistrate and the priest, encroached upon the special spiritual governance between Christ and the individual, and violated the terms on which political society subsisted, for religious uniformity was possible only by employing the coercive power of magistrates beyond their rightful jurisdiction – that is, through tyranny. *Their* positions were incompatible with legitimate government. Turning the tables on Baxter once again, Stubbe was able to argue that the political and religious opinions of the Presbyterians rendered them as intolerable as they themselves held Roman Catholics and Quakers to be. The Good Old Cause carried forward the banner of Reformation in revolutionary England. Baxter and his allies were enemies of this project, not its instruments. After such an ingenious, and intensely provoking hatchet-job, it is small wonder that Baxter, in his autobiography, would

---

[54] A point made in John Locke to S. H. [Henry Stubbe], [Mid-September 1659] in *The Correspondence of John Locke,* ed. E. S. de Beer, 8 vols (Oxford, 1976–89), I, pp. 109–12.
[55] Henry Stubbe, *A Letter to an Officer in the Army concerning a Select Senate* (London, 1659), p. 54.
[56] The entrenched association of Baxter with Presbyterianism is now contested by Baxter scholars. See Tim Cooper, 'Polity and peacemaking: To what extent was Richard Baxter a congregationalist?', in *Church Polity and Politics in the British Atlantic World, c. 1635–66,* eds Elliot Vernon and Hunter Powell (Manchester, 2020), pp. 200–21.
[57] Stubbe, *A Light Shining,* p. 90.

seek to retaliate by representing Stubbe to posterity as a petty little nobody who drowned in a puddle.[58]

Stubbe, the Indulgence, and the study of Islam

In 1659, Stubbe employed his enviable scholarly gifts to take the disparate conceptual materials associated with the Good Old Cause to which he subscribed and to reformulate them in terms that cast the supposedly holy ideals of Baxter and other opponents of the Cause as not merely erroneous but as antithetical to the Protestant faith itself. He condemned the marriage of the temporal and spiritual, connected liberty of conscience to the nature of true Christianity, extolled the necessity of toleration for the sake of both conscience and temporal peace, and attacked those who claimed *jure divino* authority in ecclesiastical matters. At the Restoration, he was stripped of his studentship at Oxford and his job at the Bodleian Library. Stubbe was dispatched to Jamaica for two years by the new regime, in part to sweat out his sins, whereupon he formally renounced his former allies and appeared eager for a new start. His circumstances, as well as those of the English church and polity, had changed quite dramatically, but his aims in his writing remained the same – to diagnose where Christianity had gone astray and to identify how a religiously plural Christian nation might peacefully exist. This shift in circumstances inevitably changed Stubbe's polemical targets: the enemy was no longer Baxter, discountenanced by the new regime, deprived of his Kidderminster living and contemplating emigration. Stubbe and Baxter were only two of many who had seen the hopes of the 1650s dashed before their eyes and had to adjust their expectations and approaches accordingly.

Stubbe's *An Account of the Rise and Progress of Mahometanism*, a product of his new situation, built upon intellectual foundations laid in 1659. As recent scholarship has emphasised, an interest in Islam (and other religions more broadly) in mid-seventeenth-century England was in no sense indicative of scepticism about religion or Christianity more narrowly.[59] In the *Account*, Stubbe found in early Islam the materials he needed to extend his views on the peaceful distribution of political and religious power whilst simultaneously broadening and intensifying his criticisms of the contemporary condition of Christianity. Both Christianity and Islam originated in precepts that emphasised religion as a primarily spiritual affair,

---

[58] Richard Baxter, *Reliquiae Baxterianae*, eds N. H. Keeble et al, 5 vols (Oxford, 2020), I, p. 386.
[59] In addition to notes 7 and 8 above, see also William J. Bulman, *Anglican Enlightenment: Orientalism, Religion and Politics in England and its Empire, 1648–1715* (Cambridge, 2015); Alexander Bevilacqua, *The Republic of Arabic Letters: Islam and the European Enlightenment* (Cambridge, MA, 2018).

the sincerity of personal faith for salvation and the need for simple public worship giving thanks to God as creator. However, Christianity had become coercive and superstitious. By contrast, Islam had maintained its primitive purity. Mahomet was a model statesman who understood the bounds of his jurisdiction and how effectively to advance the common good within those limitations. Islam was not a superior substitute for Christianity. Rather, Stubbe wished to show just how far-removed Christendom had become was from the sanctity of its original teachings.

The *Account* was written sometime during the early 1670s, a period of intense public debate concerning the direction of the Church of England after Charles II issued the Declaration of Indulgence in 1672 – affording toleration to Dissenters in place of the state policy of religious comprehension codified in the Clarendon Code – and concern over the involvement of England in war against the Dutch. During this period, Stubbe enjoyed the patronage of Henry Bennet, Earl of Arlington and Charles's secretary of state, and he would publicly defend the Crown on both fronts. As Jacqueline Rose has demonstrated, it is a mistake to reduce these debates to a dichotomous choice between comprehension and toleration. There were complex questions surrounding economic advantage, liberty of conscience, *raison d'État*, and political prudence, the answers to which could, as a matter of material coincidence, unite thinkers as diverse as Baxter (now a leading figure in Nonconformity) and Stubbe. It is not clear that either would have revelled in the proximity, however temporary.[60]

Given the feverish atmosphere and the increasingly heated pamphlet exchanges, it is not surprising to find Stubbe at the forefront of public debate once more. The conclusions he had arrived at in 1659 concerning the relations between the temporal and the spiritual, the connections of liberty of conscience and toleration to the nature of true Christianity, and his use of the authority of the early Church were easily adaptable and readily answerable to meet the demands of this new situation. Moreover, the discourse surrounding the Indulgence enabled Stubbe to affirm the validity of the claims he had already formulated.

For example, in one tract attacking the political ecclesiology of Andrew Marvell and Samuel Parker, we find Stubbe once more defending the principle of toleration as the basis of social and spiritual order via reference to ecclesiastical history and the authority of the early Church. Stubbe denounced their Erastianism, observing that if 'we look into *ancient Governments* ... there is no such *Connexion* betwixt the CROWN and MITRE, that *Ecclesiastical* and *Civill power* should be INSEPARABLE'.[61] The

---

[60] Jacqueline Rose, *Godly Kingship in Restoration England: The Politics of the Royal Supremacy, 1660–1688* (Cambridge, 2011), pp. 171–4. For Baxter and nonconformity, see Lamont, *Baxter and the Millennium*, chapter 4.

[61] Henry Stubbe, *Rosemary & Bayes: or, Animadversions upon a Treatise called, The Rehearsall Trans-posed* (London, 1672), p. 3.

Emperor Julian 'gave an *universal indulgence*, re-called the *exil'd Orthodox*, protected the *Christian Churches*, and severely forbid that *Christians* should be enforced to *Paganism*'.[62] These arguments contributed to a broader critique of the condition of Christianity in England, whereupon he rather sarcastically observed that many of the self-appointed defenders of religious orthodoxy in the present age would, '[w]ere Bishop *Whitgift* and *Jewel*, *Whitaker* and *Perkins* alive now ... be accounted *Fanaticks*, *Hereticks* and *Brambles*'.[63] In fact, Stubbe had already opened a second front in his assault on contemporary Christendom in his attacks on the philosophy of the Royal Society, where he defended '[t]hose *Metaphysicks* which the *constant policy of Christendom* hath found so advantageous ... out of which we do so confound the *Papists*'.[64] The mechanical philosophy of the new science threatened to create scepticism about all truths, disposing 'mens minds afterwards to *Atheism*, or an *Indifference* in *Religion*'.[65] Though neither man acknowledged their shared concerns, it is ironic that Stubbe's criticisms of the Royal Society were similar to those of Baxter.[66]

To meet these threats, Stubbe increasingly looked to the stabilising role that might be played by a virtuous human lawgiver. He had first begun to ruminate on this idea in the final months before the Restoration. In an intemperate tract, *The Commonwealth of Oceana put into the ballance, and found too light* (1660), he attacked the republicanism of Harrington. The matter of his arguments, crude and narrow, fell below his normal standards of scholarship. Their manner was typically robust. Both qualities reflected the frustration of his hopes for the Good Old Cause. He disputed Harrington's contention that republics were founded on popular rule by highlighting the role of Lycurgus, who served as a sort of Machiavellian lawgiver to the Spartan republic through his virtue and wisdom. Stubbe now developed this line of thought in support of the Declaration of Indulgence, which Bennet regarded as a useful means of keeping nonconformists peaceable during the coming war, venerating the wisdom and virtue of Charles II. The King, said Stubbe,

> expresseth himself to be the *common Father of His People*, at the same time *He* demonstrateth himself likewise a zealous and perfect *Son of the Church*. He revives the *Primitive Policy of Constantine*, and acteth like a *Bishop* over

---

[62] *Ibid.*, p. 9.
[63] *Ibid.*, p. 16.
[64] Henry Stubbe, *Legends no Histories: or, A Specimen of some Animadversions upon the History of the Royal Society* (London, 1670), Preface.
[65] Henry Stubbe, *A Specimen of some Animadversions upon a Book, Entituled, Plus Ultra* (London, 1670), p. 17.
[66] See David S. Sytsma, *Richard Baxter and the Mechanical Philosophers* (Oxford, 2017).

those that are without, whilst he defends and owns the *Orthodox Bishops over those that are within*.[67]

In the early Church, the '*Arians*, and other Sects [abounded], yet there were *Hereticks* openly tolerated in the *Empire* untill the dayes of *Justinian*, with their Churches richly adorned'.[68] Stubbe presented Charles's enactment of the Indulgence as evidence that 'the *Ancient Politicks* concur with the *modern prudence* of *His Majesty*' and demonstrated there was cause for optimism, for 'if the *Orthodox Church* did advance itself in the *Primitive* Ages, amidst *those circumstances*, there is no fear that the *Church of England* (which takes that *Antiquity* for its pattern as to *Doctrine* and *Discipline*) should be *ruined amidst much better conditions*'.[69] Stubbe showcased his willingness to move with the times in order to realise his ends.

This brings us to Stubbe's *Account* of Islam, written, surely not coincidentally, around the same time he was defending the Indulgence. The text tells a tale of two faiths – Christianity and Islam. Both originally adhered to a similar minimalist, millenarian doctrine based solely on faith and revelation. Yet whilst Christianity declined into outward pomp and superstition, Islam retained its primitive purity. As in his printed works from this period, so too in the *Account* we find Stubbe reaffirming conclusions he had arrived at in his earlier works.

That is not to say that he arrived by the same route. Stubbe now extended his survey of the early Christian Church to embrace the nature and consequences of Constantine's conversion to Christianity. The de-centralised congregationalist apparatus that distinguished the primitive Church had been superseded by the installation of Christianity as the state religion of the Roman Empire, replaced by a rigidly centralised and hierarchical system of governance. Stubbe identified two disastrous consequences. First, the doctrine of Trinitarianism was institutionalised via the decrees of the First Council of Nicaea, which in their admixture of religion and heathen philosophy moved Christianity away from its faith-based origins. Stubbe fiercely criticised Trinitarians as 'enemies to all human learning' whose 'religion consisted rather in an outside service than inward piety'. Trinitarians cynically mystified faith, particularly the doctrine of the Trinity, wherein 'the vulgar became prone to embrace superstition'.[70] Christianity from hereon in was characterised by trickery and outward pomp, not by the Word:

---

[67] Henry Stubbe, *A further iustification of the present war against the United Netherlands* (London, 1673), p. 32.
[68] *Ibid.*, p. 58.
[69] *Ibid.*, pp. 62–3.
[70] Stubbe, *An Account*, p. 100.

> Religion now was no longer in the purity of the mind, but in the performance of certain outward ceremonies... and men testified their Christianity not so much by amending their lives as by exterior and bodily gestures... and a zealous adherence to the party they owned.[71]

The second calamity Stubbe identified was the admixture of temporal and spiritual powers and the wielding of the composite power that resulted by a single individual. As he observed, 'many Christian doctors have held that Christianity may be enforced and that it is a just cause for one prince to invade and conquer another's territories to propagate the true religion'. Christian imperialism conceives of Christian Emperors and Kings as viceroys of God, endowed with a duty and a power 'to execute wrath upon such as do evil' and 'to assert the glory, cause, and sovereignty of God to be everywhere submitted to'.[72] As the guardian and nurturer of religious truth, the godly magistrate was now endowed with jurisdiction over the individual's conscience in the name of the sanctity of public conscience.

Through this juxtaposition of Christianity and Islam, Stubbe sought to challenge the long-standing assumption within Christian thought that Islam was a religion of the sword. On the contrary, he argues, Islam is a pure faith based on the teachings of the Word through the Quran and liberty of conscience guided by the Spirit (Rūh), doctrinally defined by the fundamental beliefs that 'there was one God, that He had no associates, that there was a providence and a retribution hereafter proportionate to the good or evil actions of men'.[73] Islam recognises that 'the wisdom and felicity of man chiefly consisted in serving the great God, that joy of this world was but imposture', and that the natural life of man is so short and uncertain, it is a mistake to 'take pleasure in anything but what is agreeable to His will'.[74]

Complementing this interpretation of Islam was Stubbe's analysis of Mahomet as a lawgiver. Mahomet, said Stubbe, rightly recognised that tolerance was a demand of God for the peaceful existence of human societies. He describes it as 'a vulgar opinion that Mahomet did propagate his doctrine by the sword and not only compelled the Arabians at first to receive his doctrine but obliged his successors by a perpetual vow or precept to endeavour the extirpation of Christianity and all other religions'.[75] Mahomet attacked idolatry and preached a faith whose defining requirements consisted of '[t]he confession, there is no God besides God, and Mahomet is the apostle of God; In a constant saying of the prayers according to appointment; In giving alms; In performing a religious

---

[71] Ibid., p. 187.
[72] Ibid., pp. 177–8.
[73] Ibid., p. 177.
[74] Ibid., p. 137.
[75] Ibid., p. 177.

pilgrimage to Mecca; And in observing the fast of the month of Ramadam'.[76] Whilst sincere subscription to the first two was essential for salvation, the last three were preached by Mahomet as public aspects of worship necessary for maintaining conditions under which salvation might be peacefully pursued. Moreover, when Mahomet expanded the empire of Islam, he did so for consciously political purposes, permitting toleration to the faiths of those who were conquered (except atheists), allowing 'the unbelievers to hold their own religion and declares that every of them – Jew, Christian, or other – might be saved if he hold that there was one God, creator, a day of judgment, and lived justly and uprightly'.[77] Stubbe's polemical suggestion was that this demonstrated it was indeed possible for people of different faiths to co-exist peacefully within the one political society while taking their own, different ways to heaven. Mahomet preached a faith whose doctrines and demands had much in common with Christianity as it had originally been proclaimed by Jesus and the Apostles, but little in common with Christianity as it was formulated and practised in the present day. The comparison was not flattering. Stubbe's analysis attempted to demonstrate that Christianity was by now so far distant from the Word of God that it had become all the things Christians demonised Islam for being.

Towards the end of his treatise, Stubbe paused to reflect

> [w]hat a discourse might be made upon [Mahoment's] uniting the civil and ecclesiastical powers in one sovereign, upon his rejecting all the Christian scripture rather than decide amidst so great uncertainty of books and so difficult rules to judge of the right and to reconcile the different sects and tenets. Was it not prudently foreseen that it would be more easy to introduce a new religion than to reform such a one, and well conjectured that all interested parties would more willingly submit to a novel doctrine than yield themselves to have been all in error except one party?[78]

It is tempting to read this passage as evidence of Stubbe's final judgement on both the wisdom and the folly of Hobbes's attempts to bring Christianity under the control of the sovereign.[79] But this temptation should be resisted. It would be attempting to locate his views without the co-ordinates needed to map them accurately. It is enough to say that the *Account* probes questions about the nature of magisterial authority, and the character and extent of its authority over the church. In his defences of the Indulgence, Stubbe argued simultaneously that the Crown and Mitre were to be separated and that a single individual might prudently and justly police the boundaries of toleration. Similarly in the *Account*, he condemned any who

---

[76] *Ibid.*, p. 197.
[77] *Ibid.*, p. 180.
[78] *Ibid.*, p. 207.
[79] Jacob, *Henry Stubbe*, pp. 154–60.

would use the sword of Christian magistracy to build a holy society. His analysis of Mahomet confirmed what he already knew: that the magistrate's role in God's divine economy was largely negative and that he fulfilled his Scriptural duty to act as father to God's truth by providing the necessary temporal conditions for individuals to pursue salvation as their consciences directed.

Texts are evidence of an author's footprints, not always their ultimate destination. Quite where Stubbe would have gone next is mere guess work. His premature death means that we will never know. Nevertheless, and for all the apparent zig-zagging between positions that he attempted to explain away after the Restoration as dutiful deference to the whims of his patrons,[80] a general tendency and trajectory can be discerned. All the evidence suggests that Stubbe spent most of his adult life attempting to work out what the necessary conditions for the peaceful pursuit of salvation were and how they might be realised. An obvious point is that such evidence is what is, or ought to be, of primary interest to intellectual historians, whose role it is to make sense of the texts that claim their attention in terms that root them in the time and place from which they issued and capture their twists and turns and the complex intentions of their authors. Those intentions tend to respond as much to their author's immediate wants, circumstantial needs, prejudices, and personality traits as anything else. At all times and in all places, thinkers have their own peculiar narrowness, because all have lives to live of their own, and those lives are lived in relation to others: behind even classic thinkers there is an unpreventable locality which leaves its mark upon the supposedly universal messages they contribute to thought. This is as true of a Hobbes or a Locke as it is of a Baxter or a Stubbe.

The limits of early modern civil religion

The portrait of Henry Stubbe which emerges from James R. Jacob's monograph is of a swashbuckling iconoclast who brazenly assaulted the intellectual presuppositions of seventeenth-century Christendom, through a form of religious scepticism, and asserted in its place a secular civil religion characterised by an extreme Erastian disintegration of autonomous spiritual authority and a distinctly natural understanding of the world, one which foreshadowed and may even have influenced the age of 'Enlightenment'. Stubbe's positions were so extreme that he often had to resort to subtle rhetoric and trickery to conceal their true nature. This chapter has reconstructed a contrasting picture of Stubbe's thought. Rather than presenting a composite notion of Stubbe's thought, this chapter has preferred to follow the development of his thinking through the pages

---

[80] Wood, *Athenae Oxonienses*, III, cols 1069–72.

of his texts. It has interpreted Stubbe as a neo-Calvinist thinker whose thought developed from the fundamental dictum that sincere faith in God is necessary for salvation and the very essence of worship and belief. Such faith is arrived at exclusively via the revelations of the Holy Spirit operating on the individual's conscience. God permitted fallible men liberty of conscience to freely submit their wills to His. The governance of faith occurred within the conscience between the individual believer and Christ. These theological presuppositions directly informed Stubbe's understanding of the relationship between civil and ecclesiastical powers. Truth was beyond the faculties of men. Magistrate and pastor alike had no greater access to this truth than any other man, thereby demonstrating that each had no spiritual role in the economy of salvation whatsoever: their purpose was to realise and nurture the necessary conditions in this life for men to peacefully pursue their salvation for the next life. Stubbe understood his own views to be compatible with the Reformed tradition and he deployed them to refute an alternative vision of the Reformation and relationship of the temporal and spiritual most grievously exemplified in the works of Richard Baxter during the late 1650s. When the realities of English politics, religion, and society changed upon the Restoration, Stubbe continued to subscribe to these postulates, but he adapted them to meet his and the nation's new circumstances. His famous analysis of Islam was not meant to be the terminus of his thought, but rather yet another step in diagnosing Christianity's ailments and proscribing appropriate solutions. Stubbe was a thinker *of* the Protestant Reformation, not a terror to it.

Jacob's interpretation of Stubbe wedded him and 'civil religion' together as one. This chapter has not made the same definitive connection. Whether one chooses to think about the language of 'civil religion' as the replacement of Christianity with a new theory of morality necessary for political order or as the construal of the secular polity as the instrument of spiritual reformation, Stubbe's desiderata do not fit easily under the rubric of 'civil religion'. How are we to account for this lack of fit? One response is to say that it simply confirms that his status as a relatively minor figure in the intellectual history of seventeenth-century England is merited. A more interesting and rewarding response is to utilise the opportunity this case study of Stubbe offers and to question the categories in terms of which we, as historians, approach questions about the relationships between church and state, and the temporal and the spiritual more broadly, and to ask ourselves whether and how far we are approaching them in the spirit of our own age rather than as they were approached in the past.[81]

The key political and religious questions facing Christian Europe in the early modern period principally concerned the content and practical

---

[81] For a critique of how the assumptions of historians can shape their interpretations of early modern thought, see Timothy Stanton, 'Authority and freedom in the interpretation of Locke's political theory', *Political Theory*, 39 (2011), pp. 6–30.

consequences of Christianity, with understandings of the former structuring the answers to the latter. These questions, and the further issues asking them raised about the relationship between human reason and divine revelation, in turn shaped responses to subsidiary questions concerning the scope of human authority and the proper responsibilities of those in power.[82] The analysis of Stubbe provided throughout this chapter provides an insightful reminder that answers to these questions were shaped in no small part by discrete contexts peculiar to the enormous variety and number of thinkers who engaged with them and produced a kaleidoscope of responses more protean than many have been able or willing to recognise. Such complexities and nuances problematise both over-simplified and over-ecumenical explanations of historical identity and conceptual change. The present volume invites scholars to diversify and expand our understanding of 'civil religion'. It is no less important to consider the limitations involved in thinking through concepts of this kind and to recall that there are different modes of understanding by which we make sense of the world, of which the historical is only one.[83] One eminent historian has rightly lamented that scholarship on early modern European political thought has been fixated for too long on the languages of natural jurisprudence and classical republicanism, causing other languages of equal importance and prominence in the architectonics of early modern political thinking to be grossly neglected, one of which he identifies as 'sacred history, or civil religion'.[84] *How* they should be studied is another question, though it is one that all the contributors to this volume are answering in their own ways. It is for readers to decide in whose footsteps to follow.

---

[82] John Dunn, 'The claim to freedom of conscience: freedom of speech, freedom of thought, freedom of worship?', in *The History of Political Theory and other essays* (Cambridge, 1996), pp. 100–20; Tim Stuart-Buttle, *From Moral Theology to Moral Philosophy: Cicero and Visions of Humanity from Locke to Hume* (Oxford, 2019).
[83] Michael Oakeshott, *Experience and its Modes* (Cambridge, 1933), chapter 3.
[84] Mark Goldie, 'The Ancient Constitution and the Languages of Political Thought', *The Historical Journal*, 62 (2019), pp. 5–6.

7

Civil Religion on the Ground: Theory and Practice in Early Pennsylvania

Andrew R. Murphy and Christie L. Maloyed

After a decade and a half of energetic but often disappointing efforts on behalf of toleration – during which he had emerged as a leading Quaker controversialist, public figure, and theorist of toleration, yet achieved few concrete victories over the persecuting Restoration regime – William Penn set out on an ambitious new undertaking: an American colony committed to liberty of conscience. In 1682, fifteen years after his Quaker convincement, Penn sailed for America, armed with a plan for the colony's government that, in his mind, would ensure the attainment of the long-elusive goal of toleration and would pave the way for a prosperous and civil public sphere. Penn's longstanding commitment to religious liberty and reflection on the components of legitimate government had yielded a plan that included representative institutions, jury trials, and minimal doctrinal requirements for public office holding, thus making possible, he hoped, what had long been merely theoretical in England. 'There may be room there, though not here', he wrote in a famous letter to Lancashire Quaker James Harrison, 'for such an holy experiment'.[1]

In what follows, we use the founding of Pennsylvania as a window into two related issues that have long animated debates over civil religion. First, Christie L. Maloyed has emphasized Penn's dual commitment to promoting liberty of conscience and suppressing moral vice, identifying them as key components of a 'liberal civil religion' that he framed in response to events in England and later hoped to bring into existence in America.[2] Maloyed's argument grew out of an engagement with Ronald Beiner's claim that 'there is such a thing as a liberal civil religion, although

---

[1] To James Harrison, 25 August 1681, in *The Papers of William Penn*, eds Richard S. Dunn and Mary Maples Dunn, 5 vols (Philadelphia, 1981-6), II, p. 108 [hereafter *PWP*, vol: pg].

[2] Christie L. Maloyed, 'A Liberal Civil Religion: William Penn's Holy Experiment', *Journal of Church and State*, 55 (2012), 669–89.

its existence as an intellectual possibility seems at first glance paradoxical', a claim that we hope to trouble in this essay.[3] Relatedly, Andrew R. Murphy has argued for Penn's inclusion in the canon of early modern political thinkers alongside such contemporaries as Hobbes, Locke, and Sidney. On this view, Penn's ideas fit well within a broader current of Restoration tolerationist theory, and his role as colonial founder provides fruitful ground for exploring the interplay between political theory and practice.[4] We explore the aspects of Penn's thought that provide a sense of his social vision and the ways in which it proposes a kind of civil religion, focusing especially on the importance of 'civil interest' and 'general religion' within his broader campaign for liberty of conscience. Next, we discuss a few specific aspects of Pennsylvania politics and society, aspects that Penn hoped would realize this civil religion in practice. Finally, we look at the colony's early years and ask to what extent that system set down roots in the ordinary lived experience of Pennsylvanians. In other words, we look not only at the way Penn's political framework and hopes might constitute a recognizable civil religion, but also at the early returns on those plans in concrete terms. If he did have something like a liberal civil religion in mind, how did he think it would be maintained, or enforced, in Pennsylvania society? What might the evidence from the colony's early years have to say about the extent to which his aspirations did or did not make the transition from theory to practice?

Penn's 'civil religion': Liberty of conscience, suppression of vice, civil interest, and general religion

Although the term 'civil religion' does not appear in William Penn's corpus, his work does evince the broader aspiration of theorists of civil religion: namely, as Beiner puts it, 'the empowerment of religion...for the sake of enhanced citizenship'.[5] Furthermore, a closer examination of two important concepts in Penn's lexicon – 'civil religion' and 'general and practical

---

[3] Ronald Beiner, *Civil Religion: A Dialogue in the History of Political Philosophy* (Cambridge, 2011), p. 418. Beiner mentions Tocqueville and Montesquieu as two exceptions that prove the rule, and in several intriguing footnotes invokes Voltaire's praise of Penn and Pennsylvania, though Penn is not his focus.

[4] Andrew R. Murphy, *Liberty, Conscience, and Toleration: The Political Thought of William Penn* (Oxford, 2016), chapter six; Andrew R. Murphy, *William Penn: A Life* (Oxford, 2019).

[5] Beiner, *Civil Religion*, p. 2. We demur from a phrase taken out by the ellipsis in this passage: 'not for the sake of religion but...' since it suggests a clear distinction between 'religious' and 'non-religious' purposes (and thus that the use of 'religion' in civil religion is of instrumental value only, or in some way not 'really' religious). For some thinkers this might be the case; as we shall see, it is not so with Penn, or at least the binary nature of Beiner's claim obscures more than it reveals when applied to Penn.

religion' – suggest that he was aiming at something analogous to civil religion as he envisioned a society characterized by liberty of conscience and moral virtue, first in England (1670s) and later in Pennsylvania (1680s). Through the first of these two terms, as we shall see below, Penn set out to reconceptualize British identity as *civil* rather than *ecclesiastical*, proclaiming the notion of civil interest, rather than religious uniformity, as the glue of common civic membership. With regard to the second, Penn called on civil magistrates to promote a general, practical religion that rewarded works of charity and mercy rather than exercising coercive powers against those who dissented on doctrinal matters. Both terms played a central role in Penn's larger campaign for liberty of conscience, the cause to which he dedicated his entire public career.

In *One Project for the Good of England* (1679), published in the midst of the Popish Plot crisis (and just prior to his 1680 petition for a colonial charter), Penn argued that although some might hope for a religiously unified society, a more realistic prospect would be to 'recur to some lower but true principle for the present'. He called that principle 'civil interest' and described it as 'the foundation and end of civil government.... a legal endeavour to keep rights, or augment honest profits, whether it be in a private person or a society'. Building upon the firm foundation of civil interest would lead governments to 'preserv[e]...civil rights, according to the free and just laws of the land', and to acknowledge that 'the good of the people is properly the civil interest of the people'. Furthermore, government's attention to civil interest was *in its own interest*: when people are confident that their rulers are committed to safeguarding their rights, he argued, 'they chearfully yield their obedience, and pay their contribution to the support of that government'. Such an understanding not only points individuals toward clear and reasonable standards of justice, but does so in a way that holds irrespective of differences in matters of faith. A commitment to civil interest is a key element of legitimate government and, although it aims 'lower' than religious union, Penn nonetheless called it a 'true principle'.[6]

Several points are worth bearing in mind about this idea of civil interest. First, civil interest played a key role in Penn's notion of legitimate government, linked with territorial integrity and national security and more broadly with the peace and prosperity of the political community. In this sense, civil interest referred to a *type* of governmental function, an emphasis on the civil power's responsibility to oversee certain aspects of social life (e.g., preserving 'honest profits', or upholding legal rights). Thus, civil interest can be threatened by two different sets of actors: a government that overreaches and legislates on things not properly civil (e.g., the persecuting Restoration

---

[6] William Penn, *One Project for the Good of England* (1679), in *William Penn: Political Writings*, ed. Andrew R. Murphy (Cambridge, 2021), p. 213.

regime) or an external actor that seeks to undermine the civil government and substitute its own interests for those of the political community (e.g., the French king, or the pope). Each one of these potential threats loomed large in English political rhetoric during these years, and Penn intended civil interest as a way to unify a divided political community.

Second, Penn argued that a legitimate government, pursuing the legitimate goal of safeguarding civil interest, posed no threat to religion properly understood. To the contrary, he insisted, in keeping with longstanding English anti-Catholic rhetoric, ecclesiastical claims to political power were evidence of a distorted understanding of Christianity. Since, for Penn, religion in the true sense is about loving God above all, and one's neighbour as oneself – faith is grounded in love, and epitomized by the Sermon on the Mount, the Golden Rule, and Christ's commandment to 'love one another'[7] – then by virtue of its claims to its members' political allegiance, Catholicism is not only a religion 'degenerated from the Scriptures' but also a political threat.[8] (Whether Catholic authorities did in fact make such claims is a separate question; English anti-Catholicism took as given that they did).[9]

This particular interpretation of civil interest, offered in the midst of a tumultuous time, was a variant on an argument that Penn made throughout his career: civil loyalty and unity were compatible with religious difference, and an excessive focus on the things that purportedly divided the nation along religious lines played into the hands of those who sought to undermine the common civil good.[10] More than a decade earlier, for example, while imprisoned in the Tower of London on a blasphemy charge, Penn had written to Lord Arlington, the Secretary of State, 'What if I differ from some religious apprehensions publicly imposed? Am I therefore incompatible with the well- being of human societies?' This argument about civil interest often carried a singularly economic aspect,

---

[7] Penn, *One Project*, in *Political Writings*, p. 212; see also Penn, *An Address to Protestants* (London, 1679), pp. 81, 99–104. On civil interest more generally, see Murphy, *Liberty, Conscience, and Toleration*, pp. 188–94.

[8] Penn, *One Project*, in *Political Writings*, p. 215. This sentiment dates back to Penn's first published work, *A Seasonable Caveat against Popery* (London?, 1670).

[9] On the important topic of English anti-Catholicism, see Peter Lake, 'Anti- Popery: The Structure of a Prejudice', in *Conflict in Early Stuart England: Studies in Religion and Politics 1603–1642*, eds Richard Cust and Ann Hughes (London, 1989), pp. 72–106; Adam Morton, 'Anti-Catholicism: Catholics, Protestants, and the "Popery" problem', in *A Companion to Catholicism and Recusancy in Britain and Ireland*, eds Robert E. Scully and Angela Ellis (Leiden, 2022), pp. 410–48; Adam Morton, 'Anti-popery', in *The Oxford History of British and Irish Catholicism*, eds John Morrill and Liam Temple (Oxford, 2023), II, pp. 170–89. More generally, see *Against Popery: Britain, Empire, and Anti-Catholicism*, ed. Evan Haefeli (Charlottesville, 2020).

[10] Thus, Penn became one of the key figures in what Scott Sowerby calls 'anti-anti-popery' ('Opposition to Anti-Popery in Restoration England', *Journal of British Studies*, 51 (2012), 26–49).

given Quakers' frequent invocation of their own sober industriousness. As he put it in his letter to Arlington, 'No man is wont to come and ask at any shop of what religion the master is, in order to a bargain, but rather what's the price of this or that commodity'.[11] Penn's identification of civil interest with property rights, prosperity, and protection from violence and injury drew on a line of Whig argument that would find its most noted exposition in Locke's *Letter Concerning Toleration*, where Locke famously defined the commonwealth as a 'society of men constituted only for the procuring, preserving, and advancing their own civil interests'.[12] It formed a longstanding element not only of Penn's private correspondence, but of his published works as well.[13]

Although much of the language in which Penn discussed civil interest was political and legal in nature, his social vision also contained a deep ethical and religious dimension, and he argued in the Preamble to the Pennsylvania *Frame of Government* (1682) that government was 'a part of Religion itself, a thing Sacred in its Institution and End'.[14] Earlier, in *Englands Present Interest Discover'd* (1675), Penn had urged the government to undertake 'a sincere promotion of general and practical religion', the core elements of which he presented as 'the Ten Commandments' and 'Christ's Sermon upon the Mount'. The reason for focusing on such core teachings, he thought, was clear: they reinforce ethical bonds, producing 'mutual *Desires* to be assistent to one another in a better Sort of Living'. In other words, 'general and practical religion' would refocus attention where it ought to be focused: encouraging this-worldly acts of love, service, and charity, and de-emphasizing doctrinal arguments regarding the world to come. Penn built this notion of general and practical religion upon what he considered an inclusive sociological foundation; he insisted that it 'takes in all the religious persuasions of the kingdom'. As such, it was (in his view) a nonsectarian notion of religion: 'so many Orders of Christians...unite in the Text', he insisted in *A Perswasive to Moderation* of 1685, 'and differ only in the Comment'. He listed, as evidence, 'The Church of England, Roman-Catholicks, Grecians, Lutherans, Presbyterians, Independents, Anabaptists, Quakers, Socinians', which one can charitably call an overly charitable reading of the English landscape. Yet to Penn, such a promotion of 'general and practical religion' would not simply repeat the persecuting tendencies common to the governments of his day. Although he did not give much detail about specific statutes or policies – nor did he clarify who, with the possible exception of the most vocal atheists, might be excluded

---

[11] Penn to Lord Arlington, 19 June 1669, in *PWP*, I: 91, 93.
[12] John Locke, *Letter Concerning Toleration* (1689), ed. James Tully (Indianapolis, 1983), p. 26.
[13] See, for example, Penn, *The Guide Mistaken, and Temporizing Rebuked* (London, 1668), pp. 62–3; *The Great Case of Liberty of Conscience* (1670), in *Political Writings*, p. 179.
[14] *Frame of Government* (1682), Preamble, in *Political Writings*, p. 316.

from such a formulation – Penn insisted that such a promotion of general religion would 'brin[g] back again ancient *Virtue*', producing 'Honest, Trusty and and Temperate' men who would display 'good Neighbourhood and Cordial Friendship'.[15] Substantively, these two concepts, civil interest and general religion, yielded a dual commitment to liberty of conscience and the promotion of moral virtue.

Penn's 1679 *Address to Protestants*, published in the same year as *One Project*, which introduced the notion of civil interest, amplified these themes of general religion, emphasizing a broadly based charitable morality including meekness, humility, and the love of God and neighbour. Such, in Penn's view, were the marks of a true Christian, and such should be the extent of governmental concern.[16]

Then again, critics of toleration liked to point out, if 'merely' civil interest grounded civil government, how would magistrates be able to maintain the basic moral standards necessary to ensure civil peace? Penn and other tolerationists held that such fears were groundless, and his *Address to Protestants* attempted to balance liberty of conscience with the role of civil government in policing immoral behaviour. Using the commotion surrounding the Popish Plot to call for national self-examination and repentance, Penn lamented that sin and impiety were rampant in the kingdom, and called on his readers to note the two forms taken by communal sin: those connected with the state, and those connected with the church.

Impieties particularly relating to the state, Penn wrote, included 'drunkenness, whoredoms and fornication; excess, in apparel, in furniture, and in living; profuse gaming; and finally oaths, prophaneness, and blasphemy'.[17] Most of these state-related impieties, in Penn's view, had a twofold dimension: their morally objectionable qualities included both their effect on the individuals partaking in them as well as the broader social effects that they left in their wake as they spread throughout society. For example, drunkenness

> is not only a violation of God's law, but of our own natures; it doth… rob us of our reason, deface the impressions of virtue, and extinguish the remembrance of God's mercies and our own duty: It fits men for that,

---

[15] Penn, *Englands Present Interest Discover'd* (1675), in *Political Writings*, pp. 133–4, 136; *A Perswasive to Moderation* (1685), in *Political Writings*, p. 269. This distinction between doctrinal matters and ethical behaviour built upon another one in Penn's thinking (common to many thinkers in the tolerationist tradition), in which 'true religion' was internal and focused on an individual's salvation ('the life to come'), while politics referred to 'matters of an external nature'; see Penn's *Great Case of Liberty of Conscience* (1670), in *Political Writings*, pp. 170–1.

[16] Penn, *An Address to Protestants* (London, 1679), pp. 116–20.

[17] *An Address to Protestants*, p. 7.

which they would abhor, if sober.... [I] t spoils health, weakens the human race, and above all provokes the just God to anger.[18]

But it is not only these moral consequences *for the drunkard* that Penn found relevant to the political question of drunkenness: it is the wasted resources that drunkenness represents, the way its prevalence betrayed a more fundamental callousness at the heart of English society. He lamented 'that such excesses should be, while the backs of the poor are almost naked, and their bellies pinched with hunger'.[19] He lodged similar objections against gluttony and luxuriousness: though there is nothing untoward about the wearing of clothes, the essence of excess lies in its abuse of lawful enjoyments. The resources expended on excessive and luxurious furnishings, Penn observed, 'might probably maintain the poor of a numerous parish', and excess in feasting 'destroys hospitality and wrongs the poor'.[20] Penn also denounced sexual immorality, especially in and around the capital (where the loose manners of France had been enthusiastically adopted by the English, he insisted, undermining marriage and true affection), and gaming, as undermining people's willingness to labour honestly.

So (as Ethan Shagan has ably pointed out) alongside a limitation of the magistrate's power in the arena of religious worship, Penn proved himself an austere moralist in other regards, more than willing to countenance an expansion of the magistrate's power over matters of morality beyond the church doors. In Shagan's words, 'When we look more deeply at Penn's discussion of state sins... we see how thoroughly his vision of toleration was dependent on a coequal prosecution of vice'.[21] For his part, however, Penn insisted that such restrictions did not represent 'troubling Men for Faith, nor perplexing People for Tenderness of Conscience; for there can be no Pretence of Conscience to be Drunk, to Whore, to be Voluptuous, to Game, Swear, Curse, Blaspheme and Profane....These are Sins against Nature; and against Government'.[22] While such austere moralizing might strike twenty-first century eyes as merely trading one set of orthodoxies for another, Penn was hardly alone in his simultaneous combination of an expansive understanding of religious conscience with a more orthodox understanding of appropriate human behaviour in other realms.[23] Penn considered moral

---

[18] *Ibid.*, p. 7.
[19] *Ibid.*, p. 9.
[20] *Ibid.*, pp. 17, 18.
[21] Ethan Shagan, *Rule of Moderation: Violence, Religion and the Politics of Restraint in Early Modern England* (Cambridge, 2011), p. 308.
[22] Penn, *Address to Protestants*, p. 33. In his 1668 letter to Arlington, cited above, Penn had claimed that it did not take a great deal of scholastic subtlety to understand that 'whoredom, perjury, lying, cozening, intemperance, injustice, etc. are unlawful, or destructive of good order' (*PWP*, I: 93).
[23] I explore this phenomenon in more depth in Andrew R. Murphy, '"Religion", "Politics", and the Theory and Practice of Toleration: The Case of William Penn', in

virtue as both the foundation of good government and the only means by which it could be maintained.[24]

For Penn, the protection of liberty of conscience and the promotion of virtue went hand in hand. Governments that protect religious freedom have more religious citizens and hence more virtuous citizens. A government run by corrupt individuals will inevitably fail to protect the rights and liberties of its citizens. As such, he argued that government must have a role in promoting virtue, since it is vital to the protection of liberty. He had the opportunity to combine his dual interest in liberty and virtue in the construction of Pennsylvania government and society and, as we shall see, he attempted to design a government that both protected liberty of conscience and cultivated civic virtue among its citizens. While Beiner may indeed call the idea of a liberal civil religion 'at first glance paradoxical', it seems a valuable way of attempting to gain some clarity on the lessons that Penn drew from his English campaigns as he turned his attention across the Atlantic Ocean.

Plans for Pennsylvania

Unfortunately for Penn and his fellow Quakers (to say nothing of Dissenters more generally), persecution persisted in England throughout the 1670s, leading him to petition for a colonial charter in 1680. He received it in 1681, parlaying a royal debt to his deceased father into a massive grant of land between New York and Maryland, and journeyed in person to America a year later.[25] Although, as mentioned above, Penn never used the term civil religion to describe his own project, his stated objectives in founding Pennsylvania shared many of the same goals as a civil religion: the promotion of civic virtue and common interest, fostered and maintained using religious language and commitments. As J. William Frost has put it, Penn envisioned Pennsylvania's government as resting 'upon the virtue of subjects and religious observances remained the most effective creators

---

Secularization, Desecularization, and Toleration: Cross-Disciplinary Challenges to a Modern Myth, eds Vyacheslav Karpov and Marcus Svensson (London, 2020), pp. 81–99. We might also note the Lockean distinction between liberty and license in *Second Treatise*, section six as another example of this sort of distinction.

[24] *An Address to Protestants*, p. 34.

[25] For the details of this process, see Murphy, *Liberty, Conscience, and Toleration*, chapter five. Since this chapter focuses more on the substantive components of early Pennsylvania life, we say little about the basic architecture of the government, which was characterized by representative institutions elected by the freemen of the colony. This aspect of Pennsylvania's design reflects Penn's Whig sympathies and his longstanding view of representative institutions as the embodiment of popular consent.

of such virtue'.[26] That said, which institutions or entities did Penn expect to buttress, or enforce, the public morality of his American society? How was this liberal civil religion, this 'non-coercive Quaker establishment', supposed to be enacted and maintained on the ground?[27] What particular contribution might Quakerism – as a movement that eschewed many of the doctrinal disputes that often consumed other Protestants – have to make to those efforts?

In keeping with his broader commitments, Penn's plans for Pennsylvania involved a government deeply involved with both discouraging vice and promoting virtue. Penn highlighted the significance of a virtuous populace in the Preamble to the *Frame of Government*, stressing the importance of 'Men of Wisdom and Virtue' to his government; qualities, he wrote, 'that because they descend not with Worldly Inheritances, must be carefully propagated by a *virtuous Education* of Youth'.[28] Accomplishing such a task required, among other things, a clear commitment to education and the formation of virtuous individuals, and Chapter 12 of the *Frame* empowered the Governor and Council to 'erect and order all public schools'. Furthermore, within the colony's Provincial Council, the *Frame* provided for 'A *Committee* of Manners, Education and Arts', which had two charges: 'that all Wicked and Scandalous Living may be prevented, and that *Youth* may be successively trained up in *Virtue* and *useful Knowledge* and *Arts*'.[29] Supporting virtuous education of youth and preventing 'wicked and scandalous living' were two sides of the same coin and, implicitly at least, progress on the former goal would aid in the attainment of the latter. Penn's insistence that 'though good laws do well, good men do better' in the Preface to the *Frame* provides a clear indication of the importance he placed on such wisdom and virtue, and on preventing Pennsylvanians from becoming a 'loose and depraved people'.[30]

Liberty of conscience, Penn's ultimate political objective since his emergence as a Quaker controversialist in the late 1660s, clearly resonated with this commitment to virtuous living, since it would enable individuals to live out their deepest commitments free from fines, prison, and other punishments. Nowhere, perhaps, was the simultaneous protection of liberty of conscience and punishment of vice more evident than in the *Laws Agreed upon in England*, which Penn published along with the *Frame of Government*

---

[26] J. William Frost, 'Secularization in Colonial Pennsylvania', in *Seeking the Light: Essays in Quaker History in Honor of Edwin B. Bronner*, eds J. William Frost and John M. Moore (Wallingford and Haverford, PA, 1986), p. 108.

[27] The phrase is taken from J. William Frost, 'Religious Liberty in Early Pennsylvania', *Pennsylvania Magazine of History and Biography*, 105 (1981), p. 449.

[28] *Frame of Government*, in *Political Writings*, p. 318.

[29] Ibid., p. 321.

[30] Ibid., p. 318.

in spring 1682, shortly before he sailed for America. Law 35 extended explicit protection for liberty of conscience to all who confessed belief in the 'One Almighty and Eternal God', a far more expansive range of protection than currently on offer in England (even if, in practice, most early Pennsylvanians landed somewhere on the Christian spectrum). Immediately following these protections, in Law 36, Penn directed that all individuals should observe the first day of the week by abstaining from labour, in order to 'better dispose themselves to Worship God according to their understanding'.

Echoing his earlier claims (in *An Address to Protestants*) about the government's role in preventing vice, Law 37 prohibited crimes like murder, rape, incest, and sedition, but also

> all such offences against God, as swearing, cursing, lying, prophane talking, drunkenness, drinking of healths, obscene words, incest, sodomy, rapes, whoredom, fornication, and other uncleanness... all treasons, misprisions, murders, duels, felony, seditions, maims, forcible entries, and other violences...all prizes, stage-plays, cards, dice, May-games, gamesters, masques, revels, bull-battings, cock-fightings, bear-battings, and the like, which excite the people to rudeness, cruelty, looseness, and irreligion.

The corrupting nature of these actives, for Penn, removed them from the sphere of private concern due to their potential to incite people to act in vicious ways in public, and subjected them to the authority of the civil government acting through the colony's courts. Other laws relevant to this nascent civil religion included Law 28, which ensured the education of children in a skill or trade; and Law 30, which punished 'scandalous and malicious reporters, backbiters, defamers and spreaders of false news'.[31] Penn considered the enforcement of all these laws by the civil courts and the legislature to be essential to the flourishing of the colony. A functioning civil government acting properly within its limits formed a key component of a good society.

Then again, Penn never understood the colonial government to be the sole promoter of a civil religion in Pennsylvania. He expected that the influence of a socially dominant, though not legally established, Quakerism (Frost's 'non-coercive Quaker establishment') to foster and maintain the cohesive effects of such a system, and colonial society more generally. Although Penn welcomed 'sober people of all sorts' to join in the project of building Pennsylvania, he also envisioned the social influence of a Quaker majority as serving a positive function in modelling civil behaviour and integrity.[32] Indeed, it was this aspect of Pennsylvania society on which Voltaire focused, calling Penn the 'new sovereign... [and] at the same time the legislator of

---

[31] The Laws are reprinted in Penn, *Political Writings*, pp. 325–31.

[32] The phrase 'sober people of all sorts' is from the Fundamental Constitutions of Pennsylvania (1681, unpublished), in *William Penn: Political Writings*, p. 301.

Pennsylvania'.[33] In the *Laws Agreed in England*, Pennsylvania's marriage law (Law 19), which provided that all marriages 'shall be solemnized, taking one another as husband and wife before credible witnesses', and a prohibition on swearing of oaths in legal settings (Law 26) aimed to further bolster the public influence of Quakers and Quaker principles. A prohibition on swearing oaths had long been part of Quaker practice, and Law 26 attempted to use public shame, rather than enforced oaths, to ensure truth-telling in legal settings. 'In case any Person...shall afterwards be convicted of Wilfull Falsehood', the law held, 'such Person shall suffer...such Damage or Penalty as the Person or Persons, against whom he or she bore false Witness, did or should undergo, and shall also make Satisfaction to the Party wronged, and be publickly exposed as a *False Witness*, never to be credited in any Court or before any Magistrate in the said Province'.[34]

Civil religion on the ground: Early Pennsylvania society and politics

But planning a society, or formulating elements of a civil religion in theory, is one thing; carrying out those plans is another thing entirely. When Penn arrived in America in late October 1682, he embarked on the challenge of translating his grand vision into practical reality. Looking at the colony's earliest history – roughly speaking, from Penn's arrival through his departure in mid-1684, when he returned to England to defend against a border challenge from Lord Baltimore, proprietor of Maryland and his southern neighbour – provides an up-close view of the accomplishments and setbacks in this process. As we shall see, in addition to the active role played by governing institutions in upholding the main components of Pennsylvania's civil religion, the colony's Quakers also exercised authority, guiding and, where necessary, disciplining their members.

Penn's first Assembly, held at Chester in December 1682, shortly after his arrival, passed the colony's 'Great Law', which built upon the *Laws Agreed upon in England* until a General Assembly could be convened. It reaffirmed some of the central commitments of the *Frame*, ensuring liberty of conscience to all believers and commanding observance of the Sabbath 'to the End that Looseness, Irreligion and Atheism may not creep in under pretence of Conscience', and restricting office holding to professing Christians.[35] The Great Law also contained a prohibition on religious insult and invective, proclaiming that 'if any person shall abuse or deride any other for his or her different persuasion and practice in matters of religion

---

[33] François Marie Arouet de Voltaire, *Letters on the English*. The Harvard Classics, vol. 34, pt. 2 (New York, 1910), Letter 4. Online at www.bartleby.com/34/2/
[34] *Laws Agreed upon in England*, in *Political Writings*, pp. 327–9.
[35] 'The Great Law,' in *The Statues at Large of Pennsylvania in the Time of William Penn*, ed. Gail McKnight Beckman (New York, 1976), I, p. 6.

such shall be looked upon as a disturber of the peace and be punished accordingly'. Such a provision reflected Penn's frank acknowledgment of the fundamental importance of mutual restraint in the project of living together peacefully with one's neighbours in this multi-religious, multi-ethnic American undertaking. Certainly, Penn and his fellow Quakers had long experience with the importance of church discipline over members' behaviour ('Gospel Order' in Quaker parlance). Such practices were internal to faith communities, however, and friction and conflict could easily ensue between groups that lacked conversational guardrails, which the prohibition aimed to provide. (That said, it remains unclear whether this provision was ever brought to bear against anyone in the colony, and the Great Law would ultimately take a back seat after the adoption of a new Frame of Government the following April.) Subsequent chapters of the Great Law took up the morals legislation outlined in Law 37 of the *Laws Agreed upon in England*, including punishments for sexual immorality (prohibitions on adultery, bestiality, incest, rape, fornication, and bigamy), drunkenness, duelling, and engaging in 'rude and riotous sports and practices' or 'playing at cards, dice, [or] lotteries'.[36]

Over the ensuing months, Penn set out to establish the institutions of Pennsylvania government and society, and it became clear that the press of business (to say nothing of the still-inchoate nature of the colony's public life) prevented him from exercising the kind of close oversight he might have preferred on these matters. The aforementioned Provincial Council committee overseeing 'Manners, Education and Arts' was an early casualty; the Council voted in its first session that the work of all its committees would 'be performed by the Council for the time being, in such a way and manner as their numbers will give leave'.[37] (Other than hiring Enoch Flower as the colony's schoolmaster 'for the instruction and sober education of youth in the town of Philadelphia' more than nine months later, it is not clear that the committee ever really took up the charge that the proprietor had given it, or exercised more than nominal oversight of the colony's education).[38]

Penn had empowered the colonial government to pursue the social goals he felt his civil religion ought to foster. And during his time in Pennsylvania, he did work with and through the colony's government (primarily, though not exclusively, the Provincial Council) to punish public drunkenness, address disorder in public houses, control the conditions under which taverns operated in the colony, and deal with disruptive public speech. (The standard fine for 'being disordered in drink'

---

[36] *Ibid.*, chapters 9–18, 28–30, pp. 8–11, 13–14.
[37] Council Minutes, 13 March 1683, in *Minutes of the Provincial Council of Pennsylvania*, ed. Samuel Hazard (Harrisburg, PA, 1838), I, p. 3.
[38] Council Minutes, 26 December 1683, in *Minutes*, I, p. 36.

seems to have been five shillings).³⁹ On two occasions in the colony's early months, Penn and the Council attempted to take action to curtail 'disorder in public houses' in an attempt to 'see good orders kept'.⁴⁰ More than a year later, such issues persisted, leading Penn to appeal to the Council to 'be sure above anything to suppress lewdness and all manner of wickedness' and to act against 'unlicensed houses selling liquor without license'.⁴¹ The Council worked in other ways to suppress vice and division in the colony, addressing business disputes, conflicts between masters and servants, counterfeiting, and even overseeing a witchcraft trial, with the proprietor himself presiding.⁴² The lower House (Assembly), for its part, lacked legislative initiative and thus did not have a very active role in these matters, although they frequently agitated for a greater role in the colony's governance; during these early years their actions consisted largely of endorsing the measures passed by the Council.⁴³ Much of this activity, though, resembles the sort of actions one might find in any settlement; and one looks in vain for evidence that political institutions were heavily invested in the particularly 'religious' aspects of civil religion except insofar as they contributed to public order.

But Pennsylvania had something that other colonies lacked: the dominance of Quakers at the highest levels of society and government, and the corresponding influence of the Quaker Meeting as an extra-governmental tool of social discipline over members. As we shall see below, the Meeting often took behavioural matters into its own hands, though its enforcement capacity only worked as long as Friends showed themselves willing to accept its legitimacy over their actions. Friends would have been primed, from their experiences in England, to exercise disciplinary functions and oversee members' conduct, and Pennsylvania allowed the prospect of scaling those operations up, so to speak. As J. William Frost has put it, 'Friends saw themselves as the proprietors of Pennsylvania, responsible for establishing and maintaining a distinctive way of life. The meeting gained power in Pennsylvania members could not have dreamed of possessing in England'.⁴⁴ Penn clearly aspired for his colony to evoke the spirit of unity of the (ideal) Quaker Meeting; in Jane Calvert's words, the colonial government 'was conceived in the spirit of the Quaker meeting for

---

[39] Fines levied on John Richardson (15 March 1683), *Minutes*, I, p. 5; and Timothy Metcalf (28 March 1683), *Minutes*, I, p. 12.
[40] May 1683, *Minutes*, I, p. 18; 9 June 1683, *Minutes*, I, p. 20.
[41] July 1684; *Minutes*, I, pp. 63, 64.
[42] See *Minutes*, I, pp. 3–40.
[43] See *Votes and Proceedings of the House of Representatives of the Province of Pennsylvania* (Pennsylvania Archives: Eighth Series, Volume I: December 4, 1682 - June 11, 1707), ed. Gertrude MacKinney (Philadelphia, 1752).
[44] Frost, 'Secularization in Pennsylvania', p. 199.

business, the administrative assembly of the ecclesiastical polity'.[45] When Penn wrote to English Quaker John Alloway a year into his first stay in Pennsylvania, his euphoric description of 'scarce one law that did not pass nemine contradicente', which was likely as aspirational as it was empirical, evoked the attachment to unity so central to Friends.[46]

In another clear gesture toward Friends' practices, the first Assembly adopted a law providing for 'common peacemakers', whose 'arbitrations may be as valid as the judgments of the courts of justice', to mediate private disputes. Provided that the parties affirmed their submission, the peacemakers' judgment 'shall be as conclusive, as a sentence given by the county court', and should be registered in the courts as well.[47] The early Council records show this phenomenon in action several times. On two occasions during the first session of the General Assembly in March 1683, disputes were referred to prominent Friends (who were also Council members), in similar manner to the ways in which Friends dealt with such disputes within the Meeting. In the March 1683 dispute between Nathaniel Allen and Henry Bowman, for example, the Council 'ordered that Wm. Clarke, John Simcox & James Harrison, should speak to Henry Bowman concerning this matter'. Eight months later, in a clear reference to the Quaker emphasis on attempting to keep their disputes out of civil courts, the Council ordered that the petition of Richard Wells 'be referred to the Peace makers, and in Case of Refusall to the County Court, according to Law'.[48]

Beyond the colony's governmental institutions, moreover, the records of early Pennsylvania Quaker meetings show these aspects of discipline over a range of cases. Often political and ecclesiastical institutions worked in tandem: After being punished by the Council for circulating counterfeit money in October 1683, Charles Pickering appeared before the Meeting offering 'to do anything that the Meeting should order which might remove any scandal that the Truth was likely to suffer through him'. The wide availability of complete sets of Meeting minutes is enormously promising in terms of seeing how civil religious aims, which are often framed in broad or general ways, are enacted in the operations of social institutions in the day to day lives of communities.[49]

---

[45] Jane E. Calvert, *Quaker Constitutionalism and the Political Thought of John Dickinson* (Cambridge, 2009), p. 105.
[46] Penn to John Alloway, 29 November 1683, PWP, II: 503; the N.C.D. does appear frequently in the records of the Assembly (see *Votes and Proceedings*).
[47] Law 65, in *Charter to William Penn, and Laws of the Province of Pennsylvania*, eds Staughton George, Benjamin M. Mead, and Thomas McCamant (Harrisburg, 1879), p. 128. This law was abrogated by the Crown in 1693.
[48] March 1683, *Minutes*, I, p. 7 (see also I, p. 11); 7 November 1683, *Minutes*, I, p. 34.
[49] Council session 24 and 26 October 1683, *Minutes*, I, pp. 29–33; Philadelphia Monthly Meeting, 6 November 1683. All of the references and quotations are taken from Meeting minutes available online at https://www.ancestry.com/search/collections/2189/

THEORY AND PRACTICE IN EARLY PENNSYLVANIA

Quaker meetings – chiefly Philadelphia, for our purposes in this chapter, but also the Chester and Falls Monthly and/or Quarterly Meetings – actively oversaw Friends' behaviour in four overarching domains: care for widows, orphans, and the needy; the management of interpersonal disputes; issues relating to marriage, family, and children; and incidents of disreputable conduct or personal misbehaviour. In each of these areas, Friends in America built upon the disciplinary functions they had created in England, although the nascent quality of the colony's public life and the outsized influence of Quakers in Pennsylvania offered the possibility of doing so more effectively.

Providing for the needs of Friends in want or facing economic hardship had long characterized Quaker practice in England – Penn himself contributed to such appeals on a number of occasions – and it continued to be the case in Pennsylvania.[50] The Chester meeting approved payment for the lodging of a widow, while the Falls meeting reimbursed one of its members for his expenses in purchasing a cow and calf for a Friend in want.[51] The Philadelphia Monthly and Quarterly Meetings similarly provided for widows and children, and in late 1683 assigned four Friends to 'make enquiry into the necessity of the poor and needy, and supply their wants'.[52]

Beyond these needs for care, there was no shortage of disputes between Friends, whether interpersonal, business, or land related. Meetings frequently assigned mediators in attempts to bring about acceptable agreements between the parties. On one occasion, the Chester meeting mediated the provision of 'a two year old heifer' in order to reconcile two disputing Friends.[53] Numerous boundary disputes (which were ubiquitous in early Pennsylvania, given the often-unsettled nature of land claims and purchases), the recovery of goods in dispute between parties in exchanges or sales, and disputed contracts regarding payments to servants: meetings attempted not only to resolve disagreements between Friends, but also to avoid the public airing of intra-Quaker grievances.[54] The nature of some of these disputes remains opaque from the surviving documentary record: in September 1684, for example, the Philadelphia Quarterly Meeting considered the conflicts that had arisen between Griffith Jones and

---

[50] In summer 1673, for instance, Penn was listed as contributing £5 to help John Gigger (or Giggour), a Friend who had signed the Penns' marriage certificate and whose son was the servant of Penn's wife Gulielma, pay off some of his debts. See Murphy, *William Penn: A Life*, p. 112.
[51] Chester Monthly Meeting minutes, 11 June 1683, and 4 July 1683.
[52] Philadelphia Quarterly Meeting minutes, 4 December 1683.
[53] Chester Monthly Meeting minutes, 1 December 1684.
[54] See the following: boundary dispute, Falls Monthly Meeting, 4 March 1685; dispute over payment for goods, Falls Monthly Meeting, 1 July 1685, Falls Monthly Meeting, 2 December 1685; dispute over payment of a servant, Philadelphia Monthly Meeting, 1 July 1684; dispute over fulfillment of a contract, Philadelphia Monthly Meeting, 3 April 1683 and Philadelphia Quarterly Meeting, 5 June 1683.

James Atkinson, assigning several of its members to 'hear and compose all differences betwixt them, as much as in them lies'. The next month's Monthly Meeting reported the differences 'composed'.[55]

Friends had concerned themselves with their members' marriages since the movement's earliest days. George Fox's attempts to establish a coherent structure of meetings during the 1670s had a number of goals, but especially important among them was more effective oversight of the Society's marriages. In fact, Fox issued no fewer than sixty epistles on the subject during his lifetime. Worries about marriage outside the sect were as common among Friends as in any other community concerned about preserving its distinctive character (including 'clearness' committees and, at the outer limit, disownment for marrying outside the meeting), and those concerns traveled from England to America. Evaluating proposed matches developed as one of the important tasks that Friends performed for other Friends in early Pennsylvania.[56]

Proposals of couples' intention to marry, and the assignment of Friends to investigate the 'clearness' of each member of the couple, dominate the early minutes of the Philadelphia, Falls, and Chester meetings. Meetings often sought to withhold their approval of proposed marriages until they could be sure of the couple's suitability, but in this new environment, such functions could be difficult to carry out. For example, in May 1683, at 'the first [Falls Monthly Meeting] after our arrival in these parts', Samuel Darke proposed his marriage to Ann Knight for the meeting's consideration. The meeting put off granting its approval, as it had yet to hear from the Burlington (New Jersey) meeting, where the couple had resided previously. A month later, they were still waiting, and in July 1683 two Friends reported having heard from Burlington that Darke and Knight 'have disorderly and contrary to the Truth which they made profession to take each other in marriage'.[57] Furthermore, the meeting became aware that a number of Falls Friends had attended the marriage, which added another layer of controversy to the situation.[58] At the September 1683 Monthly Meeting, Darke brought 'his pass of condemnation', which was read and accepted by the meeting.[59] (It seems likely, though, that the marriage continued.) The following spring, the meeting took up the issue of Roger

---

[55] For the Jones-Atkinson dispute, see Philadelphia Quarterly Meeting, 2 September 1684; Philadelphia Monthly Meeting, 7 October 1684.
[56] See Murphy, *William Penn*, pp. 93–4.
[57] Falls Monthly Meeting, May–July 1683. The Burlington meeting explained itself to Falls Friends by pointing out that many Friends had arrived from England seeking marriages, and that for a time it had approved those marriages while expressing its frustration at their lack of certificates from their English meetings (Falls Monthly Meeting, 1 August 1683).
[58] See also Falls Monthly Meeting, 1 August 1683.
[59] Falls Monthly Meeting, September 1683.

Hawkins, who had taken a wife who was not a Friend. The meeting ordered two Friends to speak with Hawkins, who reported a month later that 'as yet [they] have not had a satisfactory answer'.[60]

Finally, meetings took up questions of disreputable behaviour and personal conduct (including sexual misconduct, drunkenness, and disruptiveness). In December 1683, the Falls Meeting received a report that Ann Millton 'doth keep a disorderly house and sells liquors to English and Indians'; it charged William Biles to speak with her 'and also about her daughter Mary's loose carriage which is reported she is addicted to'. Millton 'disowned the reports' of disorderly walking, but promised to exercise greater care in the future.[61] The same meeting received a report that John Hough 'hath been drunk and fought and abused [a widow] and her daughter' and sent several Friends to speak with him. Hough promised to come to the Meeting and accept discipline, but then failed to show up.[62] Six months later, the meeting was still waiting for him to confess regarding his 'fighting, drinking, and misbehavior'.[63] Finally, in January 1685, Hough promised to bring the Meeting a written document acknowledging his fault and promising amendment, though he did not actually deliver the document until June of that year.[64]

Sometimes action had to be taken after the fact, as when the Philadelphia Meeting received 'a certain certificate dated from Clanbrazill in the County of Armah in Ireland...James Atkinson...his coming into this province contrary to the confession of Friends of the Meeting whereunto he belonged, whom Friends by the aforesaid certificate signified to be very much in debt'. Over the next few months, the Meeting sent representatives to Atkinson, 'to give Friends satisfaction touching his arrival in this province', and later decided to correspond with Friends in Ireland 'touching [Atkinson's] departure out of England and Ireland into Pennsylvania'.[65] Shortly after Charles Pickering appeared before the Philadelphia Meeting following his conviction on charges of counterfeiting (mentioned above), Penn himself wrote to the Meeting, 'counselling [Friends] to be careful in their behavior for the Truth's sake, that so the Lord might not be dishonored, and the Truth evilly spoken of amongst men'.[66]

Though the Quaker Meeting did not hold the force of law, its disciplinary function, when situated within a pluralistic public sphere, demonstrates how a nascent civil religion might contribute to the maintenance of early colonial Pennsylvania society. Combining Penn's ideals of civil interest and general

---

[60] Falls Monthly Meeting, May and June 1684.
[61] Falls Monthly Meeting, December 1683; 6 February 1684.
[62] Falls Monthly Meeting, 2 June 1684; 30 July 1684.
[63] Falls Monthly Meeting, 3 December 1684.
[64] Falls Monthly Meeting, 7 January 1685; 3 June 1685.
[65] Philadelphia Monthly Meeting, 3 April 1683; 5 June 1683; 3 July 1683.
[66] Philadelphia Monthly Meeting, 1 January 1684.

religion, the Quaker Meetings aimed to both protect liberty of conscience and promote a consensus around community standards of moral conduct. Though imperfect in achieving that goal, the Meetings did shape narratives around what it meant to be both a good Quaker and a good Pennsylvanian. Of course, as was soon to become clear, although Quakers dominated Pennsylvania's public life, they were far from the only group present in the colony, and religious and cultural diversity would present a significant challenge to peaceful social order.

Bumps in the Road: Civil Religion and Pennsylvania Practice

William Penn had ambitious plans for a virtuous government that simultaneously promoted moral virtue and protected liberty of conscience, overseeing a harmonious society characterized by a commitment to the common good even under conditions of religious diversity. As we have seen, the importance of the Quaker meeting structure to early Pennsylvania society provides important insights into the broader processes by which civil religious tenets and commitments might manifest themselves in everyday civic life. But as was often the case in other colonies, Pennsylvania did not develop in ways that aligned with its founder's original vision. Several factors conspired to frustrate Penn's attempts to instantiate his civil religion and to exercise effective control over the colony.

The first of these factors was personal: despite his early claims that he was 'like to be an adopted American',[67] Penn's first stay would be relatively brief. He returned to England in mid-1684 to pursue a legal dispute with Lord Baltimore, his southern neighbour, over the boundaries of their respective colonies. Despite frequent protestations of his desire to return, Penn quickly found himself pressed into service in England, part of King James II's plan to secure liberty of conscience for all the realm's Dissenters. That program, of course, came to an abrupt end with William of Orange's invasion, the 1688 Revolution, and James's expulsion from the throne and flight to France. For much of the next decade, Penn found himself in varying degrees of disrepute and legal jeopardy (he went into hiding, and had the colony stripped from him entirely, for several years), and only returned to Pennsylvania in 1699. It is impossible to know, of course, how Pennsylvania's social, political, and economic institutions would have developed had Penn stayed in the colony as he had planned; but his fifteen-year absence made it nearly impossible for the proprietor to shape events on the ground.

Secondly, insofar as one of Penn's aspirations lay in making Pennsylvania a hospitable home for Quakers, cultural diversity would soon complicate the smooth functioning of the colony under Quaker control. The idea

---

[67] Penn to Lord Culpeper, 5 February 1683, *PWP*, II: 350.

that civil religion expresses some deeper level of consensus has long played a role in its presentation as a unifying force, from Machiavelli and Rousseau to Durkheim and Bellah. Penn attempted a thinner version of civil religion than those associated with republican thinkers, one that sought unity while also preserving religious freedom. But the increasing number of Anglicans in Pennsylvania and the demographic contrast between Pennsylvania proper and the 'Lower Counties' (later the independent colony of Delaware), where Quakers were far fewer and a diverse range of European nationalities were represented, undermined attempts at cohesion and introduced tensions along religious and ethnic lines. For example, the prohibition of oaths in the colony's courts – part and parcel of a Quaker approach to public life – caused no end of tension with Pennsylvania's Anglicans, who bitterly complained to ecclesiastical and civil authorities in England in ways that posed an ongoing threat to Penn's proprietorship.[68]

One of Penn's proudest moments in the settlement's early history was the passage of the Act of Union and Naturalization in December 1682, which brought the colony and the Lower Counties under a common government, aiming to establish 'the union of two distinct people...under one governor'.[69] Relatively soon after Penn's departure, however, the colony descended into open sectarian conflict; the social and political dominance of Philadelphia Quakers aroused deep resentment among the territories' other inhabitants and contributed to the eventual secession of the Lower Counties into the separate colony of Delaware. By the early 1690s, some Pennsylvania Quakers were tracing the roots of the colony's difficulties back to the earliest days of settlement, offering as evidence none other than the Act of Union and Naturalization. One Pennsylvania correspondent called the Act a 'Pandora's box' that had produced 'innumerable miseries' upon its opening. 'Had it not been for this', he went on, Penn 'would never have had to return to England...and we had been blessed still with thy company'. A joint letter from the Council and Assembly lamented that 'we are forsaken by all our stepbrethren of the Lower Counties...so that we are at present by reason of their absenting themselves incapable of making laws' and referred to inhabitants of the Lower Counties as 'both strangers to ourselves and [our] principles'.[70]

William Penn clearly aspired to something like a civil religion in his colonizing enterprise in America. Informed by the failure of the tolerationist

---

[68] On these tensions, see Murphy, *William Penn: A Life*, chapters 11, 12.

[69] Act of Union and Naturalization, *Statutes at Large*, I, p. 2.

[70] From Joseph Growden, *PWP*, III: 309; From the Provincial Council and Assembly, 18 May 1691, *PWP*, III: 316, 317. For broader background on the growing rift between Pennsylvania and the Lower Counties see Robert W. Johannsen, 'The Conflict Between the Three Lower Counties on the Delaware and the Province of Pennsylvania, 1682-1704', *Delaware History*, 5 (1952), 96-132.

movement in England during the 1670s, he sought to overcome that country's persistent political divisions along religious lines by creating a doctrinally minimal public sphere with particular distinguishing features favourable to Quakerism. Difficulties posed both by external rivals like Baltimore and the border controversy, and internal factors like ethnic and religious diversity, combined to frustrate his ambitious aspirations. As a kind of case study in the historical career of the concept of civil religion, the early history of Pennsylvania provides important insights into the various institutional ways in which civil religion does, or does not, take root in the everyday lives of citizens.

8

John Locke and Civil Religion

John Marshall

Locke, 'Latitudinarianism', Comprehension, and Toleration

As he spent the last two decades of his life composing and publishing the host of political, epistemological, religious, economic and educational writings that made him celebrated in his own time and profoundly influential in eighteenth-century Britain and America, John Locke was a member of the Church of England. He was close to a number of ministers and lay members of its low-church or 'Latitudinarian' tolerant and eirenic strands. These included Archbishop John Tillotson; bishops Edward Fowler and Gilbert Burnet; ministers Samuel Bold and William Stephens; and lay Anglicans Robert Boyle, Edward Clarke, James Tyrrell, Damaris Cudworth Masham, Thomas Firmin, Isaac Newton, William Popple, and Matthew Tindal. The last several of these were increasingly Unitarian or deistically influenced; the Church of England remained for them the most congenial church communion. Even though Locke himself had become privately Unitarian and clashed publicly in the later 1690s with Bishop Edward Stillingfleet over the implications of his epistemology for theology and his refusal to testify publicly to his own belief in the Trinity, Locke asserted his membership of the Church of England in his defences of his *Letter Concerning Toleration*, and recommended works by many of these 'Latitudinarian' Anglicans and their major associates and influences Ralph Cudworth, Benjamin Whichcote, and William Chillingworth. Significantly, the Church of England was led after 1689 by Archbishop Tillotson, whom Locke personally consulted on 'doubtful theological matters'. From Tillotson Locke obtained permission for the dedication of the *History of the Inquisition* by Philipp Van Limborch, Locke's close Dutch friend, himself an important advocate of religious toleration, and Locke's initial addressee of his *Letter Concerning Toleration* itself. Tillotson supported the religious toleration provided in 1689 and declared of the damnatory Trinitarian Athanasian Creed that he wished the Church were 'well rid of it'.[1]

By the 1690s Locke had long supported religious toleration through 'comprehension' within the Church of England as well as outside of the bounds of that Church. At the end of his final draft of his 1667-71 'Essay Concerning Toleration' Locke explicitly supported 'latitudinism', declaring his intention to show 'how it comes to passe that Christian religion hath made more factions wars, and disturbances in civil societys then any other, and whether tolleration and Latitudinisme would prevent those evills' and that

> Toleration conduces noe otherwise to the settlement of a government then as it makes the majority of one minde and incourages vertue in all, which is donne by makeing and executing strict lawes concerning vertue and vice, but makeing the termes of church communion as large as may be, ie that your articles in speculative opinions be few and large, and ceremonys in worship few and easy, which is Latitudinisme.

In a lengthy 1681 manuscript of criticisms of Edward Stillingfleet's *Mischief of Separation* and *Unreasonableness of Separation* Locke advocated measures to make the church comprehend and unite the vast majority of Protestant Dissenters alongside providing toleration for those Protestants who remained outside and was critical of Presbyterians' and Independents' intolerance and intransigence. In correspondence in 1689 Locke declared to Limborch that 'Toleration' was under consideration in England under two names, both desirable, 'Comprehension', which meant widening the boundaries of 'the publick established church' in the nation so that it could accommodate almost all Protestants, and 'indulgence' for those Protestants who would nonetheless remain outside of its boundaries.[2]

---

[1] John Marshall, 'John Locke and Latitudinarianism', in *Philosophy, Science and Religion in England, 1640-1700*, eds Richard Kroll, Richard Ashcraft, and Perez Zagorin (Cambridge, 1992), pp. 253-82; John Marshall, 'The Ecclesiology of the Latitude-Men, 1660-1689', *Journal of Ecclesiastical History*, 36 (1985), 407-27; John Marshall, *Locke, Resistance, Religion and Responsibility* (Cambridge 1996); John Marshall, *Locke, Toleration and Early Enlightenment Culture* (Cambridge 2006); John Marshall, 'Locke, Socinianism, "Socinianism" and Unitarianism', in *English Philosophy in the Age of Locke*, ed. M. A Stewart (Oxford, 2000), pp. 111-82; Mark Goldie, 'John Locke, Jonas Proast and Religious Toleration 1688-1692', in *The Church of England c1689-1832: From Toleration to Tractarianism*, eds John Walsh, Colin Haydon and Steven Taylor (Cambridge, 1993), pp. 147-71; Mark Goldie, 'Priestcraft and the birth of Whiggism', in *Political Discourse in Early Modern Britain*, eds Nicholas Phillipson and Quentin Skinner (Cambridge, 1993), pp. 209-31; Stephen Snobelen, 'Socinianism, Heresy and Locke's *Reasonableness of Christianity*', *Enlightenment and Dissent*, 20 (2001), 88-125; Diego Lucci, *John Locke's Christianity* (Cambridge, 2021).
[2] John Locke, *An Essay Concerning Toleration*, eds John Milton and Philip Milton (Oxford, 2006), pp. 301-2; Marshall, 'Latitudinarianism'; Marshall, *Locke, Toleration*;

Locke was deeply hostile in his epistemology in the closing decades of his life to religious 'enthusiasm', which he saw as a form of religious 'madness' opposite to the calm moderation of his own commitment to 'reasonable Christianity', and as making unfounded and illimitable claims to inspired religious certainty. And Locke was fiercely opposed in the 1690s to the 'blind faith' and 'superstitious' ignorance that he saw as fostered by self-interested priests of many denominations who had generated an 'Empire of Darkness' of centuries of religious impositions and violence. For Locke, such 'priestcraft' centred in Roman Catholicism, but all Christian sects included 'papistical' Christians who were itching to impose alongside laudably 'evangelical' Christians who did not seek to impose their interpretations on others. To counteract the forces of 'enthusiasm', 'papistical' ignorance, and 'priestcraft', Locke composed an epistemological program to 'conduct the understanding' in order to eliminate false claims to certainty of 'knowledge' about matters that were instead matters of 'belief' capable of reasonable disagreement; an educational program that stressed civility, the inculcation of habits of enquiry and holding to the 'plain words of Scripture'; and an hermeneutics of biblical interpretation which asserted the centrality of morals and an afterlife of rewards for moral behaviour and legitimized individual interpretations and 'paraphrases', and not creeds or rituals. In these cumulative commitments to support for comprehension and toleration and personal and principled preference for a particularly capacious established church with a minimal creed and an allowed latitude of interpretations and opinions alongside emphasis on moral performance, Locke supported much that could be termed a 'civil religion'.[3]

Atheism and Roman Catholicism

Emphasising such creedal minimalism and moralism, toleration was emphatically not extended to atheists by Locke – nor by any other otherwise broadly tolerant 'Latitudinarian' Anglican. Locke had stressed punishment for atheism and the requirements of oaths across many decades. In his 1669 *Discourse of Ecclesiastical Polity* Samuel Parker had argued for duties of obedience to an established religion, holding that religion played a foundational role in society: 'without it the most absolute and unlimited

---

Nicholas Jolley, *Toleration and Understanding in Locke* (Oxford, 2016); Teresa Bejan, *Mere Civility* (Cambridge, MA, 2017); Goldie, 'Locke, Proast'; Lucci, *Locke's Christianity*.

[3] Marshall, *Locke, Toleration*; Marshall, 'Locke and latitudinarianism'; Marshall, *Locke: Resistance*; Mark Goldie, 'John Locke, the early Lockeans, and priestcraft', *Intellectual History Review*, 28:1 (2018), 125-44; Mark Goldie, 'Civil Religion', this volume, pp. 42-70; Lucci, *Locke's Christianity*; Sami SavoniusWroth, 'Corruption and Regeneration in the Political Imagination of John Locke', in *Politics, Religion and Ideas in Seventeenth and Eighteenth Century Britain*, eds Justin Champion, John Coffey, Tim Harris, and John Marshall (Woodbridge, 2019), pp. 141-59.

Powers in the World must be forever miserably weak and precarious, and lie always at the mercy of every Subjects Passion and Private Interest'. As J. C. Walmsley and Felix Waldmann have shown recently, in some newly discovered manuscript notes on Parker that provide important evidence of Locke's significant engagement with Parker's thought in 1669, Locke transcribed Parker's wording at this point, and then registered as his query 'whether this extends any farther then a beleife of god in general. but not of this particular worship'. Locke's 'query' here thus emphasised as necessary to the security of political society perhaps only the most minimal of creedal beliefs of all, 'belief of God in general', simultaneously with thereby placing atheists firmly outside the boundaries of toleration.[4]

The first of the religious articles in the 1669 *Fundamental Constitutions of Carolina* declared that everyone was required to 'acknowledge a God, and that God is publicly and solemnly to be Worshipped'. David Armitage, Mark Goldie, John Milton, and most recently, meticulously, and powerfully, James Farr have suggested that Locke contributed as secretary and at significant moments also as author and reviser of the drafting of the provisions and parts of the language of parts of the *Constitutions* in 1669–70 and again in 1682. This provision of the *Constitutions* excluding atheists from toleration was placed at the very head of a series of articles listing those to whom toleration was then in contrast to be provided. Locke was probably author of the content and phrasing of these articles. In his own 'Essay Concerning Toleration', several drafts of which Locke seems to have been composing from 1667 to 1671, and so just before and then alongside his participation in the 1669–70 drafts of the *Constitutions*, Locke declared that 'the belief of a deitie is not to be recond amongst purely speculative opinions for it being the foundation of all morality and that which influences the whole life and actions of men without which a man is to be counted noe other than one of the most dangerous wild beasts and so incapable of all society'.[5]

---

[4] J. C. Walmsley and Felix Waldmann, 'John Locke, Toleration, and Samuel Parker's *A Discourse of Ecclesiastical Politie* (1669): A New Manuscript', *Modern Intellectual History*, 19 (2022), 997–1032.

[5] John Locke, *Political Essays*, ed. Mark Goldie (Cambridge, 1997), pp. 160–81; John Locke, *An Essay Concerning Toleration*, eds John Milton and Philip Milton (Oxford 2006), pp. 45, 308. In his brilliant and meticulous article, '"Absolute Power and Authority": John Locke and the Revisions of the *Fundamental Constitutions of Carolina*', *Locke Studies*, 20 (2020), 1–49, James Farr has recently noted that several contemporaries indicated Locke's extensive roles in composition of the *Constitutions*; that Locke was official Secretary of the Lords Proprietors from 1668 to 1675 (having been personal secretary since 1666 to Shaftesbury, the driving force behind colonization among the Lords Proprietor of the Carolinas); that Locke was appointed an absentee 'landgrave' (a member of the senior and hereditary nobility of the Province); and that Locke handled enormous quantities of the correspondence with and about the Colony. Most importantly of all, Farr argues powerfully that the documentary trail of the multiple manuscript drafts and revisions and excisions from the 1660s to 1680s shows that Locke's role in composition and revisions of many of the articles in the *Constitutions*

Locke declared some two decades later in the *Letter Concerning Toleration* – in William Popple's pithy translation into English – that atheists were intolerable because 'promises, covenants and oaths, which are the bonds of human society can have no hold upon an atheist. The taking away of God, but even in thought, dissolves all'. An atheist 'can have no pretence of religion whereupon to challenge the privilege of a toleration'. In his 1695 *Vindication of the Reasonableness of Christianity* Locke held that atheism was a crime 'which, for its madness, as well as guilt, ought to shut a man out of all sober and civil society'. In a 1690s manuscript entry, Ethica B, Locke declared that 'If man were independent he could have noe law but his own will noe end but himself. He would be a god to himself, and the satisfaction of his own the sole measure and end of all his actions'. In defending his *Letter Concerning Toleration* Locke declared to his controversial opponent Jonas Proast that he did not 'blame your zeal against atheism'. Condemning atheists for immorality, in the 1690s Locke supported the campaigns of the Societies for the Reformation of Manners, which targeted drunkenness, idleness, and 'sodomy' as 'immoral', and supported royal and local magistrates transporting, whipping, mutilating, and incarcerating the 'idle' and 'lewd' who had failed to be appropriately 'honest' and 'industrious'. Here, then, was commitment to an often fiercely punitive civic morality anchored in an explicitly religious morality of belief in God as part and parcel of the moral mortar of society for Locke.[6]

Such life-long hostility to atheism was combined by Locke with decades of denial of toleration to Roman Catholics, even though Locke repeatedly suggested that for their 'speculative' opinions and manner of worship alone Catholics would deserve toleration, and at a very few moments seems at least to have attempted to find ways to extend toleration to some English Catholics. In 1659 Locke asserted that liberty to Catholics was inconsistent with the 'security of the Nation' because they could not 'obey two different authoritys' with contrary interests and where one that was 'destructive' of the peace was further backed by 'an opinion of infallibility and holiness'. In a 1667-8 manuscript recently discovered and interpreted by J. C. Walmsley and Felix Waldmann, 'Reasons for tolerating Papeists equally with others', which Locke wrote in significant part as reflections on the arguments of Charles Wolseley's *Liberty of conscience the magistrate's interest*, Locke canvassed a number of arguments that might be given

---

and much of their language was very considerable, even as Farr notes that Locke should not therefore be said to have been *the* author of the text. See also David Armitage, 'John Locke, Carolina, and the *Two Treatises of Government*', *Political Theory*, 32 (2004), 602-27; Mark Goldie, 'Locke and America', in *A Companion to Locke*, ed. Matthew Stuart (London, 2016), pp. 27-44; John R. Milton, 'John Locke and the *Fundamental Constitutions* of Carolina', *Locke Newsletter*, 21 (1990), 111-33.

[6] Locke, *Letter*, in *The Works of John Locke*, 10 vols (London, 1823), VI, pp. 47, 416; Marshall, *Locke, Toleration*, p. 540; John Marshall, 'London, Locke, and 1690s Provisions for the Poor in Context; Beggars, Spinners and Slaves', in *Politics, Religion and Ideas*, eds Champion et al, pp. 181-200; John Dunn, *The Political Thought of John Locke* (Cambridge, 1969); Jeremy Waldron, *God, Locke and Equality* (Cambridge, 2002).

for tolerating Catholics. He suggested that 'I doubt whether upon Protestant principles we can justifie punishing of Papists for their speculative opinions as Purgatory, transubstantiation &c if they stopd there'. But Locke then continued in a vein that he was to mine time and again in following decades:

> But possibly noe reason nor religion obliges us to tolerate those whose practicall principles necessarily lead them to the eager persecution of all opinions, & the utter destruction of all societys but their owne, soe that it is not the difference of their opinion in religion, or of their ceremonies in worship; but their dangerous and factious tenents in reference to the state, which are blended with and make a part of their religion that excludes them from the benefit of a toleration.

Following Wolseley in seeing the 'variety of opinions in religion' among Protestants as the consequences of Princely encouragement of 'Knowledge', Locke held that 'papists' followed instead 'an implicit faith and acquiesce in ignorance' and were 'obliegd to propagate their religion by force'. For Locke, a Catholic could not 'be thought to be punished meerly for conscience who ownes himself at the same time the subject and adherent of an enemy prince'. Catholics made it 'a part of their religion to pay an implicit subjection to a foraigne infallible power'. They were not 'fit to tolerate'.[7]

In his 1667-71 'Essay Concerning Toleration', which Walmsley and Waldmann have now very persuasively suggested was influenced by Locke's 'Reasons for tolerating Papists equally with others', was perhaps partially composed in tandem, and echoed parts of its language at moments, Locke declared that Catholics took up their religion 'in grosse' and that this included political principles inimical to obedience and security, including papal authority to 'dispense with all their oaths, promises, and the obligations they have to their prince, especially being an heretic'. Catholics 'where they have power', Locke asserted, 'think themselves bound to deny it to others'. It was 'impossible...to make Papists, whilst Papists, friends to your government being enemies to it both in their principles and interest' and owing a 'blind obedience' to the Pope, 'I thinke that they ought not to enjoy the benefit of toleration'. For Locke, having 'adopted into their religion as fundamental truths, several opinions, that are opposite and destructive to any government but the Popes', [Catholics] 'have no title to toleration'.[8]

In writing the *Letter Concerning Toleration* in the Netherlands in the midst of the influx of thousands of Protestant refugees fleeing French Catholic persecution following the Revocation of the Edict of Nantes, Locke argued that there was no right to toleration for those who held that 'faith need not be kept with heretics', for those who held that kings 'excommunicated forfeit their kingdoms' or for

---

[7] John Locke, *The Correspondence of John Locke*, ed. Esmond de Beer, 8 vols (Oxford 1976-82), I, III; J. C. Walmsley and Felix Waldmann, 'John Locke and the Toleration of Catholics: a new manuscript', *Historical Journal*, 62 (2019), 1-23; Marshall, *Locke, Toleration*.
[8] Walmsley and Waldmann, 'Locke and the Toleration of Catholics'; Locke, *Essay Concerning Toleration*, pp. 28, 39-41, 45, 51, 284, 288-92, 305-7, 309; Marshall, *Locke, Toleration*.

a church constituted such 'that all those who enter into it, do thereby, *ipso facto*, deliver themselves up to the protection and service of another prince'. In 1690 Locke viewed the pitched battles fought in Ireland between the forces of William III and James II as battles between 'popery' and 'slavery' on the one side and 'liberty' and 'property' on the other, with the fate of Christendom hanging very precariously in the balance. With Locke's support, the religious toleration provided in and after 1689 in England excluded Catholics from worship and office – as did the severely restrictive Protestant 'penal regime' established in Ireland over the majority Catholic population in the 1690s.[9]

The fierceness of Locke's commitment to anti-Catholicism as for him quite literally a battle to the death for the existence of the Protestant religion needs to be underlined. In his lengthy 1681-2 manuscript reply to Edward Stillingfleet's *Mischief of Separation* and *Unreasonableness of Separation*, even though at one moment Locke briefly mentioned the possibility of a 'regulated toleration' of English Catholics but not priests, Locke stressed instead that Catholics were 'subjects to a Prince [the Pope] that hath declared enmity and war to us', and he declared forcefully that 'all Protestants ought now by all ways to be stirred up against (Catholics) as People that have declared themselves ready by blood violence and destruction to ruine our Religion and Government'. Part of Locke's argument for toleration of Protestant Dissenters at that moment was the urgent need to unite Protestants against Catholics – a theme that had been sounded as an argument for toleration of Protestant Dissenters in Locke's reading of Wolseley's *Liberty of Conscience* in 1667-8. Catholics, Locke declared, could be looked on as 'nothing but either enemyes in our bowels or spies among us, whilst their General Commanders whom they blindly obey declare war, and an unalterable design to destroy us'. Locke wrote these words calling for Protestants to be 'stirred up' against Catholics, it needs once again to be underlined, in the midst of a Protestant Parliamentary propagandist campaign led by Locke's political patron, Shaftesbury, to exclude James, Duke of York from the succession as a Catholic and to challenge the growth of royal absolutism in England. In the fervid and ferocious anti-Catholic atmosphere fostered and fuelled by Shaftesbury and his political clients, many innocent Catholics were tried and executed, including the aged Archbishop Oliver Plunkett, who probably suffered the fate of most declared 'traitors' by being castrated and disemboweled before his death through public execution on the streets of London in 1681. Locke's mature commitment to religious toleration was deeply if often implicitly Protestant as it focused on beliefs, on individuals, and on churches communicating as consequences of consenting communicants' shared understandings of their duties to worship publicly; it was also at moments deeply and explicitly Protestant as it was very violently anti-Catholic.[10]

---

[9] Locke, *Letter*, pp. 45–6; Marshall, *Locke, Toleration*; Mark Goldie, 'John Locke on the Glorious Revolution: A New Document', *History of Political Thought*, 42 (2012), 74–97.

[10] Locke, *Political Essays*, p. 152; MS Locke c34, 7–11; John Marshall, 'The Trial and Execution of Oliver Plunkett', in *The State Trials and the Politics of Justice in Later Stuart*

JOHN MARSHALL

Persecuting Priesthoods and Mistaken Magistrates

If support for a 'civil religion' means rendering Christianity a religion 'stripped of creedal excess, intellectual bigotry, and priestcraft', as Mark Goldie has put it, or what Ashley Walsh has termed a 'Christian civil religion' growing in part from Locke's arguments in the British long eighteenth century, then Locke's project in the 1690s was an important one of advancing a Christian 'civil religion', and close in temperament and temperature to the most capacious and tolerant strands of publicly established low Church Anglicanism. It needs to be understood, however, as simultaneously very fiercely anti-Catholic and anti-atheist, with Locke calling at moments for populations and magistrates to be 'stirred up' with 'zeal' to the use of force against Catholics and atheists in order to establish the religious toleration that Locke supported against those whom he termed intolerant and immoral.[11]

In his multiple commitments to undermining the power of persecuting priesthoods Locke joined hands with parts of what is more usually diagnosed as a fully political 'civil religion', supported by a number of political theorists from Machiavelli to Rousseau and articulated most extensively by Rousseau in the *Social Contract*. Rousseau celebrated Hobbes as his most important predecessor as an advocate of 'civil religion', and some parts of Locke's thought were in proximity to elements of Hobbes's thought even as late as the 1690s. Locke's own theological beliefs increasingly attenuated towards Unitarianism, with a commitment in the 1695 *Reasonableness of Christianity* to morality as the central requirement of Christianity and to belief that 'Jesus was the Messiah' as the only belief required of anyone for entry into Christianity, and thus the only belief absolutely required of every Christian for salvation. Such creedal minimalism brought upon Locke charges of 'Hobbism' for its similarity to the creed specified by Hobbes in *Leviathan*.[12]

As has been underlined by many scholars, most recently by Jeffrey Collins' important *In The Shadow Of Leviathan*, in Locke's earliest lengthy writings, his *Two Tracts*, Locke was close indeed to Hobbes' thinking about 'civil religion' in asserting the authority of the magistrate to command religious ceremonial in

---

England, eds Brian Cowan and Scott Sowerby (Woodbridge, 2021), pp. 93–102; Marshall, *Locke, Resistance*, p. 110; Marshall, *Locke, Toleration*, pp. 686–94 and *passim*.

[11] Mark Goldie, 'The civil religion of James Harrington', in *The Languages of Political Theory in Early Modern Europe*, ed. Anthony Pagden (Cambridge, 1987), pp. 197–224; Mark Goldie, 'civil religion', this volume, pp. 49–52, 55–9; Ashley Walsh, *Civil Religion and the Enlightenment in England 1707–1800* (Woodbridge, 2020); for analysis of Locke's and Hobbes' similar creedal minimalism as among Locke's many associations with Hobbes, see Jeffrey Collins, *In the Shadow of Leviathan* (Cambridge, 2020).

[12] For other accounts of Locke's relations to 'civil religion' see, persuasively, Ronald Beiner, *Civil Religion* (Cambridge, 2011), pp. 147–55 and 156–75 and Elizabeth Pritchard, *Religion in Public* (Stanford, 2014), p. 56; also, Michael Zuckert, *Launching Liberalism* (Lawrence, KS, 2002) and Steven Frankel and Martin Yaffe (ed.), *Civil Religion in Modern Political Philosophy* (Penn State, PA, 2020), pp. 94–113.

ways that were probably influenced by Locke's careful reading of Hobbes; such careful reading of Hobbes by Locke has been suggested by Felix Waldmann's recent identification of Locke's friend James Tyrrell as indicating – albeit in a very much later account – that Locke 'almost always' had Hobbes's *Leviathan* on his table at Oxford in the late 1650s or early 1660s. In his 1660-2 *Two Tracts* Locke asserted the 'absolute authority' of magistrates over religious and civil indifferent matters, including the manner, form, and time of worship, identifying this as necessary when people considered God 'dishonoured upon every small deviation from that way of worship which either education or interest hath made sacred to them'. At the beginning of the 1660s, Locke was, like Hobbes, supportive of magisterial authority over religion as a consequence of viewing intolerance as the only route to political security.[13]

But even if it is important to see the significant convergence between Locke and Hobbes at this moment of Locke's *Two Tracts*, there came to be many striking and especially crucial divergences between Hobbes and Locke as Locke's thought developed, which increased considerably after Locke's composition of his drafts of his 1667-71 'Essay Concerning Toleration', and which especially intensified and deepened by the 1680s in Locke's manuscript opposition to Stillingfleet and then in his key statement of rights to toleration, the *Letter Concerning Toleration*, as Locke came clearly and adamantly to uphold the right and need for expression of beliefs and of actions in worship as any individual interpreted these as true and necessary to hold and perform publicly, and as Locke came to see religious toleration and not magisterially commanded uniformity as the essential route to civil peace. The distance between Locke and Hobbes became considerable as Locke became a supporter of individual rights of resistance to tyranny in composing the *Two Treatises of Government*. Locke had, moreover, clearly set himself directly against Hobbes as a moral thinker in proclaiming in 1677 that Hobbes's 'principle of self-preservation, whereof himself is to be judge, will not easily admit a great many plain duties of morality'. As brilliant scholarship by John Dunn, Mark Goldie, Jeremy Waldron, and Teresa Bejan has shown very clearly, Locke's mature ethical, political and religious thought was structured around the central axiom of God's ownership of humans and humans' consequent extensive duties to others. And even at Locke's most authoritarian moment in the *Two Tracts* in the early 1660s, as Jacqueline Rose, Nicholas Jolley, Felix Waldmann, and others have indicated, his approach towards Hobbes was incomplete: Locke did not render the magistrate supreme pastor and interpreter of the public meaning of Scripture. His composition of the evolving drafts of the "Essay Concerning Toleration" clearly show that Locke had some significant difficulty in trying to think through how much toleration was possible as an eminently

---

[13] Collins, *In the Shadow of Leviathan*; Felix Waldman, 'John Locke as a Reader of Thomas Hobbes' *Leviathan*: A New Manuscript', *Journal of Modern History*, 93 (2021), 245-82; John Locke, *Two Tracts Upon Government*, ed. Philip Abrams (Cambridge, 1969); see also this author's review of Collins' book in *Hobbes Studies*, 33 (2020), 177-81.

practical political question, and in years when there is also some evidence that Hobbes was himself moving towards a complicatedly Erastian tolerance and moving in some overlapping Cabal circles to Locke. But in the wake of Walsmley and Waldmann's manuscript discoveries, Locke's direct influence by Wolseley here now seems much more significant than that of Hobbes at this moment, and there is reason to understand Locke as himself thinking that he had decisively rejected Hobbes in his tolerationist effort to find ways for people to 'quietly permit one another to choose their way to heaven' amidst a wide diversity of beliefs and practices as based on Locke's increasing conviction, contra Hobbes, that it was the attempt to impose uniformity and to assert magisterial authority that posed the greatest threat to civil peace. Locke had praised people for permitting one another to 'choose their own way to heaven' on a diplomatic mission to Cleves in 1665, in writing to his close 'Latitudinarian' Anglican friend Robert Boyle. In his manuscript expression of tolerationist opposition to Samuel Parker's *Discourse of Ecclesiastical Polity* in 1669 Locke directly understood himself as challenging an argument by Parker as problematic precisely because Parker's assertion of magisterial command over the externals of religion as necessary for peace had made Parker's argument, Locke commented, indistinguishable from 'Mr Hobbs's doctrine'.[14]

In order to underline the increasing distance between Locke on the one hand and the central projects of political civil religion's subordination of religion to the power of the state, including those of Hobbes, it is especially important to stress that in Locke's evolving writings on toleration, it is increasingly an overriding fear of magistrates, even more than hostility to the handmaiden priests who flattered their magisterial authority in order to increase their own power, that becomes the dominant motif in Locke's arguments. While Locke never argued for the disestablishment of the Church of England and remained a communicant until his death, Locke became diametrically opposed to 'national' religions being backed by 'force' and 'laws' – and in that very important sense diametrically opposed to his own earlier Hobbesian-flavoured authoritarianism of the *Two Tracts*. In his extensive 1681 manuscript of 'Critical Notes' on Edward Stillingfleet, Locke condemned religion becoming 'a business of state' and the dependence of ecclesiastical government 'upon the secular arm', with ecclesiastical governors forcing men to what they called 'true religion' but which was actually 'such opinions as pleased at court, and best suited the designs and interest of secular domination'. In his *Letter Concerning Toleration* Locke suggested that the church was 'for the most part more apt to be influenced by the Court, than the court by the Church'. Ecclesiastics 'hardly every let

---

[14] Dunn, *Political Thought*; Waldron, *God, Locke*; Bejan; *Mere Civility*; the extensive oeuvre of Mark Goldie on Locke; Jacqueline Rose, 'John Locke, "matters indifferent" and the Restoration of the Church of England', *Historical Journal*, 48 (2005), 601–21; Jolley, *Toleration*; Walmsley and Waldman, 'Locke, Toleration'; Collins, *Shadow*; Richard Tuck, 'Hobbes and Locke on Toleration', in *Thomas Hobbes and Political Theory* (Lawrence, KS, 1990), pp. 153–71; Jon Parkin, *Taming the Leviathan* (Cambridge, 2007).

loose their zeal for God...unless where they have the civil magistrate on their side'; it was when 'court favour has given them the better end of the staff, and they begin to feel themselves the stronger' that then 'charity' was 'laid aside'. It was then, Locke's *Letter* intoned in William Popple's flowing English rendition, that by 'flattering the ambition and favouring the dominion of princes and men in authority, they endeavor with all their might to promote that tyranny in the commonwealth which otherwise they should not be able to establish in the Church'. For Locke's *Letter*, this twinned tyranny in state and church needed to be ended by a firm distinction between the 'business' of churches and the 'business of the state'. Locke restricted the precedent of the Mosaic commonwealth, declaring that 'there is absolutely no such thing, under the Gospel, as a Christian Commonwealth'. Christ had 'instituted no commonwealth' nor put 'the sword into any magistrate's hand'.[15]

Locke backed this set of declarations with chronologically sweeping arguments on the fate of Christianity if one accepted mistaken theories that asserted magisterial power over religion. The fate of the Church under 'the vicissitude of orthodox and Arian emperors' Locke declared 'well known' and the point further 'illustrated' by the 'fresher examples' of English history of 'Henry the 8th, Edward the 6th, Mary and Elizabeth':

> how easily and smoothly the clergy changed their decrees, their articles of faith, their form of worship, everything, according to the inclination of those kings and queens. Yet were those kings and queens of such different minds, in point of religion, and enjoined thereupon such different things, that no man in his wits (I had almost said none but an atheist) will presume to say that any sincere and upright worshipper of God could, with a safe conscience, obey their several decrees.

And Locke supported this argument not just with a sweeping chronological vision but also with a sweeping global vision in condemning 'national' religions backed by the force of magistrates as far more likely to condemn than to support 'truth'. Writing the *Letter Concerning Toleration* in the immediate aftermath of the Revocation of the Edict of Nantes in 1685, and its defences immediately after largely French Catholic forces backed James II in Ireland and Locke saw international Protestantism as in danger, Locke focused unsurprisingly on French Catholic intolerance to make his case that one should not empower any magistrate. In a 'neigbouring country', he remarked acidly, the prince 'declares he will have all his dissenting subjects saved and pursuant thereunto has taken away the lives of many of them. For thither at last persecution must come'. For Locke, magisterial force would 'promote popery in France, as protestantism

---

[15] Locke, *Letter*, in *The Works of John Locke*, pp. 9–12, 20, 37–8, 54 and passim; Marshall, *Locke, Toleration*; Marshall, *Locke, Resistance*.

in England' and 'excuse the late barbarous usage of the Protestants in France, designed to extirpate the reformed religion there'.[16]

Across decades, Locke's extremely negative figuring of the problems of subjecting religion to political authority utilized conjoined images of 'extirpation' or 'slavery' and the questioning not only of Catholic rulers but of what Islamic rulers could do if magistrates were empowered in religion. Locke thus asked in the *Letter* what would happen if magistrates had power to impose their understanding of a true religion 'if in another country, to a Mahometan or a pagan prince, the Christian religion seem false and offensive to God; may not the Christians for the same reason, and after the same manner, be extirpated there'. In the work in which Locke first argued for religious toleration, the 'Essay Concerning Toleration', in a section on force as ineffective in changing opinions and as instead causing hostility to those using force, Locke illustrated his argument by invoking an image then central to many widely circulated English condemnations of Islamic intolerance and slavery in pointing to the 'gally slaves who return from Turky' after having endured 'all manner of miserys rather than part with their religion'. Had their 'chains given them leave', Locke wrote, they would have 'cut the throats of those cruell patrons who used them so severely'. In the initial draft of the 'Essay Concerning Toleration' Locke declared that it would be 'a hazardous attempt for those who designe it, to bring this island to the condition of a gally where the greater part shall be reduced to the condition of slaves, be forced with blows to row the vessel, but share in none of the ladeing or be allowed soe much as a cabin unless they will make chaines, for all those who are to be used like Turks and persuade them also to stand still whilst they put them upon 'em'. The enslavement of some Christians under Ottoman rule came to Locke's mind again in March 1679 when he recorded a passage from Sagard's *History of Canada* on those brought up as captives among Indian tribes who fought against their parents. He then added, signed with his initials to indicate that it was his view: 'We see the same in the Janissaries' – that is, among the elite Turkish troops taken from Christian parents as children and were brought up as Muslim slaves who then fought against their parents and their original country 'as heartily as any'. In the *Two Treatises*, the political slavery that Locke condemned as the threatening potential future fate of England under absolutism was imaged through a ship sailing to Algiers, home of the Barbary pirates who had captured and enslaved many Christians.[17]

Locke thus imaged and condemned across many years in his writings on toleration and against absolutism the use of magisterial authority to

---

[16] Locke, *Letter*, in *Works*, pp. 27, 35; *Second Letter* in *Works*, VI, pp. 64, 69, 72, 77, 87, 89; *Third Letter* in *Works*, VI, pp. 152, 181, 193, 194, 251, 366, 400, 413; Marshall, *Locke, Toleration*, p. 556.

[17] Locke, *Essay*, pp. 178, 294; Locke, *Political Essays*, p. 273; John Locke, *Two Treatises of Government*, ed. Peter Laslett (Cambridge, 1988), II, p. 210; Nabil Matar, *Turks, Moors and Englishmen in the Age of Discovery* (New York, 1999); Bernard Capp, *British Slaves and Barbary Corsairs 1580–1750* (Oxford, 2022).

command worship among Christians in part by raising the spectre of Islamic absolutism and intolerance towards Christians. In a further passage in the *Letter* on the intolerability of subjects who profess allegiance to foreign rulers Locke declared that

> It is ridiculous for anyone to profess himself to be a Mahometan only in religion, but in everything else a faithful subject to a Christian Magistrate, whilst at the same time he acknowledges himself bound to yield blind obedience to the Mufti of Constantinople, who himself is entirely obedient to the Ottoman emperor, and frames the feigned oracles of that religion according to his pleasure. But this Mahometan, living amongst Christians, would yet more apparently renounce their government, if he acknowledged the same person to be head of his church who is the supreme magistrate in the state.[18]

Once again, then, Locke has here figured intolerant magistrates as those commanding their religious acolytes to issue dictates backing their authority. Noel Malcolm's *Useful Enemies* has recently identified the trope of the obedience of the Mufti to the Ottoman Sultan as having been developing extensively in a series of seventeenth-century works that Locke can be shown to have owned, read, and recommended, and in a series of crucial articles on Locke and the toleration and endenization of Muslims Nabil Matar has pointed to some of these works as influences on Locke and as possessed by Locke. In his 1703 'Some thoughts concerning reading and study by a gentleman' Locke recommended George Sandys' 1615 *Relation of a Journey*, a work which spoke of the Ottoman Sultan ruling by his will 'although sometime for forme he useth the assent of the never gainsaying Mufti'. In the early 1680s Locke read Paul Rycaut's *Present State of the Ottoman Empire*, which described the Mufti as 'that Authority wherein their Religion hath placed an ultimate power of decision in all their controversies', but declared that in matters of state the Sultan, who was 'above the Law, and the Oracle and Fountain of Justice' 'demands his opinion...either to appear more just and religious, or to incline the people more willingly to obedience'. Rycaut recorded that the Sultan could disagree with the Mufti and dismiss and execute him at will. In *Political Reflections Upon the Government of the Turks*, Francis Osborne identified Muhammad as having forbidden anyone to interpret the Koran other than the Mufti, and the Sultan as having honored the Mufti in public, but 'for show' as 'true Reason of State'. The Mufti could be executed if he countermanded the Sultan. According to Osborne, the people viewed the Mufti as 'sanctified', but he was a 'weather-cock pointing onely that way which the breath of *Policy* blows'. In his *A Description of the Grand Signior's Seraglio* John Greaves described the Mufti as a 'Circumcised pope' who 'yields an infallible obedience to all the Emperor inspires him with'. It is clear that what Locke added to this strain of thinking about the Mufti as

---

[18] Locke, *Letter*, p. 47; Marshall, *Locke, Toleration*, chapter 19.

legitimating what he was ordered to declare by the Ottoman Sultan, then, was Locke's characteristic phrasing condemning those who gave 'blind obedience' to religious figures.[19]

While this issue was in Locke's *Letter* presented as a conceptual issue about Christian rulers being unable to tolerate subjects of a foreign prince, Locke wrote this in the winter of 1685, and it was published in 1689, in the midst of a major war between Christian and Ottoman forces 'legitimated' by the Mufti as a religious war on the Sultan's orders. The period around the Siege of Vienna of 1683 had witnessed a concerted campaign in the Netherlands for international Christian forces to be raised to fight against the Ottomans. There was extensive propaganda celebrating the Christian victory in September 1683, and then about the continued military campaigns against the Ottomans, including the 1686 'liberation' of Buda. In 1689 a Grand Alliance was formed, participated in by the Dutch and the English, and signed by William III, to fight against both the Ottomans and the French. In March 1684 Locke wrote to his close friend Edward Clarke from exile in the Netherlands about the growth of 'tares and divisions' among Christians, wishing that 'beati pacifici would pass among Christians for good gospel, as I think it would be good policy in defence of Christendom against the great event of war with the Turk'. And in 1689 Locke corresponded with Carey Mordaunt, Lady Peterborough, about the desirability of the Grand Alliance against the Ottomans and the French. A supporter of the war in Ireland in 1689–90 that was largely composed of international Protestant forces fighting against the largely French Catholic forces backing James II, Locke was also a supporter in 1689 of an alliance of Christians against the Ottoman forces.[20]

It is extremely important to underline in saying this that Locke knew that there were many contemporary Muslims who were not subjects of the Sultan, and even more important still to underline that Locke was explicit and adamant in the *Letter Concerning Toleration* and its defences that all Muslims who did not subscribe to 'blind obedience' to the Mufti and thus to the Ottoman Sultan as a foreign prince deserved toleration. Inter alia, Locke explicitly discussed Persian Muslims in his *Third Letter on Toleration*; read and sought information about Muslims in India; discussed the visit of the Moroccan ambassador to England; and discussed in manuscripts the 'traditions' of Muslim 'priests' which he paralleled to the traditions of Catholics and Jews without any

---

[19] Noel Malcolm, *Useful Enemies* (Oxford, 2019), pp. 288–9, 296–302; Nabil Matar, 'John Locke and the "turbaned nations"', *Journal of Islamic Studies*, 2 (1991), 67–77 and 76; Nabil Matar, 'England and Religious Plurality: Henry Stubbe, John Locke and Islam', *Studies in Church History*, 51 (2015), 181–203; Marshall, *Locke, Toleration*.

[20] John Locke, *The Correspondence of John Locke*, ed. Esmond de Beer, 8 vols (Oxford 1976–82), II, p. 612; Nabil Matar, 'Britons and Muslims in the early modern period: from prejudice to (a theory of) toleration', *Patterns of Prejudice*, 43 (2009), 213–31; Hendrilk Van Nierop, *The Life of Romeyn de Hooghe 1645–1708* (Amsterdam, 2018), pp. 191–216; Andrew Wheatcroft, *The Enemy at the Gate* (New York, 2008).

mention of Muftis. Locke had very considerable awareness of the wide range of commitments, practices, polities, and individuals within contemporary Islam. Locke did not support in the *Letter* the exclusion of Muslims from toleration *as* Muslims, nor did he articulate any general association of Islam as a religion with intolerance or absolutism; Locke's exclusion from rights to toleration was only of those subjects said to offer 'blind obedience' to a specific religious authority in one Empire who was himself said to obey an absolutist political authority.

Very importantly indeed, in the *Letter* itself Locke declared directly that the commonwealth 'embraces indifferently all men that are honest, peaceable, and industrious' and that 'If we may openly speak the truth' then 'neither pagan, nor Mahometan, nor Jew ought to be excluded from the civil rights of the commonwealth because of his religion'. Locke had put the same idea forward as early as the 1667 'Essay Concerning Toleration': 'If I observe the Friday with the Mahometan, or the Saturday with the Jew, or the Sunday with the Christian...I see noe thing in any of these that can of itself make me either the worse subject to my prince, or worse neighbor to my fellow subject'. And in his defence of the *Letter Concerning Toleration*, Locke explicitly and repeatedly supported toleration of Muslims when challenged by Jonas Proast for doing precisely that. In 1692 Locke declared 'ill-grounded' Proast's 'pretence against admitting Jews, Mahometans, and Pagans, to the civil rights of the commonwealth', noting that no law in England made any converting to those religions 'forefeit the civil rights of the commonwealth'. In his posthumously published *Fourth Letter* Locke declared of 'a Brahmin, a Mahometan' just as he did of a Quaker or Lutheran that 'you are no more a judge for any of them than they are for you. Men in all religions have equally strong persuasions, and every one must judge for himself, nor can anyone judge for another, and you last of all for the magistrate'. Locke's one restriction on the toleration of Muslims was contingently, not intrinsically, related to Islam; and to particular subjects of one particular regime within Islam, and not to Islam itself. Stressing Locke's distinction between Muslims in general and the specific regime of the Ottoman Sultans, Nabil Matar has recently suggested that Locke 'knew how the cooperation of North African regions would be crucial to British navies and grounds forces fighting against France' in the Nine Years War, and provision to England by Morocco, Algeria, Tunisia, and Libya of wheat, corn, horses and leather, inter alia. Matar even suggests that this was perhaps why Locke 'sought accommodation for Muslims'.[21]

In the *Letter* Locke moreover invoked the toleration that he recognized as provided for most religions in Constantinople, then the most multi-religious city in Europe, as he supposed for his Arminian friend Limborch two churches, 'the one of Arminians, the other of Calvinists, residing in the city of

---

[21] Locke, *Letter*, in *Works*, pp. 31, 36, 40, 52, 232 and 561 ; Locke, *Essay Concerning Toleration*, p. 234; Marshall, *Locke, Toleration*; chapter 19; Denise Spellman, *Thomas Jefferson's Qur'an* (New York, 2013), pp. 72-9; Lucci, *Locke's Christianity*; Matar, 'John Locke and the "turbaned nations"', pp. 67-77; Matar, 'Britons and Muslims', p. 228.

Constantinople', and declared that no one would then say that 'either of these churches' had 'the right to deprive the members of the other of their estates and liberty' because of differences of 'doctrines or ceremonies'. The Turks, Locke observed, would 'silently stand by, and laugh to see with what inhuman cruelty Christians then rage against Christians'. Locke continued that no one would

> say that any right can be derived unto a Christian Church, over its brethren, from a Turkish Emperor....An infidel, who has himself no authority to punish Christians for the articles of their faith, cannot confer such an Authority upon any society of Christians, nor give unto them a right that he does not have himself. This would be the case at Constantinople. And the reason of the thing is the same in any Christian kingdom. The civil power is the same in every place, nor can that power, in the hands of a Christian prince, confer any greater authority upon the Church, than in the hands of a heathen, which is to say, just none at all.[22]

Here, it needs to be emphasized, Locke was pointing towards Islamic practices of tolerance as far greater than Christian practices had been and then were, in order to mock Christian practices, arguments, and pretensions, and in making his central claim that no ruler, Christian or Islamic should impose their own understanding of 'truth' on any subjects in their realms.

Locke and America, religious toleration, and slavery

Locke's strong assertion in the *Letter* that Muslims should receive toleration equally with those of other religions was taken up in the decades of the American Revolution by many who defined and defended religious toleration in late eighteenth-century America, whether they saw this with Thomas Jefferson and James Madison as requiring the separation of church and state or held, with George Washington and Patrick Henry, that a tax supported state and even a national religion was permissible as long as it provided truly extensive toleration outside of its boundaries. In his extensive notetaking from Locke's *Letter* Jefferson recorded in 1776 that Locke 'sais neither pagan nor Mahamedan nor Jew ought to be excluded from the civil rights of the Commonwealth because of his religion'. As Denise Spelman has shown, Jefferson then noted Locke's specific exclusion of Muslims who were obedient to the Mufti who was obedient to the Sultan, and Locke's exclusions of Catholics and atheists, but held that unless one acknowledged obedience to a foreign prince one could be a good citizen and deserved toleration. Condemning the 'impious presumption' of rulers assuming 'dominion over the faith of others', Jefferson's and Madison's Virginia Statute for Religious Freedom drew heavily from Locke, asserting that the fundamental natural

---

[22] Locke, *Letter* in *Works*, pp. 18–19.

right of conscience had been reserved by individual citizens when they left the state of nature for civil society and enacting that 'no man shall...suffer on account of his religious opinions or belief'. George Washington argued that 'any man, conducting himself as a good citizen, and being accountable to God alone for his religious opinions, ought to be protected in worshipping the Deity according to the Dictates of his own conscience'. Identifying the bosom of America as open to receive 'the Oppressed and Persecuted of all Nations and Religions, whom we shall welcome to a participation of all our rights and privileges', Washington declared that 'they may be Mohometans, Jews or Christians of any sect, or they may be Atheists'.[23]

It is extremely important to recognize the extensiveness of the toleration supported by Jefferson, Madison, Washington, and others, who created considerable freedom of worship and belief in late eighteenth-century America, and who were significantly influenced by reading Locke's arguments, while seeing themselves as 'going beyond' Locke on some points, such as toleration for atheists. It is simultaneously extremely important to stress, as Denise Spelman does powerfully, that Jefferson, Madison, Washington, and others were owners of enslaved people. Some of the people owned by Washington, such as 'Fatimer' and 'Little Fatimer', were surely Muslim, and it seems likely that this was true of some people owned by Jefferson and Madison also. But such enslaved people were denied free practice for their worship, and freedom itself. It is on this important issue in Locke's own thought and practice that we will close this essay.[24]

Locke was an extremely active, acquisitive, avid English imperialist who supported the extension of religious toleration in English colonies in the Americas and West Indies from the 1660s until his death, and simultaneously through many actions supported the massive expansion of slavery in English colonies in the Americas and West Indies. From the 1660s Locke supported an imperialism based significantly on the expansion of religious toleration in English colonies such as Carolina. As noted earlier, the *Constitutions* for Carolina provided that to be accounted a church or religious profession it was necessary to assert that there is a God and worship God publicly, but the *Constitutions* had then allowed churches to set down their 'external way' of worship, with none to 'disturb or molest any religious assembly' and 'no person whatsoever shall disturb, molest, or persecute another for his speculative opinions in religion, or his way of worship'. In what Teresa Bejan has shown became a repeated part of

---

[23] Vincent Philip Munoz, *Religious Liberty and the American Founding* (Chicago, 2022); Jack Racove, *Beyond Belief, Beyond Conscience: the radical significance of the free exercise clause* (Oxford, 2020); Spelman, *Jefferson's Qur'an*; 'Notes on Locke and Shaftesbury', in *The Papers of Thomas Jefferson*, ed. Julian Boyd (Princeton 1953), I, pp. 544–51. For a recent fascinating and important discussion of Locke's arguments and contemporary issues of toleration for Muslims, see Pooyan Tamimi Arab, *Why do religious forms matter?* (London, 2022), chapter 3.

[24] Spelman, *Jefferson's Qur'an*.

religious provisions in British Atlantic colonies in the later seventeenth century, the *Constitutions* further asserted that none was to 'use any reproachful, reviling, or abusive language, against any religion of any church or profession' as this was a 'certain way of disturbing the peace' and 'of hindering the conversion of any to the truth'. The articles stressed 'good usage and persuasion' to win over to the 'truth' as many as possible of 'Jews, Heathens and other Dissenters from the purity of Christian religion'. And the *Constitutions* declared that:

> since the Natives of that Place, who will be concerned in our Plantation, are utterly strangers to Christianity, whose Idolatry, Ignorance, or Mistake gives us no right to expel or use them ill; and those who remove from other parts to Plant there will unavoidably be of different Opinions concerning Matters of Religion, the liberty whereof they will expect to have allowed them, and it will not be reasonable for us, on this account to keep them out.

Locke seems very likely to have been the primary author of this set of provisions, and of much of its language.[25]

In the *Constitutions* it was simultaneously explicitly provided that the enslaved population in the Carolinas could worship freely, but would not be freed as the result of their belief or worship:

> Since Charity obliges us to wish well to the Souls of all Men, and Religion ought to alter nothing in any Man's Civil Estate or Right, It shall be lawful for Slaves, as well as others, to Enter themselves and be of what Church of Profession any of them shall think best, and thereof be as fully Members as any Freeman. But yet, no Slave shall hereby be exempted from that Civil Dominion his Master has over him, but be in all other things in the same State and Condition he was in before.

The end of this passage echoes language, James Farr has stressed, that Locke himself composed about the separation of civil and religious status such that Christian commitments do not change one's status as a slave in Locke's own compositions across many decades, from his early authoritarian *Two Tracts* right until his posthumously published *Paraphrases on the Epistles of St Paul*, composed at the very end of his life. This passage in the *Constitutions* was written, Farr notes, before a single slave had yet been brought forcibly to Carolina. It was also written during years when a number of British colonies in the Americas were passing significant legislation to ensure that baptism or conversion to Christianity would not free enslaved people.[26]

---

[25] Locke, *Political Essays*, pp. 160–81; Bejan, *Civility*; Farr, "Absolute".

[26] Locke, *Political Essays*, pp. 160–81; Farr, "Absolute"; Jon Sensbach, 'Slaves to Intolerance: African-American Christianity and Religious Freedom in Early America', in *The First Prejudice*, eds Chris Beneke and Christopher S. Grenda (Philadelphia, PA, 2011), pp. 195–217. For an alternate view, Holly Brewer, 'Slavery, Sovereignty,

In a 1669 variation of the *Constitutions*, again as Farr has recently documented and as Armitage had earlier indicated, a separate paragraph was added to this provision which declared that 'Any freeman of Carolina, who hath Slaves, shall have an absolute arbitrary Power, over the Lives Liberties and Persons of his Slaves, and their Posterities, to punish them with Death or otherwise, whom and for what cause soever he shall think fit'. This paragraph was withdrawn in the next 1669 manuscript variation of the articles, but the articles of the *Constitutions* were then revised to declare that 'Every freeman of Carolina shall have absolute authority over his Negro Slaves, of what opinion or religion soever', and that was then further revised by the addition of two further words, 'power and' before 'authority', in a manuscript version, and thereafter in the printed version of 1670. In manuscript revisions of the *Constitutions* in January and August 1682, the text remained with that wording, and though it mysteriously disappeared in a version of the articles sealed in August 1682, that text was restored in the final version in 1698 (with which Locke may or may not have been associated but about which he was probably at least aware) so that in all but one version of the *Constitutions* from 1670 to 1698 the *Constitutions* declare that 'Every freeman of Carolina shall have absolute power and Authority over his Negro Slaves, of what Opinion or Religion soever'. As David Armitage and James Farr have indicated, Locke was probably author of this horrifying specific provision, and of its additions, amendments, and phrasing.[27]

In the same period of the late 1660s that we saw earlier that Locke was attempting to identify grounds to support and to expand religious toleration in England in his 'Essay Concerning Toleration', Locke was thus very deeply involved in the expansion of slavery in British colonies. In the very same texts in which he advanced many provisions for religious toleration in the Carolinas, he also advanced the expansion of slavery in the Carolinas. In the same period in the 1690s that Locke wrote the series of works advancing religious toleration in the program of epistemological, educational, economic, and hermeneutic works focusing on expanding individuals' rights to believe and worship freely with which this essay started, Locke was a major figure in England's colonial administration and significantly involved in the massive expansion of slavery in England's colonies, especially in the West Indies. Locke's support for religious toleration was in some ways expansive, including Jews, Muslims, 'heathens' and 'pagans' alongside toleration of many denominations of Christians. But it did not include atheists or Catholics, the intolerant, and many whom Locke held to be immoral. And it was combined with Locke having undertaken many actions that led not only to the

---

and "Inheritable Blood": Reconsidering Locke and the Origins of American Slavery', *American Historical Review*, 122 (2017), 1038–78.

[27] Locke, *Political Essays*, pp. 160–81; Farr, "Absolute"; Armitage, 'Locke and Carolina'.

expansion of colonial practices of religious toleration but also simultaneously, horrifyingly, to massively increasing enslavement.[28]

In the same period of the late 1660s in which, as we saw earlier, Locke was coming to identify religious toleration and not magisterially imposed uniformity as essential to civil peace in the drafts of his 'Essay Concerning Toleration', Locke was involved in the expansion of religious toleration and simultaneously of slavery in the Americas in helping to draft the *Constitutions* – acting among those who could be termed overarching legislators for the colony of Carolina. The claim that one's religious commitments did not affect one's civil status was made in these *Constitutions* both a ground for toleration of diverse beliefs and worships *and* for not being freed by becoming a Christian. In the same period in the 1690s that Locke published the series of epistemological, educational, economic, and hermeneutic works advancing religious toleration and comprehension with which this piece started, Locke was a major figure in England's colonial administration in years of the massive expansion of slavery in English colonies in the Americas and especially in the West Indies. For Locke, the wealth and power brought to Britain from those colonies aided defence of the recently established English Protestant toleration against immediate threats of Catholic absolutist tyranny and religious 'slavery'. Locke's support for religious toleration was in some ways expansive, including Jews, and the vast majority of Muslims, as well as many Christian denominations, and 'heathens', but it did not include atheists or Catholics, nor those whom Locke held to be intolerant and immoral, and it involved expansion of colonial practices not only of toleration but also of slavery.

---

[28] Farr, Locke'; Armitage, Locke and Carolina', Marshall, 'Beggars'; Goldie, 'Locke and America'; Marshall, *Locke, Toleration*; Pritchard, *Religion*. We await very important forthcoming scholarship on Locke, slavery, and colonialism from Mark Goldie and David Armitage.

9

Civil Religion and Early Modern Views of the Anglo-Saxon Church

Jacqueline Rose

'The most valuable part of the laws, the constitution, and the religion of England, is undoubtedly built on a SAXON foundation'. The man who made this claim went on to bemoan the 'abject vassalage' suffered under the Norman 'usurpation'. It was these Normans and their 'minions' who had introduced the *iure divino* hereditary monarchy that had subverted the free constitution and elective kingship of the Saxons, whose rulers had done nothing without their great council, the micel-gemot. Indeed, he argued, ecclesiastical as well as civil laws had a Saxon foundation, and King Alfred's care for his people was shown by his translating 'various ... works of piety' into the vernacular for their benefit.

Initially it is surprising to find that these claims do not come from an early modern polemical text. Their author was, in fact, James Ingram, the third professor of Anglo-Saxon at the University of Oxford, writing at the dawn of the nineteenth century. Furthermore, while early modern authors might have recognised each one of Ingram's claims, the particular combination in which he offered them would have been hard for any author between the sixteenth and early eighteenth centuries to swallow wholesale. Ingram's assertion that the Church of England's kinship with Saxon times 'satisfactorily prove[s] the purity of our primitive church' and the doctrine and discipline of the Reformation sounds like the arguments made by the circle of the Reformed Protestant Archbishop Matthew Parker, early in Elizabeth I's reign, yet he cited the non-juror George Hickes and the High Church Anglican Elizabeth Elstob.[1] His argument for the importance of great councils and elective monarchy sounds whiggish, albeit Ingram lighted

---

[1] James Ingram, *An Inaugural Lecture on the Utility of Anglo-Saxon Literature* (Oxford, 1807), pp. 25–6; the passages mentioned in the first paragraph of this article are found on pp. iv, 3, 14n, 23–4, 20, and 25. On the lectureship, see David Fairer, 'Anglo-Saxon Studies', in *The History of the University of Oxford: V: The Eighteenth Century*, eds L. S. Sutherland and L. G. Mitchell (Oxford, 1986), pp. 827–9.

on the most inappropriate whig example in saying that 'the principles of [Anglo-Saxon constitutional] common sense' had been revived 'by the genius of a Locke', given Locke's avoidance of the type of historical forays his fellow whigs often engaged in. Nevertheless, his reference to Norman tyranny echoed a more radical Leveller account of a Norman Yoke, rather than stressing – as moderate parliamentarians and whigs did – continuity before and after 1066.[2] Finally, that his claim that religion was received from a Roman church 'less corrupt' than it would later become sat alongside his observation of the 'striking contrast' between the 'domineering spirit of the Romish priesthood and the affectionate concern of King Alfred for the religious welfare of his subjects' marked an unease at how to praise Anglo-Saxon religion while knowing it derived from Roman missionaries.[3]

This chapter explores some of Ingram's themes, triangulating between three established historiographies: first, that on the Elizabethan Protestant recovery and use of Anglo-Saxon Christianity; second, the seventeenth-century debate on the origin of parliaments; and third, the location of Anglo-Saxon, Old English, and septentrional studies in a narrative of the development of historical scholarship. Almost nobody has yet examined the topic that links all of these: Anglo-Saxon ecclesiastical constitutionalism. Colin Kidd comes nearest in delineating, first, the place of Saxonism in different views of the ancient constitution and second, the value polemicists found in deploying both a British and Saxon ecclesiastical ancestry.[4] However, he does not probe the relationship between the two – i.e., whether, and if so how, they could combine in a claim for a Saxon civil religion. What did it mean that Anglo-Saxon councils contained a strong cohort of ecclesiastical members? What conclusions might be drawn from the indistinguishability of synods and great councils? Was the intermingling of civil and ecclesiastical law and lawcourts a model for early modern England?

Many of these aspects of Anglo-Saxon politics and religion remain difficult to pronounce on conclusively now. Ecclesiastical and civil authority were closely related, but the extent of their interdependence and how it changed over time is harder to chart.[5] The mid- to late ninth-century king Edgar ordered that bishops and ealdormen sit in shire courts, but how different types of law interacted is 'complex and largely hidden from

---

[2] Ingram, *Inaugural Lecture*, pp. 14 and n., 24.
[3] *Ibid.*, p. 25.
[4] Colin Kidd, *British Identities before Nationalism* (Cambridge, 1999), chapters 4–5.
[5] See Patrick Wormald, 'Archbishop Wulfstan and the Holiness of Society', in his *Legal Culture in the Early Medieval West* (London, 1999), esp. pp. 241–4, on the difficulties of separating legal and homiletic texts; Peter Hunter Blair, *An Introduction to Anglo-Saxon England* (Cambridge, 1970), p. 162, on a decline of the interdependence of church and state by the mid-eighth century; and Catherine Cubitt, 'Bishops and Councils in Late Saxon England: The Intersection of Secular and Ecclesiastical Law', in *Recht und Gericht in Kirche und Welt um 900*, ed. Wilfried Hartmann (Munich, 2016), pp. 154–8, on the specific contextual reasons for excommunication appearing in law codes.

view'.[6] Councils that included both lay and ecclesiastical members are tricky to categorise; whether to apply the term synod or witenagemot is unclear, 'often a matter of the historian's judgment', the two being, perhaps, 'different names for the same thing'.[7] Even the frequency of such meetings is hard to trace, too dependent on the exigencies of source survival, while the relative significance of Roman and Celtic missions in making converts to Christianity may be 'impossible' to assess. A similar challenge arises regarding succession and rituals of king-making.[8] Such ambiguities marked out the Anglo-Saxon period as a potential battleground for early modern writers. How should this era, so awkwardly poised between the pristine apostolic age and the high tide of late medieval papal authority, be treated? What relationship did it have with the earlier British church, whose history was even harder to evidence? Was Christianity present in England by the time of King Lucius, in the second century, or did it arrive with Joseph of Arimathea,[9] or through the apostles themselves? Or were the English church's origins to be found in Augustine's mission, ordered by Rome in the 590s, with its early progress and development therefore a part of a Saxon, more than a British, story?

This chapter argues that the ecclesiastical-temporal relationships of the seventh to eleventh centuries were potentially useful to early modern authors, but that the full realization of such potential was strikingly rare. Occasional hints that the Anglo-Saxon church might prove useful to radical critics of the established Church of England often remained undeveloped, while the degree to which the positions the Anglo-Saxon church was invoked to uphold constituted a form of civil religion is also open to question. Indeed, as this chapter shows, while the Anglo-Saxon period was a usable past, it was also a recalcitrant one. In exploring how it was approached by early modern authors, this chapter asks whether its apparently closely connected church and state could be read as an example of civil religion, and whether, if not, that tells us something important about the meanings of civil religion and the limits of its utility as an analytical category.

---

[6] Cubitt, 'Bishops and Councils', p. 158.

[7] *Ibid.*, p. 153; Blair, *Introduction*, p. 216. For attempts to define and describe assemblies, see Catherine Cubitt, *Anglo-Saxon Church Councils, c.650-c.850* (London, 1995), pp. 2-6 and chapter 1; Blair, *Introduction*, pp. 214-22.

[8] Blair, *Introduction*, pp. 125, 204.

[9] A mid-thirteenth-century version of William of Malmesbury's twelfth-century history of Glastonbury claimed that Joseph of Arimathea, said to have requested and buried Christ's body, came to England with the Holy Grail and founded the first church at Glastonbury: *The Oxford Dictionary of the Christian Church*, ed. F. L. Cross, 3rd edn (Oxford, 1997), s.v. Joseph of Arimathea, St. See also Justin Champion, *The Pillars of Priestcraft Shaken: The Church of England and its Enemies, 1660-1730* (Cambridge, 1992), pp. 55-7.

I

Ambivalence over the religious value of the Anglo-Saxon period was deeply rooted. Anglo-Saxon history occupied 'a peculiar and difficult position' in the English Protestant imagination, even from the point at which study of it burgeoned in the 1560s.[10] Early English evangelicals dated the end of the primitive church to around 600 or the following century and the coincidence of this date with Augustine's mission to Kent in 597 associated Augustine with the decline rather than revival or foundation of English Christianity.[11] Dispatched to England by Pope Gregory I, Augustine was seen as importing Romish hierarchy, superstition, and persecution. For some, the story of the slaughter at Bangor of the British monks who had resisted Rome's authority made the mission a precursor to the Marian burnings, not the Reformed Church of England. As late as 1685, the Protestant preacher and future bishop of Worcester Edward Stillingfleet described a Christianity established by St Paul and upheld by the British church against Augustine.[12]

Catholics, not Protestants, celebrated Augustine's mission and the patriotic virtues of the Anglo-Saxon church. The Catholic exile Thomas Stapleton underlined Bede's Englishness in his translation of the church historian published in 1565, while Richard Verstegan emphasised the Saxon, not British, origins of Englishness.[13] A very English Catholic Anglo-Saxon church lived long, and by the later seventeenth century could be attractively un-papal in the hands of men such as the Benedictine convert Serenus Cressy, whose version of its history reflected a way in which 'religious consciousness' could be 'nourished' by 'ruminations on the ancient matter of Christian Britain'.[14] The title page of Cressy's *Church-History of Brittany* proudly announced 'That the present Roman-Catholick Religion hath from the Beginning, without interruption or change been professed in this our Island' and ended, over a thousand pages later, by arguing that changes of government from the sixth to eleventh centuries did not alter the English

---

[10] Benedict Scott Robinson, 'John Foxe and the Anglo-Saxons', in *John Foxe and his World*, eds Christopher Highley and John N. King (Aldershot, 2002), p. 56.

[11] Rosamund Oates, 'Elizabethan Histories of English Christian Origins', in *Sacred History: Uses of the Christian Past in the Renaissance World*, eds Katherine van Liere, Simon Ditchfield, and Howard Louthan (Oxford, 2012), pp. 168–70.

[12] Bale's letter to Matthew Parker, 30 July 1560, in Timothy Graham and Andrew G. Watson, *The Recovery of the Past in Early Elizabethan England: Documents by John Bale and John Joscelyn from the Circle of Matthew Parker* (Cambridge, 1998), p. 23; Edward Stillingfleet, *Origines Britannicae* (1685), pp. 356–64. Bede's account of Bangor has Augustine predicting divine vengeance wrecked on the monks through the hands of Æthelfrith: *Ecclesiastical History of the English People*, eds Bertram Colgrave and R. A. B. Mynors (Oxford, 1969), II.2.

[13] Robinson, 'Foxe and the Anglo-Saxons', pp. 58, 66–72.

[14] Gabriel Glickman, 'Gothic History and Catholic Enlightenment in the Works of Charles Dodd (1672–1743)', *Historical Journal*, 54 (2011), 347–69, at p. 352.

church, which had been 'as constant as Rome it self'.[15] The Benedictine acknowledged some early roots of British Christianity, though seized the opportunity to point out that Joseph of Arimathea, that iconic figure of the early British church, linked ancient faith in Britain to monasteries. Although pointing to monasteries and masses in the sixth century, Cressy depicted the condition of Britain on the eve of the Saxon invasions as 'miserable'.[16] The British clergy had singularly failed to reform the country and, according to Cressy, were so bad that they might have deterred rather than attracted converts; by contrast, the missions from Rome led to a 'new seed of pious *Princes*, zealous *Bishops*, immaculate *Virgins*, devout *Monks*', and the truth of Augustine's message was evidenced by miracles associated with his mission.[17] Admitting that the terminology used for assemblies in the following centuries could only ever be inexact, Cressy still argued that kings and clergy had worked together to legislate, with mixed law courts from the 960s to 1066, and fines for peacebreaking used as evidence for the equal esteem given to kings and bishops.[18] His history included impious kings and samples of clerical rebukes to erring rulers, even of excommunications.[19] Yet it also offered much exemplary royal piety: the removal of idols, gifts to Rome (even when royal coffers were running low), baptisms at and pilgrimages to Rome, royal attention to the interests of the church, and royal foundations of monasteries. '*Piety* and munificence to *Gods Church* was the ordinary employment & business of the *Kings* of this age'.[20]

By the eighteenth century, the Catholic priest and historian Charles Dodd was not averse to acknowledging a pre-Saxon English Christianity, while also showing the compatibility of the Roman mission and pre-existing British church by reducing the differences between them to matters indifferent. Dodd's depiction of an Anglo-Saxon Christian monarchy with extensive powers over synods, laws, and consecrations echoed the godly rulers whom James II's preachers cited as examples.[21] He tactically alluded to the vague origins of Christianity in the British Isles and, although noting the role of Joseph of Arimathea was 'best attested', focused instead on how knowledge of the true faith came from a 'continual correspondence

---

[15] Serenus Cressy, *The Church-History of Brittany from the Beginning of Christianity to the Norman Conquest* (1668), t.p. and p. 1002.
[16] Cressy, *Church-History*, pp. 17, 19, 31, 236, 272, 201. The Saxons, he said, were terrible but – unlike Protestants – chaste: pp. 202–3.
[17] Ibid., pp. 282, 279, 287–8, 304.
[18] Ibid., pp. 479, 492, 775, 801, 869, 479.
[19] Ibid., pp. 323, 488, 751–2, 852–4, 865, 810.
[20] Ibid., 357, 409, 781–2, 467, 571, 718–19, 741, 476, 519. His unusual suggestion (p. 357) that the king of Kent's removal of idols was encouraged by the queen marks his distinctive attention to female royal piety, a feature of a work dedicated to Catherine of Braganza.
[21] Glickman, 'Gothic History', 362–4. Dodd was therefore able to pair Catholicism with the language of Saxon liberties: *ibid.*, 365–6.

between *Great Britain* and *Rome*'.²² Yet his account of the fifth-century British church was negative, 'a dismal scene of confusion', paralleled by indolent and immoral kings. The more learned and disciplined British church in Wales only derived, he said, from a few who withdrew there in the 580s and meditated on their troubles – and Dodd had no sympathy for their 'whimsical' objections to Augustine.²³ For him the Saxon church provided a more positive picture, having 'obtain'd a perfect establishment under archbishops, bishops and monastick discipline, before the close of the seventh century'.²⁴ Familiar images recurred: the expulsion of paganism from Kent by the king, royal conversions, Edwine of Northumbria discussing his new faith with his nobles (albeit, perhaps, to identify the best time to announce this rather than whether to adopt it), lawmaking for both church and state.²⁵ Yet there were also clear markers of Catholicism: accounts of miracles and monasteries, the establishment and re-foundation of an English College at Rome, King Kenulphus of Mercia – a great example of integrity and ability, Dodd said – asking the pope about the liberties of Canterbury.²⁶ Here was a civil religion built upon Constantinian principles, in which a king might rebuke the sins of the clergy, as in 969, when the monarch declared in a synod 'that as he held the sword of *Constantin*, so they held the sword of *Peter*, and therefore they ought to join in concert, and purge the house of God', but also where good kings deferred to the advice of the clergy and did penance when told of their sins.²⁷ Pointedly stating that the fortunes of civil government and religion rose and fell together, Dodd – although declaring an intent to refrain from commenting on 1066 – alluded to the possibility that this was when the struggle between church and state began, a battle that would culminate in the disastrous instability of Tudor religion 'that, almost every month ... put on a new face'.²⁸

Anglo-Saxon godly rule served the Catholic convert king of 1685 rather than the Protestant queen of 1585.²⁹ Texts produced throughout the intervening century nevertheless engaged with one another: in the 1660s, Cressy was still critiquing work on the Anglo-Saxon church produced by Elizabethan Protestant clergy in the 1560s.³⁰ As previous scholars have pointed out, it was Elizabeth I's first archbishop of Canterbury Matthew Parker and his circle who provided a new impetus to English Protestant Anglo-Saxon studies, partly in response to requests made by the Magdeburg Centuriators

---

[22] Charles Dodd, *The Church History of England*, 3 vols (Brussels, 1737), I, p. 2.
[23] *Ibid.*, I, pp. 6, 8, 9, 11.
[24] *Ibid.*, I, p. 11; he claimed monks were present in the mid-fourth century (p. 5).
[25] *Ibid.* I, pp. 13, 15, 18, 23.
[26] *Ibid.*, I, pp. 11, 16, 24, 17.
[27] *Ibid.*, I, pp. 28, 25, 27.
[28] *Ibid.*, I, pp. 31–2, xii.
[29] Oates, 'Elizabethan Histories', p. 184.
[30] Cressy, *Church-History*, pp. 282, 912–13.

for information, partly because of Thomas Stapleton's translation of Bede, printed in 1565. Stapleton's dedicatory epistle to Elizabeth prominently and repeatedly insisted on the value of reading Bede as a way to defeat 'the misse informations of a fewe for displacing the aunceint and right Christen faith', continued for almost a thousand years since Augustine's mission, but now uprooted by 'the pretended refourmers of the church' who 'haue departed from the patern of that sounde and catholike faith'. Reading Bede was presented as a remedy for 'present schismes', troubled consciences, and 'an open pathe to returne to the faith'. The preface reiterated the claim that Bede told the story of 'the primitive church of the english nation', a narrative of patriotic Catholicism retold in 'this history of the church of England (our dere countre) containing ... the historical narration of the coming in of vs Englishmen into this lande, and of attaining to the faith off Christ'. Stapleton also included a seven-page list of 'Differences betwene the primitive faithe of England continewed almost these thousand yeres, and the late pretensed faith of protestants'.[31]

While the response of Parker and his circle was not an unambiguous embracing of Anglo-Saxon Christianity, it also marked a new determination not to cede the era to the Church of England's Catholic opponents. Investigation of the period may also have acquired its own scholarly momentum, as Parker's research team sought and compared manuscripts.[32] Exploring the past might be, as John Bale suggested, valuable in generating 'knowledge of thynges necessary in thys fall of Antichriste to be knowne' as well as a natural wish (which he regretted was not stronger) to preserve 'the olde monumentes of [a] nacyon'.[33] Parker's circle showed both instincts, taking more care of Anglo-Saxon than they did Norman manuscripts, refusing to let the former leave their care while being willing to entrust the latter to the dangers of the printshop.[34]

For Parker and his associates, the study of Anglo-Saxon religion was a necessary but hazardous project, and their works demonstrate, to a greater or lesser extent, the lack of enthusiasm these men, renowned as early scholars of Anglo-Saxon history, felt for the church between 597 and 1066. John Joscelyn, Parker's secretary, gave warning about its imperfections in the preface to his edition of the sermon on the sacrament by Ælfric, the late tenth/early eleventh-century Benedictine abbot of Eynsham. Foxe purged further sections of this, the first Old English text to be printed, when

---

[31] *The History of the Chvrch of Englande compiled by Venerable Bede, Englishman*, trans. Thomas Stapleton (Antwerp, 1565), Stapleton's ep. ded., preface, and list of 'Differences'.
[32] This is emphasised by Madeline McMahon, 'Matthew Parker and the Practice of Church History', in *Confessionalisation and Erudition in Early Modern Europe*, eds Nicholas Hardy and Dmitri Levitin, Proceedings of the British Academy, 225 (Oxford, 2019), pp. 116-53.
[33] Bale to Parker, 30 July 1560, in Graham & Watson, *Recovery of the Past*, pp. 17, 21.
[34] McMahon, 'Parker and the Practice of Church History', pp. 145-6.

editing a version for the 1570 edition of the *Acts and Monuments*.[35] Broadly, the conclusion reached was that the Anglo-Saxon era contained too many errors, and numerous traces of popery, but not quite as many as later on. If not the pure British church, nor was it sixteenth-century Catholicism. For Foxe, its Christianity was of a 'certaine Romish sort, yet notwithstanding somewhat more tollerably, then were the times, which after followed'.[36] 'Some godly men' existed, Bale wrote, 'though they than erred in many thinges'.[37] Only in 1623 did William L'Isle describe the 'good old trees' in the Saxon 'orchard of the old English church'. While L'Isle's precise theological stance may be difficult to discern, the title page of his book included the proudly Protestant announcement that the use of vernacular scripture stretched back 'so long agoe' as the time of King Edgar, seven centuries past, when the Church of England had used scripture 'in her Mother-tongue'.[38]

Elizabethan clergy may therefore have bequeathed their ambivalence as well as their scholarship to later generations. The latter clearly continued to be valued. 150 years after Parker's deployment of Ælfric's sermon on the sacrament, Elizabeth Elstob used it as a model for her edition of Ælfric's homily on the birthday of Pope Gregory the Great. Her claims about vernacular prayers and scripture, credal orthodoxy, and rejection of transubstantiation and papal authority led her to treat the Church of England's kinship with the Saxons as 'one of the greatest Advantages we can boast of'.[39] It is worth noting that Elstob saw this as applying to the 'Discipline' as well as doctrine of that church, 'so early planted, and purely

---

[35] Robinson, 'Foxe and the Anglo-Saxons', pp. 63, 65; Theodore H. Leinbaugh, 'Aelfric's *Sermo de sacrificio in die pascae*: Anglican Polemic in the Sixteenth and Seventeenth Centuries', in *Anglo-Saxon Scholarship: The First Three Centuries*, eds Carl T. Berkhout and Milton Gatch (Boston, MA, 1982). Leinbaugh also describes (pp. 59–62) further attempts to deal with this text in the seventeenth century.

[36] Quoted in Robinson, 'Foxe and the Anglo-Saxons', p. 56; see also Benedict Scott Robinson, '"Darke speech": Matthew Parker and the Reforming of History', *Sixteenth Century Journal*, 29 (1998), 1061–83. Foxe took a similar line on monasticism under Edgar (r. 943/4–975): Jesse M. Lander, 'The Monkish Middle Ages: Periodization and Polemic in Foxe's *Acts and Monuments*', in *Renaissance Retrospections: Tudor Views of the Middle Ages*, ed. Sarah A. Kelen (Kalamanzoo, 2013), p. 106.

[37] Quoted in McMahon, 'Parker and the Practice of Church History', p. 133.

[38] William L'Isle, *A Saxon Treatise concerning the Old and New Testament* (1623), sig. [b4]r and title page.

[39] Elizabeth Elstob, *An English-Saxon Homily on the Birth-day of St Gregory* (London, 1709), 2nd pag., xxxi and ff, pp. 3, xiii. There is a growing literature on Elstob: see Michael Murphy, 'The Elstobs, Scholars of Old English and Anglican Apologists', *Durham University Journal*, 58 (1966), 131–8; Mechtild Gretsch, 'Elizabeth Elstob: A Scholar's Fight for Anglo-Saxon Studies', *Anglia*, 117 (1995), 163–201, 481–524; Sarah H. Collins, 'The Elstobs and the End of the Saxon Revival', in *Anglo-Saxon Scholarship*, eds Berkhout and Gatch, pp. 107–18; Kathryn Sutherland, 'Elizabeth Elstob', in *Medieval Scholarship: Biographical Studies on the Formation of a Discipline*, ed. Helen Damico (New York, 1998), II, pp. 59–73. For her brother, see Timothy Graham, 'William Elstob's

reformed ... in and with Bishops'.[40] In Elstob's eyes the Anglo-Saxon church was far superior to the 'dismal' British church, and her sympathies lay with Augustine rather than with the previous Christians who had defied him. This departure from her contemporaries who nuanced or fudged their works so as to incorporate both British and Saxon ecclesiastical ancestry demonstrated Elstob's impatience with zealous Protestant as well as Roman Catholic opponents. She criticised violent prejudices against the Church of England's links to Rome, arguing that the Rome of Gregory's time was 'sound and uncorrupt'. For her, to say otherwise was not merely ingratitude, but also ceded the crucial case for antiquity to Catholics.[41]

When dedicating her edition to Queen Anne, Elstob seized an obvious opportunity to celebrate royal women who had supported the church: Helena, mother of Constantine; Berhta, Christian wife of Æthelberht, the king of Kent who received Augustine's mission; and Elizabeth I. She also spoke without qualification of the Anglo-Saxon ecclesiastical calendar being regulated by synods and great councils or parliaments.[42] Yet for many of her contemporaries the balance between these elements created far more of a constitutional quandary. As shown below, discussed in temporal terms, Saxon constitutionalism had frequently been employed to limit royal authority. Yet the widespread acceptance that Anglo-Saxon councils included a significant role for the clergy became extremely problematic for those who sought to limit priestcraft as well as kingship. Far from embracing a Saxon civil religion, radical authors briefly invoked the unity of ecclesiastical and temporal courts and then avoided delving into details. Saxon history was far more pertinent to those involved in debating the succession of calls, first, in the 1690s, for convocation to meet; then, in the early eighteenth century, about the relationship between its Upper and Lower Houses. This argument reflected and contributed to the inflammatory question of the relationship between church and state in the aftermath of the Revolution of 1688–9, which pointedly demonstrated the interplay of matters civil and religious: the overthrow of a Catholic monarch and the non-juring schism; relationships between the Church and nonconformists – the shape of the new religious settlement, occasional conformity, and toleration – and high profile controversies over church-state relations provoked by Benjamin

---

Planned Edition of the Anglo-Saxon Laws: A Remnant in the Takamiya Collection', *Poetica*, 73 (2010), 109–41.

[40] Elstob, *Homily*, sigs. [A4]v–ar, p. xiv (and p. 28 on Augustine as the first archbishop of Canterbury). Elstob's text leaves open the question of whether bishops were established *iure divino* or by long custom; pp. xxxix–xliv offer a familiar Protestant line on Peter representing all the apostles rather than having a particular superiority to them (apropos Matt 16:18), but she also said nothing to unchurch non-episcopal churches and commented (p. xliv) that catholic communion could continue 'under any other Apostle or Bishop'.

[41] Elstob, *Homily*, pp. xv–xxiii, ix-x, 2nd pag., xxx–xxxi, liii.

[42] *Ibid.*, sigs. [A3]r, [A4]r, appx, p. 28.

Hoadley, bishop of Bangor. What sustained attention to the ecclesiastical dimensions of Saxon councils in the years after 1688 was not the early Enlightenment, but the convocation controversy, for it was in that debate that the interaction between civil and religious authorities, and how that played out in conciliar structures, had to be confronted. And, as will be shown, that did not require a discourse of civil religion, for the rhetoric of royal supremacy was pluriform enough without it.

II

First, though, it is useful to recollect the extent of Saxon secular ancient constitutionalism, to demonstrate its potential utility for those advocating quite varied political positions. Claims for the antiquity of parliaments and their role in governing the church were partly provoked by the need to defend the Elizabethan Settlement of 1559, legislated by statute despite the dissenting voices of the Marian bishops of the House of Lords.[43] Arguing that the bishops sat as individual barons rather than representatives of the church, defenders of the Settlement asserted its place in a tradition of parliamentary decisions on religion stretching back to Anglo-Saxon times. Such claims grew in significance from the 1570s, given they provided a justification of parliament, rather than the monarch alone, deciding the shape of national worship – and therefore a way to overcome monarchical opposition to further reformation. They relied, nevertheless, on muddling together various Anglo-Saxon assemblies and indiscriminately labelling almost any such meeting a parliament, as Catholic and crypto-Catholic critics such as Thomas Stapleton and Arthur Hall pointed out.[44] But even at this point there were varied views among Protestants as to how far parliament had changed over time, and a willingness to draw on examples from after as well as before 1066. Conflicts over these aspects of the ancient constitution grew in the seventeenth century.

If the ancient constitution has received less attention than some other languages of political thought, recent work on it has nevertheless detected a more variegated discourse than that famously depicted in J. G. A. Pocock's classic account. This language had many dialects; Kidd outlines eight strategies for using it, while Goldie tellingly introduces his review of the topic by emphasizing that 'a political language ... is protean, malleable, and not prescriptive ... in use, it might lead to quite contrary positions'.[45] United by

---

[43] This paragraph summarises some of the findings of Alexandra Gajda, 'The Elizabethan Church and the Antiquity of Parliament', in *Writing the History of Parliament in Tudor and Early Stuart England*, eds Paul Cavill and Alexandra Gajda (Manchester, 2018), pp. 77–105.
[44] *Ibid.*, pp. 83–4, 92–3.
[45] Kidd, *British Identities*, pp. 79–81; Mark Goldie, 'The Ancient Constitution and the Languages of Political Thought', *Historical Journal*, 62 (2019), 3–34, at 3; J. G. A. Pocock,

their attention to a history of particular customs, laws, and institutions, ancient constitutionalists were capable of advocating moderate limited monarchy or offering more radical views associated with resistance and contract. Preserving the ancient constitution could take the form of a revolutionary restoration of Saxon or Gothic liberties, with a populist and participatory edge to it, especially in the realm of local governance.[46] Nor was its use incompatible with the deployment of other political languages. We should not assume, therefore, that a discourse of Saxon civil religion was doomed to incoherence.

The ecclesiology of the ancient constitution was by necessity a conciliar one. Ancient constitutionalists agreed that Anglo-Saxon councils had played a fundamental role in political decision-making, either by continuing a parliamentary tradition from the Britons, or by a Gothic adherence to liberty. Tacitus' claim that a large council debated major questions and a restricted group more minor matters was echoed by seventeenth-century authors. The Parliamentarian Nathaniel Bacon sharply pointed out that no wittanagemot would implement idolatry.[47] The whig historian James Tyrrell cited the common example of King Eadwine of Northumbria consulting with his great council before converting to Christianity.[48] John Sadler not only noted that the British would not conform to Roman ecclesiastical rituals without the consent of their councils but also rejoiced, given his aim to defend the regicide, in how Edgar's parliaments 'did often Oppose, and Depose, the King Himselfe'.[49] While others said less about the removal of kings once in power, ancient constitutionalists emphasised their election by councils – Bacon even explored the territory of stipulation and contract – and that this had been continued under the early Normans, including in 1066.[50] While the debate in

---

The Ancient Constitution and the Feudal Law (Cambridge, 1957; reissued with a retrospect, 1987).

[46] E.g. Janelle Greenberg, 'The Confessor's Laws and the Radical Face of the Ancient Constitution', *English Historical Review*, 104 (1989), 611-37; Janelle Greenberg, *The Radical Face of the Ancient Constitution: St Edward's 'Laws' in Early Modern Political Thought* (Cambridge, 2001); Ashley Walsh, 'The Saxon Republic and Ancient Constitution in the Standing Army Controversy, 1697–1699', *Historical Journal*, 62 (2019), 663-84; Ashley Walsh, 'John Streater and the Saxon Republic', *History of Political Thought*, 39 (2018), 57-82; Mark Goldie, 'The Unacknowledged Republic: Officeholding in Early Modern England', in *The Politics of the Excluded, c.1500–1850*, ed. Tim Harris (Houndmills, 2001), p. 182.

[47] Nathaniel Bacon, *An Historicall Discourse on the Uniformity of the Government of England* (London, 1647), pp. 61, 97.

[48] James Tyrrell, *Bibliotheca Politica* (1694), p. 368. The account derives from Bede, and – in the words of one modern scholar – provides 'some of the most memorable prose' in his text: Rosemary Cramp, 'Eadwine (c. 586–633)', *Oxford Dictionary of National Biography* (24 May 2008) [accessed 15 April 2022], including the comparison of human life to a sparrow's brief flight through a lighted hall. Bede, *Ecclesiastical History*, II, p. 13.

[49] John Sadler, *Rights of the Kingdom* (London, 1649), 2nd pag., pp. 81, 92.

[50] Sadler, *Rights*, pp. 60ff; Bacon, *Historicall Discourse*, pp. 47-8, 53, 55; Humphrey Hody, *A History of English Councils and Convocations* (London, 1701), part 1, p. 96.

the 1680s over the origins of the rights of the Commons to sit in parliament mainly focused on later medieval history, some of the leading figures on each side, like William Petyt and Robert Brady, felt it necessary to include briefer accounts of Saxon parliaments and rules of succession.[51]

Although early modern writers were divided over the relative powers of king and council, and over whether the lay commons had sat in Anglo-Saxon assemblies, they agreed that those councils included ecclesiastical members. Many authors explained that it was hard to distinguish between a 'synod' and a 'great council' or 'parliament' in Saxon times, and almost all allowed clergy to be members of the latter.[52] Brady scorned Petyt's claim that King Ine and a council had legislated on marriage, but he also mocked his opponent for praising conciliar bodies that were so dominated by priests.[53] While Bacon at one point said it had taken decades for the clergy to enter the grand council (in contrast with the laity sitting in synods until after 1066), he also argued that it was hard to distinguish this from the general synod and that 'all the Church Laws in the Saxons times were made in the *Micklemote*'.[54] Thus legislation as well as titles and membership was cited to demonstrate the intermingling of ecclesiastical and temporal issues. Humphrey Hody, chaplain to two archbishops of Canterbury, and regius professor of Greek at Oxford from 1698, pointed out that the 'synodalia decreta' passed in 1009 were made by the king and council, and included temporal matters, while many of the tenth-century King Edmund's 'purely Ecclesiastical' laws were made 'partly in a Parliamentary Council'. Tyrrell argued that bishops were chosen by the rest of the episcopate and invested by the king, but that such appointments were only valid when confirmed 'in a full Synod or *Parliament*'. And Hody charted how Northumbrian synods and senates had decided whether to restore or remove the archbishop of York in the years around 700.[55]

---

[51] William Petyt, *The Antient Right of the Commons of England Asserted* (London, 1680), preface, pp. 6–12; Robert Brady, *An Introduction to the Old English History* (London, 1684), pp. 3, 7, 358–63.

[52] Tyrrell, *Bibliotheca Politica*, p. 546; Brady, *Introduction*, p. 10; Hody, *History of English Councils*, part 1, p. 14 and part 3, pp. 1–2 (though p. 124 of part 1 does mention different names).

[53] Brady, *Introduction*, pp. 5–6, 3; cf. Petyt, *Antient Right*, preface, p. 8. The law code of Ine, king of the West-Saxons, dates from 688–94. See also Sadler, *Rights*, p. 83.

[54] Bacon, *Historicall Discourse*, ch. 20 (qu. p. 59); Nathaniel Bacon, *The Continuation of an Historicall Discourse of the Government of England* (London, 1651), sig. [B3]v. He argued otherwise for constitutional continuity in 1066: *Historicall Discourse*, pp. 110, 115–16, chapters 46, 55–6.

[55] Hody, *History of English Councils*, part 1, pp. 90, 71, 28–32; Tyrrell, *Bibliotheca Politica*, pp. 368–9.

III

The potential for this interweaving of church and state to be used to rein in the autonomy of early modern clergy manifested itself most sharply in common lawyers' attacks on separate ecclesiastical courts, and ecclesiastical regulation of marriage. In the 1630s, Bulstrode Whitelocke gave a charge to the Oxford Quarter Sessions on the power of temporal courts in ecclesiastical questions '& the antiquity thereof' and later argued that there had been mixed ecclesiastical/temporal courts before 1066.[56] Fighting one of his periodic battles with the church hierarchy, the maverick clergyman Edmund Hickeringill attributed the existence of distinct ecclesiastical courts to the popish William I, for before 1066 such jurisdiction had been incorporated into the hundredal court, in which, he said, cases were judged by the laity. He therefore concluded that there was no common law basis for church courts, and that their jurisdiction depended on statute.[57] In reply, the presbyterian-turned-episcopalian Francis Fullwood claimed that it was no detriment to the Church if its courts were established by the king, for that still endowed them with the authority of law and wove civil and ecclesiastical power together. Fullwood cited bishops and lords meeting to discuss church and state under king Æthelberht and claimed the laity attended, but did not decide, cases in the hundredal court.[58] A decade later, the whig lawyer Robert Washington would shift the emphasis again, to argue that William's separation of ecclesiastical courts was an act of king-in-parliament. Although not offering a detailed survey of Anglo-Saxon history, Washington asserted that an ecclesiastical power distinct from temporal supremacy that included the *ordines regni* was inconceivable for a nation descended from the Saxons. 'The whole Fabrick of the *English Saxon Church* was built upon Acts of Parliament'. Yet his primary aim was to ensure that parliament had a role in governing the church, not that it pushed the clergy out.[59]

The radical potential of the Anglo-Saxon church was rarely developed. When in 1721 Robert Molesworth defined a 'real Whig' as one who strictly upheld the 'true old Gothick constitution' he talked about the three estates of king, lords, and commons and a fiduciary and accountable executive.

---

[56] BL, Add. MS 37343, fol. 131r; Bulstrode Whitelocke, *Essays Ecclesiastical and Civil* (London, 1706), pp. 3-5. William Temple, *An Introduction to the History of England*, 3rd edn (London, 1708), p. 158, offers a passing mention of judgments by ealdermen, bishops, and juries, but without detailing mixed courts.

[57] Edmund Hickeringill, *A Vindication of the Naked Truth, the Second Part* (London, 1681), pp. 13-14, 32.

[58] Francis Fullwood, *Leges Angliae* (London, 1681), sigs. A8r-v, ar-v, pp. 48-50; Francis Fullwood, *A Dialogue betwixt Philautus and Timotheus* (London, 1681), p. 21.

[59] Robert Washington, *Some Observations upon the Ecclesiastical Jurisdiction of the Kings of England* (London, 1689), pp. 26-7, 14-22, 40, 20 (qu.).

Even as Molesworth angrily denounced the persecutory spirit that infected all churches, he sidestepped the question of what the clergy had done in the Gothic constitution.[60] Bacon's book encapsulated the problem. He firmly endorsed the 'beautifull composure' of the Anglo-Saxon constitution, whose monarchical veneer was laid atop the foundations of popular sovereignty. He thought Anglo-Saxon bishops' governance of the church was 'stated and regulated by publique Councell' (synods), that excommunication was 'pronounced' by the church but 'determined' by parliament, and that the civil magistrate had ultimate authority over marriage, and penalties for incest, adultery, and bastardy.[61] Yet Bacon's Saxon clergy were very far from being civic patriots, unlike the pastorate envisaged by a civil religion, i.e. one that upholds patriotic virtues, or at least prevents religion conflicting with these. Bacon was deeply unhappy about churchmen's role in Anglo-Saxon government, asserting that their place in public councils had been a cunning strategy to seize authority and subvert the commonwealth. Siphoning off public money to fund the church rather than national defence, 'they so intoxicated the domestique counsels ... as they generally staggered and many times came short'.[62] In denying that the Danes had overthrown the Saxon constitution, Bacon questioned whether 'Lord Dane or Lord Bishop was the greater burden'. For him, the pure church was British, not Saxon: i.e., that founded in the first century or two after Christ, with bishops (from Constantine's time) who enjoyed 'no great pompe', and no archbishops until Augustine, the emissary of the by-then nearly antichristian Rome. In introducing papal authority, Bacon claimed, Augustine brought 'more trouble to this Isle than either Pict or Saxon'.[63] Afterwards, the rising tide of clerical pride marked not a godly episcopate but a creeping prelacy – and one that Bacon denounced, in Shaftesburian terms, as forging an alliance with kings to suppress liberty. Nothing summarises better his ambivalence than his suggestion that Saxon kings took care not to betray Saxon principles when making concessions to the church.[64]

Other authors shared these concerns. William Temple likewise acknowledged the significant influence of the clergy, but sarcastically stated that their greater learning compared to the rest of the population did not necessarily mean that they enjoyed much wisdom, and that they were united in a single mission: to protect themselves. For their 'one common Interest ... was pretended to be the Greatness of the holy Church, but indeed was their own, and the Honours, Power, and Riches of the Church-men, rather than

---

[60] Robert Molesworth, preface to trans. of *Francogallia*, 2nd edn (1721), in *An Account of Denmark*, ed. Justin Champion (Indianapolis, 2011), pp. 174, 178, 182, 156 (cf. p. 157).
[61] Bacon, *Historicall Discourse*, pp. 111–12, 36, 95, 41–2. Page 85 noticeably fails to expound the idea of mixed courts.
[62] Ibid., pp. 38, 30, 22–3.
[63] Ibid., pp. 112 (quotation), 3–4, 7–9, 11, 17–19.
[64] Ibid., pp. 26–7, 322, chapter 15 (especially pp. 44–5), p. 52.

of the Church'.⁶⁵ Sadler turned to the Druids rather than the Saxons for a constitutional clergy.⁶⁶ As Nicholas von Maltzahn has demonstrated, despite Milton's positive reference to the Saxons in some of his political pamphlets, his *History of Britain* refrained from praising Saxon constitutionalism and scathingly denounced both Saxon and British clergy, kings, and people.⁶⁷ Frequently, what might be seen as praiseworthy pious behaviour was treated ambivalently by Milton. He admitted that some were converted by the holy life of Augustine and his fellow clergy but insisted that that mission's apostolic zeal was mingled with superstition and a pride that rapidly elevated archbishops to the level of kings, both being buried at Canterbury with equal pomp. (He refrained, at least in the final version, from pronouncing on whether Augustine had ordered or simply prophesied the slaughter of the monks at Bangor.)⁶⁸ The king of Kent's expulsion of idols was laudable *if* it was thorough – strongly implying that it was not. Eadwine had correctly taken instruction before being baptized, but his taking counsel on the subject was, for Milton, far from a moment of triumph, for he claimed that councillors had simply said what they knew the king wanted to hear.⁶⁹ He bemoaned the 'ridiculous' quarrels over tonsures and the late Saxon contests between the seculars and regulars that had embroiled the nobility too.⁷⁰ If the whole is more restrained than might be anticipated, the cause could have been the censorship and self-censorship that the *History* underwent before its printing in 1671. It was said that the censor had removed some (now lost) passages and that Milton had been advised to pare others back.⁷¹ Royal piety also earned no praise from Milton, who criticised Æthelwulf for going on pilgrimage to Rome in 855 when he should have been defending the realm. Indeed, any praise for monarchs was treated sceptically in the *History*, as Milton saw it as resulting from churchmen writing the histories on which he reluctantly depended.⁷²

---

⁶⁵ Temple, *Introduction*, pp. 128–31.
⁶⁶ Sadler, *Rights*, p. 38, 2nd pag., p. 77.
⁶⁷ Nicholas von Maltzahn, *Milton's History of Britain: Republican Historiography in the English Revolution* (Oxford, 1991), pp. 197, 200, 210–15.
⁶⁸ John Milton, *The History of Britain*, ed. French Fogle, in *Complete Prose Works*, V, part I (New Haven, 1971), pp. 187–95; the topic was one of his planned British tragedies, and the treatment in the *History* may have been toned down: von Maltzahn, *Milton's History*, pp. 163–5.
⁶⁹ Milton, *History*, pp. 207, 200, 202. This was another topic for a British tragedy, *ibid.*, p. 200, n. 74.
⁷⁰ *Ibid.*, pp. 215, 329–30.
⁷¹ von Maltzahn, *Milton's History*, pp. 13–16; as he points out (p. 159) what was left in regarding the British clergy suggests that the comments on the Saxons must have been far worse.
⁷² Milton, *History*, pp. 265–6, 321. For Milton's comments on clerical chronicles, see pp. 127–8, 229–30 of the *History*.

Rather than glorying in the Saxon constitution, Milton instead depicted a nation full of civil and religious vices: luxury, sloth, ceremonies, relics, monks, masses, and idols.[73] By 1066, this was fitted for conquest – as the country of his day might also be, and as it seemed the British might ever be. For even the pre-Saxon Britons offered a lesson in failure: men offered 'such a manumission as never subjects had a fairer' after the Romans left, but who could not bear the burden of self-government and who thus 'shrunk more wretchedly under the burden of thir own libertie, than before under a foren yoke'.[74] For the British church was no better for Milton than the Saxon one, its clergy corrupt, drunk, proud, envious, unlearned, impudent, lying, flattering, inventing superstitious trifles to justify their role while suppressing true religious knowledge; the victory of the pagan Saxons was a message as to what God had thought of them.[75] If Milton did not use the word priestcraft, it might have seemed inherent in his similar criticisms of the ambitious and barbarous Druids; no civil religion here either.[76] He did adhere to a claim for the early preaching of the gospel in Britain, and to the conversion of Lucius, the supposed second-century king whose conversion and correspondence with Rome had been a motif of sixteenth-century religious debates. Yet again his earlier more positive account of Lucius mutated here to a puncturing not only of the account of his 'improbable Letter' to Rome, but also of the merits of his Christianity – praiseworthy only if sincere and persevering, and laudable in his subjects only if they genuinely believed rather than merely practising outward conformity.[77]

Thus the Anglo-Saxon church was too priest-ridden to be utilised for a programme of priest-riddance. But if there was no Anglo-Saxon civil religion, there could be found instead a royal supremacy. William Prynne's vast tomes of the mid-1660s complained of the tendency of all types of clergy to usurp sovereign kings, demonstrating a worry about priestcraft, but his solution was the old one of royal supremacy. Arguing that this was inherent in all rulers, even pagan ones, he adhered to claims that Christianity had been preached in Britain by the apostles and established by King Lucius.[78]

---

[73] Ibid., p. 259.

[74] Milton, 'Digression', in History, pp. 441, 450; and in the History itself pp. 402–3, 129–31, 139.

[75] Milton, History, pp. 140, 175, 183 (in contrast to his earlier praise for the British church, on which see von Maltzahn, Milton's History, p. 144). Similarly, the positive remark on the poverty of the British bishops (History, p. 116) was geared to denounce presbyterians seeking rich livings.

[76] Milton, History, p. 61; again a change of view: von Maltzahn, Milton's History, pp. 113–15.

[77] Milton, History, pp. 96–7. On uses of Lucius, see Felicity Heal, 'What can King Lucius do for you? The Reformation and the Early British Church', English Historical Review, 120 (2005), 593–614.

[78] William Prynne, The First Tome of an Exact Chronological Vindication and Historical Demonstration of our British, Roman, Saxon, Danish, Norman, English Kings Supreme

His account of Saxon times showed a familiar ambivalence, charting the rise of popery and resistance to it. Popes had usurped the emperor's right to bestow a pall, so Gregory giving one to Augustine was a crafty way to increase his authority.[79] This era saw the first appeal to Rome (in 678) and assertions of the first papal excommunication of a monarch, although also resistance to such claims.[80] The dominant message in Prynne's book was royal power: it was Æthelberht who founded the archbishopric of Canterbury, monarchs who chose, consecrated, changed, and invested bishops and archbishops. They removed idols.[81] Kings issued anathemas and excommunications 'like a Pope or Bishop'; Erastianism, Prynne said, was no innovation.[82] They consulted with their councils – enter the stock figure of Eadwine, mulling over conversion – and they and their councils made and received ecclesiastical laws.[83] William I, whatever his reputation, had resisted the pope's infringement of his sovereignty and it was his 'Absolute Royal Ecclesiastical Authority' that separated church courts and regulated them and their use of canon law.[84] Prynne could still argue that these separate church courts were a tool for papal usurpation, and urge that they now exercise jurisdiction in the name of the king, under the royal seal, and under the supervision of a vicegerent in spirituals.[85] Nevertheless, these remedial measures against clerical subversion – like Prynne's Saxon history – were reached through discourses on royal supremacy that were not unfamiliar by the 1660s.

Initially I anticipated that this chapter would chart the shift from the Elizabethan Protestant invocation of Saxon Christianity to show how the period was used to defend royal supremacy, and then outline how in the seventeenth century this account splintered and become a resource for more radical theorists of civil religion. But even in the latter part of the period we find instead a continuation of the type of discourse used by Prynne. In 1704, the royal chaplain John Inett (acknowledging a mixed British-Saxon ancestry for the Church of England), likewise delineated a history of English Christianity shaped by royal action. Augustine could only preach once permitted by Æthelberht. While Gregory the Great had wrongly endorsed the incorporation of pagan images in worship, it was King Eorcenberht of Kent who had banned idolatry. In Inett's narrative, the rise and fall of Christianity and paganism depended on royal conversions,

---

Ecclesiastical Jurisdiction (1666), sig. [d2]v, pp. 134 and book II, chapters 1–2.
[79] Prynne, *First Tome*, book II, chapters 6–7, pp. 153–60.
[80] Ibid., pp. 186, 197, 245.
[81] Ibid., pp. 150, 163, 168, 173–4, 344–5, 167.
[82] Ibid., pp. 223 (qu.), 200, 231, 250, 274.
[83] Ibid., pp. 162, 164, 142, 219–20, 229, 298, 299, 303.
[84] Ibid., pp. 353, 366–7.
[85] Ibid., sigs. [i2]v–kv.

dynastic alliances, and the deaths of kings.[86] Both Inett and Hody were writing to defend the Williamite church against the attacks made on it in the convocation controversy. Hence Hody also emphasised the royal summoning of synods and his denial that the commons were members of them was not Bradyite royalism, but a way of rejecting Francis Atterbury's claims about the lesser clergy's powers in convocation.[87] These men had more of an agenda than their works initially betray, but their concern was with the high church, not the radical Enlightenment. In pursuing it, they turned not to civil religion but to the royal supremacy, which held the comparative advantage of being both an established political language and one flexible enough to accommodate different voices.[88]

IV

In conclusion, this material offers a salutary reminder of the dangers of employing civil religion too loosely or too often. Earlier accounts of civil religion treated it as a precursor to or facet of a totalitarian state.[89] Even more recent genealogies, interested in it as a route to reflecting on modern liberalism more than the history of the relationship between religion and politics, have sometimes offered a narrative of canonical thinkers such as Machiavelli, Hobbes, and Rousseau.[90] By contrast, more historically sensitive definitions have emerged that have incorporated a widening array of thinkers, albeit sharing the premise that the liberal separation of church and state was neither historically inevitable nor a phenomenon that can be explained purely through a narrative of secularisation.[91] Such

[86] John Inett, *Origines Anglicanae* (London, 1704), pp. 18, 54, 24, 40, 50–1. R. J. Smith characterises Inett's work as 'the Gothic theory in a surplice': *The Gothic Bequest: Medieval Institutions in British Thought, 1688–1863* (Cambridge, 1987), p. 30. Eorcenberht ruled from 640 to 664 and ordered the destruction of idols and fasting in Lent: S. E. Kelly, 'Eorcenberht (d. 664)', *Oxford Dictionary of National Biography* (23 Sept. 2004) [accessed 15 Apr. 2022]; Bede, *Ecclesiastical History*, III.8.
[87] Hody, *History of English Councils*, pp. 19, 53, 81, and *passim*. For Hody's significance see Mark Goldie, 'The Nonjurors, Episcopacy, and the Origins of the Convocation Controversy', in *Ideology and Conspiracy: Aspects of Jacobitism, 1689–1759*, ed. Eveline Cruickshanks (Edinburgh, 1982), especially pp. 17, 21.
[88] For some examples of how conflicting accounts of supremacy were used to justify different positions on convocation, see Jacqueline Rose, 'By law established: The Church of England and the Royal Supremacy', in *The Later Stuart Church, 1660–1714*, ed. Grant Tapsell (Manchester, 2012), pp. 34–6; Goldie, 'Nonjurors'.
[89] As noted by Mark Goldie, 'The Civil Religion of James Harrington', in *The Languages of Political Theory in Early Modern Europe*, ed. Anthony Pagden (Cambridge, 1987), p. 197.
[90] Ronald Beiner, *Civil Religion: A Dialogue in the History of Political Philosophy* (Cambridge, 2011).
[91] Partly stimulated by Goldie, 'Civil Religion of James Harrington'.

accounts describe a project of making religion less uncivil, bringing it into accord with the state and society to create a virtuous, polite, sociable piety.[92] Still associated with Enlightenment writers, this discourse is nevertheless treated as fundamentally rooted in Reformation principles. Its sentiment was restorative: less the triumph of Reason than the reversion to a purer primitive Christianity,[93] though this was coupled with a militantly vigorous desire for the purgation of superstition and priestly power. Its tone was redolent of the debates of the Reformation, with a recurrent invocation of the principle that the church was the congregation of all believers rather than a particular priestly caste, a nagging concern about *praemunire* damaging *imperium*, and thus incorporating an inclination to praise godly monarchy for rooting out superstition as much as an impulsion towards liberty of conscience.[94] If this association with Reformation concerns makes civil religion potentially widespread, it is important not to underestimate its putative radical force. While 'the cult of reason was never performed in Westminster Abbey',[95] the energetic pursuit of priestcraft might challenge political, social, and cultural norms as insidiously as if religion itself were the target. Yet civil religion, in this guise, is 'exasperating[ly]' difficult to pin down.[96] It becomes indeterminate, perhaps a plural rather than singular entity, so that by the eighteenth century its multiple manifestations included – but were far from represented by – that of the radical Enlightenment. Some limits to capaciousness may nevertheless be valuable. Endeavours to map the 'varieties of civil religion'[97] must locate it in relation to its long Reformation landmarks, pairing historiographical attention to similarities with an acknowledgement of differences.

Early modern accounts of the Saxon church may assist in this regard. They offer tantalising hints of themes that link the Reformation with the Enlightenment critique of clerisy, such as the rise of prelacy or the question

---

[92] Colin C. Kidd, 'Constructing a Civil Religion: Scots Presbyterians and the Eighteenth-Century British State', in *The Scottish Churches and the Union Parliament, 1707–1999*, ed. James Kirk (Edinburgh, 2001), p. 5; Ashley Walsh, *Civil Religion and the Enlightenment in England, 1707–1800* (Woodbridge, 2020), p. 4; Mark Goldie, 'John Locke, the Early Lockeans, and Priestcraft', *Intellectual History Review*, 28 (2018), 125–44, at 131.

[93] Mark Goldie, 'Civil Religion and the English Enlightenment', in *Politics, Politeness and Patriotism*, eds Gorden J. Schochet, Patricia E. Tatspaugh, and Carol Brobeck (Washington, DC, 1993), p. 35; Walsh, *Civil Religion*, pp. 4–5.

[94] Gaby Mahlberg, 'Machiaevelli, Neville, and the Seventeenth-Century English Republican Attack on Priestcraft', *Intellectual History Review*, 28 (2018), 79–99, at p. 87; Goldie, 'Lockeans', p. 138; Goldie, 'Civil Religion', p. 35; Walsh, *Civil Religion*, pp. 5, 11, 21; Mark Goldie, 'Priestcraft and the Birth of Whiggism', in *Political Discourse in Early Modern Britain*, eds Nicholas Phillipson and Quentin Skinner (Cambridge, 1993), p. 215.

[95] Goldie, 'Civil Religion', p. 31; Goldie, 'Lockeans', p. 130; Walsh, *Civil Religion*, p. 17 characterises it as anti-sacerdotal rather than anticlerical.

[96] As per Goldie's comment on Locke's religion: 'Lockeans', p. 133.

[97] Walsh, *Civil Religion*, p. 36.

of ecclesiastical jurisdiction. But they may also show how Reformation royal supremacy might be the root of Enlightenment civil religion without the two being the same thing, highlighting the differences as well as similarities between them; or, if pursuing the alternative strategy of identifying moderate as well as radical versions of civil religion, pose the question of when to apply the terminology of civil religion rather than the taxonomy of the long Reformation. Royal supremacy protected the jurisdictional authority of the king, or of crown-in-parliament, while still leaving a space for clergy of some description to define the core principles of Christianity and wield spiritual authority over monarch and subjects. It did not separate church and state, but proposed two complementary hierarchies: one jurisdictional, where the monarch governed the church, and the other spiritual, where the monarch deferred to the authority of the clergy. Theorists of civil religion were perhaps more concerned by the social and cultural power of the clergy and for them a jurisdictional measure like royal supremacy did not go far enough; at times, it was deemed necessary to erode the church's authority, reducing it to a department of state, and denying its independence. Theorists of royal supremacy looked to Reformation laws and church history, and while these could be exploited in remarkably varied ways, they set limits to claims. Advocates of civil religion were willing to employ pagan antiquity and to look beyond Christianity. Their strategy of extending Reformation attacks on popery into a wider denunciation of an array of practitioners of priestcraft – so that *no* godly clergy was possible – was an example of one political language borrowing from another, not of the two being the same discourse.

Early modern accounts of the Saxon church help us to sharpen our sense of these divisions. The Anglo-Saxon mixture of lay and clerical members of councils and courts, and its intermingling of civil and ecclesiastical business, could be and was exploited in the religious politics of the long Reformation. It was a useful resource for those defending the Reformed Church of England and advocating the royal supremacy, while examples could be found to support Erastian (properly so-called) civil control of excommunication.[98] Yet the Saxon godly bishop would never mutate into the patriot priest. If the core of early modern civil religion was an attack on priestcraft, the Anglo-Saxon era was of limited use as a model to follow. The impossibility of disaggregating church and state gave it radical potential, but its history was high-risk, threatening to demonstrate how unified church-state institutions could lead to the church dominating or undermining the state rather than generating a religion orientated to patriotic virtues. Those in search of a pious time ere priestcraft did begin would have to look elsewhere for inspiration.

---

[98] On the meaning of Erastianism, see J. Neville Figgis, 'Erastus and Erastianism', *Journal of Theological Studies*, 2 (1901), 66–101; Jacqueline Rose, *Godly Kingship in Restoration England: The Politics of the Royal Supremacy, 1660–1688* (Cambridge, 2011), pp. 203–5.

Bibliography

Manuscript Sources

The National Archives, Kew

SP 16/103/39.
SP 16/138/10, 23, 90.
SP 16/142/114.

The British Library, London

Additional MS 37343.
Additional MS 41162.

Bodleian Libraries, University of Oxford

Clarendon MS 60.
Douce MSS 173.
MS Locke c. 34.

Hertfordshire Record Office

DE/P/F31.

Queen's College, University of Oxford

MS 215.

Trinity College Dublin

MS 140.

Printed Primary Sources

The Fifth Monarchy, or Kingdom of Christ, in Opposition to the Beast's, Asserted (London, 1659).
The Folly of Priestcraft (London, 1690).
The Humble Proposals of Mr. Owen, Mr. Tho. Goodwin, Mr. Nye, Mr. Sympson, and other ministers, who presented the petition to the Parliament, and other persons, Febr. II under debate by a committee this 31. of March, 1652 for the furtherance and Propagation of the Gospel in this Nation... (London, 1652).

Priestcraft Expos'd (London, 1691).

Ames, William, *A fresh suit against human ceremonies in God's worship* (Amsterdam, 1633).

——, *A reply to Dr. Mortons generall Defence of three innocent ceremonies* (Amsterdam, 1622).

Augustine *City of God*, trans. Henry Bettenson (New York. 1984).

Bacon, Francis, *New Atlantic and Great Instauration*, ed. Jerry Weinberger (Arlington, IL, 1989).

——, *The Works of Francis Bacon*, eds J. Spedding, R. L. Ellis, and D. D. Heath (London, 1861).

——, *The Charge ... whether the Doctrine ... Touching Deposing, and Killing, of Kings Excommunicated, were True, or No*, in *Resuscitatio* (1657).

Bacon, Nathaniel, *An Historicall Discourse on the Uniformity of the Government of England* (London, 1647).

——, *The Continuation of an Historicall Discourse of the Government of England* (London, 1651).

Baker, Philip and Vernon, Elliot (eds), *The Agreements of the People, the Levellers and the Constitutional Crisis of the English Revolution* (Basingstoke, 2012).

Barnes, Barnabe, *Foure Bookes of Offices* (London, 1606).

Baron, Richard, *Pillars of Priestcraft Shaken*, 4 vols (1768).

Baxter, Richard, *Reliquiae Baxterianae*, eds N. H. Keeble et al, 5 vols (Oxford, 2020).

——, *A Holy Commonwealth, or Political Aphorisms* (London, 1659).

——, *A Key for Catholicks* (London, 1659).

——, *One Sheet against the Quakers* (Kidderminster, 1657).

——, *The Saints Everlasting Rest* (London, 1650).

——, *Aphorismes of Justification* (London, 1649).

Beard, Thomas, *The theatre of Gods judgements* (London, 1597).

Beckman, Gail McKnight (ed.), *The Statues at Large of Pennsylvania in the Time of William Penn* (New York, 1976).

Bede, *Ecclesiastical History of the English People*, eds Bertram Colgrave and R. A. B. Mynors (Oxford, 1969).

Bede, *The History of the Chvrch of Englande compiled by Venerable Bede, Englishman*, trans. Thomas Stapleton (Antwerp, 1565).

Benson, G., *A Collection of Tracts* (London, 1748).

Bilson, Thomas, *De perpetua Ecclesiae Christi gubernatione* (London, 1611).

——, *The True Difference between Christian Subjection and Unchristian Rebellion* (1585).

Black, Joseph L. (ed.), *The Martin Marprelate Tracts* (Cambridge, 2008).

Blair, Hugh, *Gods Soveraignity, His Sacred Majesties Supremacy, the Subjects Duty* (Glasgow, 1661).

Blount, Charles, *The Oracles of Reason* (London, 1693).

——, *Great is Diana of the Ephesians* (London, 1680).

BIBLIOGRAPHY

Blount, Thomas Pope, *Essays on Several Subjects* (1691).
Bond, John, *Eschol, or Grapes (among) thorns* (London, 1648).
Boys, John, *Remaines of That Reverend and Famous Postiller, Iohn Boys, Doctor in Divinitie, and Late Deane of Canterburie* (London, 1631).
Bray, Gerald (ed.), *Tudor Church Reform: The Henrician Canons of 1535 and the 'Reformatio Legum Ecclesiasticarum'*, Church of England Record Society 8 (Woodbridge, 2000).
—— (ed.), *Documents of the English Reformation*, 3rd edn (Cambridge, 2019).
Brady, Robert, *An Introduction to the Old English History* (London, 1684).
Burnet, Gilbert, *A History of his Own Times*, 2 vols (London, 1838).
Burton, Henry, *A Divine Tragedy* (London, 1636).
Burton, Thomas, *The Diary of Thomas Burton*, ed. John Towill Rutt (London, 1828).
Calendar of State Papers Domestic: Charles I, 1628–29 (London, 1859).
Calendar of State Papers Domestic: Charles I, 1629–31 (London, 1860).
Cobbett, W. (ed.), *Cobbett's Complete Collection of State Trials*, 34 vols (1808–28).
Cosin, John, *An apologie for svndrie proceedings by iurisdiction ecclesiasticall* (London, 1593).
Cressy, Serenus, *The Church-History of Brittany from the Beginning of Christianity to the Norman Conquest* (1668).
Crook, Samuel, *Ta Diapheronta, or, Divine Characters* (1658).
[Croope, John?], *Panarmonia. Or the Agreement of the People* (London, 1659).
Cromwell, Oliver, *Writings and Speeches of Oliver Cromwell*, ed. W. C. Abbott, 4 vols (Cambridge, MA, 1937—47).
Cusa, Nicholas of, *Nicholas of Cusa on Interreligious Harmony: Text, Concordance and Translation of De Pace Fidei*, ed. and trans. James E. Biechler (Lewiston, NY, 1991).
Dacres, Edward, 'Animadversion', in *Machiavel's Discourses upon the First Decade of T. Livius* (London, 1636).
Dennis, John, *Priestcraft Distinguished from Christianity* (London, 1715).
——, *The Danger of Priestcraft* (London, 1702).
Dodd, Charles, *The Church History of England*, 3 vols (Brussels, 1737).
Downame, George, *A Treatise Vpon John 8.36. Concerning Christian Libertie* (London, 1609).
Du Moulin, Lewis, *Proposals, and Reasons ... Presented to the Parliament* (London, 1659).
Eliot, John, *The Monarchie of Men*, ed. A. B. Grosart (London, 1879).
Elstob, Elizabeth, *An English-Saxon Homily on the Birth-day of St Gregory* (London, 1709).
Fenner, Dudley, *A short and profitable treatise, of lawfull and unlawfull recreations* (Middelburg, 1590).
Firth, C. H. (ed.), *The Clarke Papers: Selections from the Papers of William Clarke, I-II* (Orig, 1891, 1894, London, 1992).

Frere, W. H. and Douglas, C. E. (eds), *Puritan Manifestoes* (London, 1954).
Fulke, William, *A briefe and plaine declaration...a learned discourse* (1574).
Fuller, Thomas, *The Holy State* (Cambridge, 1642).
Fullwood, Francis, *A Dialogue betwixt Philautus and Timotheus* (London, 1681).
——, *Leges Angliae* (London, 1681).
Gardiner, S. R. (ed.), *The Constitutional Documents of the Puritan Revolution, 1625-1660* (Oxford, 1906).
—— (ed.), 'Speech of Sir Robert Heath, Attorney-General, in the case of Alexander Leighton in the Star Chamber, June 4, 1630', Camden Society New Series, Vol. 14 (1875).
George, Staughton, Mead, Benjamin M., and McCarment, Thomas (eds) *Charter to William Penn, and Laws of the Province of Pennsylvania* (Harrisburg, 1879).
Goodall, Charles, *The Royal College of Physicians of London, founded and established by law...* (London, 1684).
Goodwin, John, *Basanistai. Or the Triers or Tormentors Tried and Cast* (1657).
——, *Triumviri* (1658).
Graham, Timothy and Watson, Andrew, *The Recovery of the Past in Early Elizabethan England: Documents by John Bale and John Joscelyn from the Circle of Matthew Parker* (Cambridge, 1998).
Grosart, A. B. (ed.), *De jure maiestatis, or, Political treatise of government (1629-30) and the Letter-Book of John Eliot (1625-1632)* (London, 1882).
Grotius, Hugo, *De imperio summarum potestatum circa sacra*, ed. and trans. Harm-Jan van Dam, 2 vols (Leiden, 2001).
Hammond, Henry, *A Letter of Resolution to Six Quaeres, of Present Use in the Church of England* (London, 1653).
Harrington, James, *The Political Works of James Harrington*, ed. J. G. A. Pocock (Cambridge, 1977).
——, *Aphorisms Political*, 2nd edn (London, 1659).
——, *The Art of Law-giving* (London, 1659).
——, *The Prerogative of Popular Government* (London, 1658).
——, *Pian Piano. Or, Intercourse between H. Ferne, Dr in Divinity and J. Harrington, Esq. Upon occasion of the Doctors Censure of the Common-Wealth of Oceana* (London, 1656/1657).
——, *The Common-Wealth of Oceana* (London, 1656).
Hazard, Samuel (ed.), *Minutes of the Provincial Council of Pennsylvania*, 3 vols (Harrisburg, PA, 1838).
Hegel, G. F., *The Philosophy of History*, ed. C. J. Friedrich (New York, 1956).
Herbert, E., *De Religione Laici*, ed. H. T. Hutcheson (Yale, 1944).
——, *The Antient Religion of the Gentiles* (1705).
Hewit, John. *Repentance and Conversion, the Fabrick of Salvation* (London, 1658).
Heylyn, Peter, *A Help to English History* (London, 1671).

———, *Ecclesia Restaurata: The History of the Reformation of the Church of England* (London, 1661).
Hickeringill, Edmund, *The History of Priestcraft* (London, 1705).
———, *A Vindication of the Naked Truth, the Second Part* (London, 1681).
Hill, Joseph, *The Interest of These United Provinces* (Middleburg, 1673).
Hobbes, Thomas, *Leviathan*, ed. Richard Tuck (Cambridge, 1991).
———, *A True Ecclesiastical History* (1722).
Hobson, Paul, *A Garden Inclosed* (London, 1647).
Hody, Humphrey, *A History of English Councils and Convocations* (London, 1701).
Hooker, Richard, *The Folger Library Edition of the Works of Richard Hooker*, 6 vols (Cambridge, MA, 1977–93).
———, *Of the Laws of Ecclesiastical Polity*, ed. Christopher Morris (London, 1954).
———, *The Works of Mr. Richard Hooker* (London, 1666).
Howard, Robert, *A History of Religion* (London, 1696).
Hume, David, *Dialogues concerning natural religion ; and, The natural history of religion*, ed. J.C.A Gaskin (Oxford/New York, 1993).
Inett, John, *Origines Anglicanae* (London, 1704).
L'Isle, William *A Saxon Treatise concerning the Old and New Testament* (1623).
Jackson, Thomas, *Diverse Sermons: With a Short Treatise Befitting These Present Times* (Oxford, 1637).
Jacob, Henry, *A Declaration* (Middleburg, 1612).
Jewel, John, *The works of John Jewel, Vol. IV*, ed. J. Ayre (Cambridge, 1850).
———, *Defence of the Apologie of the Churche of England* (London, 1567).
Journal of the House of Commons: Volume 2, 1640–1643 (London, 1802).
King, Peter, *An Enquiry into the Constitution ... of the Primitive Church* (London, 1691).
Leighton, Alexander, *An Epitome or Brief Discoverie, from the beginning to the ending, of the many and great troubles Dr. Leighton suffered in his body, estate, and family* (London, 1646).
———, *A decade of grievances, presented and approved to the right honourable and High Court of Parliament* (London, 1641).
———, *An Appeal to the Parliament; or Sions Plea against the Prelacie* (Amsterdam, 1628).
———, *A shorte treatise against stage-playes* (Amsterdam, 1625).
———, *Speculum belli sacri, or, The Looking Glass of the Holy War* (Amsterdam, printed by the successors of Giles Thorp, 1624).
Livy, Titus, *The Early History of Rome*, trans. Aubrey De Sélincourt (London, 2002).
Lloyd, David, *Cabala, or, The mystery of conventicles unvail'd in an historical account of the principles and practices of the nonconformists, against church and state* (London, 1664).
Locke, John, *The Correspondence of John Locke*, ed. Esmond de Beer, 8 vols (Oxford 1976–82).

——, *An Essay Concerning Toleration*, ed. John Milton and Philip Milton (Oxford, 2006).
——, *Political Essays*, ed. Mark Goldie, (Cambridge, 1997).
——, *Two Treatises of Government*, ed. Peter Laslett (Cambridge 1988).
——, *Letter Concerning Toleration* (1689), ed. James Tully (Indianapolis, 1983).
——, *Two Tracts Upon Government*, ed. Philip Abrams (Cambridge 1969).
Machiavelli, Niccolò, *Discourses on Livy*, trans. Harvey C. Mansfield and Nathan Tarcov (Chicago, 1996).
——, *The Chief Works and Others*, vol. I, trans. Allan H. Gilbert (Durham, NC, 1965).
——, *The Works of Nicholas Machiavel, Secretary of State to the Republic of Florence*, vol. 2, ed. and trans. Elias Farneworth (London, 1762).
——, *The Works of the Famous Nicolas Machiavel, Citizen and Secretary of Florence*, trans. J. B. (London, 1675).
MacKinney, Gertrude (ed.), *Votes and Proceedings of the House of Representatives of the Province of Pennsylvania (Pennsylvania Archives: Eighth Series, Volume I: December 4, 1682 - June 11, 1707* (Philadelphia, 1752).
Milton, John, *Complete Prose Works*, ed. French Fogle (New Haven, 1971).
Molesworth, Robert, *An Account of Denmark*, ed. Justin Champion (Indianapolis, 2011).
——, *An Account of Denmark* (London, 1694).
Montesquieu, Charles de Secondat baron de, *The Spirit of Laws* (Cambridge/New York, 1989).
Nedham, Marchamont, *The Great Accuser Cast Down, or A Publick Trial of Mr John Goodwin of Coleman-Street, London, at the Bar of Religion and Right Reason* (1657).
——, *The Excellencie of a Free State* (1656).
——, *A True State of the Case of the Common-wealth* (1654).
——, *The Case of the Common-wealth of England stated* (1650).
Neville, Henry, *Plato Redivivus: Or, A Dialogue Concerning Government* (London, 1681).
Notestein, W. and Relf, F. H., *Commons Debates for 1629* (Minneapolis, 1921).
Nuttall, Geoffrey F. and Keeble, N. H. (eds), *The Calendar of the Correspondence of Richard Baxter*, 2 vols (Oxford, 1991).
Owen, John, *The Works of John Owen*, 16 vols (London, 1850–3).
Parker, Henry, *The True Grounds of Ecclesiastical Regiment* (London, 1641).
Penn, William, *Political Writings*, ed. Andrew R. Murphy (Cambridge, 2021).
——, *The Papers of William Penn*, eds Richard S. Dunn and Mary Maples Dunn, 5 vols (Philadelphia, 1981–6).
——, *Rule of Moderation* (1685)
——, *An Address to Protestants* (London, 1679).
——, *A Seasonable Caveat against Popery* (London, 1670).
——, *The Guide Mistaken, and Temporizing Rebuked* (London, 1668)

Perkins, Williams, *A Golden Chaine, or, The Description of Theologie* (London, 1621).
——, *A Graine of Mustard-seed* (London, 1611).
——, *A Treatise of Mans Imaginations* (Cambridge, 1607).
Petyt, William, *The Antient Right of the Commons of England Asserted* (London, 1680)
Plato, *The Laws*, ed. Trevor J. Saunders (Harmondsworth, 1970).
Prothero, G. W., *Select Statutes and other Constitutional Documents illustrative of the reigns of Elizabeth and James I*, 4th edn (Oxford, 1964).
Prynne, William, *The First Tome of an Exact Chronological Vindication and Historical Demonstration of our British, Roman, Saxon, Danish, Norman, English Kings Supreme Ecclesiastical Jurisdiction* (London, 1666).
——, *The Re-publicans and Others Spurious Good Old Cause … Anatomized* (London, 1659).
——, *The true good old cause rightly stated, and the false un-cased* (London, 1659).
——, *New Discovery of Free-State Tyranny* (London, 1655).
——, *Canterburies Doome* (London, 1646).
——, *A New Discovery of the Prelates Tyranny* (London, 1641).
——, *The humble petitions of Mr. Burton, Dr. Bastwicke, Mr Prynne, presented to the honorable knights, citizens, and burgesses of the Commons* (London, 1641).
——, *The humble petition of Mr. Prynne, late exile, and close prisoner in the Ile of Jersey* (London, 1641).
——, *Histrio-mastix, or, the player's scourge* (London, 1633).
Rainolds, John, *Th'Overthrow of Stage-Playes, by the Way of Controversie betwixt D. Gager and D. Rainoldes* (Middelburg, 1599, reprinted in Oxford, 1629).
Randall, John *Tvventy Nine Lectures of the Church* (London, 1631).
Robertson, John, *Rusticus Ad Clericum, or, The Plow-Man Rebuking the Priest* (Aberdeen, 1694).
Robbins, C. (ed.), *Two Republican Tracts* (Cambridge, 1969).
Rogers, John, *Ohel of Beth-shemesh, A tabernacle for the sun* (1653).
Ross, Alexander, *Pansebia: Or a view of all Religions in the World*, 6th edn (London, 1696).
Rousseau, Jean-Jacques, *The Social Contract*, ed. Victor Gourevitch (Cambridge, 1997).
Rushworth, John (ed.), *Historical Collections of Private Passages of State: Volume 4, 1640–42* (London, 1721).
Sadler, John, *Rights of the Kingdom* (London, 1649).
St German, Christopher, *Treatise Concerning the Division between the Spirituality and Temporality* (London, 1532).
——, *Doctor and Student* (London, 1528).

Saunders, Thomas, John Okey, and Matthew Alured, *The Humble Petition of Several Colonels of the Army* (London, 1654)

South, Robert, *Interest Deposed, and Truth Restored, or, A Word in Season, Delivered in Two Sermons* (Oxford, 1660).

Spinoza, Barruch, *Tractatus theologico-politicus*, trans. Samuel Shirley, 2nd edn (Leiden/New York, 1991).

Starkey, John, 'The Publisher to the Reader Concerning the Following Letter', in *The Works of the Famous Nicolas Machiavel, Citizen and Secretary of Florence* (London, 1675)

Stillingfleet, Edward, *Origines Britannicae* (London, 1685).

Stubbe, Henry, *Henry Stubbe and the Beginnings of Islam: The Originall & Progress of Mahometanism*, ed. Nabil Matar (New York, 2014).

——, *An Account of the Rise and Progress of Mahometanism*, ed. Hafiz Mahmud Khan Shairani (London, 1911).

——, *A further iustification of the present war against the United Netherlands* (London, 1673).

——, *Rosemary & Bayes: or, Animadversions upon a Treatise called, The Rehearsall Trans-posed* (London, 1672).

——, *A Specimen of some Animadversions upon a Book, Entituled, Plus Ultra* (London, 1670).

——, *Legends no Histories: or, A Specimen of some Animadversions upon the History of the Royal Society* (London, 1670).

——, *A Light Shining out of Darkness*, 2nd edn (London, 1659).

——, *A Letter to an Officer in the Army concerning a Select Senate* (London, 1659).

——, *An Essay in Defence of the Good Old Cause* (London, 1659).

——, *A vindication of that prudent and honourable knight, Sir Henry Vane, from the lyes and calumnies of Mr. Richard Baxter, minister of Kidderminster* (London, 1659).

Temple, William, *An Introduction to the History of England*, 3rd edn (London, 1708).

Tindal, Matthew, *Christianity as Old as the Creation* (1731).

Toland, John, *Nazarenus Or, Jewish, Gentile, and Mahometan Christianity* (1718).

——, *Anglia Libera* (London, 1701).

——, *Clito* (London, 1700).

——, *Christianity Not Mysterious* (London, 1696).

Travers, Walter, *A full and plaine declaration of Ecclesiasticall Discipline owt off the word off God* (Heidelberg, 1574).

Trenchard, John, *A Natural History of Superstition* (London, 1709).

Trenchard, John and Gordon, Thomas, *Cato's Letters; Or Essays on Liberty, Civil and Religious*, 4 vols (London, 1737).

Tyndale, William, *The Obedience of a Christen Man* (1528).

Tyrrell, James, *Bibliotheca Politica* (London, 1694).

Ussher, James, *The Correspondence of James Ussher* ed. Elizabethanne Boran, 3 vols (Dublin, 2015).

BIBLIOGRAPHY

Vane, Henry, *A Healing Question Propounded* (London, 1656).
——, *A Needful Corrective of Ballance in Popular Government, Expressed in a Letter to James Harrington* (London, 1660).
Vernon, G. (ed.), *Historical and Miscellaneous Tracts* (1681).
Voltaire, François Marie Arouet de, *Letters on the English*. The Harvard Classics, vol. 34, pt. 2 (New York, 1910).
Washington, Robert, *Some Observations upon the Ecclesiastical Jurisdiction of the Kings of England* (London, 1689).
Whetstone, George, *A Mirour for Magestrates* (London, 1584).
Whitelocke, Bulstrode, *Essays Ecclesiastical and Civil* (London, 1706).
Williams, Roger, *The Complete Writings of Roger Williams*, 7 vols (New York: 1963).
——, *The Hirelings Ministry None of Christ's* (London, 1652).
——, *The Bloudy Tenent Yet More Bloudy* (London, 1652).
——, *A Key into the Language of America* (London, 1644).
——, *The Bloudy Tenent of Persecution* (London, 1644).
Wilson, G. (ed.), *The Reports of Sir Edward Coke, knt. (1572–1617) in English, in thirteen parts complete* (London, 1777).
Wolfe, Don M. (ed.), *Leveller Manifestoes of the Puritan Revolution* (New York, 1944).
Wood, Anthony, *Athenae Oxonienses: an exact history of all the writers and bishops who have had their education in the University of Oxford*, ed. Philip Bliss, 3 vols (London, 1813–20).
Woodhouse, A. S. P. (ed.), *Puritanism and Liberty: Being the Army Debates (1647–49) from the Clarke Manuscripts* (Orig. 1938, London, 1992).
Young, C. D. (ed.), *The Treatises of Marcus Cicero* (1853).

Secondary Works

Achinstein, Sharon and Sauer, Elizabeth (eds), *Milton and Toleration* (Oxford, 2007).
Agamben, Giorgio, *The Kingdom and the Glory: For a Theological Genealogy of Economy and Government* (Stanford, 2011).
Alford, Stephen, 'The Political Creed of William Cecil', in *The Monarchical Republic of Early Modern England*, ed. John McDiarmid (Aldershot, 2007), pp. 75–90.
Almasy, Rudolph, 'The "Public" of Richard Hooker's Book 7 of the *Laws*: Stitching Together the Unjoined', *Renaissance and Reformation*, 41:1 (2018), 131–61.
——, 'Richard Hooker and places of Worship – 'In due season they are all pleasaunt and good'" *Anglican and Episcopal History*, 85 (2016), 306–30.
Anderson, Martin, 'Royal Idolatry: Peter Martyr and the Reformed Tradition', *Archiv fur Reformationsgeschichte*, 69 (1978), 451–69.

Apetrei, Sarah, *Women, Feminism, and Religion in Early Enlightenment England* (Cambridge, 2010).

Arab, Pooyan Tamimi, *Why do religious forms matter?* (London, 2022).

Armenteros, Carolina, *The French Idea of History: Joseph de Maistre and his Heirs, 1794-1854* (Ithaca, 2011).

Armitage, David, 'John Locke, Carolina, and the *Two Treatises of Government*', *Political Theory*, 32 (2004), 602-27.

Asad, Talal, *Formations of the Secular: Christianity, Islam, Modernity* (Stanford, 2003).

——, *Genealogies of Religion: Discipline and Reasons of Power in Christianity and Islam* (Baltimore, 1993).

Ashcraft, Richard, 'Anticlericalism and Authority in Lockean Political Thought', in *The Margins of Orthodoxy*, ed. Roger Lund (Cambridge, 1995), pp. 73-96.

Aston, Nigel and Cragoe, Matthew (eds), *Anticlericalism in Britain, c.1500-1914* (Stroud, 2000).

Avis, Paul (ed.), *Neville Figgis: His Life, Thought, and Significance* (Leiden, 2022).

Baker, John, *The Reinvention of Magna Carta 1216-1616* (Cambridge, 2017).

Barducci, Marco, 'Clement Barksdale, Translator of Grotius: Erastianism and Episcopacy in the English Church, 1651-1688', *The Seventeenth Century*, 25 (2010), 265-80.

Barish, Jonas, *The Antitheatrical Prejudice* (Berkeley, 1981).

Barnett, S. J., *Idol Temples and Crafty Priests: The Origins of Enlightenment Anticlericalism* (New York, 1999).

Bartolucci, G., 'The Hebrew Republic in Sixteenth-century Political Debate: The Struggle for Jurisdiction', in *Ancient Models in the Early Modern Republican Imagination*, eds W. Velema and A. Weststeijn (Leiden, 2017), pp. 214-33.

Bauer, Thomas, *A Culture of Ambiguity: An Alternative History of Islam* (New York, 2021).

Beard, Mary, North, John, and Price, Simon, *Religions of Rome*, 2 vols (Cambridge, 1998).

Beiner, Ronald, 'Civil Religion and Anticlericalism in James Harrington', *European Journal of Philosophy*, 13 (2014), 388-407.

——, 'James Harrington on the Hebrew Commonwealth', *The Review of Politics*, 76 (2014), 169-93.

——, *Civil Religion: A Dialogue in the History of Political Philosophy* (Cambridge, 2011).

——, 'Machiavelli, Hobbes, ad Rousseau on Civil Religion', *Review of Politics*, 55 (1993), 613-38.

Beiser, Frederick, *The Sovereignty of Reason: The Defense of Rationality in the Early English Enlightenment* (Princeton, 1996).

BIBLIOGRAPHY

Bejan, Teresa, *Mere Civility: Disagreement and the Limits of Toleration* (Cambridge, MA, 2017).

Bell, Duncan, 'What is Liberalism?', *Political Theory*, 42 (2014), 682–715.

Bellah, Robert, *The Broken Covenant: American Civil Religion in Time of Trial* (Chicago, 1992).

——, 'Religion and the Legitimation of the American Republic' in *Varieties of Civil Religion*, eds R. N. Bellah and P. E. Hammon (New York, 1980)

——, 'Civil Religion in America', in *Beyond Belief* (New York, 1970), pp. 168–91.

——, 'Civil Religion in America', *Daedalus, Journal of the American Academy of Arts and Sciences*, 96 (1967), 1000–21.

Bellah, R. N. and Hammon, P. E. (eds), *Varieties of Civil Religion* (New York, 1980).

Bendlin, Andreas, 'Religion in Rome', in *Themes in Roman Society and Culture*, eds M. Gibbs, M. Nicolic, and P. Ripat (Oxford, 2021), pp. 246–76.

Berger, Peter, *The Desecularization of the World* (Washington, DC, 1999).

Berman, David, 'Disclaimers as Offence Mechanism in Charles Blount and John Toland' in *Atheism from the Reformation to the Enlightenment*, eds Michael Hunter and David Wootton (Oxford, 1992), pp. 255–72.

——, *A History of Atheism in England* (London, 1987).

Bevilacqua, Alexander, *The Republic of Arabic Letters: Islam and the European Enlightenment* (Cambridge, MA, 2018).

Bingham, Matthew, 'On the Idea of a National Church: Reassessing Congregationalism in Cromwellian England', *Church History*, 88 (2019), 27–57.

Black, Anthony, *Council and Commune* (London, 1979).

——, 'Christianity and Republicanism: from St Cyprian to Rousseau', *American Political Science Review*, 91 (1997), 647–56.

Black, Robert, *Machiavelli: From Radical to Reactionary* (London, 2022).

Blair, Peter Hunter, *An Introduction to Anglo-Saxon England* (Cambridge, 1970).

Botvar, Pål Ketil, 'Civil Religion or Nationalism? The National Day Celebrations in Norway', *Religions*, 12 (2021), 1–15.

Brachlow, Stephen, 'The Elizabethan Roots of Henry Jacob's Churchmanship: Refocusing the Historiographical Lens', *Journal of Ecclesiastical History*, 36:2 (1985), 228–54.

Braddick, Michael J, *God's Fury, England's fire: a new history of the English Civil Wars* (London, 2008).

Breidenbach, Michael, *Our Dear-Bought Liberty: Catholics and Religious Toleration in Early America* (Cambridge, MA, 2021).

——, 'Conciliarism and the American Founding', *William and Mary Quarterly*, 73 (2016), 467–500.

Bremer, Francis, 'Dissent in New England', in *The Oxford History of Protestant Dissenting Traditions, vol. I: The Post-Reformation Era, c. 1559–1689*, ed. John Coffey (Oxford, 2020), pp. 244–66.

Brewer, Holly, 'Slavery, Sovereignty, and "Inheritable Blood": Reconsidering Locke and the Origins of American Slavery', *American Historical Review*, 122 (2017), 1038–78.

Brooks, Christopher, *Law, Politics and Society in Early Modern England* (Cambridge, 2009).

Bruce, Steven, *Secularization: In Defence of an Unfashionable Theory* (Oxford, 2011).

Bulman, William J., *Anglican Enlightenment: Orientalism, Religion and Politics in England and its Empire, 1648–1715* (Cambridge, 2015).

Bulman, William and Ingram, Robert (eds), *God and the Enlightenment* (Oxford, 2016).

Burgess, Glenn, *British Political Thought, 1500–1660* (New York, 2009).

Burke, Peter, 'William Dell, the Universities and the Radical Tradition', in *Reviving the English Revolution*, eds Geoff Ely and William Hunt (London, 1988), pp. 181–9.

Burson, Jeffrey and Lehner, Ulrich (eds), *Enlightenment and Catholicism in Europe* (Notre Dame, 2014).

Bush Jr, Sargent (ed.), *The Correspondence of John Cotton* (Chapel Hill, NC, 2001).

Calvert, Jane E., *Quaker Constitutionalism and the Political Thought of John Dickinson* (Cambridge, 2009).

Capp, Bernard, *British Slaves and Barbary Corsairs 1580–1750* (Oxford, 2022).

——, *England's Culture Wars: Puritan Reformation and Its Enemies in the Interregnum, 1649–1660* (Oxford, 2012).

Cargill Thompson, W. S. J, 'The Philosopher of the Politic Society: Richard Hooker as a Political Thinker', in *Studies in the Reformation: Luther to Hooker*, ed. C. W. Dugmore (London, 1980), pp. 131–91.

——, 'The Philosopher of the 'Politic society': Richard Hooker as a Political Thinker', in *Studies in Richard Hooker*, ed. W. Speed Hill (Cleveland, 1972), pp. 3–76.

——, 'Sir Francis Knollys' Campaign Against the *Jure Divino* Theory of Episcopacy', in *The Dissenting Tradition: Essays for Leland H. Carlson*, ed. C. R. Cole and M. Moodie (Ohio, 1975), pp. 39–69.

Champion, Justin A. I, '"I remember a Mahometan story of Ahmed ben Edris": freethinking uses of Islam from Stubbe to Toland', *Al-Qantara*, 31 (2010), 443–80.

——, 'Decoding the *Leviathan*: Doing the History of Ideas through Images, 1651–1714', in *Printed Images in Early Modern Britain*, ed. Michael Hunter (Farnham, 2010), pp. 255–75.

——, *Republican Learning: John Toland and the Crisis of Christian Culture, 1696–1722* (Manchester, 2003).

——, '"Religion's Safe, with Priestcraft is the War": Augustan Anticlericalism', *The European Legacy*, 5 (2000), 547–61.

——, 'Legislators, Impostors, and the Politic Origins of Religion: English Theories of 'Imposture' from Stubbe to Toland', in *Heterodoxy, Spinozism, and Free Thought in Early-Eighteenth-Century Europe*, eds Silvia Berti, Françoise Charles-Daubert and Richard H. Popkin (Dordrecht, 1996), pp. 333–56.

——, *The Pillars of Priestcraft Shaken: The Church of England and its Enemies, 1660–1730* (Cambridge, 1992).

Champion, Justin, Coffey, John, Harris, Tim and Marshall, John (eds), *Politics, Religion, and Ideas in seventeenth- and eighteenth- century Britain: essays in honour of Mark Goldie* (Woodbridge, 2019).

Chapman, Alister, Coffey, John and Gregory, Brad (eds), *Seeing Things Their Way: Intellectual History and the Return of Religion* (Notre Dame, 2009).

Chinnici, Joseph P., *The English Catholic Enlightenment: John Lingard and the Cisalpine Movement, 1780–1850* (Shepherdstown, WV, 1980).

Clark, J. C. D., 'Secularization and Modernization: The Failure of a Grand Narrative', *Historical Journal*, 55 (2012), 161–94.

Coffey, John, 'How Religious Freedom became a Natural Right: The Case of Post-Reformation England', in *From Toleration to Religious Freedom: Cross-Disciplinary Perspectives*, eds Marietta van der Tol, Carys Brown, John Adenitire, and E. S. Kempson (Oxford, 2021), pp. 23–56.

——, '"The Brand of Gentilism": Milton's Jesus and the Augustinian Critique of Pagan Kingship, 1649–71', *Milton Studies*, 48 (2014), 67–95.

——, 'Between Reformation and Enlightenment: Presbyterian Clergy, Religious Liberty and Intellectual Change, 1647 to 1788', in *Insular Christianity: Alternative Models of the Church in Britain and Ireland, c.1550-c.1750*, eds R. Armstrong and T. O'Hannrachain (Manchester, 2013), pp. 252–71.

——, 'John Owen and the Puritan Toleration Controversy, 1646–59', in *The Ashgate Research Companion to John Owen's Theology*, ed. Kelly Kapic and Mark Jones (Farnham, 2012), pp. 227–48.

——, 'European Multiconfessionalism and the English Toleration Controversy, 1640–1660', in *A Companion to Multiconfessionalism in the Early Modern World*, ed. Thomas Max Safley (Leiden, 2011), pp. 340–65.

——, 'The Martyrdom of Sir Henry Vane the Younger: From Apocalyptic Witness to Heroic Whig' in *Martyrs and Martyrdom in England, c. 1400–1700*, ed. Thomas Freeman (Woodbridge, 2007), pp. 221–39.

——, *John Goodwin and the Puritan Revolution* (Woodbridge, 2006).

——, *Persecution and Toleration in Protestant England, 1558–1689* (Harlow, 2000).

——, 'Puritanism and Liberty Revisited: The Case Toleration in the English Revolution', *Historical Journal*, 41 (1998), 961–85.

Cogswell, Thomas, 'England and the Spanish Match', in *Conflict in Early Stuart England*, eds Richard Cust and Ann Hughes (Harlow, 1989), pp. 107–33.
Colish, Marcia L., 'Republicanism, Religion, and Machiavelli's Savonarolan Moment', *Journal of the History of Ideas*, 60:4 (1999), 597–616.
Collins, Jeffrey R., *In the Shadow of Leviathan: John Locke and the Politics of Conscience* (Cambridge, 2020).
——, 'Restoration Anti-Catholicism', in *England's Wars of Religion Revisited*, eds Glenn Burgess and Charles Prior (Farnham, 2011), pp. 281–306.
——, *The Allegiance of Thomas Hobbes* (Oxford, 2005).
——, 'Thomas Hobbes and the Blackloist Conspiracy of 1649', *Historical Journal*, 45 (2002), 305–31.
——, 'The Church Settlement of Oliver Cromwell', *History*, 87 (2002), 18–40.
——, 'The Restoration Bishops and the Royal Supremacy', *Church History: Studies in Christianity and Culture*, 68:3 (1999), 549–80.
——, 'Quentin Skinner's Hobbes & the neo-Republican project', *Modern Intellectual History*, 6 (2009), 343–67.
Collins, Sarah H., 'The Elstobs and the End of the Saxon Revival', in *Anglo-Saxon Scholarship*, eds Carl T. Berkhout and Milton Gatch (Boston, MA, 1982), pp. 107–18.
Collinson, Patrick, *Richard Bancroft & Elizabethan Anti-Puritanism* (Cambridge, 2013).
——, 'Ecclesiastical Vitriol: Religious Satire in the 1590s and the Invention of Puritanism', in *The Reign of Elizabeth I: Court and Culture in the Last Decade*, ed. John Guy (Cambridge, 1995), pp. 150–70.
——, *The Birthpangs of Protestant England: Religion and cultural change in the sixteenth and seventeenth centuries* (Basingstoke, 1988).
——, *The Religion of Protestants: The Church in English Society, 1559–1625* (Oxford, 1982).
——, 'If Constantine, then also Theodosius: St Ambrose and the Integrity of the Elizabethan Ecclesia Anglicana', *Journal of Ecclesiastical History*, 30 (1979), 205–29.
——, *The Elizabethan Puritan Movement* (London, 1967).
Connell, Philip, *Secular Chains: Poetry and the Politics of Religion from Milton to Pope* (Oxford, 2016).
Cook, Sarah G., 'The Congregational Independents and the Cromwellian Constitutions', *Church History*, 46 (1977), 335–57.
Cooper, Tim, 'Polity and peacemaking: To what extent was Richard Baxter a congregationalist?', in *Church Polity and Politics in the British Atlantic World, c. 1635–66*, eds Elliot Vernon and Hunter Powell (Manchester, 2020), pp. 200–21.

Corns, Thomas N., 'John Milton, Roger Williams, and the Limits of Toleration', in *Milton and Toleration*, eds Sharon Achinstein and Elizabeth Sauer (Oxford, 2007), pp. 72–85.
Cressy, David, 'Puritan Martyrs in Island Prisons', *Journal of British Studies*, 57:4 (2018), 736–54.
Cristi, Marcela, *From Civil to Political Religion: The Intersection of Culture, Religion, and Politics* (Waterloo, ON, 2001).
Cristi, Marcela and Dawson, Lorne L., 'Civil Religion in Comparative Perspective: Chile under Pinochet (1973–1989)', *Social Compass*, 43 (1996), 319–38.
Crockett, Clayton, *Radical Political Theology: Religion and Politics after Liberalism* (New York, 2011).
Cromartie, Alan, 'Democracy, Toleration, and the Interests of the People', in *Democracy and Anti-Democracy in Early Modern England 1603–1689*, eds Cesare Cuttica and Markku Peltonen (Leiden, 2019), pp. 45–65.
——, *Sir Matthew Hale, 1609–1676* (Cambridge, 1995).
Cross, Clare, 'The Church in England, 1646–1660', in *The Interregnum*, ed. Gerald Aylmer (London, 1972), pp. 99–120.
Cross, F. L. (ed.), *The Oxford Dictionary of the Christian Church*, 3rd edn (Oxford, 1997).
Cubitt, Catherine, 'Bishops and Councils in Late Saxon England: The Intersection of Secular and Ecclesiastical Law', in *Recht und Gericht in Kirche und Welt um 900*, ed. Wilfried Hartmann (Munich, 2016).
——, *Anglo-Saxon Church Councils, c.650–c.850* (London, 1995).
Cummings, Brian, *Mortal Thoughts: Religion, Secularity, and Identity in Shakespeare and Early Modern Culture* (Oxford, 2013).
Damrosch, Leo, *The Sorrows of the Quaker Jesus: James Nayler and the Puritan Crackdown on the Free Spirit* (Cambridge, MA, 1996).
——, 'Hobbes as Reformation Theologian', *Journal of the History of Ideas*, 40 (1979), 339–52.
Dandelet, Thomas, 'Creating a Protestant Constantine: Martin Bucer's *De Regno Christi* and the Foundations of English Imperial Political Ideology', in *Politics and Reformations*, ed. Christopher Ocker (Leiden, 2007), pp. 539–50.
Danielson, Leilah, 'Civil Religion as Myth, Not History', *Religions*, 10 (2019), 1–16.
Davidson, G., 'Robert Leighton, his family and his library', *Transactions of the Society of the Friends of Dunblane Cathedral* (1959), 44–9.
Davie, Grace, 'Global Civil Religion: A European Perspective', *Sociology of Religion*, 62 (2001), 455–73.
Davies, Horton, *The Worship of the American Puritans, 1629–1730* (London/New York, 1990).
Davis, C. T., *Dante and the Idea of Rome* (Oxford, 1957).

Davis, J. C., 'Religion and the Struggle for Freedom in the English Revolution', *The Historical Journal*, 35:3 (1992), 507-30.

Deenan, Patrick, 'The Great Combination: Modern Political Thought and the Collapse of the Two Cities', in *Political Theology*, ed. Michael Kessler (Oxford, 2013), pp. 43-61.

Dickens, A. G., *The English Reformation* (London, 1964).

Dickey, Laurence, *Hegel: Religion, Economics, and the Politics of Spirit, 1770-1807* (Cambridge, 1987).

Diehl, Huston, *Staging Reform, Reforming the State: Protestantism and Popular Theatre in Early Modern England* (Cornell, 1997).

Duffy, Eamon, *The Stripping of the Altars: Traditional Religion in England, 1400-1580* (New Haven, 1992).

——, 'The Godly and the Multitude in Stuart England', *The Seventeenth Century*, 1:1 (1986), 31-55.

Dunn, John, 'The claim to freedom of conscience: freedom of speech, freedom of thought, freedom of worship?', in *The History of Political Theory and other essays* (Cambridge, 1996), pp. 100-20.

——, *Interpreting Political Responsibility* (Princeton, 1990).

——, *The Political Thought of John Locke* (Cambridge, 1969).

Durkheim, Emile, *The Elementary Forms of Religious Life*, trans. Karen G. Fields (New York, 1995).

Dzelzainis, Martin, 'Milton, Sir Henry Vane the Younger, and the Toleration of Catholics', in *Milton and Catholicism*, eds Ronald Corthell and Thomas N. Corns (Notre Dame, IN, 2017), pp. 65-83.

——, 'Harrington and the Oligarchs: Milton, Vane and Stubbe', in *Perspectives on English Revolutionary Republicanism*, eds Dirk Wiemann and Gaby Mahlberg (Abingdon, 2014).

East, Katherine, '*Superstitionis Malleus*: John Toland, Cicero, and the War on Priestcraft', *History of European Ideas*, 40 (2014), 965-83.

Eccleshall, Robert, *Order and Reason in Politics: Theories of Absolute and Limited Monarchy in Early Modern England* (Oxford, 1978).

Elton, G. R., *Tudor England*, 3rd edn (London, 1991).

——, *Reform and Reformation: England, 1509-1558* (London, 1977).

——, *Reform and Renewal* (Cambridge, 1973).

Fairer, David, 'Anglo-Saxon Studies', in *The History of the University of Oxford: V: The Eighteenth Century*, eds L. S. Sutherland and L. G. Mitchell (Oxford, 1986), pp. 807-29.

Farr, James, '"Absolute Power and Authority": John Locke and the Revisions of the *Fundamental Constitutions of Carolina*', *Locke Studies*, 20 (2020), 1-49.

Figgis, J. Neville, *From Gerson to Grotius, 1414-1625* (Cambridge, 1907).

——, 'Erastus and Erastianism', *Journal of Theological Studies*, 2 (1901), 66-101.

Forst, Rainer, *Toleration in Conflict: Past and Present* (Cambridge, 2003).

Fortin, Ernest, 'Augustine and Roman Civil Religion: Some Critical Reflections', in *Classical Christianity and the Political Order: Ernest Fortin's Collected Essays*, ed. J. Brian Benestad (Lanham, MD, 1996), II, pp. 238–56.

Foster, A., 'Church Policies of the 1630s' in *Conflict in Early Stuart England: Studies in Religion and Politics, 1603–1642*, eds Richard Cust and Ann Hughes (Harlow, 1989), pp. 193–223.

——, 'The Clerical Estate Revitalized', in *The Early Stuart Church, 1603–1642*, ed. Kenneth Fincham (Basingstoke, 1993), pp. 139–60.

Foster, Stephen, *Notes from the Caroline Underground: Alexander Leighton, the Puritan Triumvirate, and the Laudian Reaction to Nonconformity* (Hamden, CT, 1979).

Foxley, Rachel, *The Levellers: Radical Political Thought in the English Revolution* (Manchester, 2013).

Frankel, Steven and Yaffe, Martin (eds), *Civil Religion in Modern Political Philosophy* (Penn State, PA, 2020).

Freeman, Thomas, '"The Reformation of the Church in this Parliament": Thomas Norton, John Foxe and the Parliament of 1571', *Parliamentary History*, 16:2 (1997), 131–47.

Frost, J. William, 'Secularization in Colonial Pennsylvania', in *Seeking the Light: Essays in Quaker History in Honor of Edwin B. Bronner*, eds J. William Frost and John M. Moore (Wallingford and Haverford, PA, 1986), pp. 105–28.

——, 'Religious Liberty in Early Pennsylvania', *Pennsylvania Magazine of History and Biography*, 105 (1981), 419–51.

Gajda, Alexandra, 'The Elizabethan Church and the Antiquity of Parliament', in *Writing the History of Parliament in Tudor and Early Stuart England*, eds Paul Cavill and Alexandra Gajda (Manchester, 2018), pp. 77–105.

Gazal, A. A., '"A Christian prince hath the charge of both tables": John Jewel's biblical doctrine of the royal supremacy' in *Reformation faith: exegesis and theology in the Protestant reformations*, ed. Michael Parsons (Exeter, 2014), pp. 57–70.

Gildin, Hilail, *Rousseau's Social Contract: The Design of an Argument* (Chicago, 1983).

Glickman, Gabriel, 'Gothic History and Catholic Enlightenment in the Works of Charles Dodd (1672–1743)', *Historical Journal*, 54 (2011), 347–69.

Goff, Philip, Haberski, Raymond, and Williams, Rhys (eds), *Civil Religion Today: Religion and the American Nation in the Twenty-First Century* (New York, 2021).

Goldie, Mark, 'Sarah Cowper's "Character" of John Locke', *Locke Studies*, 21 (2021), 1–25.

——, 'The Ancient Constitution and the Languages of Political Thought', *Historical Journal*, 62 (2019), 3–34.

——, 'John Locke, the Early Lockeans, and Priestcraft', *Intellectual History Review*, 28:1 (2018), 125–44.

——, *Roger Morrice and the Puritan Whigs, The Entring Book 1677–1691* (Woodbridge, 2016).

——, 'Locke and America', in *A Companion to Locke*, ed. Matthew Stuart (London, 2016), pp. 27–44.

——, 'John Locke on the Glorious Revolution: A New Document', *History of Political Thought*, 42 (2012), 74–97.

——, 'Toleration and the Godly Prince in Restoration England', in *Liberty, Authority, and Formality*, eds John Morrow and Jonathan Scott (Exeter, 2008), pp. 45–66.

——, 'The Unacknowledged Republic: Officeholding in Early Modern England', in *The Politics of the Excluded, c.1500–1850*

Graham, Timothy, 'William Elstob's Planned Edition of the Anglo-Saxon Laws: A Remnant in the Takamiya Collection', *Poetica*, 73 (2010), 109-41.

Grazia, Sebastian de, *Machiavelli in Hell* (Princeton, 1989).

Greenberg, Janelle, *The Radical Face of the Ancient Constitution: St Edward's 'Laws' in Early Modern Political Thought* (Cambridge, 2001).

———, 'The Confessor's Laws and the Radical Face of the Ancient Constitution', *English Historical Review*, 104 (1989), 611-37.

Gregory, Eric, 'Before the Original Position: the Neo-Orthodox Theology of the Young John Rawls', *Journal of Religious Ethics*, 35 (2007), 175-206.

Gretsch, Mechtild, 'Elizabeth Elstob: A Scholar's Fight for Anglo-Saxon Studies', *Anglia*, 117 (1995), 163-201, 481-524.

Gribben, Crawford, *John Owen and English Puritanism: Experiences of Defeat* (New York, 2016).

Grimsley, Ronald, *Rousseau and the Religious Quest* (Oxford, 1968).

Gunnoe, C., *Thomas Erastus and the Palatinate* (Leiden, 2010).

Gunther, Karl, *Reformation Unbound: Protestant Visions of Reform in England, 1525-1590* (Cambridge, 2014).

Guy, John, 'Introduction: The 1590s: the second reign of Elizabeth I?', in *The Reign of Elizabeth I: Court and Culture in the Last Decade*, ed. John Guy (Cambridge, 1995), pp. 1-19.

Guy, John (ed.), *The Reign of Elizabeth I: Court and Culture in the Last Decade* (Cambridge, 1995).

Ha, Polly, 'Discovering Orthodoxy? Rethinking the Purpose and Impact of the Synod of Dordt' in *The Synod of Dordt: A Landmark in Turbulent Times*, eds Henk van den Belt, Willem van Vlastuin, and Klaas-Willem de Jong (Göttingen, 2022), pp. 37-54.

———, 'The Elizabethan Wars of Religion', in *Reformed Government*, eds Polly Ha, Jonathan D. Moore, and Edda Frankot (Oxford, 2022), pp. xiii-xxii.

———, 'Leveraging Historical Contingency: Christian Antiquity and Late Elizabethan Society', in *Reformed Government*, eds Polly Ha, Jonathan D. Moore, and Edda Frankot (Oxford, 2022), pp. xxxix-liii.

———, 'Who Owns the Hebrew Doctors?', *Journal of Medieval and Renaissance Studies*, 53:1 (January 2023), 55-85.

———, *English Presbyterianism 1590-1640* (Stanford, 2010).

Ha, Polly, Moore, Jonathan D., and Frankot, Edda (eds), *Reformed Government* (Oxford, 2022).

——— (eds), *The Puritans on Independence* (Oxford, 2017).

Habermas, Jürgen and Ratzinger, Joseph, *The Dialectics of Secularization* (San Francisco, 2006).

Haberski, Ray, *God and War: American Civil Religion Since 1945* (New Brunswick, 2012).

Hadfield, Andrew, *Lying in Early Modern English Culture: From the Oath of Supremacy to the Oath of Allegiance* (Oxford, 2017).

———, 'Milton and Catholicism', in *Milton and Toleration*, eds Sharon Achinstein and Elizabeth Sauer (Oxford, 2007), pp. 186–200.

Haefeli, Evan (ed.), *Against Popery: Britain, Empire, and Anti-Catholicism* (Charlottesville, 2020).

———, *New Netherland and the Dutch Origins of American Religious Liberty* (Philadelphia, 2012).

Hageman, Elizabeth, 'John Foxe's Henry VIII as *Justitia*', *Sixteenth Century Journal*, 10 (1979), 35–43.

Haivry, Ofir, *John Selden and the Western Tradition* (Cambridge, 2017).

Halkett, John, *Milton and the Idea of Matrimony* (New Haven, 1970).

Hall, David D., *A Reforming People: Puritanism and the Transformation of Public Life in New England* (Chapel Hill, NC, 2012).

Haller, William, *Foxe's Book of Martyrs and the Elect Nation* (London, 1963).

Halverson, Jeffry R., Rushton, Scott W., and Tretherway, Angela, 'Mediated Martyrs of the Arab Spring: New Media, Civil Religion, and Narrative in Tunisia and Egypt', *Journal of Communication*, 63 (2013), 312–32.

Hammersley, Rachel, *James Harrington: An Intellectual Biography* (Oxford, 2019).

———, 'Rethinking the Political Thought of James Harrington: Royalism, Republicanism and Democracy', *History of European Ideas*, 39:3 (2013), 357–70.

———, 'The Commonwealth of Oceana & the Republican Tradition', in *The Oxford Handbook of Literature and the English Revolution*, ed. Laura L. Knoppers (Oxford, 2012), pp. 534–50.

Hammill, Graham, *The Mosaic Constitution: Political Theology and Imagination from Machiavelli to Milton* (Chicago, 2012).

Hamill, Graham and Lupton, Julia (eds), *Political Theology and Early Modernity* (Chicago, 2012).

Hann, Chris, 'Problems with the (De)privatization of Religion', *Anthropology Today*, 16 (2000), 14–20.

Harris, Tim, Seaward, Paul, and Goldie, Mark (eds), *The Politics of Religion in Restoration England* (Oxford, 1990).

Heal, Felicity, 'What can King Lucius do for you? The Reformation and the Early British Church', *English Historical Review*, 120 (2005), 593–614.

———, *Reformation in Britain and Ireland* (Oxford, 2003).

Heinemann, Margot, *Puritanism and Theatre: Thomas Middleton and Opposition Drama under the Early Stuarts* (Cambridge, 1980).

Helmholz, R. H., 'Origins of the Privilege Against Self-Incrimination: The Role of the European *Ius Commune*', *New York University Law Review*, 65:4 (1990), 962–91.

Herberg, Will, 'America's Civil Religion: What it is and Whence in Comes', in *American Civil Religion*, eds Russell E. Richey and Donald G. Jones (New York, 1974), pp. 76–88.

Herold, Aaron, 'John Locke's Theology of Toleration and his Case for Civil Religion', *Review of Politics*, 76 (2014), 195–221.
Hill, Christopher, *The Economic Problems of the Church* (Oxford, 1956).
Holmes, Geoffrey S., *The Trial of Doctor Sacheverell* (London, 1973).
Holt, P. M., 'A Seventeenth-Century Defender of Islam: Henry Stubbe (1632–76) and his book', *Friends of Doctor Williams Library*, 26 (1972), 1–30.
Höpfl, Harro (ed.), *Luther and Calvin on Secular Authority* (Cambridge, 1991).
Hoppit, Julian, *A Land of Liberty? England, 1689–1727* (Oxford, 2000).
Hovey, Craig and Phillips, Elizabeth (eds), *The Cambridge Companion to Christian Political Theology* (Cambridge, 2015).
Hughes, Ann, '"The Public Profession of these Nations": The National Church in Interregnum England', in *Religion in Revolutionary England*, eds Christopher Durston and Judith Maltby (Manchester, 2006), pp. 93–114.
Hulme, Harold, *The Life of Sir John Eliot, 1592–1632: The struggle for parliamentary freedom* (London, 1957).
Hunter, Ian, *The Secularization of the Confessional State: The Political Thought of Christian Thomasius* (Cambridge, 2007).
Hutchinson, Mark A. and Stanton, Timothy, 'On liberalism, liberty of conscience, and toleration: some historical and theoretical reflections', in *Toleration and the Challenges to Liberalism*, eds Johannes Drerup and Gottfried Schweiger (London and New York, 2020), pp. 53–76.
Hwan Cha, Seong, 'Korean Civil Religion and Modernity', *Social Compass*, 47 (2000), 467–85.
Iliffe, Rob, *Priest of Nature: The Religious Worlds of Isaac Newton* (Oxford, 2017).
Ingram, James, *An Inaugural Lecture on the Utility of Anglo-Saxon Literature* (Oxford, 1807).
Ingram, Robert, *Reformation without End: Religion, Politics, and the Past in Post-Revolutionary England* (Manchester, 2018).
Innocenti, Piero and Rossi, Marielisa, 'Introduzione', in *Bibliografia Delle Edizioni Di Niccolò Machiavelli* (Rome, 2015), III, p. ix–lxxvii.
Israel, Jonathan, *Radical Enlightenment* (Oxford, 2001).
Jacob, James R., *Henry Stubbe, Radical Protestantism and the Early Enlightenment* (Cambridge, 1983).
Jacob, Margaret, *The Radical Enlightenment* (London, 1981).
James, Margaret, 'The Political Importance of the Tithes Controversy in the English Revolution, 1640–1660', *History*, 26 (1941), 1–18.
Jenkinson, Sally, 'Two Concepts of Tolerance: Or why Bayle is not Locke', *Journal of Political Philosophy*, 4 (1996), 302–21.
Johnson, A. F., 'The Exiled English Church at Amsterdam and its Press', *The Library*, Fifth Series, 5:4 (1951), pp. 219–42.

Johannsen, Robert W., 'The Conflict Between the Three Lower Counties on the Delaware and the Province of Pennsylvania, 1682–1704', *Delaware History*, 5 (1952), 96–132.

Jolley, Nicholas, *Toleration and Understanding in Locke* (Oxford, 2016).

Jones, Norman, *Faith by Statute: Parliament and the Settlement of Religion, 1559* (London, 1982).

Judson, Margaret, *The Political Thought of Sir Henry Vane the Younger* (Philadelphia, 1969).

Kelly, Ryan, 'Reformed or Reforming? John Owen and the Complexity of Theological Codification for Mid-Seventeenth-Century England', in *The Ashgate Research Companion to John Owen's Theology*, eds Kelly Kapic and Mark Jones (Farnham, 2012), pp. 3–30.

Kelley, Maurice, 'Milton and Machiavelli's "Discorsi"', *Studies in Bibliography*, 4 (1951), 123–7.

Kessler, Michael (ed.), *Political Theology for a Plural Age* (Oxford, 2013).

Kidd, Colin C., 'Constructing a Civil Religion: Scots Presbyterians and the Eighteenth-Century British State', in *The Scottish Churches and the Union Parliament, 1707–1999*, ed. James Kirk (Edinburgh, 2001), pp. 1–21.

——, *British Identities before Nationalism* (Cambridge, 1999).

——, 'Civil Theology and Church Establishments in Revolutionary America', *Historical Journal*, 42 (1999), 1007–26

Killeen, Kevin, *The Political Bible in Early Modern England* (Cambridge, 2017).

Kirby, Torrance, 'Peter Martyr Vermigli on the Unity of Civil and Ecclesiastical Jurisdiction', *Archiv fur Reformationsgeschichte* (2014), 161–93.

——, *The Zurich Connection and Tudor Political Theology* (Leiden, 2007).

——, 'Lay Supremacy: Reform of the canon law of England from Henry VIII to Elizabeth I (1529–1571)', *Reformation and Renaissance Review: Journal of the Society for Reformation Studies*, 8:3 (2006), 349–70.

Kirwan, Michael, *Political Theology: A New Introduction* (London, 2008).

Kishlansky, Mark, 'Martyrs' Tales', *Journal of British Studies*, 53:2 (2014), 334–55.

——, 'A whipper whipped: the sedition of William Prynne', *Historical Journal*, 56:3 (2013), 603–27.

Knights, Mark, 'John Starkey and Ideological Networks in Late Seventeenth-Century England', *Media History*, 11:1/2 (2005), 127–45.

Knox, T. M. (ed.), *The Philosophy of Right* (Oxford, 1967).

Koch, Bettina, 'Priestly Despotism: The Problem of Unruly Clerics in Marsilius of Padua's *Defensor Pacis*', *Journal of Religious History*, 36 (2012), 165–83.

Kolakowski, Leszek, *Modernity on Endless Trial* (Chicago, 1990).

Koontz, T. J., 'Religion and Political Cohesion: John Locke and Jean-Jacques Rousseau', *Journal of Church and State*, 23 (1981), 95–115.

Laborie, Lionel, *Enlightening Enthusiasm: Prophecy and Religious Experience in Early Eighteenth-Century England* (Manchester, 2015).
Lake, Peter, 'Puritanism, (Monarchical) Republicanism, and Monarchy: or John Whitgift, Puritanism and the "Invention" of Popularity', *Journal of Medieval and Early Modern Studies*, 40:3 (2010), 463–95.
———, '"Anti-Puritanism": The Structure of a Prejudice' in *Religious Politics in Post-Reformation England*, eds Kenneth Fincham and Peter Lake (Woodbridge, 2006), pp. 80–97.
———, 'Deeds against nature: cheap print, Protestantism and murder in early seventeenth century England', in *Culture and politics in early Stuart England*, eds Kevin M. Sharpe and Peter Lake (London, 1994), pp. 257–83.
———, 'Anti- Popery: The Structure of a Prejudice', in *Conflict in Early Stuart England: Studies in Religion and Politics 1603–1642*, eds Richard Cust and Ann Hughes (London, 1989), pp. 72–106.
———, *Anglicans and Puritans? Presbyterianism and English Conformist Thought from Whitgift to Hooker* (London, 1988).
———, 'Constitutional consensus and Puritan opposition in the 1620s: Thomas Scott and the Spanish Match', *Historical Journal*, 25 (1982), 805–25.
Lamont, William Montgomerie, 'The Religion of Andrew Marvell', in *The Political Identity of Andrew Marvell*, eds Conal Condren and A. D. Cousins (Aldershot, 1990), pp. 135–56.
———, *Richard Baxter and the Millennium: Protestant Imperialism and the English Revolution* (Washington, DC, 1979).
———, *Godly Rule: Politics and Religion, 1603–1660* (London, 1969).
———, *Marginal Prynne* (London, 1963).
Lander, Jesse M., 'The Monkish Middle Ages: Periodization and Polemic in Foxe's *Acts and Monuments*', in *Renaissance Retrospections: Tudor Views of the Middle Ages*, ed. Sarah A. Kelen (Kalamanzoo, 2013), pp. 93–110.
Larsen, Timothy, *Friends of Religious Equality: Nonconformist Politics in Mid-Victorian England* (Woodbridge, 1999).
Lehmberg, Stanford E., *Reformation Parliament 1529–36* (Cambridge, 1970).
Lehner, Ulrich, *The Catholic Enlightenment* (Oxford, 2016).
Leinbaugh, Thoedore H., 'Aelfric's *Sermo de sacrificio in die pascae*: Anglican Polemic in the Sixteenth and Seventeenth Centuries', in *Anglo-Saxon Scholarship: The First Three Centuries*, eds Carl T. Berkhout and Milton Gatch (Boston, MA, 1982), pp. 51–68.
Leites, Edmund (ed.), *Conscience and Casuistry in Early Modern Europe* (Cambridge, 1988).
Levitin, Dimitri, *Ancient Wisdom in the Age of the New Science: Histories of Philosophy in England, c1640–1700* (Cambridge, 2015).
———, 'From Sacred History to the History of Religion: Paganism, Judaism, and Christianity in European Historiography from Reformation to "Enlightenment"', *The Historical Journal*, 55:4 (2012), 1117–60.

——, 'Matthew Tindal's *Rights of the Christian Church* (1706) and the Church-State Relationship', *Historical Journal*, 54 (2011), 717–40.
Lewis, Bradley V., 'Gods for the City and Beyond: Civil Religion in Plato's Laws', in *Civil Religion in political thought: its perennial questions and enduring relevance in North America*, eds Ronald L. Weed and John von Heyking (Washington, DC, 2010), pp. 19–46.
Lilla, Mark, *The Stillborn God: Religion, Politics, and the Modern West* (New York, 2007).
Lockwood, Shelley, 'Marsilius of Padua and the Case for the Royal Ecclesiastical Supremacy', *Transactions of the Royal Historical Society*, 1 (1991), 89–119.
Losonczi, Peter et al (eds), *The Future of Political Theology* (Farnham, 2011).
Lucci, Diego, *John Locke's Christianity* (Cambridge, 2021).
MacCabe, David, 'John Locke and the Argument against Strict Separation', *Review of Politics*, 59 (1997), 233–58.
MacCulloch, Diarmaid (ed.), *The Reign of Henry VIII: Politics, Policy and Piety* (New York, 1995).
Macguire, M. H., 'Attack of the Common Lawyers on the Oath *Ex Officio* as Administered in the Ecclesiastical Courts of England', in *Essays in History and Political Theory in Honour of Charles Howard McIlwain*, ed. C. F. Wittke (Cambridge, MA, 1936), pp. 199–229.
Maclear, J. F., 'Popular Anticlericalism in the Puritan Revolution', *Journal of the History of Ideas*, 17 (1956), 443–70.
Mahlberg, Gaby, 'Machiavelli, Neville, and the Seventeenth-Century English Republican Attack on Priestcraft', *Intellectual History Review*, 28:1 (2018), 79–99.
——, 'Henry Neville and the Toleration of Catholics during the Exclusion Crisis', *Historical Research*, 83:222 (2010), 617–34.
——, *Henry Neville and English Republican Culture in the Seventeenth Century: Dreaming of Another Game* (Manchester, 2009)
——, 'Historical and Political Contexts of The Isle of Pines', *Utopian Studies*, 17:1 (2006), 111–29.
Mahmood, Saba, 'Religious Reason and Secular Affect: An Commensurable Divide?', *Critical Enquiry*, 35 (2009), 836–62.
Malcolm, Noel, *Useful Enemies: Islam and The Ottoman Empire in Western Political Thought, 1450–1750* (Oxford, 2019).
Maloyed, Christie L., 'A Liberal Civil Religion: William Penn's Holy Experiment', *Journal of Church and State*, 55 (2012), 669–89.
Maltzahn, Nicholas von, *Milton's History of Britain: Republican Historiography in the English Revolution* (Oxford, 1991).
Marchant, Ronald A., *The Church under the Law: Justice, Administration, and Discipline in the Diocese of York, 1560–1640* (Cambridge, 1969).

Marshall, John, 'The Trial and Execution of Oliver Plunkett', in *The State Trials and the Politics of Justice in Later Stuart England*, eds Brian Cowan and Scott Sowerby (Woodbridge, 2021), pp. 93–102.

——, 'London, Locke and 1690s provision for the poor in context: beggars, spinners and slaves', in *Politics, Religion and Ideas in seventeenth- and eighteenth-century Britain: essays in honour of Mark Goldie*, eds Justin Champion, John Coffey, Tim Harris, and John Marshall (Woodbridge, 2019), pp. 181–200.

——, *John Locke, Toleration and Early Enlightenment Culture* (Cambridge, 2006).

——, 'Locke, Socinianism, "Socinianism" and Unitarianism', in *English Philosophy in the Age of Locke*, ed. M. A. Stewart, (Oxford, 2000), pp. 111–82.

——, *John Locke, Resistance, Religion and Responsibility* (Cambridge, 1996).

——, 'John Locke and Latitudinarianism', in *Philosophy, Science and Religion in England, 1640–1700*, eds Richard Kroll, Richard Ashcraft, and Perez Zagorin (Cambridge, 1992), pp. 253–82.

——, 'The Ecclesiology of the Latitude-Men, 1660–1689', *Journal of Ecclesiastical History*, 36 (1985), 407–27.

Martin, Craig, *Masking Hegemony: A Genealogy of Liberalism, Religion, and the Private Sphere* (Abingdon, 2010).

Martinich, A. P., 'Interpreting the Religion of Thomas Hobbes', *Journal of the History of Ideas*, 70 (2009), 143–63.

Marty, Martin, 'Two Kinds of Civil Religion', in *American Civil Religion*, ed. Russell E. Richey (New York, 1974), pp. 139–60.

Marvin, Carolyn and Ingle, David W., 'Blood Sacrifice and the Nation: Revisiting Civil Religion', *Journal of the American Academy of Religion*, 64 (1996), 767–80.

Masters, Ronald D., *The Political Philosophy of Rousseau* (Princeton, 1968).

Masuzawa, Tomoko, *The Invention of World Religions* (Chicago, 2005).

Matar, Nabil, 'England and Religious Plurality: Henry Stubbe, John Locke and Islam', *Studies in Church History*, 51 (2015), 181–203.

——, 'Britons and Muslims in the early modern period: from prejudice to (a theory of) toleration', *Patterns of Prejudice*, 43 (2009), 213–31.

——, *Turks, Moors and Englishmen in the Age of Discovery* (New York, 1999).

——, 'John Locke and the "turbaned nations"', *Journal of Islamic Studies*, 2 (1991), 67–77.

——, 'The Ecclesiology of the Latitude Men, 1660–1689', *Journal of Ecclesiastical History*, 36 (1985), 407–27.

Mathieson, James, 'Twenty Years After Bellah: Whatever Happened to American Civil Religion?', *Sociological Analysis*, 50 (1989), 129–46.

Mayer, Ruth, *1659: The Crisis of the Commonwealth* (Woodbridge, 2004).

McGee, S., *The Godly Man in Stuart England, Anglicans, Puritans, and the Two Tables, 1620–1670* (Yale, 1976).

McGovern, J., 'The Political Sermons of Lancelot Andrewes', *Seventeenth Century*, 34:1 (2019), 3–23.
McGrath, Patrick, *Papists and Puritans under Elizabeth I* (London, 1967).
McLaren, Anne, 'Elizabeth I as Deborah: Biblical Typology, Prophecy, and Political Power', in *Gender, Power, and Privilege in Early Modern Europe*, eds Jessica Munns and Penny Richards (Harlow, 2003), pp. 90–107.
McMahon, Madeline, 'Matthew Parker and the Practice of Church History', in *Confessionalisation and Erudition in Early Modern Europe*, eds Nicholas Hardy and Dmitri Levitin, *Proceedings of the British Academy*, 225 (Oxford, 2019), pp. 116–53.
Meinecke, Friedrich, *Machiavellism: The Doctrine of Raison d'État and its Place in Modern History*, trans. Douglas Scott (London, 1957).
Melzer, A., *The Natural Goodness of Man: On the System of Rousseau's Thought* (Chicago, 1990).
Milbank, John, *Theology and Social Theory: Beyond Secular Reason* (London, 1993)
Mills, R. J. W., 'Alexander Ross's *Pansebia* (1653), religious compendia and the seventeenth-century study of religious diversity', *Seventeenth Century*, 31 (2016), 285–310.
Milton, Anthony, *England's Second Reformation: The Battle for the Church of England, 1625–1662* (Cambridge, 2021).
——, 'A Missing Dimension of European Influence on English Protestantism: The Heidelberg Catechism and the Church of England, 1563–1663', *Reformation & Renaissance Review*, 20:3 (2018), pp. 235–48.
——, *Laudian & Royalist Polemic in seventeenth-century England: the career & writing of Peter Heylyn* (Manchester, 2007).
——, 'Licensing, Censorship, and Religious Orthodoxy in early Stuart England', *The Historical Journal*, 41:3 (1998), 625–51.
——, *Catholic and Reformed: The Roman and Protestant Churches in English Protestant Thought, 1600–1640* (Cambridge, 1995).
Milton, John R., 'John Locke and the *Fundamental Constitutions* of Carolina', *Locke Newsletter*, 21 (1990), 111–33.
Mohammed, Feisal G., 'Milton, Sir Henry Vane, and the Brief but Significant Life of Godly Republicanism', *Huntington Library Quarterly*, 76 (2013), 83–104.
Moots, Glenn A., 'John Cotton and Roger Williams', in *Great Christian Jurists in American History*, eds Daniel L. Dreisbach and Mark Hall (Cambridge, 2019), pp. 16–36.
Morrison, Jeffrey, 'John Witherspoon and the Public Interest of Religion', *Journal of Church and State*, 41 (1999), 551–73.
Mortimer, Sarah, *Reason and Religion in the English Revolution: The Challenge of Socinianism* (Cambridge, 2010).

Morton, Adam, 'Anti-popery', in *The Oxford History of British and Irish Catholicism*, eds John Morrill and Liam Temple (Oxford, 2023), II, pp. 170–89.

——, 'Anti-Catholicism: Catholics, Protestants, and the "Popery" problem', in *A Companion to Catholicism and Recusancy in Britain and Ireland*, eds Robert E. Scully and Angela Ellis (Leiden, 2022), pp. 410–48.

Moyn, Samuel, 'Jacques Maritain, Christian New Order, and the Origins of Human Rights', in *Intercultural Dialogue and Human Rights*, eds Luigi Bonanante et al (Washington, DC, 2011).

Munoz, Vincent Philip, *Religious Liberty and the American Founding* (Chicago, 2022).

Murphy, Andrew R., '"Religion", "Politics", and the Theory and Practice of Toleration: The Case of William Penn', in *Secularization, Desecularization, and Toleration: Cross-Disciplinary Challenges to a Modern Myth*, eds Vyacheslav Karpov and Marcus Svensson (London, 2020), pp. 81–99.

——, *William Penn: A Life* (Oxford, 2019).

——, *Liberty, Conscience, and Toleration: The Political Thought of William Penn* (Oxford, 2016)

Murphy, Michael, 'The Elstobs, Scholars of Old English and Anglican Apologists', *Durham University Journal*, 58 (1966), 131–8.

Murry, Gregory, 'Anti-Machiavellianism and Roman Civil Religion in the Princely Literature of Sixteenth Century Europe', *The Sixteenth Century Journal*, 45:2 (2014), 331–50.

——, 'The Best Possible Use of Christianity: The Rhetorical Stance of Machiavelli's Christian Passages', *History of Political Thought*, 36:2 (2015), 262–80.

Nederman, Cary J. and Lahoud, Nelly, '"This Is the Way I Pray": Precatory Language in the Writings of Niccolò Machiavelli', *Intellectual History Review*, 31 (2021), 1–22.

Nelson, Eric, *The Hebrew Republic: Jewish Sources and the Transformation of European Political Thought* (Cambridge, MA, 2010).

Nierop, Hendrilk Van, *The Life of Romeyn de Hooghe 1645–1708* (Amsterdam, 2018).

Nobbs, D., 'Philip Nye on Church and State', *Cambridge Historical Journal*, 5 (1935), 41–59.

Noll, Mark, *America's God: From Jonathan Edwards to Abraham Lincoln* (New York, 2002).

Nongbri, Brent, *Before Religion: A History of a Modern Concept* (Cambridge, 2015).

North, John, *Roman Religion* (Oxford, 2000).

Nuttall, Geoffrey, *Visible Saints: The Congregational Way, 1640–1660* (Oxford, 1957).

Oakeshott, Michael, *Experience and its Modes* (Cambridge, 1933).

Oakley, Francis, *The Conciliarist Tradition* (Cambridge, 2003).

Oates, Rosamund, 'Elizabethan Histories of English Christian Origins', in *Sacred History: Uses of the Christian Past in the Renaissance World*, eds Katherine van Liere, Simon Ditchfield, and Howard Louthan (Oxford, 2012), pp. 165–85.

Olsen, V. Norskov, *John Foxe and the Elizabethan Church* (Berkeley, CA, 2022: original 1973).

Oresko, Robert, 'The House of Savoy in Search for a Royal Crown', in *Royal and Republican Sovereignty*, eds Robert Oresko et al (Cambridge, 1997), pp. 294–301.

Orr, D. Alan, *Treason and the State: Law, Politics and Ideology in the English Civil War* (Cambridge, 2002).

———, 'Sovereignty, Supremacy and the Origins of the English Civil War', *History*, 87:288 (2002), 474–90.

Overhoff, Jurgen, 'The Lutheranism of Thomas Hobbes', *History of Political Thought*, 18 (1997), 604–23.

Owen, Evivion, 'Milton and Selden on Divorce', *Studies in Philology*, 43 (1946), 233–57.

Pagden, Anthony, *The Enlightenment and Why it Still Matters* (Oxford, 2015).

Parkin, Jon, *Taming the Leviathan* (Cambridge, 2007).

Parel, Anthony, *The Machiavellian Cosmos* (New Haven, 1992).

Parnham, David, *Sir Henry Vane, Theologian: A Study in Seventeenth-Century Religious and Political Discourse* (Cranberry, NJ, 1997).

Parsons, Gerald, *The Cult of St Catherine of Siena: A Study in Civil Religion* (London, 2017).

———, *Perspectives on Civil Religion* (Aldershot, 2002).

Patterson, Annabel, *Marvell and the Civic Crown* (Princeton, 1978)

Patterson, Annabel et al (eds), *The Prose Works of Andrew Marvell*, 2 vols (New Haven, 2003).

Perry, John, *The Pretences of Loyalty: Locke, Liberal Theory, and American Political Theology* (Oxford, 2011).

Phillips, H. E. I., 'The Last Years of the Court of Star Chamber 1630–41: (The Alexander Prize Essay)', *Transactions of the Royal Historical Society*, 21 (1939), 103–31.

Pierce, Helen, *Unseemly Pictures: Graphic Satire and Politics in Early Modern England* (New Haven, 2008).

Pocock, J. G. A., *The Ancient Constitution and the Feudal Law* (Cambridge, 1957; reissued with a retrospect, 1987).

———, *The Machiavellian Moment: Florentine Political Thought and the Atlantic Republican Tradition* (Princeton, 1975).

Polizotto, Carolyn, 'The Campaign against The Humble Proposals of 1652', *Journal of Ecclesiastical History*, 38 (1987), 569–81.

Powell, Hunter, 'Cromwellian Calvinism: England's Church and the End of the Puritan Revolution', in *The Oxford Handbook of Calvin and Calvinism*, eds Bruce Gordon and Carl Trueman (Oxford, 2021), pp. 339–58.

——, *The Crisis of British Protestantism: Church Power in the Puritan Revolution, 1638–44* (Manchester, 2015).
Primus, John, *Holy Time: Moderate Puritanism and the Sabbath* (Macon, 1989).
Prior, Charles, 'Hebraism and the Problem of Church and State in England, 1642–1660', *The Seventeenth Century*, 28 (2013), 37–61.
——, *A Confusion of Tongues: Britain's War of Reformation, 1625–1642* (Oxford, 2012).
Prior, Charles W. A. and Burgess, Glenn (eds), *England's wars of Religion, revisited* (Farnham, 2011).
Pritchard, Elizabeth, *Religion in Public: Locke's Political Theology* (Stanford, 2014).
Quantin, Jean-Louis, *The Church of England and Christian Antiquity: The Construction of a Confessional Identity in the 17th Century* (Oxford, 2009).
Quinn, Timothy Sean, 'Machiavelli, Christianity, and Civil Religion', in *Civil Religion in Modern Political Thought: Machiavelli to Tocqueville*, eds Steven Frankel and Martin D. Yaffe (Penn State, PA, 2020), pp. 13–33.
Raab, Felix, *The English Face of Machiavelli: A Changing Interpretation, 1500–1700* (London, 1964).
Racove, Jack, *Beyond Belief, Beyond Conscience: the radical significance of the free exercise clause* (Oxford, 2020).
Rahe, Paul Anthony, *Against Throne and Altar: Machiavelli and Political Theory under the English Republic* (Cambridge, 2008).
Ray, John, 'Rousseau's Civil Religion "Problem"' in *Civil Religion in Modern Political Thought: Machiavelli to Tocqueville*, eds Steven M. Frankel and Martin D. Yaffe (Penn State, PA, 2020), pp. 183–97.
Reay, Barry, 'Quaker Opposition to Tithes, 1652–60', *Past and Present*, 86 (1980), 98–120.
Reeh, Niels, 'A Shining City on Another Hill: Danish Civil Religion as State Mythology', *Social Compass*, 58 (2011), 235–46.
Regan, Daniel, 'Islam, Intellectuals, and Civil Religion in Malaysia', *Sociological Analysis*, 37 (1976), 95–110.
Richy, R. E. and Jones, D. G. (eds), *American Civil Religion* (New York, 1974).
Robertson, John, 'Sacred History and Political Theory', *Historical Journal*, 56 (2013), 1–29.
——, *The Case for the Enlightenment* (Cambridge, 2005).
Robbins, Jeffrey, *Radical Democracy and Political Theology* (New York, 2011).
Robinson, Benedict Scott, 'John Foxe and the Anglo-Saxons', in *John Foxe and his World*, eds Christopher Highley and John N. King (Aldershot, 2002), pp. 54–72.
——, '"Darke speech": Matthew Parker and the Reforming of History', *Sixteenth Century Journal*, 29 (1998), 1061–83.
Rose, Jacqueline, 'Roman *Imperium* and the Restoration Church', *Studies in Church History*, 54 (2018), 159–75.

———, 'The Debate over Authority: Adiaphora, the Civil Magistrate, and the Settlement of Religion', in *Settling the Peace of the Church*, ed. N. H. Keeble (Oxford, 2014), pp. 29–56.

———, 'By law established: The Church of England and the Royal Supremacy', in *The Later Stuart Church, 1660–1714*, ed. Grant Tapsell (Manchester, 2012), pp. 21–45.

———, *Godly Kingship in Restoration England: The Politics of the Royal Supremacy, 1660–1688* (Cambridge, 2011).

———, 'John Locke, "matters indifferent" and the Restoration of the Church of England', *Historical Journal*, 48 (2005), 601–21.

Rosenblatt, Helen, 'On the Intellectual Sources of Laïcité', *French Politics, Culture, and Society*, 25 (2007), 1–18.

———, *Rousseau and Geneva* (Cambridge, 1997).

Rosenblatt, Jason, *Renaissance England's Chief Rabbi: John Selden* (Oxford, 2006).

Rowe, Valerie, *Sir Henry Vane the Younger: A Study in Political and Administrative History* (London, 1970).

Rummel, Erika, *The Confessionalization of Humanism in Reformation Germany* (Oxford, 2000).

Rüpke, Jörg, *Pantheon: A New History of Roman Religion* (Princeton, 2018).

——— (ed.), *Companion to Roman Religion* (Oxford, 2007).

Russell, Conrad, *King James VI and I and His English Parliaments: The Trevelyan Lectures Delivered at the University of Cambridge, 1995*, eds Richard Cust and Andrew Thrush (Oxford, 2011).

———, 'Parliament, the Royal Supremacy and the Church', *Parliamentary History*, 19 (2000), 27–37.

———, 'Whose Supremacy? King, Parliament and the Church, 1530–1640', *Lambeth Palace Library Annual Review* (1995), 53–64.

———, *Parliaments and English Politics, 1621–29* (Oxford, 1979).

———, 'Arguments for Religious Unity in England, 1530–1650', *Journal of Ecclesiastical History*, 18 (1967), 201–26.

Sanderson, Mary, 'Limited Liberties: Catholics and the Policies of the Pitt Ministry', *Journal of British Studies*, 59 (2020), 737–63.

SavoniusWroth, Sami, 'Corruption and Regeneration in the Political Imagination of John Locke', in *Politics, Religion and Ideas in Seventeenth and Eighteenth Century Britain*, eds Justin Champion, John Coffey, Tim Harris, and John Marshall (Woodbridge, 2019), pp. 141–59.

Sawada, P. A., 'Two Anonymous Tudor Treatises on the General Council', *Journal of Ecclesiastical History*, 12 (1961), 197–214.

Schochet, Gordon et al (eds), *Political Hebraism* (Jerusalem, 2008).

Scott, Jonathan, *Algernon Sidney and the English Republic 1623–1677* (Cambridge, 2005).

———, *Commonwealth Principles: Republican Writing of the English Revolution* (Cambridge, 2004).

Scott Pearson, A. F., *Church and State: Political Aspects of Sixteenth Century Puritanism* (Cambridge, 1928).
Sensabaugh, George F., *Milton in Early America* (Princeton, NJ, 1964).
Sensbach, Jon, 'Slaves to Intolerance: African-American Christianity and Religious Freedom in Early America', in *The First Prejudice*, eds Chris Beneke and Christopher S. Grenda (Philadelphia, PA, 2011), pp. 195-217.
Shagan, Ethan, *The Rule of Moderation: Violence, Religion and the Politics of Restraint in Early Modern England* (Cambridge, 2011).
——, 'The English Inquisition: Constitutional Conflict and Ecclesiastical Law in the 1590s', *Historical Journal*, 47 (2004), 541-65.
Sharpe, Kevin, *Personal Rule of Charles I* (New Haven, 1992).
Sheehan, Jonathan, *The Enlightenment Bible* (Princeton, 2007).
——, 'Enlightenment, Religion, and the Enigma of Secularization', *American Historical Review*, 108 (2003), 1061-80.
Sher, Richard, *Church and University in the Scottish Enlightenment* (Edinburgh, 1985).
Shuger, Debora, *The Renaissance Bible* (Berkeley, 1994).
Siedentop, Larry, *Inventing the Individual: The Origins of Western Liberalism* (London, 2014).
Silk, Mark, 'Numa Pompilius and the Idea of Civil Religion', *Journal of the American Academy of Religion*, 72 (2004), 863-96.
Smith, David Chan, 'Remembering Usurpation: the common lawyers, Reformation narratives, and the prerogative, 1578-1616', *Historical Research*, 86 (2013), 619-37.
Smith, R. J., *The Gothic Bequest: Medieval Institutions in British Thought, 1688-1863* (Cambridge, 1987).
Snobelen, Stephen, 'Socinianism, Heresy and Locke's *Reasonableness of Christianity*', *Enlightenment and Dissent*, 20 (2001), 88-125.
Solt, Leo F., 'Anti-Intellectualism in the Puritan Revolution', *Church History*, 25 (1956), 306-16.
Sommerville, Johann, 'Hobbes and Independency', *Rivista di Storia della Filosofia*, 59 (2004), 155-73.
——, 'Hobbes, Selden, Erastianism, and the History of the Jews', in *Hobbes and History*, eds G. A. J. Rogers and Tom Sorell (New York, 2000), pp. 160-88.
——, 'The Royal Supremacy and Episcopacy Jure Divino, 1603-1640', *Journal of Ecclesiastical History*, 34:4 (1983), 548-58.
Sowerby, Scott, 'Opposition to Anti-Popery in Restoration England', *Journal of British Studies*, 51 (2012), 26-49.
Spaans, Joke and Touber, Jetze (eds), *Enlightened Religion* (Leiden, 2019).
Spalding, J. C., 'The *Reformatio Legum Ecclesiasticarum* of 1552 and the Furthering of Discipline in England', *Church History*, 39:2 (1970), 162-71.
——, *The Reformation of the Ecclesiastical Laws of England, 1552* (Kirksville, MO, 1992).

Spellman, Denise, *Thomas Jefferson's Qur'an* (New York, 2013).
Spitz, Lewis, 'Luther's Ecclesiology and his Concept of the Prince as Notbischof', *Church History*, 22 (1953), 113–41.
Springborg, Patricia, 'Thomas Hobbes and Cardinal Bellarmine: *Leviathan* and the Ghost of the Roman Empire', *History of Political Thought*, 16 (1995), 503–21.
Springsted, Eric, *Simone Weil for the Twenty-First Century* (South Bend, IN, 2021).
Sprunger, Keith, *The Learned Doctor William Ames* (Urbana, IL, 1972).
Spurr, John, *The Restoration Church of England, 1646–89* (New Haven, 1991).
Stanton, Timothy, 'John Locke and the Fable of Liberalism', *Historical Journal*, 61 (2018), 597–622.
———, 'Authority and freedom in the interpretation of Locke's political theory', *Political Theory*, 39 (2011), 6–30.
Stedman Jones, Gareth, *Karl Marx* (London, 2016).
Stocker, Margarita, *Apocalyptic Marvell* (Brighton, 1986).
Strousma, Guy, *A New Science: The Discovery of Religion* (Cambridge, MA, 2010).
Strauss, Leo, *Persecution and the Art of the Writing* (Chicago, 1952).
Strauss, Leo, *Thoughts on Machiavelli* (Chicago, 1995).
Stuart-Buttle, Tim, *From Moral Theology to Moral Philosophy: Cicero and Visions of Humanity from Locke to Hume* (Oxford, 2019).
Sullivan, Vickie B., *Machiavelli's Three Romes* (Ithaca, 2020).
———, *Machiavelli, Hobbes, and the Formation of a Liberal Republicanism in England* (Cambridge, 2004).
Sutherland, Kathryn, 'Elizabeth Elstob', in *Medieval Scholarship: Biographical Studies on the Formation of a Discipline*, ed. Helen Damico (New York, 1998), II, pp. 59–73.
Svensson, Manfred, 'John Owen and John Locke: Confessionalism, Doctrinal Minimalism, and Toleration', *History of European Ideas*, 43 (2017), 302–16.
Sytsma, David S., *Richard Baxter and the Mechanical Philosophers* (Oxford, 2017).
Tadmor, Naomi, *The Social Universe of the English Bible* (Cambridge, 2010).
Talmon, Jacob, *The Origins of Totalitarian Democracy* (London, 1952).
Taylor, Charles, *A Secular Age* (Cambridge, MA, 2007).
Taylor, Stephen, 'William Warburton and the Alliance of Church and State', *Journal of Ecclesiastical History*, 43 (1992), 271–86.
Tenney, M. F, 'Tacitus in the politics of early Stuart England', *Classical Journal*, 37:3 (1941), 151–63.
Thomas, Keith, *In Pursuit of Civility: Manners and Civilization in Early Modern England* (New Haven, 2018).
Tierney, Brian, *Religion, Law, and the Growth of Constitutional Thought, 1150–1650* (Cambridge, 1982).
———, *Foundations of the Conciliar Theory* (Cambridge, 1955).

Thornbury, Walter, 'New Palace Yard and Westminster Hall', *Old and New London: Volume 3* (London, 1878), pp. 536–44.

Tipton, Steven M., 'Civil Religion and Public Theology', in *The Anthem Companion to Robert Bellah*, ed. Matteo Bortolini (London, 2019), pp. 63–80.

Todd, Margo, *Christian Humanism and the Puritan Social Order* (Cambridge, 1988).

Toomer, Gerald J., *John Selden: A Life in Scholarship* (Oxford, 2009).

Tuck, Richard, 'The Civil Religion of Thomas Hobbes', in *Political Discourse in early modern Britain*, ed. Nicholas Phillipson and Quentin Skinner (Cambridge, 1993), pp. 120–38.

———, 'Hobbes and Locke on Toleration', in *Thomas Hobbes and Political Theory* (Lawrence, KS, 1990), pp. 153–71.

Turner, Jack, 'John Locke, Christian Mission, and Colonial America', *Modern Intellectual History*, 8 (2011), 267–97.

Tutino, Stefania, *Thomas White and the Blackloists* (Aldershot, 2008).

Tyacke, Nicholas, 'The Puritan Paradigm of English Politics, 1559–1642', *The Historical Journal*, 53 (2010), 527–50.

——— (ed.), *England's Long Reformation, 1500–1800* (London, 1996).

———, *Anti-Calvinists: The Rise of English Arminianism 1590–1640* (Oxford, 1990).

Ullmann, Walter, *The Growth of Papal Government in the Middle Ages* (London, 1955).

Underdown, David, *Fire from Heaven: Life in an English Town in the Seventeenth Century* (London, 1992).

Van Baumer, Franklin Le, 'Christopher St German: The Political Philosophy of a Tudor Lawyer', *American Historical Review*, 42 (1937), 631–51.

Van Kley, Dale, 'Piety and Politics in the Century of Lights', in *The Cambridge History of Eighteenth-Century Political Thought*, eds Mark Goldie and Robert Wokler (Cambridge, 2006), pp. 110–43.

———, *The Religious Origins of the French Revolution* (New Haven, CT, 1996).

Vatter, Miguel, 'Machiavelli and the Republican Conception of Providence', *Review of Politics*, 75 (2013), 605–23.

——— (ed.), *Crediting God: Sovereignty and Religion in the Age of Global Capitalism* (New York, 2011).

Verkamp, Bernard, *The Indifferent Mean: Adiaphorism in the English Reformation* (Athens, OH, 1977).

Vernon, Elliot, *London Presbyterians and the British Revolutions, 1638–1664* (Manchester, 2021).

Viroli, Maurizio, *Machiavelli's God*, trans. Antony Shugaar (Princeton, 2010).

Vopa, Anthony La, 'A New Intellectual History? Jonathan Israel's Enlightenment', *Historical Journal*, 52 (2009), 717–38.

Waldman, Felix, 'John Locke as a Reader of Thomas Hobbes' *Leviathan*: A New Manuscript', *Journal of Modern History*, 93 (2021), 245–82.

Waldron, Jeremy, *God, Locke and Equality* (Cambridge, 2002).

Walmsley, J. C. and Waldmann, Felix, 'John Locke, Toleration, and Samuel Parker's *A Discourse of Ecclesiastical Politie* (1669): A New Manuscript', *Modern Intellectual History*, 19 (2022), 997–1032.

——, 'John Locke and the Toleration of Catholics: a new manuscript', *Historical Journal*, 62 (2019), 1093–1115.

Walsh, Ashley, *Civil Religion and the Enlightenment in England, 1707–1800* (Woodbridge, 2020).

——, 'The Saxon Republic and Ancient Constitution in the Standing Army Controversy, 1697–1699', *Historical Journal*, 62 (2019), 663–84.

——, 'John Streater and the Saxon Republic', *History of Political Thought*, 39 (2018), 57–82.

Walsham, Alexandra, 'The godly and popular culture', in *The Cambridge Companion to Puritanism*, eds John Coffey and Paul C. H. Lim (Cambridge, 2008), pp. 277–93.

——, *Charitable Hatred: Tolerance and Intolerance in England 1500–1700* (Manchester, 2006).

——, '"A Very Deborah?": The Myth of Elizabeth I as a Providential Monarch', in *The Myth of Elizabeth*, eds Susan Doran and Thomas Freeman (Basingstoke, 2003), pp. 143–68.

Warburg, Margrit, 'The Danish Reformation Celebrations as Civil Religion', *Journal of Church and State*, 61 (2018), 222–41.

Warren, Rebecca, 'The Ecclesiastical Patronage of Oliver Cromwell, c. 1654–1660', in *Church and People in Interregnum Britain*, ed. Fiona McCall (London, 2021), pp. 65–86.

Webster, Tom, 'Early Stuart Puritanism', in *The Cambridge Companion to Puritanism*, ed. John Coffey and Paul C. H. Lim (Cambridge, 2008), pp. 48–66.

Weed, Ronald L. and Heyking, John von (eds), *Civil Religion in political thought: its perennial questions and enduring relevance in North America* (Washington, DC, 2010).

West, Brad, 'Enchanting Pasts: The Role of International Civil Religious Pilgrimage in Reimagining National Collective Memory', *Sociological Theory*, 26 (2008), 258–70.

Wheatcroft, Andrew, *The Enemy at the Gate* (New York, 2008).

Williams, Rhys H. and Fuist, Todd Nicholas, 'Civil Religion and National Politics in a Neoliberal Era', *Sociology Compass*, 8 (2014), 929–38.

Willis, Jonathan, *The Reformation of the Decalogue* (Cambridge, 2017).

Winship, Michael, *Godly Republicanism: Puritans, Pilgrims and a City on a Hill* (Cambridge, MA, 2012).

——, 'Algernon Sidney's Calvinist Republicanism', *Journal of British Studies*, 49 (2010), 753–73.

———, 'Godly Republicanism and the Origins of the Massachusetts Polity', *William and Mary Quarterly*, 63 (2006), 427–62.

———, *Making Heretics: Militant Protestantism and Free Grace in Massachusetts, 1636–1641* (Princeton, NJ, 2002).

Wolterstorff, Nicholas, *The Might and the Almighty: An Essay in Political Theology* (Cambridge, 2012).

Woolrych, A. H., 'The Good Old Cause and the Fall of the Protectorate', *The Cambridge Historical Journal*, 13 (1957), 133–61.

Wootton, David, *Paulo Sarpi: Between Renaissance and Enlightenment* (Cambridge, 1983).

Worden, Blair, *God's Instruments: Political Conduct in the England of Oliver Cromwell* (Oxford, 2012).

———, *Roundhead Reputations: The English Civil Wars and the Passions of Posterity* (London, 2001).

———, 'The Question of Secularisation', in *A Nation Transformed: England after the Restoration*, eds Alan Houston and Steve Pincus (Cambridge, 2001), pp. 20–70.

Wormald, Patrick, *Legal Culture in the Early Medieval West* (London, 1999).

Wuthnow, Robert, *The Restructuring of American Religion: Society and Faith since World War II* (Princeton, 1988).

Young, B. W., *Religion and Enlightenment in Eighteenth-Century England* (Oxford, 1998).

Yule, George, *The Independents in the Civil War* (Cambridge, 1958).

Zakai, Aviku, 'Religious Toleration and its Enemies: the Independent Divines and the Issue of Toleration during the English Civil War', *Albion*, 21 (1989), 1–33.

Zuckert, Michael, *Launching Liberalism: On Lockean Political Philosophy* (Lawrence, KS, 2002).

Zurbuchen, Simone, 'Republicanism and Toleration', in *Republicanism: A Shared European Heritage*, eds Martin van Gelderen and Quentin Skinner, 2 vols (Cambridge, 2002), II, pp. 47–72.

Unpublished PhD Theses

Brown, A. J., 'Anglo-Irish Gallicanism, 1635–1685' (PhD, University of Cambridge, 2004).

Counsell, Esther, 'Protestant Jurisdictionalism and the Nature of Puritanism, 1560–1642' (PhD, Cambridge, forthcoming)

McCallum, Charlotte Lucy Lorraine, 'English Translations of Machiavelli's Political Works 1560–1675' (PhD, Queen Mary University of London, 2022).

Moussa, Mohamed, 'Divisive Rights: Constitutional Wrongs' (PhD, University of Cambridge, 2022).

BIBLIOGRAPHY

Robinson, Connor, '1659 and the Quest for Settlement: George Lawson, Richard Baxter, and Henry Stubbe at the Twilight of the Puritan Revolution' (PhD, University of York, 2021).

Sachs, Leslie R., 'Thomas Cranmer's *Reformatio legum ecclesiasticarum* of 1553 in the context of English church law from the later Middle Ages to the canons of 1603' (JCD thesis, Catholic University of America, 1982).

Sommerville, J. P., 'Jacobean Political Thought and the Controversy over the Oath of Allegiance' (PhD, University of Cambridge, 1981).

Index

Act of Toleration (1650) 142
Act of Union and Naturalisation
   (1682) 201
Æthelberht 227–8
Æelfric 229, 230
Æthelwolf 237
Alfred, King of England 183–202,
   223, 224
Alloway, John 196
America
   Religion in 157–8, 218–22
Ames, William 141
Anne I, Queen of Britain 231
Anglo-Saxon Church 223–42
   Protestant views of 229–30, 239–40
   Structure of 224–5, 228, 231, 233–4
   Whig views of 233–4, 235
Anti-Catholicism 55–6, 57–9, 65, 71,
   186, 205, 207–8, 214, 216, 239
Anti-Clericalism 14, 21, 25, 32, 68,
   70, 107–8
Antinomianism 164
Apostolic Church 20, 21, 26, 67
Athanasian Creed 28
Atterbury, Francis 240
Augustine 3, 139

Bacon, Francis 234, 236
Baptists 142
Barnes, Barnaby 128
Baxter, Richard 18, 22, 37–8, 122,
   162, 171–2
   Aphorisms of Justification (1649) 164,
   165–9, 180
   *A Holy Commonwealth, or Political
   Aphorisms* (1659) 164, 165
   A Key for Catholicks (1659) 164, 165
Bede 226, 229
Beiner, Ronald 2, 4, 5, 7, 47–8, 120,
   127, 183–4, 190

Bejan, Teresa 220
Bellah, Robert 2, 10–12
Bennet, Henry, Earl of Arlington 175
Bishops 80, 82–4, 99–100, 107,
   110–18
Black, Robert 119
Blasphemy Act (1650) 150
Blount, Thomas Pope 27
Bold, Samuel 203
Boyle, Robert 203, 212
Boys, John, Dean of Canterbury 128
Brady, Robert 234
British Revolutions (1640–1660) 5,
   17–23, 35–6
Bucer, Martin 52, 113
Bulman, William 157
Burlington, New Jersey 198
Burnet, Gilbert 25, 203

Calvert, Jane 195
Canossa 59
Carolina 220–2
Cartwright, Thomas 15
Catholicism 13, 14, 55–6, 57–61, 65,
   172–3, 187
Champion, Justin 13, 27, 31, 119
Charles I, King of England, Scotland
   and Ireland 148
Charles II, King of England, Scotland
   and Ireland 175, 176
Chester, Pennsylvania 193, 198
Chillingworth, William 203
Church of England 13–17, 66, 78, 88
   Anglo-Saxon origins of 39–40,
   223–42
   Augustine's mission to 225–6, 229,
   236, 237
   Elizabethan Religious
   Settlement 33, 71, 110, 232–3

INDEX

Roman Catholic origins of 224, 225, 227, 232, 237
Royal Supremacy 13, 14, 16, 34, 40, 84, 91, 241–2
Cicero 29–31, 134
Clarendon Code 24
Clarke, Edward 203
Coke, Sir Edward 114–16
Colish, Marcia L 127
Collins, Jeffrey 19, 21, 93–4, 210
Congregationalists 141–5
Constantine, Roman Emperor 13, 28, 38, 52–3, 170, 176, 177
Cosin, John 85–6
Cotton, John 141, 142, 145, 146
Cowper, Sarah 70
Cressy, Serenus 226–7
Cromwell, Oliver 19, 22, 38, 140, 141, 142, 144, 153, 154, 165
Cromwell, Richard 165
Cudworth, Ralph 203
Cusa, Nicholas of 129

Dacres, Edward 126
Davis, Colin 18
Dodd, Charles 227–8
Durkheim, Emile 10, 201

Eadwine, King of Northumbria 233, 239
Edgar, King of England 223, 230
Edict of Nantes 213
Eliot, Sir John 100–2
Elizabeth I, Queen of England 13, 15, 71, 231, 232
Elstob, Elizabeth 230–1
Eorenberht, King of Kent 239
Episcopacy *see* Bishops
Erastianism 7, 13–17, 20–1, 32, 34–5, 39, 61–2, 93–4, 116–18, 133, 158, 159, 160, 210–12, 239
Erastus, Thomas 61, 145, 149

Ferne, Henry 26
Fifth Monarchists 142, 153
Fox, George 198
Foxe, John 13, 50, 59, 230
Fowler, Edward 203

Frost, J. William 195
Fuller, Thomas 128

Goldie, Mark 17, 112
Goodwin, Thomas 141, 142–3, 146, 148, 153, 154
Gordon, Thomas 69
Greaves, John 215
Gregory I, Pope 226, 239

Hall, Arthur 232
Hall, John 152
Hall, Joseph 128
  The Interests of These United Provinces (1673) 128
Harrington, James 17, 19–22, 36, 121, 140, 141, 151, 153, 158, 160
  Oceana 154–6, 176
  Pian Piano 6
Heath, Robert, Attorney General 95, 100
Hegel, Georg 56–7
Henry VIII, King of England 13, 34
Hickeringill, Edmund 235
Hickes, George 223
Hoadley, Benjamin 232
Hobbes, Thomas 17, 19–22, 63, 140, 160, 162, 168, 180, 184, 210, 211, 212, 240
Hody, Humphrey 234, 240
Hooker, Richard 16, 33, 53, 73–9, 82–5, 86–9, 129–30, 131
Howard, Robert 28
Humble Petition and Advice (1657) 145, 164

Independent congregations 18–19, 22, 141–4, 145, 146–51, 154, 187, 204
  Debates between magisterial and radical factions 36, 146–9
  and The Instrument of Government (1653) 144
Inett, John 239
Islam 37–8, 160–1, 178–9

Jacobs, James R. 159–60, 162, 181

280

INDEX

James II and VII, King of England, Scotland and Ireland 209, 213, 216, 227, 231-2
Jefferson, Thomas 218
Jewel, John 13, 52
Joseph of Arimathea 225, 227
Julian, Roman Emperor 176

Keckerman, Bartholomew 169
Kidd, Colin 224, 232
Kishlansky, Mark 104
Kolakowski, Leszak 119

L'Isle, William 230
Lacroze, Jean Cornand de 137-8
Laud, William, Archbishop of Canterbury 16, 34, 93, 95, 98, 101, 117
Leighton, Alexander 34-5, 92-3, 94-6, 97-118
Leuytt, John 125, 130-1
Levellers 147, 224
Levitan, Dmitri 161
Liberalism 8, 44-7, 48, 240
Liberty of Conscience 18, 20, 23-4, 166-8, 170-1, 174-5
Lilburne, John 147
Limborch, Philip van 203, 204, 217
Livy 125, 128, 136
Locke, John 6, 39, 46, 64-9, 140, 173, 180, 184, 203-22
  and Anglo-Saxon Church 224
  and Catholics 207-8, 221-2
  and the Church of England 203, 210, 211-13
  and civil religion 205, 206-7, 210, 220
  and comprehension 204
  and Erastianism 210-12
  'Essay Concerning Toleration' 204, 206, 208, 211, 214, 220-1
  and *Fundamental Constitution of Carolina* (1669) 206, 219-20, 221
  and international Protestantism 213-14
Latitudinarianism 203

Letter Concerning Toleration (1689) 187, 203, 207, 208-9, 211-12, 216, 217
Toleration 204, 207-8, 214-18
Two Tracts 210-11, 214, 220
Vindication of the Reasonableness of Christianity (1695) 207
Lucius, King of the Britons 225, 238
Luther, Martin 136, 168

Machiavelli, Niccolò 7, 8-9, 63, 140, 146, 176, 210, 240
  Anti-Christianity of 35, 119-20, 123-4, 126-7
  and civil religion 119-38
  Discourses on Livy (1517/1531) 119, 124-6, 128, 131-2, 134, 135
  and Paganism 128-30
  The Prince (1532) 120, 124, 135
  and Republicanism 121
  and secularisation 120-1
Madison, James 218-19
Mahomet *see* Mohamed
Malcolm, Noel 161, 214
Martin Marprelate tracts 15, 82
Maryland 193
Massachusetts Bay 142, 148, 149, 158
Matar, Nabil 214, 217
Medici, Cosimo de 137
Milton, Anthony 94
Milton, John 36, 121, 140, 146, 147-8, 149-50, 151, 153, 157, 172, 237-8
Mohamed 38, 178-9
Molesworth, Robert 26-7, 56, 235-6
Moyle, Walter 30

Naylor, James 145
Nedham, Marchamont 36, 140, 141, 142, 151
  The Case of the Commonwealth of England (1650) 151
  The Excellencie of a Free State (1656) 151-2
  The Great Accuser Cast Down, or A Publick Trial of John Goodwin (1657) 152
  A True State of the Case of the Commonwealth (1654) 152-3

281

INDEX

Nelson, Eric 61–2, 156
Neville, Henry 121, 123, 137
  and Machiavelli 35, 122
  'Nicholas Machiavel's Letter to Zanobuis Buondelmontius' (1675) 122–3, 133–7
New Model Army 150
Newton, Isaac 203
Nominated Assembly 142
Noy, William, Attorney General 103
Numa Pompilius 30, 51, 125, 129, 131, 132
Nye, Philip 141, 142–3, 144, 148, 151, 152

Ordination 20–1
Owen, John 18, 141, 142–3, 144, 148, 151, 155–7
Overton, Richard 147

Paganism 176
Parker, Matthew, Archbishop of Canterbury 223, 228–9
Parker, Samuel 205, 206, 212
Patrick, Henry 218
Penn, William 38–9, 183–202
  Address to Protestants (1679) 188
  and civil interests 185, 188, 189, 192
  and civil religion 183, 184–5, 190
  Frame of Government (1682) 187, 191
  Laws agreed upon in England (1682) 191, 193, 194
  and liberty of conscience 183, 185
  One Project of the Good of England (1679) 185
  A Perswasive to Moderation (1685) 187
Perkins, William 163, 166, 176
Persecution 164, 175, 186
Petition of Right 101–2
Petyt, William 120–1, 234
Philadelphia, Pennsylvania 38, 197
Plato 3
Pocock, J.G.A. 150, 232
Popish Plot 188
Popple, William 203, 207, 213

Presbyterianism 15, 17
Priestcraft 25–8, 55–6, 205, 210, 212–13, 238, 241
Prynne, William 92–3, 96, 103–5, 117–18, 147, 238, 239
Puritans 14, 15, 33, 73, 79–81, 82–5, 90, 139–40, 142, 148, 161–2, 163

Quakers 142, 145, 148, 171–2, 173
  and civil religion 183–202
  Government of 193–200

Ranters 150
Rhode Island 148
Robinson, Henry 146
Roman Religion 3, 8–9, 29–31, 74
Ross, Alexander 28
Rousseau, Jean-Jacques 9–10, 64, 140, 201, 240
Rycaut, Paul 215

Sadler, John 233, 236–7
St Germain, Christopher 55
Secularisation 42–4, 120–1, 240
Shagan, Ethan 189
Sidney, Algernon 121
Slavery 39, 214, 218–22
Socinianism 145, 154
South, Robert 132
Spelman, Denise 218–19
Stapleton, Thomas 226, 229, 232
Starkey, John 121, 122, 124, 137
Stephens, William 203
Sterry, Peter 152
Stillingfleet, Edward 203, 212
  Mischief of Separation (1680) 204, 209
  Unreasonableness of Separation (1681) 204, 209
Stubbe, Henry 150
  Account of the Rise and Progress of Mahometanism (c.1670) 37–8, 160, 174–5, 177–9, 180
  and anti-clericalism 160
  and civil religion 159–82
  An Essay in Defence of the Good Old Cause (1659) 163, 169–70

INDEX

A Light Shining out of Darkness
  (1659) 171–2
 At the Restoration 162, 174
 and Richard Baxter 37–8, 162, 165

Temple, William 236
Theocracy 7–8, 37, 165–6
Thomas, Keith 157
Tillotson, John 203
Tindal, Matthew 69, 203
Toland, John 25, 49, 69, 160
 Nazarenus (1718) 29
Toleration 6, 8, 20, 39, 65–6
Trenchard, John 69
Tyndale, William 55
Tyrell, James 203, 233, 234

Vane, Henry 36, 140, 148–9, 150,
  168, 172, 173
Varro 139

Voltaire 192

Walsh, Ashley 13, 31
Walwyn, William 147, 150, 156
Washington, George 218, 219
Washington, Robert 235
Westminster Assembly 141
Whichcote, Benjamin 203
Whitelock, Bulstrode 235
Whitgift, John 16, 34
Wildman, John 148
William I, King of England 235, 239
William III, King of England, Scotland,
  and Ireland 200, 209, 216
Williams, Roger 142, 146–7, 151,
  156–7
Wolseley, Charles 207, 209
Worden, Blair 149

STUDIES IN EARLY MODERN CULTURAL,
POLITICAL AND SOCIAL HISTORY

I
Women of Quality
Accepting and Contesting Ideals of Femininity in England, 1690–1760
Ingrid H. Tague

II
Restoration Scotland, 1660–1690
Royalist Politics, Religion and Ideas
Clare Jackson

III
Britain, Hanover and the Protestant Interest, 1688–1756
Andrew C. Thompson

IV
Hanover and the British Empire, 1700–1837
Nick Harding

V
The Personal Rule of Charles II, 1681–85
Grant Tapsell

VI
Royalism, Print and Censorship in Revolutionary England
Jason McElligott

VII
The English Catholic Community, 1688–1745
Politics, Culture and Ideology
Gabriel Glickman

VIII
England and the 1641 Irish Rebellion
Joseph Cope

IX
Culture and Politics at the Court of Charles II, 1660–1685
Matthew Jenkinson

X
Commune, Country and Commonwealth
The People of Cirencester, 1117–1643
David Rollison

XI
An Enlightenment Statesman in Whig Britain
Lord Shelburne in Context, 1737–1805
Edited by Nigel Aston and Clarissa Campbell Orr

XII
London's News Press and the Thirty Years War
Jayne E. E. Boys

XIII
God, Duty and Community in English Economic Life, 1660–1720
Brodie Waddell

XIV
Remaking English Society
Social Relations and Social Change in Early Modern England
Edited by Steve Hindle, Alexandra Shepard and John Walter

XV
Common Law and Enlightenment in England, 1689–1750
Julia Rudolph

XVI
The Final Crisis of the Stuart Monarchy
The Revolutions of 1688–91 in their British, Atlantic and European Contexts
Edited by Stephen Taylor and Tim Harris

XVII
The Civil Wars after 1660
Public Remembering in Late Stuart England
Matthew Neufeld

XVIII
The Nature of the English Revolution Revisited
Edited by Stephen Taylor and Grant Tapsell

XIX
The King's Irishmen
The Irish in the Exiled Court of Charles II, 1649–1660
Mark R .F. Williams

XX
Scotland in the Age of Two Revolutions
Edited by Sharon Adams and Julian Goodare

XXI
Alehouses and Good Fellowship in Early Modern England
Mark Hailwood

XXII
Social Relations and Urban Space
Norwich, 1600–1700
Fiona Williamson

XXIII
British Travellers and the Encounter with Britain, 1450–1700
John Cramsie

XXIV
Domestic Culture in Early Modern England
Antony Buxton

XXV
Accidents and Violent Death in Early Modern London, 1650–1750
Craig Spence

XXVI
Popular Culture and Political Agency in Early Modern England and Ireland
Essays in Honour of John Walter
Edited by Michael J. Braddick and Phil Withington

XXVII
Commerce and Politics in Hume's *History of England*
Jia Wei

XXVIII
Bristol from Below
Law, Authority and Protest in a Georgian City
Steve Poole and Nicholas Rogers

XXIX
Disaffection and Everyday Life in Interregnum England
Caroline Boswell

XXX
Cromwell's House of Lords
Politics, Parliaments and Constitutional Revolution, 1642–166
Jonathan Fitzgibbons

XXXI
Stuart Marriage Diplomacy
Dynastic Politics in their European Context, 1604–1630
Edited by Valentina Caldari and Sara J. Wolfson

XXXII
National Identity and the Anglo-Scottish Borderlands, 1552–1652
Jenna M. Schultz

XXXIII
Roguery in Print: Crime and Culture in Early Modern London
Lena Liapi

XXXIV
Politics, Religion and Ideas in Seventeenth- and Eighteenth-Century Britain
Essays in Honour of Mark Goldie
Edited by Justin Champion, John Coffey, Tim Harris and John Marshall

XXXV
The Hanoverian Succession in Great Britain and its Empire
Edited by Brent S. Sirota and Allan I. Macinnes

XXXVI
Age Relations and Cultural Change in Eighteenth-Century England
Barbara Crosbie

XXXVII
The National Covenant in Scotland, 1638–1689
Chris R. Langley

XXXVIII
Visualising Protestant Monarchy
Ceremony, Art and Politics after the Glorious Revolution (1689–1714)
Julie Farguson

XXXIX
Blood Waters
War, Disease and Race in the Eighteenth-Century British Caribbean
Nicholas Rogers

XL
The State Trials and the Politics of Justice in Later Stuart England
Edited by Brian Cowan and Scott Sowerby

XLI
Africans in East Anglia, 1467–1833
Richard C. Maguire

XLII
Royalism, Religion and Revolution
Wales, 1640–1688
Sarah Ward Clavier

XLIII
Painting for a Living in Tudor and Early Stuart England
Robert Tittler

XLIV
Scotland and the Wider World
Essays in Honour of Allan I. Macinnes
Edited by Alison Cathcart and Neil McIntyre

XLV
Urban Government and the Early Stuart State
Provincial Towns, Corporate Liberties, and Royal Authority in England, 1603–1640
Catherine F. Patterson

XLVI
The National Covenant and the Solemn League and Covenant, 1660–1696
James Walters

XLVII
The Restraint of the Press in England, 1660–1715
The Communication of Sin
Alex W. Barber

XLVIII
Conspiracy Culture in Stuart England
The Mysterious and Strange Death of Sir Edmund Berry Godfrey
Andrea McKenzie

XLIX
Contesting the English Polity, 1660–1688
Religion, Politics, and Ideas
Mark Goldie

Printed in the United States
by Baker & Taylor Publisher Services